T0262748

Software-Defined Network Frameworks

Software-Defined Networks (SDN) work by virtualization of the network and the Cognitive Software-Defined Network (CSDN) combines the efficiencies of SDN with cognitive learning algorithms and enhanced protocols to automatize SDN. Partial deployment of SDN along with traditional networking devices forms a Hybrid Software-Defined Network (HSDN). *Software-Defined Network Frameworks: Security Issues and Use Cases* consolidates the research relating to the security in SDN, CSDN, and Hybrid SDNs. The security enhancements derived from the use of various SDN frameworks and the security challenges thus introduced, are also discussed. Overall, this book explains the different architectures of SDNs and the security challenges needed for implementing them.

Features:

- Illustrates different frameworks of SDN and their security issues in a single volume
- Discusses design and assessment of efficient SDN northbound/southbound interfaces
- Describes cognitive computing, affective computing, machine learning, and other novel tools
- Illustrates coupling of SDN and traditional networking – Hybrid SDN
- Explores services, technologies, algorithms, and methods for data analysis in CSDN

The book is aimed at researchers and graduate students in software engineering, network security, computer networks, high performance computing, communications engineering, and intelligence systems.

Computational Intelligence Techniques

Series Editor:
Vishal Jain

The objective of this series is to provide researchers a platform to present state of the art innovations, research, and design and implement methodological and algorithmic solutions to data processing problems, designing and analyzing evolving trends in health informatics and computer-aided diagnosis. This series provides support and aid to researchers involved in designing decision support systems that will permit societal acceptance of ambient intelligence. The overall goal of this series is to present the latest snapshot of ongoing research as well as to shed further light on future directions in this space. The series presents novel technical studies as well as position and vision papers comprising hypothetical/speculative scenarios. The book series seeks to compile all aspects of computational intelligence techniques from fundamental principles to current advanced concepts. For this series, we invite researchers, academicians and professionals to contribute, expressing their ideas and research in the application of intelligent techniques to the field of engineering in handbook, reference, or monograph volumes.

For more information about this series, please visit: www.routledge.com/Computational-Intelligence-Techniques/book-series/CIT

Software-Defined Network Frameworks
Frameworks
Security Issues and Use Cases

Edited by
Mandeep Kaur, Vishal Jain,
Parma Nand, and Nitin Rakesh

CRC Press
Taylor & Francis Group
Boca Raton London New York

CRC Press is an imprint of the
Taylor & Francis Group, an **informa** business

Designed cover image: www.shutterstock.com

First edition published 2024
by CRC Press
2385 NW Executive Center Drive, Suite 320, Boca Raton FL 33431

and by CRC Press
4 Park Square, Milton Park, Abingdon, Oxon, OX14 4RN

CRC Press is an imprint of Taylor & Francis Group, LLC

ISBN: 9781032450223 (hbk)
ISBN: 9781032559100 (pbk)
ISBN: 9781003432869 (ebk)

DOI: 10.1201/9781003432869

Typeset in Times
by codeMantra

Contents

Preface

Software-Defined Network (SDN) is an emerging approach as a new network innovation architecture that has overcome the limitations of traditional network architecture to adapt to dynamic environments. With SDN, the data plane can be separated from control plane and hence the system abstraction has increased. Defining and understanding the control and management software stack for SDN is indeed important. In addition to centralized network control, the current state of the OpenFlow model which is the well-known SDN protocol can also be explored. Network Function Virtualization (NFV) is another promising technology with many benefits like easy management and utilization of resources, reduction of the operational cost, and migration of network functions from a dedicated hardware scenario to virtual machines. These benefits have increased the growth of cloud services and applications to run on converged infrastructures. The analysis of SDN contributions for Cloud Computing security becomes an intrinsic part when Network Function Virtualization (NFV) is completely embedded in Cloud Computing. Since the network is automated, it becomes prone to various alerts for security threats. Studying the various security protocols, security analysis and implementation of the SDN Network Security in SDN Environments is crucial. Cognitive Software-Defined Networks (CSDN) enables the network. In another domain, SDN also augments traditional IP control planes in a wireless area network. SDN architecture also allows applying its features to alleviate the challenges of 5 vs of big data. Some potential SDN solutions address the security issues in big data and also improve the quality of service of applications with big data and SDN. The major focus of this book is to present the research related to the Cognitive SDN, SDN with Cloud Computing, SDN in WAN, SDN, and Big Data. Software-defined networking (SDN) is a network architecture approach that makes a network more programmable by separating the data plane from the control plane. This makes the control plane independent. Also, SDN completely changed the problems of traditional IP network architecture, problems such as centralized control is not feasible and switches cannot be configured dynamically, etc. Instead of manual configurations, the SDN works by virtualization of the network giving new levels of visibility, nodes are programmed dynamically. It will also become more intelligent as it assists in setting the rules network. Since the network is automated, it becomes prone to various alerts for security threats. The analysis of SDN contributions for Cloud Computing security becomes an intrinsic part when Network Function Virtualization (NFV) is completely embedded in Cloud Computing. The Cognitive Software-Defined Network (CSDN) presents to combine the efficiencies of SDN with new cognitive learning algorithms and enhanced protocols to automatize SDN. The combination of SDN and cognitive algorithms acts better to solve the issues in traditional SDNs. In today's scenario where the data plays an intrinsic role, SDN helps in improving the quality of service of applications working with big data. Software-defined networking defines IP Routing and SDN Route Control mechanisms for controlling the network. The major focus of this book is to present the research relating to the issues, challenges, and opportunities in SDN.

It also emphasizes on SDN-based Cloud Computing Networking and its issues relating to security. It discusses various tools and technologies that are required for data analysis in cognitive software-defined networks (CSDN). The simulation tools and experimental testbeds, SDN implications for research and innovation, and potential novel application of Open SDN are discussed.

Chapter 1 discusses various challenges and issues in the instance of distributed system failure and also focuses on how the distributed system detects all the issues automatically and corrects them, without disturbing the computing.

Chapter 2 gives an overview of SDN.

Chapter 3 gives a security assessment that requires login, SSL/TLS interface, and having to log audit services to enforce GUI protection. FortNOX position authorization and ciphers such as AES and DES will be utilized to encrypt data and enhance the safety of the SDN architecture.

Chapter 4 gives the descriptions of different techniques used for balancing the load of Cloud Computing with the virtualization techniques.

Chapter 5 gives the definition of consumer behavior analysis, and its significance as opposed to a common belief is explained.

Chapter 6 explores the future of Software-Defined Networking (SDN) and its potential to revolutionize the networking industry. With the increasing demand for agile, scalable, and programmable networks, SDN has emerged as a promising solution that separates the network control plane from the data plane, enabling greater network flexibility, automation, and orchestration.

Chapter 7 explores the use of SDN which helps to manage the persistent issues of network and route management along with making access-control and security a primary objective.

As an emerging connectivity paradigm, deploying SDN in WSN is covered in Chapter 8. To shed insight on upcoming developments in this subject, difficulties and open research problems are also emphasized.

Chapter 9 discusses the notion of load balancing, literature surveys on load balancing methodologies, and various measurement factors.

Chapter 10 presents a full assessment of the necessity for multiple controllers in SDN, as well as the benefits and drawbacks.

Chapter 11 examines the numerous security services built on top of this technology to address key issues in defending the SDN control plane.

Chapter 12 shows the role of IoT in the e-banking industry in depth. The major focus is on the challenges, benefits, and applications of IoT in banking.

Chapter 13 explores the security vulnerabilities and machine learning (ML) based mitigation techniques in terms of SDN.

Chapter 14 discusses the methods that ML/DL researchers have proposed to design IDS. This includes ML techniques like Support Vector Machines, Naïve-Bayes, Decision trees, Random forests, Logistic Regression, etc., and deep learning techniques like Neural networks, RNN, LSTM, and CNN.

Chapter 15 briefly examines the many characteristics of big data and its limitations, SDN for big data, the function of SDN, and the MapReduce approach.

Chapter 16 intends to put in place a defending mechanism against SDN TCP flooding attacks using statistical and ensemble machine learning-based mechanisms.

Editors

Dr. Vishal Jain is presently working as Associate Professor at the Department of Computer Science and Engineering, Sharda School of Engineering and Technology, Sharda University, Greater Noida, U. P., India. Before that, he has worked for several years as Associate Professor at Bharati Vidyapeeth's Institute of Computer Applications and Management (BVICAM), New Delhi. He has more than 16 years of experience in academics. He obtained Ph.D (CSE), M.Tech (CSE), MBA (HR), MCA, MCP, and CCNA. He has more than 1130 research citation indices with Google Scholar (h-index score 17 and i-10 index 27). He has authored more than 95 research papers in reputed conferences and journals, including Web of Science and Scopus. He has authored and edited more than 45 books with various reputed publishers. He is the series editor of ten book series. He is a life member of CSI, ISTE, and a senior member of IEEE. His research areas include information retrieval, semantic web, ontology engineering, data mining, ad hoc networks, and sensor networks. He received a Young Active Member Award for the year 2012–2013 from the Computer Society of India, Best Faculty Award for the year 2017, and Best Researcher Award for the year 2019 from BVICAM, New Delhi.

Dr. Mandeep Kaur is presently working as Associate Professor at the Department of Computer Science & Engineering, Sharda University. Dr. Kaur has completed her B.Tech in CSE from UPTU, M.Tech in CSE from PTU, and Ph.D from Sharda University. Her topic of research was "Thought Recognition: Knowledge Discovery from EEG Signals and Classifying by Classifier Ensemble." Dr Kaur has 17+ years of teaching experience in various technical universities/institutions. She is a Ph.D Coordinator (SET), IoT Program Coordinator, mentor and guiding research investigations for under-graduate, post-graduate engineering students and Ph.D scholars in areas including Image Processing, Software Engineering, Artificial Intelligence, Internet of Things, DBMS, and Soft Computing.

Prof. (Dr.) Parma Nand is PhD. in Computer Science & Engineering from IIT Roorkee, and M.Tech and B.Tech in Computer Science & Engineering from IIT Delhi. Prof Parma Nand has more than 27 years of experience both in industry and academia. He has received various awards like the best teacher award from Union Minister, best students' project guide award from Microsoft in 2015 and best faculty award from Cognizant in 2016. He has completed government-funded projects and spearheaded last five IEEE International conferences on Computing, Communication & Automation (ICCCA), IEEE students chapters, Technovation Hackathon 2019, Technovation Hackathon 2020, International Conference on Computing, Communication, and Intelligent Systems (ICCCIS-2021). He is a member Executive Council of IEEE UP section (R-10), a member Executive Committee IEEE Computer and Signal Processing Society, and a member Exec. India Council Computer Society, member Executive Council Computer Society of India, Noida section, and has acted as an observer in many IEEE conferences. He also has active memberships of ACM, IEEE, CSI, ACEEE, ISOC, IAENG, and IASCIT. He is a lifetime member of Soft Computing Research Society (SCRS) and ISTE. Currently, Prof. (Dr.) Parma Nand is Dean Academic Affairs, Sharda University, Greater Noida, India.

Prof. (Dr.) Nitin Rakesh is a recipient of IBM Drona Award and is a Top 10 State Award Winner. He is an active member of professional societies like Senior Member IEEE (USA), ACM, SIAM (USA), Life Member of CSI, and other professional societies. He is a reviewer of several prestigious journals/transactions. His research outlines an emphasis on Network Coding, Interconnection Networks and Architecture, and Online Phantom Transactions. Dr. Nitin has accorded several other awards for Best Paper Published, Session Chairs, Highest Cited author, Best Students Thesis Guide, and many others. Dr. Nitin has been instrumental in various industrial interfacing for academic research at his previous assignments at various organizations. He has 180+ publication in Scopus Indexed/SCI/High impact journals and international conferences. Dr. Nitin has guided five PhD students of various universities and industries. He has successfully guided several M.Tech and B.Tech students. Dr. Nitin has contributed to various prestigious accreditations like NAAC, NBA, QAA, WASC, UGC, IAU, IET, and others.

Contributors

V. Aanandaram
Research Scholar, Department
of Computer Applications,
Kalasalingam Academy of Research
and Education, Krishnankoil,
Tamil Nadu, India – 626126

Alok Mishra
Department of Computer Application,
BCIIT, New Delhi, India

Ambuj Kumar Agarwal
School of Engineering and Technology,
Sharda University, Greater Noida,
India

Md. Mohtab Alam
Assistant Professor, Department
of Information Technology,
Muzaffarpur Institute of Technology,
Muzaffarpur

Yusuf Alkali
Research Scholar, CV Raman Global
University Bhubaneswar Odisha,
India

Abdullah Saleh Alqahtani
King Saud University Riyadh,
Saudi Arabia

Senthil Athithan
Department of Computer Science
and Engineering, Koneru
Lakshmaiah Education Foundation,
Vaddeswaram, Andhra Pradesh,
India

Ms. K. Bavani
Kalasalingam Academy of Research
and Education

Manish Bhardwaj
Department of Computer Science and
Information Technology, KIET
Group of Institutions, Delhi-NCR,
Ghaziabad, India

Ashima Bhatnagar Bhatia
Assistant Professor, Vivekananda
Institute of Professional Studies-TC,
New Delhi, India

K. Bhavya
NMAM Institute of Technology
(NMAMIT), NITTE (Deemed
to be University), NITTE, India

Kanak Chandra Bora
University of Science and Technology,
Meghalaya

P. Deepalakshmi
Department of Computer Science
and Engineering, Kalasalingam
Academy of Research and Education,
Krishnankoil, Tamil Nadu,
India – 626126

Radhakrishna Dodmane
NMAM Institute of Technology
(NMAMIT), Nitte (Deemed to
be University), Nitte, India

N.S. Saba Farheen
Department of Electronics and
Communication, R. V. College
of Engineering Bangalore

Rupali Gill
Chitkara University Institute of
Engineering and Technology,
Chitkara University, Punjab, India

Parth Mukul Gupta
Director, ZarthCorp Tech Pvt. Ltd.,
  Greater Noida

Tahir Rashid Hakeem
King Saud University Riyadh
  Saudi Arabia

Mohd Haroon
Integral University, Lucknow
  Uttar Pradesh, India

Sardar M. N. Islam
ISILC, Victoria University, 300 Queen
  Street, PO Box 14428, Melbourne,
  VIC 8001 Australia

Vishal Jain
Department of Computer Science and
  Engineering, School of Engineering
  and Technology, Sharda University,
  Greater Noida, India

Ezhil Kalaimannan
Associate Professor/University of West
  Florida

Pankaj Kumar
SRMCEM, Lucknow Uttar Pradesh,
  India

Vivek Kumar
THDC Institute of Hydropower
  Engineering and Technology, Tehri,
  Uttarakhand

Aruna Malik
Department of Computer Science &
  Engineering, National Institute of
  Technology, Jalandhar, Punjab, India

Himani Mittal
Goswami Ganesh and Dutta; Sanatan
  Dharma College, Chandigarh

Rahul Reddy Nadikatu
Senior IEEE Member, University of the
  Cumberland, USA

P. Nagaraj
Kalasalingam Academy of Research
  and Education Krishnankoil, India

Gamze Ozel
Department of Statistics, Hacettepe
  University

K. R. Raghunandan
NMAM Institute of Technology
  (NMAMIT), Nitte (Deemed
  to be University), Nitte, India

Sindhu Rajendran
Department of Electronics and
  Communication R. V. College
  of Engineering Bangalore

Krishnaraj Rao
NMAM Institute of Technology
  (NMAMIT), Nitte (Deemed
  to be University), NITTE, India

Rashi Rastogi
CCS University, Meerut, Savya Sachi,
  Assistant Professor, Department
  of Information Technology, Lalit
  Narayan Mishra College of Business
  Management, Muzaffarpur, Bihar,
  India

Jyoti Sharma
Department of Information Technology,
  KIET Group of Institutions,
  Delhi-NCR, Ghaziabad, India

Pavika Sharma
Assistant Professor, Bhagwan
  Parshuram Institute of Technology
  under GGS IPU, New Delhi, India

Daisy Sharmah
University of Science and Technology
    Meghalaya

Surendra Shetty
NMAM Institute of Technology
    (NMAMIT), NITTE (Deemed to be
    University), NITTE, India

R. J. Shreya
Department of Electronics and
    Communication, R. V. College of
    Engineering Bangalore

Mandeep Singh
Department of Computer Science &
    Engineering, National Institute of
    Technology, Jalandhar, Punjab, India

Sathiyandra Kumar Srinivasan
Associate Vice President, V2
    Technologies Inc., 3237, Chase Point,
    Dr franklin, Tennessee, USA-37067

K. Muthamil Sudar
MepcoSchlenk Engineering College,
    Sivakasi, India

C. Swathi
Department of Electronics and
    Communication, R. V. College
    of Engineering Bangalore

Raj Gaurang Tiwari
Chitkara University Institute of
    Engineering and Technology,
    Chitkara University, Punjab,
    India

Manish Madhava Tripathi
Integral University, Lucknow
    Uttar Pradesh, India

Pawan Whig
Senior IEEE Member, Dean Research,
    Vivekananda Institute of Professional
    Studies - TC, New Delhi India

1 A System Model of Fault Tolerance Technique in Distributed System and Scalable System Using Machine Learning

Raj Gaurang Tiwari, Mohd Haroon,
Manish Madhava Tripathi, Pankaj Kumar,
Ambuj Kumar Agarwal, and Vishal Jain

1.1 FAULT-TOLERANT SYSTEM

1.1.1 HYBRID REDUNDANCY SYSTEMS (HRS)

The circuitry is tripled and voted in a triple modular redundancy (TMR) system. The TMR system fails anytime two modules in the redundant triplet generate faults, invalidating the vote. The N-modular redundancy (NMR) system, an extension of the TMR system, is an extremely effective method for increasing the dependability and fault tolerance of computer systems [1,2]. HRS is a combination of N- modular and standby redundancy. This kind of redundancy is vital in high-reliability applications such as space shuttle control systems, digital flight control systems, and radiology, where HRS systems are used to attain extremely high reliability [3].

1.1.2 DISTRIBUTED SYSTEMS

A distributed system is a subset of a cluster system, which is a group of computers capable of supporting the processing functions of any other component. A cluster is configured in a redundant n + m fashion, with n-processing nodes required to function and m-processing nodes serving as hot spares. A homogeneous distributed system is one in which all hosts, for example, workstations from the same vendor, are identical. Homogeneous distributed software/hardware systems (HDSHS) are applications of homogenously distributed software [4]. A heterogeneous distributed system (HDS) is a network of disparate hardware or software systems that are connected via gateways [5]. Due to the vast scale of distributed systems, heterogeneity is frequently unavoidable. Furthermore, heterogeneity is frequently preferred by many users since HDSs enable users to choose from a variety of computer platforms for a variety of

DOI: 10.1201/9781003432869-1

applications. A user, for example, may have the option of using a supercomputer for simulations, a Macintosh for document processing, and a UNIX workstation for program development. Distributed systems are frequently employed in a variety of mission-critical systems, including banking, military, nuclear, aerospace, and power systems. System dependability is critical for these types of systems since failures can result in significant financial and human losses. Distributed systems are frequently used to describe software that runs in identical copies on each host. Communication protocols, networking software, and distributed database management systems are all examples of such applications [6].

1.1.3 CLUSTER SYSTEMS

A cluster of computers linked to a high-speed network allows for the creation of highly scalable and available internet services. Since failing components may be easily isolated and the system can continue to operate uninterrupted, this form of loosely linked architecture is substantially more scalable, cost-effective, and dependable than a tightly coupled multiprocessor system. Additionally, highly available clusters are used to solve a wide variety of scientific, engineering, and commercial problems. However, because a cluster system is composed of numerous servers, it is necessary to address the low availability issues caused by the high probability of server software failures [7,21].

1.2 FAULT TOLERANCE SYSTEM IN THE DISTRIBUTED SYSTEM

In the context of a distributed system, cluster system, and large scalable system, fault tolerance in a system means that failure can automatically be detected and corrected. The objective of fault tolerance is only to improve the system performance and throughput, during the computing if any component and network system fail, meaning single point failure or multipoint failure, system operation cannot be disturbed. A fault tolerance system has a lot of backup resources: if node and other components fail during calculation, the backup system automatically takes responsibility, ensuring no loss of the calculation [8,9]. Fault tolerance systems are categorized into the following types [10,11]:

Hardware failure: if, at any moment, the system hardware like the server or any other machine fail amid calculation, then the equivalent system can take the responsibility; for example, if the server fails amid execution, then the identical backup server can take responsibility with all operations of the failed servers.

Software failure: if in the middle of execution, the database or any other application software fails, automatically backup software or database system will take the responsibility, that is why we are taking backups of all the calculations; for instance, a database of any customer information, will be stored or replicated to another machine, if the respondent machine data base goes down immediately the backup system database handle the issue [12,13].

Fault tolerance is strongly tied to their reliability properties in distributed systems. The following two techniques can be implemented:

- Inaccessible to application code at the architecture level: This is recognized as systematic fault tolerance. To provide fault tolerance through temporal or spatial replication of computations used to discover and conceal the errors highlighted in the fault hypothesis, the architecture must be replica deterministic.
- Application-specific fault tolerance: This type of fault tolerance is implemented at the application code level. It integrates standard processing activities with error detection and fault tolerance functions at the application level.

An error occurs when there is a discrepancy between the system's intended correct state and its actual current state. The objective of the fault-tolerant system is to detect and correct errors before they manifest as failures at the system's user service interface. The availability of knowledge about the system's nominal condition, in addition to actual state information, is required for error detection. The more a priori information on the characteristics of correct states and the temporal patterns of correct computation behavior there is, the more effective error detection algorithms become. However, by repeating the computation, several distinct combinations of hardware, software, and temporal redundancy can be used to discover various problems.

1.2.1 REPLICATION FOR AVAILABILITY

A system's availability is the likelihood that it will be operational (either at a particular time or on average). Replication is used to improve the availability of distributed systems by using a primary/standby backup or a modular redundancy approach. Only one component performs its typical functions in a primary/standby scheme; all other components are on standby. If the primary fails, one of the backup components is activated. In a modular architecture, all components perform the same purpose, and failures are hidden by voting on the outputs. Tandem's method of process pairs is the standard primary/standby architecture. A process pair consists of two processes that are performed on separate physical processors. One process is labeled as the primary, while the other is designated as the backup. The primary communicates information about its internal state to the standby in the form of a checkpoint before each request is completed. If the main fails, the checkpoint allows the standby to finish the request. For replicated items, Cornell's Isis project employs primary/standby architecture. One replica acts as the coordinator and operates each interaction within an Isis-duplicated item. The coordinator then updates the other copies using a two-phase commit mechanism. Designers of fault-tolerant computer systems are familiar with the terms TMR and NMR. Every computation in TMR is performed by one of three processors. The findings are then compared, and the value is used if at least two of them agree. Replication is combined with remote procedure calls in the Circus system to allow modular redundancy at the software module level [14,15].

1.3 FAULT TOLERANCE VERSUS AVAILABILITY OF THE SYSTEM

High availability is the kind of availability of resources to avoid the loss of computing and minimize the downtime of the execution; in most cases, both mechanisms
of fault tolerance and high availability are ensuring us to prevent and maintain the
organization, during minor failure and major faults.

Fault tolerance and high availability ensure the system functions properly. Both
have their advantages in computing jobs. Both maintain business continuity and
planning. By analogy, we can easily understand fault tolerance; flying aircraft have
two engines, and if any moment one engine fails, immediately all responsibility will
transfer to another engine, without any kind of disturbance [16].

Downtime: the high available system, means downtime is minimum, and there
is also a minimum allowed for interruption; if suppose we have a system that is not
available for five minutes every year, it means the system is down for five minutes
every year, and if we are using a fault tolerance system, which will allow a backup
scheme, once the system goes down, immediately backup portion takes responsibility and the system will not be interrupted for a bit of a second [16].

Scope: high availability can be achieved on a shared set of resources, that are
primarily used to manage failure and makes the system highly available. Once any
disaster occurs, the scope of the system automatically switches on the redundant
component of the system.

Cost: for the designing of the fault tolerance system, we must use backup components (hardware, software, firmware, switches, and so many components); for high
availability, we are also trying to minimalize downtime. For the use of redundant
components, the entire cost of the system will automatically increase [15].

Fault tolerance system for the web: in the web applications, the fault tolerance system, load balancing, and failover solution, perform well in combination,
and ensure the availability of resources via redundancy and rapid disaster recovery. Failover and load balancing both jointly work in web processing as shown in
Figure 1.1.

Load balancing is an approach by which the incoming jobs are disseminated
among all available computing nodes in a network; in the case of the web application,
processing will be going on several computing nodes, and all computing nodes are
connected to a network, load balancing allows an application to run on all connected
computing nodes, which means load balancing allows the application to run on several computers. If any moment a single point failure occurs, the web load balancer
immediately transfers a load of failed computing nodes to all available computing
nodes [16].

Application software for load balancing is running on every computing node of
the network, the load balancer is also the workload distribution of all multiple computing resources so that computing nodes become more resilient for execution and
minimized downtime [16].

In addition, a load balancing system helps us to recover single-point failure and
multiple-point failures, suppose any web-based system containing two servers, any-
how if any one of the servers fails, the production of a load balancer automatically
shifts workload in the event of an available server [16].

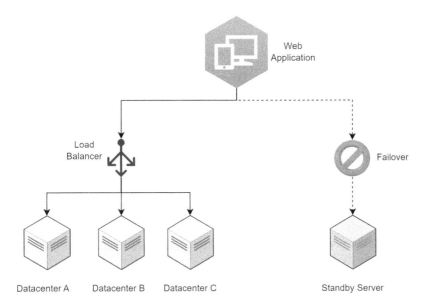

FIGURE 1.1 Fault tolerance system.

In the extreme case, if the entire system fails in web mining or web application, then the failover system is charged with auto-activating the secondary system, to keep the web application running, and meantime the primary network can be activated on standby system. Further failover can be categorized as a hot and cold failover, in the failover system, the standby system immediately takes the load of the failure system, and start to function normally, but in the case of the old failover system, the backup system will take some time to takes the responsibility.

In an extreme case, if the entire system fails in web mining or web application, then the failover system is charged with auto-activating the secondary system, to keep the web application running, and meantime primary network can be activated on a standby system. Further failover can be categorized as a hot and cold failover, in a hot failover system, the standby system immediately takes the load of the fail system, and starts functioning normally, but in the case of a cold failover system, the backup system will take some time to takes the responsibility.

1.4 FAULT TOLERANCE IN PARALLEL SYSTEM

Nowadays, a parallel computer has become a vital component in high-speed computing; parallel computers are massively used for a high amount of data computation. This computing is generally used in weather forecasting, genome sequencing, neural computation, fluid mechanics [14], and so many areas; now there are so many obstacles for the designing of parallel computers such as software issues and hardware issues. In this decade, parallel computers are used for a high amount of data computation in minimum time. In a parallel computer, there is more than one processing unit, and all the processing units are connected by some interconnection network;

various kinds of routing are also used for data communication between the processing unit. Amid of processing or computing if any kind of power or any kind of failure occurs, then the parallel computer automatically reconfigures the system which is known as reconfigurability or reliabilities. During the execution or the calculation of any kind of job, the fault tolerance system of a parallel computer will take care of responsibility. The fault may be hardware related, or software related [4], for fault tolerance system of parallel computer will take care of all the things without disturbing the execution and without the knowledge of end user. Various kinds of fault-tolerance systems are applicable in parallel computers. Generally, it is fully based on various algorithms and policies. And they have cost-effectiveness, error detection as well as an error corrections scheme, once the error is discovered by the system diagnostic the system, will recover the error and correct the error [14].

An algorithm-based fault tolerance system is a kind of fault-tolerance system in which the failed processor continuously generates wrong output; it means we must first determine the accuracy of the algorithm by some mathematical calculations. By simple linear algebra computation, we can easily determine the approach and the working of algorithms best port care system. Our further objective is to achieve a very low overhead [14].

In a parallel computer or multiprocessor, if any kind of fault occurs, then the fault tolerance system of a parallel computer cannot affect the system execution and accuracy of the result. Parallel error detection and error correction systems will work with the fault tolerance of the system; once the error occurs, the tolerance system will immediately take up the responsibility. The fault tolerance system applied in the parallel system will be based on the algorithm, and it's also cost-effective. In the early approach, error detection techniques will apply before the execution starts and when the errors have been diagnosed and corrected, the job will be initiated. But in the new fault tolerance system, parallel execution of the job and fault of the system can be handled simultaneously [14].

Algorithms-based fault tolerance system is a kind of tolerance approach, in which failed processors continue to work but generate incorrect output. This approach first determines the correctness of the algorithms or mathematical calculation. By linear algebra computation, we can easily determine the class of approach and achieve a very low overhead. Now we are considering the reconfiguring add for permanent failure, but we have assumed that once the processing unit has failed then the entire fault tolerance system will not be going to reconfigure the failed processing unit. However, the transient fault is the general fault that occurs in a parallel computer. A transient fault is the temporary fault, once any kind of computing is going on, and if a meantime error is encountered in the calculation, it means the transient fault is introduced in computing. The transient fault is temporary, and it can be easily detected and corrected by the algorithm; the primary source of the transient fault is the noise introduced inside the computing circuit [14]. The transient fault can be rectified by the concurrent error detection algorithm. Amid of execution the error detection and error correction system are also run parallel. While the execution of the job error detection and error correction is also run concurrently with that computation [15].

The major concern of a fault tolerance system in a parallel computer is that the system is affordable, has less power consumption, robustness, and is highly available once the requirement arises. For that, the new fault tolerance system will be tested by some mathematical model.

The term "redundancy" is used to describe the practice of duplicating hardware and software components with the express purpose of boosting the system's dependability. Hardware redundancy strategies use supplementary hardware components. All redundant hardware operates in parallel to carry out the same tasks, and failures may be detected and concealed using majority voting methods [15].

Software models for load balancing provide the basis of fault-tolerance strategies. In this case, a load dispatcher module is used to allocate incoming job requests to available resources. Elastic load balancing (ELB) is used by Amazon EC2 to handle incoming requests. In this setting, its primary goal is to distribute user task requests evenly among available resources to reduce the probability of system failure [17,18].

1.5 FAULT TOLERANCE IN CLOUD COMPUTING

1.5.1 METRICS FOR FAULT TOLERANCE IN CLOUD COMPUTING

The fault tolerance in the cloud system can be measured by the various parameters as follows [19,20,21]:

Throughput: throughput of the system can be considered, as how many outputs are going to be generated by the system per unit of time.

Response Time: the first response given by the processing unit to the job is known as response time. The value of response time should be minimized.

Scalability: adding more machines or nodes to a distributed system to distribute the workload across multiple resources. It aims to improve the system's capacity by scaling out, often achieved by adding more servers, nodes, or instances. Horizontal scaling usually requires mechanisms to balance and distribute the workload across these additional resources.

Performance: effectiveness of the system is known as performance; the performance of the system can be improved by the system refinement, finding the sensible cost incurred for the designing of the system.

Availability: availability means the reliability of the system, the system is available for computation, and system performance is better and better under good circumstances.

Usability: usability signifies that the output generated by the system is effective, efficient, and satisfactory.

Reliability: this component is geared for producing valid or passable outcomes in a limited amount of time.

Overhead Associated: in distributed systems, overhead refers to the additional resources, time, or complexity introduced by the system's architecture, protocols, communication, or coordination mechanisms beyond what would be required in a centralized or non-distributed environment. These overheads can impact performance, efficiency, and the overall system behavior.

Cost-effectiveness: in this case, the cost is just a monitorial cost.

S Guard: it is a rollback recovery system that can be used with HADOOP and Amazon Ec2.

Retry: of all the task-level techniques, this is the easiest. On the same cloud resource, the user resubmits the task.

Resubmission of the failed task: repeated attempts are made to complete the unsuccessful job, either on the same computer or a different one.

User-defined exception handling: in this case, the user specifies the precise action to take in the event of a task failure in a workflow.

Rescue workflow: it permits the system to resume working after a job fails until it can no longer do so without correcting the problem.

Fault Catalog: in cloud computing fault generally occurs, the reason being cloud is prone to fault. Various kinds of techniques are you in the cloud environment, some of the fault tolerance techniques are applicable at the task level, and some of the techniques are applicable at the workflow level. Fault further can be categorized as a reactive fault and a proactive fault.

  i. Reactive fault tolerance

     The reactive fault is generally known as a temporary fault. The reactive faults are used to reduce the impact of the failure of the system. When any kind of noise or minor failures occur inside the system, then it's a kind of temporary fault. It can be rectified by the policy of checking point and the policy of retransmitting data and many more [22,23].

Checkpointing/Restart: instead of starting from the beginning, the unsuccessful job is restarted from the most recent checkpoint. It is a cost-effective method for large applications.

Replication: to ensure that the work is completed successfully, many duplicates of the task are run on separate resources until the entire duplicated task is not crashed. Replication is implemented using HA Proxy, Hadoop, and AmazonEc2.

  ii. Proactive Fault Tolerance

     Proactive fault tolerance anticipates faults and replaces questionable components with other functional components, avoiding the need to recover from faults and errors. This policy is followed for preemptive migration, software rejuvenation, and so on [24].

Software Rejuvenation: the system is designed to reboot regularly, with the system starting in a new state each time [25].

Self-healing proactive fault tolerance: when running on many virtual machines, application failures are automatically managed.

Failure Detector: a software or system that can identify when a node has crashed is called a failure detector. A failure detector's dependability is determined by the accuracy of its responses. If the failure detector always produces correct results, we say that it is dependable. Unreliable failure detectors provide information that isn't always precise, and they can take a long time to discover defective processes and produce erroneous findings by suspecting processes that haven't failed. This category includes the majority of failure detectors [26].

1.5.2 Cloud Computing's Fault Tolerance Issues

Providing fault tolerance for cloud computing is a highly serious, sophisticated, and difficult task. Numerous challenges need fault tolerance. It necessitates an in-depth examination of the problem's intricacy and interdependence. This section goes into depth on the many impediments to cloud computing development, as well as measures to overcome them [27].

- **Business continuity and availability of services**
  Businesses are always concerned about the usability and availability of computer services. This enables various providers to offer cloud computing services.
- **Data safety**
  Organizations are often concerned about the utility computing service's data security and safety. This difficulty requires diverse backup solutions to keep data secure. This allows users to choose various computing ways beyond cloud computing.
- **Performance Predictability**
  Cloud computing's primary difficulty is performance. Numerous virtual machines share the physical server's CPU and memory. Due to the high strain on the real system, the performance of all virtual machines will suffer. This necessitates the enhancement of rules to allow for the management of a restricted number of virtual machines on a real server.
- **The scalable storage**
  The next issue is to offer scalability, data durability, and a high level of capability to customers that employ cloud-based utility computing services. To resolve it, fault tolerance is required.
- **Bugs in the large distributing system**
  The next issue is to keep the huge distribution system as bug-free as possible. It is a difficult task to supply clients with bug-free services. There is a need for using tools to manage issues in a big distributing system.

1.5.3 Tools Used For Implementing Fault Tolerance

To apply fault tolerance challenges and strategies, a variety of technologies have been employed. HA Proxy is used in the cloud in the case of a server failure [28]. SHelp is a lightweight virtual machine runtime system that is resistant to software failures. Additionally, it is capable of implementing checkpointing in a cloud environment. ASSURE contains rescue points for resolving difficulties foreseen by the coder. Hadoop is a data-intensive computing platform that may also serve as a fault-tolerant storage system. Cloud computing techniques, such as Amazon Elastic Compute Cloud (EC2), offer a fault-tolerant environment for executing Linux-based programs [29].

One of the primary aims of Hadoop and HDFS is to be extremely fault-tolerant. As a consequence, HDFS may be scaled to hundreds or even thousands of nodes. These nodes are outfitted with inexpensive hardware. When thousands of computer components and hundreds of network equipment components such as switches, routers, and power units are combined in these massively distributed systems, breakdowns become fairly prevalent. These systems are susceptible to failure daily. As a consequence, a distributed system like Hadoop must be very fault-tolerant. Hadoop and HDFS fault tolerance is built on data redundancy, which entails duplicating data in such a way that backup copies are accessible if one copy is destroyed [30].

Hadoop is an open-source Java-based software platform designed for use on massively dispersed networks. It is a project of the Apache Software Foundation that has gained popularity because of its open-source nature. Yahoo contributed over 80% of Hadoop's core, and other big technical businesses, including Facebook, Twitter, and LinkedIn, have utilized or are now using Hadoop. The Hadoop framework is composed of several projects, but two of the most significant are the Hadoop Distributed File System (HDFS) and Map Reduce. HDFS was designed around the Map-Reduce paradigm [31].

1.6   FUZZY LOGIC-BASED FAULT DETECTION IN DISTRIBUTED SENSOR NETWORKS

The Distributed Sensor Network (DSN) is a collection of intelligent distributed sensor nodes that operate at a high rate of speed. The DSN is expected to have a significant number of similar or mixed nodes that are dispersed logically, physically, or geographically across an environment. The dispersed sensor nodes are used to gather data from their separate surroundings logically, and this data is regularly processed and sent to the sink node through an intermediary node in the network. Sensor nodes are used in a variety of applications for data collection and processing via a network. The way nodes are exploited varies according to the application [32]. Nodes enable the acquisition and processing of data and the execution of computational activities in DSNs. While such networks have the potential to support a broad variety of applications, they confront significant problems such as frequent network disconnection, limited resources, computing power, and memory [6]. Due to these circumstances, developing an efficient and effective approach for identifying problematic nodes in the DSN is a difficult task [33].

Sensor nodes are strategically placed across dangerous and unprotected places. These deployed sensor nodes fail due to DSN factors such as fire or high heat, animal or vehicle accidents, criminal activity, or continuous usage, which results in device locations shifting over time, possibly disconnecting the network. Failures may occur at multiple levels in a DSN system, including at the node or sink node level and the network level (link failure and packet error). The sensor nodes are powered by batteries or energy. As a result, energy is a significant resource constraint for sensing and processing data in DSNs [34]. Fuzzy logic control can make judgments in real-time, even with inadequate data. A fuzzy logic system may be used to identify efficient node failures in advance of data transfer, hence avoiding network performance deterioration.

1.6.1 Design Work on Fuzzy Logic Based Fault Detection in Distributed Sensor Networks

The purpose of fault detection is to ensure that the services being given to users continue to work properly. While sensor node failures are prevalent in networks, dealing with failed nodes is the most difficult job. The failure might be a node or a connection [35]. The failed nodes are causing the network's performance to degrade. As a result, network failures must be identified in advance and appropriate actions made to maintain network functioning.

Before sending data from the source node to the sink node, the fuzzy logic technique is employed to effectively identify defects. The DSN incorporates two levels of fault tolerance. The first step is fault detection, which is used to discover and connect failing nodes in the DSN. Another step is fault recovery, during which the network is re-initialized with active nodes to build a route between the sources and sink nodes. Finally, the sink node does the action based on the information received from the sensor nodes.

Figure 1.2 illustrates the communication paradigm used in DSNs. In the presence of malfunctioning nodes in the DSNs, the communication architecture ensures uninterrupted data transfer from the source to the sink node. In this architecture, each sensor node regularly or at regular intervals transmits the heartbeat message to its neighboring nodes to indicate which nodes are active. Because each sensor node does not get a heartbeat message from its neighboring nodes, it guesses that any

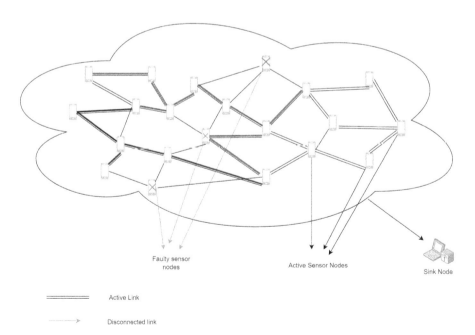

FIGURE 1.2 Fuzzy system for fault detection.

of the neighboring nodes is failing. Each sensor node stores information about its neighbors' nodes, such as their energy level, bandwidth, and connection efficiency; utilizing this information, each node identifies problematic nodes among its neighbors using fuzzy logic in the network [36] [37].

1.7   FAULT TOLERANCE USING MACHINE LEARNING

We can test a cloud/distributed system several times and keep track of which nodes fail each time. We can then apply prediction algorithms, or more precisely, classification algorithms, to the collected dataset of node failures, along with other factors like load and infrastructure that may affect the failure characteristics of a node, to predict and identify the nodes that are most likely to fail based on the data collected. Once the faulty nodes have been isolated, we may either remove them or set up a replacement node that will take over in the case of a failure, allowing the cloud system to continue functioning normally. This paradigm improves the fault tolerance and availability of cloud computing systems.

- **Evolutionary algorithms (EAs):** In fact, the model that answers the problem is a group of features known as its genotype. The model's performance is measured by a fitness function derived using a score. The subsequent iteration generates new genotypes based on model mutations and crossovers that result in more accurate predictions after computing the fitness score for all generated models. Genetic algorithms can be used to construct additional algorithms such as neural networks, credential networks, decision trees, and rule sets [38].
- **Algorithms based on the stochastic descent gradient (SGD):** These types of algorithms minimize losses defined by adjusting the model parameters to the negative gradient in the outputs of the model (the multi-variable derivative of a function). As the gradient is calculated using a randomly sampled sub-ensemble of the training data, it is dubbed stochastic. The loss feature is generally an authorization to minimize the actual error [39]. This is then the normal training procedure:
  i.   Present a random batch of training information sampled.
  ii. The model output and the desired output loss function can be calculated.
  iii. In terms of model parameters, calculate the gradient.
  iv. Adjust model parameters in the negative gradient direction, multiplied by the selected learning rate.
  v.   Repetition

For a range of ML models, SGD is the most often used training approach.
  ✓ Supporting vector machines [40]
  ✓ Perceptrons [41]
  ✓ Artificial neural networks (ANNs) [42]

ANN can be subdivided into numerous network-based subgroups:
- Deep Neural Net(DNN)

- • Convolution neural networks (CNNs/ConvNets)
- • Hopfield Networks
- • SOFMs
- • Stochastic neural networks
- • Auto-encoders
- • Generative Adversarial Networks (GANs)
- • **Rule-based machine learning (RBML) algorithms:** These algorithms are based on a set of rules that are part and parcel of the problem. Usually, these rules express a condition and a value when that condition is fulfilled. Due to the clear if-then relation, rules provide a straightforward way of interpreting ML algorithms, such as neural networks, in more abstract kinds.
  - − Association Rule Learning
  - − Classification and regressive trees, commonly termed CART trees
  - − Latent Dirichlet Allocation [43]
  - − The Naive Bayes classifiers
- • **Matrix Factorization:** These techniques can be used to detect latent components in matrix-structured data or find missing values. For example, many recommending systems are built on the User-Item Rating Matrix factorization to locate new items for users, given their evaluation of the other items [44]. A new drug discovery matrix is similarly employed to factorize Drug Compound Protein Matrix. Given the size of $O(F^3)$ with F, recent research focuses on the scaling up of such approaches to greater dimensions of function.

1.8   CONCLUSION

It is essential to provide the system with additional (redundant) resources that incorporate a fault tolerance capacity to a distributed system. Fault-tolerant and dependable computing field addresses several problems relating to various elements of system creation, operation, and maintenance. As distributed system applications continue to proliferate, problems with the reliability of systems are increasingly being addressed. Several research studies have tried to expand the standard conceptions of "fault-tolerant computing" to address the failure problem that affects the installations of distributed systems and computer networks. However, ordering the detection, diagnostic, repair, and recovery procedures in a timely manner may not be realistic for many distributed systems. No central facility for coordination of failure handling actions may be offered in a big distributed system. Instead, such fault detection technologies would probably need to be dispersed around the network, and the network fault source diagnosis would be made in a distributed way.

In this chapter, light has been thrown on various aspects of fault tolerance in a distributed environment. The aspect of machine learning which can be efficiently utilized for fault detection is also analyzed.

REFERENCES

[1]. Arifeen, T., Hassan, A.S. and Lee, J.A., 2019. A fault tolerant voter for approximate triple modular redundancy. *Electronics*, 8(3), p. 332.

[2]. Arifeen, T., Hassan, A.S. and Lee, J.A., 2020. Approximate triple modular redundancy: A survey. *IEEE Access*, 8, pp. 139851–139867.

[3]. Xu, D., Chu, C., Wang, Q., Liu, C., Wang, Y., Zhang, L., Liang, H. and Cheng, K.T., 2020, October. A hybrid computing architecture for fault-tolerant deep learning accelerators. In *2020 IEEE 38th International Conference on Computer Design (ICCD)* (pp. 478–485). IEEE.

[4]. Abdulwahab, L., Abdullahi, J.T. and Yusuf, I., 2018, November. Enhanced Markov-based model for the availability analysis of distributed software and hardware systems. In *Journal of Physics: Conference Series* (Vol. 1132, No. 1, p. 012066). IOP Publishing.

[5]. Pop, F., Iosup, A. and Prodan, R., 2018. HPS-HDS: High performance scheduling for heterogeneous distributed systems. *Future Generation Computer Systems*, 78, pp. 242–244.

[6]. Alam, M., Haidri, R.A. and Shahid, M., 2018, October. Enhanced load balancing strategy with migration cost on heterogeneous distributed systems. In *2018 3rd International Conference on Contemporary Computing and Informatics (IC3I)* (pp. 273–278). IEEE.

[7]. Akhmedov, B.A., 2021. Information technologies in cluster systems: A competence approach. *Universum: технические науки*, 4(5 (85)), p. 24.

[8]. Kumar, A., Yadav, R.S. and Ranvijay, A.J., 2011. Fault tolerance in real time distributed system. *International Journal on Computer Science and Engineering*, 3(2), pp. 933–939.

[9]. Wagle, R., Andrade, H., Hildrum, K., Venkatramani, C. and Spicer, M., 2011, July. Distributed middleware reliability and fault tolerance support in system S. In *Proceedings of the 5th ACM International Conference on Distributed Event-Based System* (pp. 335–346).

[10]. Agarwal, H. and Sharma, A., 2015, December. A comprehensive survey of fault tolerance techniques in cloud computing. In *2015 International Conference on Computing and Network Communications (CoCoNet)* (pp. 408–413). IEEE.

[11]. Bala, A. and Chana, I., 2012. Fault tolerance-challenges, techniques and implementation in cloud computing. *International Journal of Computer Science Issues (IJCSI)*, 9(1), p. 288.

[12]. Dalal, S. and Chhillar, R.S., 2012. Case studies of most common and severe types of software system failure. *International Journal of Advanced Research in Computer Science and Software Engineering*, 2(8), pp. 341–347.

[13]. Tiwari, R.G., Srivastava, A.P., Bhardwaj, G. and Kumar, V., 2021, April. Exploiting UML diagrams for test case generation: A review. In *2021 2nd International Conference on Intelligent Engineering and Management (ICIEM)* (pp. 457–460). IEEE.

[14]. Haroon, M. and Husain, M., 2013. Analysis of a dynamic load balancing in multiprocessor system. *International Journal of Computer Science Engineering and Information Technology Research*, 3(1), pp. 143–148.

[15]. Khan, R., Haroon, M. and Husain, M.S., 2015, April. Different technique of load balancing in distributed system: A review paper. In *2015 Global Conference on Communication Technologies (GCCT)* (pp. 371–375). IEEE.

[16]. Haroon, M. and Husain, M., 2015, March. Interest attentive dynamic load balancing in distributed systems. In *2015 2nd International Conference on Computing for Sustainable Global Development (INDIACom)* (pp. 1116–1120). IEEE.

[17]. Kumar, M., Dubey, K. and Sharma, S.C., 2018. Elastic and flexible deadline constraint load balancing algorithm for cloud computing. *Procedia Computer Science*, 125, pp. 717–724.

[18]. Sotiriadis, S., Bessis, N., Amza, C. and Buyya, R., 2016. Elastic load balancing for dynamic virtual machine reconfiguration based on vertical and horizontal scaling. *IEEE Transactions on Services Computing*, 12(2), pp. 319–334.

[19]. Prathiba, S. and Sowvarnica, S., 2017, February. Survey of failures and fault tolerance in cloud. In *2017 2nd International Conference on Computing and Communications Technologies (ICCCT)* (pp. 169–172). IEEE.

[20]. Shah, Y., Thakkar, E. and Bhavsar, S., 2021. Fault tolerance in cloud and fog computing—A holistic view. In *Data Science and Intelligent Applications*, Ketan Kotecha, Vincenzo Piuri, Hetalkumar N. Shah, Rajan Patel (Eds.,), (pp. 415–422). Springer, Singapore.

[21]. Asghar, H., & Nazir, B., 2021. Analysis and implementation of reactive fault tolerance techniques in Hadoop: a comparative study. *The Journal of Supercomputing*, 77, pp. 7184–7210.

[22]. Tiwari, R., Husain, M., Gupta, S. and Srivastava, A., 2010, February. Improving ant colony optimization algorithm for data clustering. In *Proceedings of the International Conference and Workshop on Emerging Trends in Technology* (pp. 529–534).

[23]. Tiwari, R.G., Husain, M., Srivastava, V. and Singh, K., 2011, February. A hypercube novelty model for comparing E-commerce and M-commerce. In *Proceedings of the 2011 International Conference on Communication, Computing & Security* (pp. 616–619).

[24]. Ray, B. K., Saha, A., Khatua, S., & Roy, S. (2020). Proactive fault-tolerance technique to enhance reliability of cloud service in cloud federation environment. *IEEE Transactions on Cloud Computing*, 10(2), pp. 957–971.

[25]. Bai, J., Chang, X., Machida, F., Trivedi, K.S. and Han, Z., 2020. Analyzing software rejuvenation techniques in a virtualized system: Service provider and user views. *IEEE Access*, 8, pp. 6448–6459.

[26]. Liu, J., Wu, Z., Wu, J., Dong, J., Zhao, Y. and Wen, D., 2017. A Weibull distribution accrual failure detector for cloud computing. *PloS One*, 12(3), p. e0173666.

[27]. Mohammadian, V., Navimipour, N.J., Hosseinzadeh, M. and Darwesh, A., 2020. Comprehensive and systematic study on the fault tolerance architectures in cloud computing. *Journal of Circuits, Systems and Computers*, 29(15), p. 2050240.

[28]. Zeebaree, S.R., Jacksi, K. and Zebari, R.R., 2020. Impact analysis of SYN flood DDoS attack on HAProxy and NLB cluster-based web servers. *Indonesia Journal of Electrical Engineering and Computer Science*, 19(1), pp. 510–517.

[29]. Gulabani, S., 2017. Hands-on elastic compute cloud. In *Practical Amazon EC2, SQS, Kinesis, and S3* (pp. 23–88). Apress, Berkeley, CA.

[30]. Elkawkagy, M. and Elbeh, H., 2020. High performance hadoop distributed file system. *International Journal of Networked and Distributed Computing*, 8(3), pp. 119–123.

[31]. Asghar, H. and Nazir, B., 2021. Analysis and implementation of reactive fault tolerance techniques in Hadoop: A comparative study. *The Journal of Supercomputing*, 77, pp. 1–27.

[32]. Wang, W., De, S., Zhou, Y., Huang, X. and Moessner, K., 2017, June. Distributed sensor data computing in smart city applications. In *2017 IEEE 18th International Symposium on a World of Wireless, Mobile and Multimedia Networks (WoWMoM)* (pp. 1–5). IEEE.

[33]. Duan, H., Zhou, Y. and Liu, M., 2017. Fault Tolerant scheduling algorithm in distributed sensor networks. *Journal of Information Hiding Multimedia Signal Processing*, 8(1), pp. 127–137.

[34]. Agarwal, H., Tiwari, P. and Tiwari, R.G., 2019, December. Exploiting sensor fusion for mobile robot localization. In *2019 Third International conference on I-SMAC (IoT in Social, Mobile, Analytics and Cloud)(I-SMAC)* (pp. 463–466). IEEE.

[35]. Dogra, R., Rani, S. and Sharma, B., 2021. A review to forest fires and its detection techniques using wireless sensor network. In *Advances in Communication and Computational Technology: Select Proceedings of ICACCT 2019*, Gurdeep Singh Hura, Ashutosh Kumar Singh, Lau Siong Hoe (Eds.,), (pp. 1339–1350). Springer, Singapore.

[36]. Talmale, R., & Bhat, M. N. (2022). Energy attentive and pre-fault recognize mechanism for distributed wireless sensor network using fuzzy logic approach. *Wireless Personal Communications*, 1–18.

[37]. Srivastava, S., Haroon, M., & Bajaj, A. (2013, September). Web document information extraction using class attribute approach. In *2013 4th International Conference on Computer and Communication Technology (ICCCT)* (pp. 17–22). IEEE.

[38]. Lilhore, U.K., Poongodi, M., Kaur, A., Simaiya, S., Algarni, A.D., Elmannai, H., Vijayakumar, V., Tunze, G.B. and Hamdi, M., 2022. Hybrid model for detection of cervical cancer using causal analysis and machine learning techniques. *Computational and Mathematical Methods in Medicine*, (Vol. 2022, Article ID 4688327, pp. 1–17).

[39]. Dogo, E.M., Afolabi, O.J., Nwulu, N.I., Twala, B. and Aigbavboa, C.O., 2018, December. A comparative analysis of gradient descent-based optimization algorithms on convolutional neural networks. In *2018 International Conference on Computational Techniques, Electronics and Mechanical Systems (CTEMS)* (pp. 92–99). IEEE.

[40]. Chauhan, M., Gupta, S. and Sandhu, M., 2022. Short-term electric load forecasting using support vector machines. *ECS Transactions*, 107(1), p. 9731.

[41]. Minsky, M. and Papert, S.A., 2017. *Perceptrons: An Introduction to Computational Geometry*. MIT Press.

[42]. Tiwari, R.G., Agarwal, A.K., Kaushal, R.K. and Kumar, N., 2021, October. Prophetic analysis of bitcoin price using machine learning approaches. In *2021 6th International Conference on Signal Processing, Computing and Control (ISPCC)* (pp. 428–432). IEEE.

[43]. Jelodar, H., Wang, Y., Yuan, C., Feng, X., Jiang, X., Li, Y. and Zhao, L., 2019. Latent Dirichlet allocation (LDA) and topic modeling: Models, applications, a survey. *Multimedia Tools and Applications*, 78(11), pp. 15169–15211.

[44]. Xue, H.J., Dai, X., Zhang, J., Huang, S. and Chen, J., 2017, August. Deep matrix factorization models for recommender systems. In *IJCAI* (Vol. 17, pp. 3203–3209).

2 An Overview of Software-Defined Network (SDN) Frameworks

Savya Sachi, Mohtab Alam, and Senthil Athithan

2.1 INTRODUCTION OF SDN

Software-Defined Networks (SDN) have emerged as a transformative technology that promises to change the way networks are managed, controlled, and secured. SDN is an architectural approach that decouples the control plane from the data plane, enabling centralized management, programmability, and agility in network operations (Table 2.1). This separation allows network administrators to dynamically configure network components, optimize traffic flow, and implement advanced security mechanisms [1] (Figure 2.1).

2.2 EVOLUTION OF SDN

The concept of SDN can be traced back to the early 2000s when researchers started exploring the idea of programmable networks (Figure 2.2).

The emergence of OpenFlow, a protocol for communication between the control plane and data plane, further propelled the development of SDN. Over the years, SDN has evolved from a research concept to a widely adopted networking paradigm, with numerous industry players contributing to its standardization and commercialization [2].

2.3 KEY COMPONENTS OF SDN ARCHITECTURE

The core components of SDN architecture are:

- Controller: The central entity responsible for managing and configuring the network. Controllers provide a platform for implementing network applications and services.
- Data Plane: Comprises network devices, such as switches and routers, responsible for forwarding traffic based on decisions made by the control plane.

DOI: 10.1201/9781003432869-2

TABLE 2.1
Comparison of Traditional Networking and SDN

Feature	Traditional Networking	Software-Defined Networking (SDN)
Architecture	Distributed control	Centralized control
Management	Device-centric	Network-centric
Configuration	Manual, device-specific	Programmable, unified
Scalability	Limited	Enhanced
Flexibility	Limited	High
Security	Device-based policies	Centralized, fine-grained policies
Traffic Analysis	Limited, passive	Real-time, dynamic
Response to Threats	Slower, manual	Faster, automated

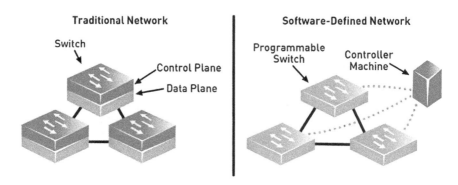

FIGURE 2.1   Software-defined networks (SDN).

- Control Plane: Communicates with the data plane through standardized protocols like OpenFlow, enabling dynamic configuration and management of network devices.
- Application Layer: Consists of various network applications and services that leverage SDN capabilities to enhance network functionality, security, and performance.

2.4   BENEFITS AND CHALLENGES OF SDN ADOPTION

SDN offers several benefits, such as:

- Centralized management: Simplifies network operations by providing a single point of control, reducing complexity, and operational costs.
- Programmability: Enables the development of custom network applications and services tailored to specific business requirements.
- Agility: Facilitates rapid network provisioning and reconfiguration to accommodate changing business needs.
- Enhanced security: Allows for the implementation of advanced security mechanisms and policies to protect the network from emerging threats.

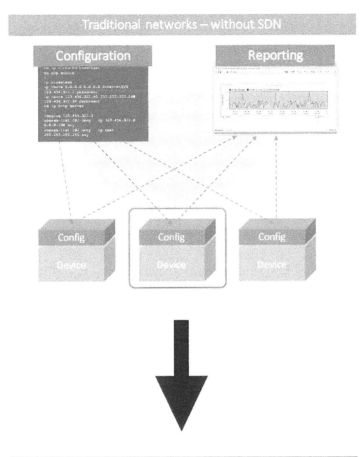

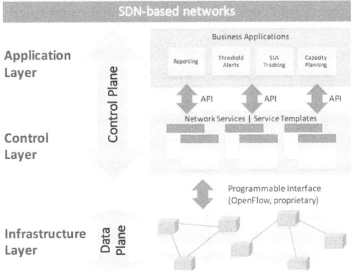

FIGURE 2.2   Traditional network and SDN.

However, SDN adoption also presents challenges, including [3]:

- Security concerns: As SDN centralizes control, it creates a single point of failure, which, if compromised, can lead to significant network disruption.
- Interoperability: Ensuring seamless integration between different SDN components and existing network infrastructure can be challenging.
- Skillset requirements: SDN adoption requires a shift in skillsets for network administrators, demanding familiarity with new tools and programming languages.

This book aims to provide an in-depth understanding of SDN security issues and explore various use cases where SDN can be effectively deployed to enhance network security [4] (Tables 2.2–2.4).

TABLE 2.2
SDN Security Mechanisms

Security Mechanism	Description
Authentication & authorization	Ensures only authorized entities can access and manage the network
Intrusion detection & prevention	Monitors and analyzes network traffic for signs of malicious activity
Security policies & rule enforcement	Governs network traffic and access to resources with fine-grained policies
Encryption & secure communication	Protects integrity and confidentiality of network data and commands

TABLE 2.3
SDN Use Cases and Security Solutions

Use Case	Security Solution
Secure data center networking	Microsegmentation, Automated threat response, Dynamic traffic analysis
Secure enterprise networks	Centralized Policy Management, Advanced Intrusion Detection, Secure Access Control
Secure cloud and edge computing	Dynamic network isolation, Automated security policy enforcement, Real-time threat mitigation

TABLE 2.4
Implementation Challenges and Best Practices for SDN-Based Security Solutions

Challenge	Best Practice
Integration with existing infrastructure	Gradually introduce SDN components, ensuring proper testing and validation
Scalability	Design SDN solutions to scale with growth without negatively impacting performance
Interoperability	Utilize open standards and protocols to ensure seamless integration
Skillset requirements	Invest in training and skill development for network administrators

2.5   SDN SECURITY ISSUES

2.5.1   Introduction to SDN Security

While SDN offers numerous benefits, it also introduces new security concerns that need to be addressed. The centralized control and programmability of SDN create unique challenges that require innovative security mechanisms and strategies.

2.5.2   Threat Landscape in SDN

The threat landscape in SDN can be categorized into the following areas:

*   Controller-level threats: As the controller is the central entity managing the network, it is a prime target for attackers. Compromising the controller can lead to the manipulation of network configurations and traffic flow, causing severe disruptions [5].
*   Data plane threats: Network devices in the data plane are also susceptible to attacks, such as Distributed Denial of Service (DDoS) and man-in-the-middle attacks, which can impact network performance and availability.
*   Control plane threats: The communication between the control plane and the data plane can be targeted by attackers to intercept, manipulate, or block network configurations and commands.
*   Application-level threats: Malicious network applications can exploit vulnerabilities in the SDN architecture to launch attacks or bypass security mechanisms.

2.5.3   Vulnerabilities in SDN Components

Each SDN component has inherent vulnerabilities that can be exploited by attackers:

*   Controller vulnerabilities: Controllers may be susceptible to vulnerabilities in their software, such as buffer overflows, SQL injection, and cross-site scripting, which can be exploited to compromise the system.
*   Data plane vulnerabilities: Network devices may have firmware vulnerabilities, weak default configurations, or insecure management interfaces that can be exploited by attackers.
*   Control plane vulnerabilities: The protocols used for communication between the control and data planes, like OpenFlow, may have security flaws that can be exploited to manipulate network traffic or launch attacks.
*   Application-level vulnerabilities: Network applications and services running on the controller may have vulnerabilities or weak configurations, allowing attackers to gain unauthorized access or perform malicious actions [6].

2.5.4 ATTACK SCENARIOS AND POTENTIAL IMPACTS

Some common attack scenarios in SDN environments include:

* Controller compromise: An attacker gains control of the SDN controller and manipulates network configurations, causing network disruptions, data leakage, or unauthorized access.
* Data plane flooding: Attackers launch a DDoS attack, overwhelming network devices and causing performance degradation or service unavailability.
* Control plane hijacking: Attackers intercept or manipulate control plane communications to redirect network traffic, bypass security policies, or gain unauthorized access to network resources.
* Malicious applications: Attackers deploy rogue network applications that exploit vulnerabilities in the SDN architecture or bypass security mechanisms to perform malicious actions.

These attack scenarios demonstrate the potential impact of security breaches in SDN environments, highlighting the importance of developing robust security mechanisms to protect the network infrastructure and maintain its integrity, availability, and confidentiality.

2.6 SECURITY MECHANISMS FOR SDN

2.6.1 OVERVIEW OF SDN SECURITY MECHANISMS

To address the security challenges and vulnerabilities associated with SDN, various security mechanisms have been proposed and developed. These mechanisms aim to protect the different components of the SDN architecture and mitigate potential threats.

2.6.2 AUTHENTICATION AND AUTHORIZATION IN SDN

Authentication and authorization are crucial for securing the SDN controller and ensuring that only authorized entities can access and manage the network. Implementing strong authentication mechanisms, such as multi-factor authentication (MFA), and enforcing role-based access control (RBAC) can help protect the controller and minimize the risk of unauthorized access.

2.6.3 INTRUSION DETECTION AND PREVENTION SYSTEMS

Intrusion detection and prevention systems (IDPS) can be employed in SDN environments to monitor and analyze network traffic for signs of malicious activity. By leveraging the centralized control and programmability of SDN, IDPS can be more efficiently deployed, allowing for dynamic configuration and updates, as well as the ability to automatically respond to detected threats [7].

2.6.4 SECURITY POLICIES AND RULE ENFORCEMENT

SDN enables the implementation of fine-grained security policies and rules that govern network traffic and access to resources. By defining and enforcing these policies centrally, network administrators can maintain consistent security across the entire network infrastructure, quickly adapt to changing threats, and minimize the risk of misconfigurations.

2.6.5 ENCRYPTION AND SECURE COMMUNICATION IN SDN

Ensuring secure communication between SDN components is essential for protecting the integrity and confidentiality of network data and commands. Implementing encryption for data-in-transit and using secure protocols, such as Transport Layer Security (TLS), can help safeguard control plane communications and prevent eavesdropping or manipulation by attackers.

2.7 USE CASE 1- SECURE DATA CENTER NETWORKING

2.7.1 INTRODUCTION TO DATA CENTER NETWORKING

Data centers are critical for the operation of many organizations, providing the infrastructure for hosting applications, storing data, and processing large amounts of information. As such, securing data center networks is of utmost importance to ensure the confidentiality, integrity, and availability of these critical resources.

2.7.2 SDN-BASED SECURITY SOLUTIONS FOR DATA CENTERS

SDN can be leveraged to enhance data center security by providing centralized control, improved visibility, and the ability to rapidly adapt to emerging threats. Some examples of SDN-based security solutions for data centers include [8]:

- Microsegmentation: SDN enables the creation of granular network segments, isolating applications and workloads, and reducing the potential attack surface.
- Automated threat response: SDN can be used to automate the response to detected threats, such as quarantining affected devices or reconfiguring the network to block malicious traffic.
- Dynamic traffic analysis: SDN can facilitate real-time traffic analysis and monitoring, allowing for the early detection and mitigation of potential security issues.

2.7.3 IMPLEMENTATION CHALLENGES AND BEST PRACTICES

Implementing SDN-based security solutions in data center networks presents challenges, such as:

- Integration with existing infrastructure: Ensuring seamless integration between SDN components and traditional data center networking devices can be complex.
- Scalability: SDN solutions must be designed to scale with the growth of data center resources and traffic, without negatively impacting performance or security.

To overcome these challenges, best practices for SDN implementation in data center networks include:

- Adopting a phased approach: Gradually introduce SDN components and solutions, ensuring proper testing and validation at each stage.
- Developing a robust security framework: Establish a comprehensive security framework that covers all aspects of SDN deployment, from authentication and authorization to encryption and secure communication.
- Leveraging open standards: Utilize open standards and protocols, such as OpenFlow and the Open Networking Foundation (ONF) specifications, to ensure interoperability and future-proofing.

2.8   CASE STUDY: SDN DEPLOYMENT IN A LARGE-SCALE DATA CENTER

In this case study, we will explore the implementation of SDN-based security solutions in a large-scale data center operated by a multinational corporation. The data center houses various critical applications and services, making security a top priority.

Challenge: The corporation faced increasing security threats, such as DDoS attacks, data breaches, and unauthorized access to network resources. They needed a solution to enhance security, improve visibility, and ensure the scalability of their data center network [9].

Solution: The corporation decided to adopt an SDN-based approach to secure their data center network. They implemented the following security solutions:

- Microsegmentation: The data center network was divided into smaller segments based on application and workload requirements, isolating traffic and reducing the attack surface.
- Automated threat response: The corporation deployed an SDN-based IDPS to monitor network traffic and automatically respond to detected threats by adjusting network configurations and blocking malicious traffic.
- Dynamic traffic analysis: SDN was utilized to enable real-time traffic analysis and monitoring, allowing the corporation to identify and mitigate potential security issues proactively.

Results: By implementing SDN-based security solutions, the corporation successfully enhanced the security of their data center network. They experienced reduced attack surfaces, improved threat detection and response, and increased visibility into network traffic. The corporation also benefited from the scalability and agility offered by SDN, which allowed them to quickly adapt to changing business requirements and emerging threats.

2.9   USE CASE 2- SECURE ENTERPRISE NETWORKS

2.9.1   INTRODUCTION TO ENTERPRISE NETWORKS

Enterprise networks are the backbone of modern organizations, connecting various devices, systems, and users within a company and facilitating communication and collaboration. As the complexity and scale of these networks continue to grow, ensuring their security becomes increasingly challenging. Traditional networking solutions often struggle to provide the flexibility, visibility, and control needed to effectively address the evolving threat landscape.

2.9.2   SDN-BASED SECURITY SOLUTIONS FOR ENTERPRISE NETWORKS

SDN offers a promising solution for securing enterprise networks by providing centralized control, improved visibility, and the ability to rapidly adapt to emerging threats. Some examples of SDN-based security solutions for enterprise networks include:

- Centralized policy management: SDN enables the implementation of consistent security policies across the entire network, simplifying management and reducing the risk of misconfigurations.
- Advanced intrusion detection: SDN-based intrusion detection systems can be more efficiently deployed and updated, allowing for improved threat detection and faster response to security incidents [10].
- Secure access control: SDN can be leveraged to enhance access control mechanisms, ensuring that only authorized users and devices can connect to the network and access sensitive resources.

2.9.3   IMPLEMENTATION CHALLENGES AND BEST PRACTICES

Implementing SDN-based security solutions in enterprise networks presents challenges, such as:

- Integration with existing infrastructure: Ensuring seamless integration between SDN components and traditional networking devices can be complex.
- Scalability: SDN solutions must be designed to scale with the growth of enterprise resources and traffic, without negatively impacting performance or security.

To overcome these challenges, best practices for SDN implementation in enterprise networks include [11]:

- Adopting a phased approach: Gradually introduce SDN components and solutions, ensuring proper testing and validation at each stage.
- Developing a robust security framework: Establish a comprehensive security framework that covers all aspects of SDN deployment, from authentication and authorization to encryption and secure communication.

- Leveraging open standards: Utilize open standards and protocols, such as OpenFlow and the Open Networking Foundation (ONF) specifications, to ensure interoperability and future-proofing.

2.10 CASE STUDY: SDN DEPLOYMENT IN A GLOBAL ENTERPRISE NETWORK

In this case study, we will explore the implementation of SDN-based security solutions in a global enterprise network operated by a multinational corporation. The organization has a complex network infrastructure, with multiple branch offices and thousands of users and devices.

Challenge: The corporation faced increasing security threats, such as phishing attacks, malware infections, and unauthorized access to network resources [12]. They needed a solution to enhance security, improve visibility, and ensure the scalability of their enterprise network.

Solution: The corporation decided to adopt an SDN-based approach to secure their enterprise network. They implemented the following security solutions:

- Centralized policy management: The corporation established a centralized policy management system, enabling consistent security policies across the entire network and simplifying administration [13].
- Advanced intrusion detection: The corporation deployed an SDN-based intrusion detection system to monitor network traffic, detect threats, and automatically respond to security incidents.
- Secure access control: SDN was utilized to enhance access control mechanisms, ensuring that only authorized users and devices could connect to the network and access sensitive resources.

Results: By implementing SDN-based security solutions, the corporation successfully enhanced the security of their enterprise network. They experienced improved threat detection and response, increased visibility into network traffic, and more effective access control. The corporation also benefited from the scalability and agility offered by SDN, which allowed them to quickly adapt to changing business requirements and emerging threats [14].

2.11 USE CASE 3- SECURE CLOUD AND EDGE COMPUTING

2.11.1 INTRODUCTION TO CLOUD AND EDGE COMPUTING

Cloud computing has revolutionized the way organizations deploy and manage applications, providing scalable, on-demand access to computing resources. Edge computing, on the other hand, brings computation and data storage closer to the location where it is needed, improving response times and reducing latency. The combination of cloud and edge computing creates new opportunities for organizations to optimize their infrastructure while maintaining a high level of performance and reliability.

However, securing cloud and edge computing environments presents unique challenges, as data and applications are often distributed across multiple locations and platforms, increasing the potential attack surface [15].

2.11.2 SDN-BASED SECURITY SOLUTIONS FOR CLOUD AND EDGE COMPUTING

SDN can be leveraged to enhance security in cloud and edge computing environments by providing centralized control, improved visibility, and the ability to rapidly adapt to emerging threats. Some examples of SDN-based security solutions for cloud and edge computing include:

- Dynamic network isolation: SDN enables the creation of on-demand, isolated network segments for cloud and edge applications, reducing the attack surface and minimizing the risk of unauthorized access.
- Automated security policy enforcement: SDN can be used to automatically enforce security policies based on the context and location of cloud and edge workloads, ensuring consistent protection across the entire infrastructure [8].
- Real-time threat mitigation: SDN allows for real-time monitoring and analysis of network traffic in cloud and edge environments, enabling the rapid detection and mitigation of potential security threats.

2.11.3 IMPLEMENTATION CHALLENGES AND BEST PRACTICES

Implementing SDN-based security solutions in cloud and edge computing environments presents challenges, such as:

- Integration with multi-cloud and edge infrastructure: Ensuring seamless integration between SDN components and a diverse set of cloud and edge platforms can be complex.
- Maintaining consistent security policies: Implementing and enforcing consistent security policies across distributed cloud and edge environments can be challenging.

To overcome these challenges, best practices for SDN implementation in cloud and edge computing include:

- Adopting a phased approach: Gradually introduce SDN components and solutions, ensuring proper testing and validation at each stage.
- Developing a robust security framework: Establish a comprehensive security framework that covers all aspects of SDN deployment in cloud and edge environments, from authentication and authorization to encryption and secure communication [7].
- Leveraging open standards: Utilize open standards and protocols, such as OpenFlow and the Open Networking Foundation (ONF) specifications, to ensure interoperability and future-proofing.

2.12 CASE STUDY: SDN DEPLOYMENT IN A HYBRID CLOUD ENVIRONMENT

In this case study, we will explore the implementation of SDN-based security solutions in a hybrid cloud environment operated by a large financial services organization. The organization uses a combination of public cloud services and on-premises infrastructure to host their applications and data [6].

Challenge – The organization faced increasing security threats, such as data breaches, unauthorized access to cloud resources, and targeted attacks on their edge infrastructure. They needed a solution to enhance security, improve visibility, and ensure the scalability of their hybrid cloud environment.

Solution- The organization decided to adopt an SDN-based approach to secure their hybrid cloud environment. They implemented the following security solutions:

* Dynamic network isolation: The organization used SDN to create on-demand, isolated network segments for their cloud and edge applications, reducing the attack surface and minimizing the risk of unauthorized access [9].
* Automated security policy enforcement: SDN was utilized to automatically enforce security policies based on the context and location of cloud and edge workloads, ensuring consistent protection across the entire infrastructure.
* Real-time threat mitigation: SDN allowed the organization to monitor and analyze network traffic in real-time, enabling rapid detection and mitigation of potential security threats.

Results: By implementing SDN-based security solutions, the organization successfully enhanced the security of their hybrid cloud environment

2.13 FUTURE TRENDS IN SDN SECURITY

2.13.1 EMERGING TECHNOLOGIES AND THEIR IMPACT ON SDN SECURITY

Emerging technologies, such as 5G, the Internet of Things (IoT), and blockchain, will have a significant impact on SDN security [12]. These technologies will bring new challenges, such as increased network complexity, a growing attack surface, and a need for more robust security mechanisms to protect networks from advanced threats.

2.13.2 INTEGRATION OF ARTIFICIAL INTELLIGENCE AND MACHINE LEARNING IN SDN SECURITY

The integration of artificial intelligence (AI) and machine learning (ML) into SDN security solutions promises to further enhance the capabilities of SDN. AI and ML can be used to analyze vast amounts of network data, identify patterns, and predict potential threats [13]. This allows for more proactive security measures, faster threat detection, and more efficient response to security incidents.

2.13.3 NEXT-GENERATION SDN SECURITY FRAMEWORKS

As SDN continues to mature and evolve, the development of next-generation SDN security frameworks will become increasingly important. These frameworks should address emerging security challenges, integrate advanced AI and ML capabilities, and provide comprehensive protection for increasingly complex and diverse network environments.

2.13.4 CHALLENGES AND OPPORTUNITIES IN SECURING FUTURE SDN DEPLOYMENTS

Securing future SDN deployments will present both challenges and opportunities. Key challenges include ensuring the interoperability of SDN components [9], maintaining consistent security policies across diverse network environments, and protecting against new and evolving threats. Opportunities include leveraging AI and ML for enhanced security capabilities, developing next-generation SDN security frameworks, and exploring innovative security solutions for emerging technologies [10].

2.14 APPLICATIONS OF SDN SECURITY SOLUTIONS

In this chapter, we will explore various applications of SDN security solutions across different industries and domains, demonstrating the potential benefits and impact of SDN security in diverse settings.

2.14.1 SDN SECURITY IN SMART CITIES

Smart cities rely on interconnected networks to manage critical infrastructure, including transportation systems, utilities, and public safety. SDN security can help protect these networks from cyberattacks and ensure the reliable operation of essential services [11]. Key applications of SDN security in smart cities include:

- Enhanced monitoring and control of critical infrastructure networks
- Improved detection and mitigation of cyber threats targeting public services
- Real-time analysis of network traffic for potential security incidents

2.14.2 SDN SECURITY IN HEALTHCARE

Healthcare networks manage sensitive patient data and support critical medical applications, making security a top priority [13,14]. SDN security can help protect healthcare networks from data breaches and ensure the confidentiality and integrity of patient information. Key applications of SDN security in healthcare include:

- Centralized management of security policies across diverse healthcare networks
- Rapid detection and response to security incidents involving patient data
- Enhanced access control for medical devices and applications

2.14.3 SDN Security in Industrial IoT

Industrial IoT (IIoT) networks connect various devices, sensors, and systems within industrial environments, such as manufacturing plants and power grids. SDN security can help protect these networks from cyber threats and ensure the reliable operation of industrial processes [14,15]. Key applications of SDN security in IIoT include:

- Real-time monitoring and control of IIoT networks
- Improved detection and mitigation of cyber threats targeting industrial systems
- Dynamic network isolation for sensitive industrial processes and devices

2.14.4 SDN Security in Telecommunications

Telecommunications networks form the backbone of modern communication and data exchange, making their security crucial. SDN security can help protect these networks from cyberattacks and ensure the availability and performance of critical communication services [16]. Key applications of SDN security in telecommunications include:

- Centralized management of security policies across diverse telecommunications networks
- Enhanced monitoring and control of network traffic for potential security incidents
- Real-time threat detection and mitigation in telecommunications infrastructure

2.14.5 SDN Security in Financial Services

Financial services organizations manage sensitive financial data and support critical transactions, making network security paramount. SDN security can help protect these networks from cyber threats and ensure the confidentiality, integrity, and availability of financial data and services. Key applications of SDN security in financial services include [17,18]:

- Centralized management of security policies across diverse financial networks
- Rapid detection and response to security incidents involving financial data
- Enhanced access control for financial applications and services

2.15 CONCLUSION

2.15.1 Recap of SDN Security Issues and Use Cases

This book has explored various aspects of SDN security, including the unique security issues associated with SDN and the use of SDN-based security solutions in diverse network environments such as data centers, enterprise networks, and cloud and edge computing.

2.15.2 Key Takeaways and Recommendations

Key takeaways from this book include the importance of understanding the unique security challenges associated with SDN, the potential benefits of implementing SDN-based security solutions, and the need for a comprehensive and proactive approach to securing SDN deployments. Recommendations for organizations considering SDN security solutions include adopting a phased implementation approach, developing a robust security framework, and leveraging open standards to ensure interoperability and future-proofing.

2.15.3 As SDN Continues to Evolve and Gain Traction in Various Industries

Its security implications will become increasingly critical. The future scope of SDN security includes several promising areas of research, development, and practical application:

1. Advanced AI and ML integration: The integration of artificial intelligence and machine learning in SDN security solutions is expected to continue advancing. This will enable the development of more proactive security measures, faster threat detection, and efficient response to security incidents.
2. Security for emerging technologies: As emerging technologies such as 5G, IoT, and blockchain gain prominence, the need for SDN security solutions tailored to these new networking paradigms will grow. Future research and development will focus on addressing the unique security challenges posed by these technologies and creating SDN-based security solutions to protect increasingly complex and diverse networks.
3. Enhanced threat intelligence and analytics: Future SDN security solutions will likely incorporate advanced threat intelligence and analytics capabilities, allowing organizations to gain deeper insights into potential threats, vulnerabilities, and attack patterns. This will enable more informed decision-making and proactive security strategies.
4. Adaptive and context-aware security: As networks become more dynamic and distributed, future SDN security solutions will need to be more adaptive and context-aware, capable of adjusting security policies and controls based on the evolving network state, user context, and threat landscape.

5. Collaboration and information sharing: The future of SDN security will involve greater collaboration and information sharing among different organizations, vendors, and security researchers. This will help create more robust, interoperable security solutions and facilitate faster response to emerging threats and vulnerabilities.

6. Security for multi-cloud and edge computing environments: As organizations continue to adopt multi-cloud and edge computing solutions, the need for SDN security solutions that can effectively protect these complex and distributed environments will grow. Future research and development in SDN security will focus on ensuring seamless integration with diverse cloud and edge platforms and maintaining consistent security policies across these environments.

7. Next-generation SDN security frameworks: The development of next-generation SDN security frameworks will become increasingly important as SDN technology matures and evolves. These frameworks should address emerging security challenges, integrate advanced AI and ML capabilities, and provide comprehensive protection for complex and diverse network environments.

By exploring these future directions, SDN security will continue to advance, enabling organizations to better protect their networks and data from increasingly sophisticated cyber threats.

REFERENCES

[1] T. Bakhshi, "Securing wireless software-defined networks: Appraising threats, defenses & research challenges," in In 2018 International Conference on Advancements in Computational Sciences (ICACS), 2018.

[2] I. Akyildiz, A. Lee, P. Wang, M. Luo, and W. Chou, "A roadmap for traffic engineering in SDN-OpenFlow networks. Computer networks," *Computer Networks*, pp. 1–30, 2014.

[3] C. Krzysztof, W. Jacek, K. Sławomir, R. Paweł, T. D. Khoa, "SDN architecture impact on network security," in Federated Conference on Computer Science and Information Systems ACSIS, Vol. 3, pp. 143–148, 2014.

[4] D. Kreutz., F. Ramos, and P. Verissimo, "Towards secure and dependable software-defined networks," in Proceedings of the Second ACM SIGCOMM Workshop on "Hot Topics in Software-Defined Networking," ACM, New York, pp. 55–60. http://dx.doi.org/10.1145/2491185.24911992013.

[5] Y. Zheng and P. Zhang, "A security and trust framework for virtualized networks and software-defined networking," *Security and Communication Networks*, pp. 3059–3069, 2016.

[6] Diego Kreutz, F. M. V. Ramos, P. E. Veríssimo, C. E. Rothenberg, S. Azodolmolky, and S. Uhlig, "Software-defined networking: A comprehensive survey," in Proceedings of the IEEE, Vol. 103, no. 1, pp. 14–76, 2015.

[7] H. Daojing, S. Chan and M. Guizani, "Securing software-defined wireless networks," *IEEE Communications Magazine*, pp. 20–25, 2016.

[8] T. N. El Moussaid and El Azhari, "Security analysis as software-defined security for SDN environment," in Fourth International Conference on IEEE, 2017.

[9] A. A., A. E. and G. A., "Securing software-defined networks: Taxonomy, requirements, and open issues," *IEEE Communications Magazine*, Vol. 53, Issue 4, pp. 36–44, 2015.

[10] B. Agborubere and E. Sanchez-Velazquez, "OpenFlow communications and TLS security in software-defined networks," in IEEE International Conference on Internet of Things (iThings) and IEEE Green Computing and Communications (Green Com) and IEEE Cyber, Physical and Social Computing (CPSCom) and IEEE Smart Data (SmartData), 2017.

[11] P. Porras, S. Shin and M. Fong, "A security enforcement Kernel for openflow networks," in Proceedings of the First Workshop on Hot Topics in Software-Defined Networks, 2012.

[12] S. T. Ali, V. Sivaraman, A. Radford, and S. Jha , "A survey of securing networks using software-defined networking," in *IEEE Transactions on Reliability*, vol. 64, no. 3, pp. 1086–1097, 2015.

[13] S. Begum, F. A. Siddique and R. Tiwari, "A study for predicting heart disease using machine learning," *Turkish Journal of Computer and Mathematics Education*, Vol. 12, Issue 10, 2021, pp. 4584–4592, e-ISSN: 1309–4653.

[14] R. Tiwari, M. Sharma and K. K. Mehta, "IoT based parallel framework for measurement of heat distribution in metallic sheets," *Solid State Technology*, Vol. 63, Issue 06, 2020, pp. 7294–7302, ISSN: 0038–111X.

[15] R. Tiwari et al., "An artificial intelligence-based reactive health care system for emotion detections," *Computational Intelligence and Neuroscience*, Vol. 2022, Article ID 8787023. https://doi.org/10.1155/2022/8787023.

[16] J. Hizver, "Taxonomic modeling of security threats in software-defined networking," In BlackHat Conference, 2015.

[17] K. Kaynar and F. Sivrikay, Distributed attack graph generation. In *IEEE Transactions on Dependable and Secure Computing*; IEEE Computer Society Press: Los Alamitos, CA, USA, 2015; Vol. 13, pp. 519–532.

[18] S.-H. S. and S. S., "A survey of security in software-defined networks," *IEEE Communications Surveys & Tutorials,* 2016.

3 Security Issues in Software-Defined Networks and Its Solutions

Pawan Whig, Ashima Bhatnagar Bhatia,
Rahul Reddy Nadikatu, Yusuf Alkali,
and Pavika Sharma

3.1 INTRODUCTION

A developing architecture called Software-Defined Networking (SDN) is dynamic, controllable, affordable, and adaptive, making it faultless for the tall bandwidth, and lively nature of nowaday's requests. The net regulator and furtherance operations are separated in this design, allowing for a straight software design of the network regulator and the concept of the underlying organization for requests and net facilities. SDN will be seen as a more mainstream, traditional kind of networking [1].

The global data center SDN marketplace will be valued over $12 billion in 2022, growing at a Compound Annual Growth Rate (CAGR) of 18.5% from 2017 to 2022. In 2017, the market brought in close to $5.15 billion, an increase of more than 32.2% from the previous year [2]. With sales of approximately $2.2 billion, or 42% of the total market revenue, the physical network accounted for the greatest portion of the global data center SDN market in 2017. However, in 2022, it was anticipated that the physical network would generate roughly $4.35 billion in revenue, which is higher than the $3.18 billion for SDN applications but rather less than the $4.67 billion credited to net virtualization SDN regulator package as shown in Figure 3.1. The majority of data center network purchasers are aware of SDN's use cases and value propositions, and an increasing amount of trades are learning that SDN products have useful advantages. The growth of SDN and the move to browser network services are helping the network regain lost territory and better match with a wave of new apps that are producing major economic advantages [3].

The greatest accurate meaning of SDN is a skill that splits the administration of net expedients' control planes from the fundamental information flat that carries out net circulation. This technology is based on the concept of programmability [4].To provide intent founded organization of the net as an entire data center, SDN systems offer software clear controllers that are isolated from the fundamental net computer hardware.

DOI: 10.1201/9781003432869-3

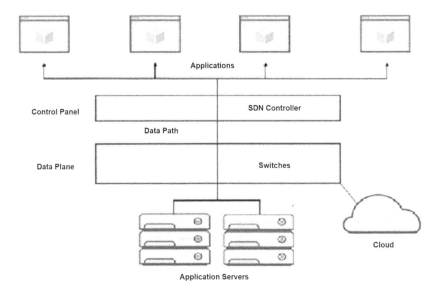

FIGURE 3.1   Virtualization overlays/SDN controller.

Several motivating principles have shaped SDN's development. For instance, it claims to simplify the administration of smoothed capitals anywhere from the data center to the campus or wide area network, as well as to greatly simplify the automation of network tasks. SDN is typically perceived as segregating the control and data planes, but its core extends beyond this. At the heart of SDN lies a centralized network, where switches and routers often possess knowledge limited to the networks adjacent to them [5].

3.1.1 SDN Assists Remote Access, IoT, and Edge Computing

Many schmoosing tendencies have contributed to the fundamental principle of SDN [6]. A properly built SDN system is simpler and more affordable to distribute calculation capitals to distant places, move data center tasks to the advantage, adopt fog calculation, and support IoT settings as shown in Figure 3.2.

For operators to more easily separate an IoT application from the production world, for instance, they can utilize dedicated network segments or Virtual Local Area Networks (VLANs) to establish distinct boundaries and enhance security measures, thereby preventing potential interferences and unauthorized access between these distinct network environments. Some SDN controllers are intelligent enough to notice when the network is becoming crowded and increase bandwidth or processing to prevent delay in edge and distant components. SDN technologies are especially helpful at dispersed locations with few IT staff members on the site, such as an initiative division office or service breadwinner-dominant workplace [7].

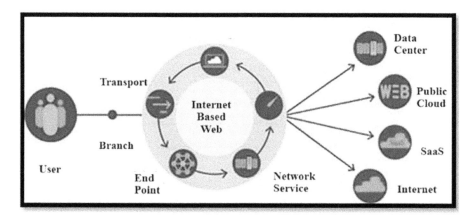

FIGURE 3.2   SDN assists remote access, IoT, and edge computing.

3.1.2   INTENT-BASED NETWORKING SUPPORTED BY SDN

To ensure that what the company wants happens, network managers must be able to declare what they want the net to fix. Automated management software must then establish the appropriate state and enforce regulations [8]. This is the basic idea behind intent-based networking (IBN), which has many different components as shown in Figure 3.3.

The provisioning paradigm and dynamic management to regulate infrastructure state is inevitably at a higher level, If a basic tenet of SDN is abstracted control over a fleet of infrastructure. Policy is moving away from the specifics of each unique device and imperative and reactive instructions, moving closer to declarative intent. Intention founded schmoosing signifies a development of SDN to attain smooth better levels of working ease, automatic intellect. Because of this, IBN marks an important step toward an independent substructure that comprises a self-driving net. This network will operate similarly to a self-driving automobile, providing desirable results based on what network operators and their companies want to achieve [9].

3.1.3   SDN BENEFITS CLIENTS IN TERMS OF SECURITY

SDN makes several security advantages possible. To have varied security settings for the various types of network traffic might gull that up. A network may contain a single, low-security network that is accessible to the public but does not handle any sensitive data as shown in Figure 3.4. Another section could have a software-based firewall and encryption settings with much finer remote access control on it, allowing sensitive data to pass through it [10].

For instance, if a client has an IoT group that doesn't feel very secure, they may partition that collection off after the important, tall worth business circulation using the SDN controller, according to Capuano. Users of SDN may tool safety rubrics through the net, after the information center to the advantage deployments can be

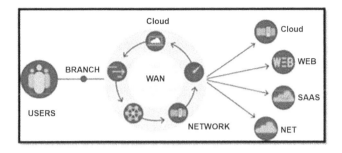

FIGURE 3.3 Intent-based networking supported by SDN.

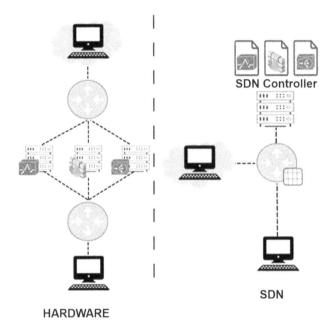

FIGURE 3.4 SDN benefit benefiting terms of security.

40 to 70 % less luxurious than those using conventional ironware [11]. One of the primary advantages of SDN is the capability to examine a group of workloads to determine whether they comply with a certain security policy, particularly when data is spread.

3.1.4 THE FUNCTION DOES SDN PLAY IN CLOUD COMPUTING

It would seem reasonable for SDN to play a part in the adoption of private clouds and hybrid clouds. Big SDN providers like Cisco offer comprehensive cloud-based solutions that integrate SDN capabilities, providing scalable and agile network infrastructures for businesses of varying sizes and complexities. The determination of initiatives encompasses the frameworks, infrastructures, and skills that support agile deployment and continuous operational management, as agility stands as a critical component of digital transformation. The necessity of digital transformation pushes the adoption of significant network automation, including SDN, in the context of data center networking, according to Casemore.

3.1.5   ROLE OF SD-WAN PLAY

An organic way to expand SDN across a WAN is via the software clear WAN. It goes beyond the SDN building, which is frequently the basis of an information center. At its most basic level, SD-WAN enables businesses to combine several network connections into a branch and to have a software organization stage that can find new locations, prioritize traffic, and establish security rules. The fundamental idea behind SD-WAN is to make it easier for large businesses to add new links [12]. Irrespective of the traffic's ingress and egress locations, and ensuring complete security, it allows networks to route traffic based on centrally defined policies or rules.

3.2   SDN ARCHITECTURE

The control and data planes are integrated as a single entity in conventional networks. The data plane is responsible for forwarding the packets in agreement with the instructions given by the switch flat. The control plane is in charge of maintaining the routing table of a switch, which determines the optimum way to deliver the network packets as shown in Figure 3.5. While in SDN, the control plane serves as a centralized controller for several data planes, the data plane is a different entity from the control plane [13].

The concept of separating the data plane (forwarding element) and control plane was initially put out by FORCES (Forwarding and Control Element Separation).

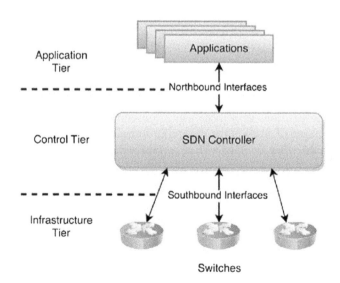

FIGURE 3.5   SDN architecture.

It is claimed that a software-based control plane manages forwarding entities that are based on hardware.

There are two approaches to applying FORCES :

Within the same network device, the forwarding element and control plane are located.

The device's control element is removed and installed in a different system.

It adheres to three standards:

3.2.1 NETWORK-LEVEL GOALS

Rather than referring to specific devices, the goals should be spoken in the footings of the entire network in instruction to eliminate the requirement for reliance on exclusive gadgets.

3.2.2 NETWORK-WIDE PERSPECTIVE

Decisions should be based on knowledge of the traffic, topology, and events occurring throughout the whole network. A network-wide perspective should be taken into account while taking action.

3.2.3 DIRECT CONTROL

The components of the control plane should have direct access to the components of the data plane. It ought to be able to set up the forwarding table on certain devices [14]. Network administrators define users' access at the network level using the Ethane protocol and the architecture of Ethane is shown in Figure 3.6. SDNs have the same antecedent as ethane .

3.2.4 FUNDAMENTALS OF ETHANE

- Policies at the highest level should examine the network.
- High-level policies should be followed during routing.
- The origin of each packet in the network should be connected to it.

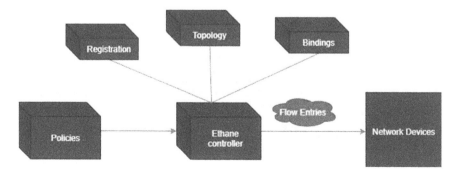

FIGURE 3.6 Architecture of ethane.

3.4   FEATURE OF THE SDN ARCHITECTURE

Being directly programmable is a feature of the SDN Architecture.

Since network control is independent of forwarding operations, it may be directly programmed.

3.4.1   AGILE

Managers can animatedly change net-wide circulation flow to suit altering stresses by conceptualizing a switch from furtherance.

3.4.2   CENTRAL MANAGEMENT

Package-founded SDN supervisors that recall a worldwide opinion of the net, which seems to request and rule trains as a solitary, rational change, are where network intellect is (logically) centralized and are shown in Figure 3.7. Net managers can

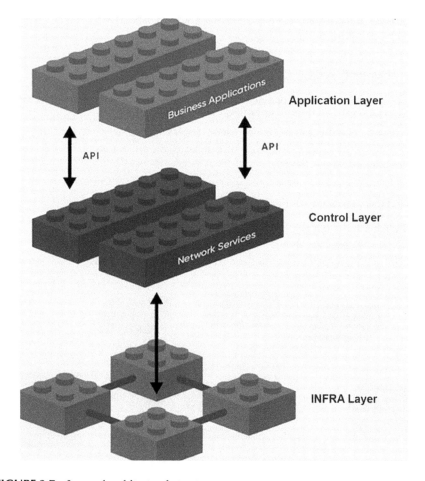

FIGURE 3.7   Layered architectural structure.

swiftly set up, manage, protect, and optimize network resources using programmatically configured SDN, thanks to dynamic, automated SDN programs that they can create on their own because they are not dependent on branded packages [15].

3.4.4 OPEN STANDARDS

SDN shortens network deployment and operational complexity when implemented using open standards since instructions are provided by SDN controllers rather than multiple, vendor-specific proprietary systems.

Even though OpenFlow was only one of the original SDN canons, it was a crucial part of the revolution in networking software. No matter which vendor built the underlying router or switch, SDN has developed into a renowned networking technology over the years since it was first introduced, and it is now sold by major manufacturers such as Cisco, VMware, Juniper, Pluribus, and Big Switch. Multiple open-source SDN technologies are also developed by the Open Networking Foundation [16].

The traditional wired design has gotten to the point where it can no longer be used to adapt to dynamic situations, such as those made possible by virtualization technologies. SDN increases system abstraction by separating the control plane from the data plane, which in turn allows for network programmability, faster operation, and popularization—in other words, the key to executing its claims and allowing it and telecom networks to advance concurrently. The SDN controller is the intelligence of the SDN construction. The SDN serves as an interface between network elements and SDN applications, which are logically positioned amongst one another. Because of its central location, it can give other SDN components a comprehensive perspective of what's going on in the network, create Network Elements (NEs) instantly, and choose the optimum route for traffic. Traditional networks use dispersed control, but SDN design uses centralized control and the SDN. Unfortunately, the SDN is a prime target for assault because of its strategic location. A logically centralized control plane, as described by ONF1, enables the upkeep of a net-wide perspective of capitals, which may subsequently be made available to the request coating. One or more NEs that interface with the SDN are used by the SDN to offer such a centralized architecture. This kind of network construction has the advantages of streamlined network administration and increased adaptability [17].

3.4.5 ADVANTAGES AND WEAKNESSES

Instead of being introduced as distinct appliances or instantiated within numerous NEs, SDN makes it easier to integrate safety applications into nets since they can be organized directly on the highest of the management plane. The centralized management method of SDN makes it possible to gather and aggregate events throughout the whole network. The resultant picture of the network's health is larger, more coherent, and more accurate, making security solutions easier to implement and manage. The advantages and disadvantages are shown in Table 3.1

It is likely to animatedly add blows and devices at different locations in the net, which improves network monitoring. Security procedures may be implemented directly on the topmost layer of the network architecture, ensuring robust protection and enforcement across all underlying network components and functionalities.

TABLE 3.1
Advantages and Weaknesses SDN

Aspect	Advantages	Weaknesses
Scalability	• Easily scales to accommodate growing network needs. • Allows for dynamic resource allocation.	• Initial setup and configuration can be complex. • Over-reliance on controller scalability.
Flexibility	• Provides flexibility in network configuration and management. • Supports rapid network changes.	• May require significant changes to existing network infrastructure. • Potential interoperability issues.
Centralized control	• Centralized control simplifies network management. • Enhances network visibility and monitoring.	• Single point of failure in the controller. • Security concerns related to controller access.
Automation	• Automates network provisioning and optimization. • Reduces manual configuration errors.	• Requires careful planning to avoid automation errors. • Initial implementation effort.
Traffic engineering	• Optimizes traffic routing for improved performance. • Supports Quality of Service (QoS) prioritization.	• Complexity in fine-tuning traffic engineering rules. • May require additional monitoring tools.
Cost Efficiency	• Can reduce operational costs by streamlining network management. • Efficient resource utilization.	• Initial investment in SDN infrastructure. • Potential costs for staff training and maintenance.
Open standards	• Based on open standards, encouraging innovation and vendor neutrality. • Supports ecosystem growth.	• Interoperability challenges with legacy hardware. • Fragmented ecosystem with varying standards.
Security	• Offers enhanced network security through granular control. • Facilitates network segmentation.	• Potential security risks associated with controller vulnerabilities. • Misconfigurations can lead to security issues.

The network can more easily identify assaults with an accurate image of its state, and the quantity of reported false positives may be decreased. In reality, SDN can direct potentially harmful traffic to an Intrusion Detection System (IDS) for examination and mitigation if a tap indicates that an endpoint is showing signs of being compromised by a bot. The SDN can filter communications that the ids deem harmful and give first-hop NE instructions [18].

3.5 SDN SECURITY

SDN network security concerns frequently resemble those that affect conventional networks. What distinguishes SDN from conventional networks is intriguing, though. In contrast to conventional nets, the parting of the switch and data hydroplanes

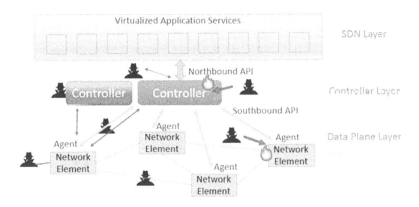

FIGURE 3.8 SDN security flow.

allows for multi-occupancy ability, and the introduction of centralized entailment and SDN security flow is shown in Figure 3.8. Tenants in this new paradigm operate SDN applications that communicate with the SDN, which directs us. One of the primary security-related distinctions between SDN and conventional systems is the capacity to share and dynamically operate the same physical network. SDN security concerns, therefore, the new control plane paradigm, and more particularly, secure inter-component communication [19].

The programmability offered by SDN grants significantly more autonomy to reduce vulnerabilities, diminishing the need for additional technologies, despite the challenges posed by factors like throughput that require resolution.

3.5.1 CENTRALIZED ADMINISTRATION

NEs are often maintained and monitored on an individual basis in conventional networks. However, network administration has grown difficult because of the load of universal protocols that can communicate with all NEs regardless of their manufacturer or generation. The SDN solution enables remote NEs to coordinate the monitoring and maintenance of forwarding rules, leading to a more adaptable management process [20]. The SDN control plane runs the danger of becoming a bottleneck, but because it can see the whole network, it can dynamically mitigate any reported fault. A DDoSat Addo, for instance, can be promptly identified and prevented by isolating the questionable traffic, networks, or hosts. SDN stands as the prime candidate for dynamically enforcing a coherent security posture due to centralized components having a broader perspective of network and performance considerations [21–23].

While it is obvious that centralization offers many advantages, it also comes with a lot of disadvantages, such as the SDNs as an attack surface.

3.5.2 DEPENDABLE CONTROL PLANE

The SDN, NEs, and SDN applications are the three core components of SDN. All messages inside the switch flat want to be viewed as vital since the network is centralized, as a successful attack might cause an outage that has business continuity.

For instance, the SDN is unable to take necessary measures. The control plane has to have more resilience built into it to prevent this [24–28]. SDN provides several interfaces for communicating with tenant applications and NEs. Depending on the kind and quantity of active applications, any or all of these interfaces can encounter high traffic loads. NEC, for instance, might affect traffic on the interfaces by forwarding packets for which they lack forwarding rules. Therefore, it would seem that older networks are more resilient in terms of reliance on the SDS. SDS-limiting NEs in footings of bandwidth and reserve ingesting, such as CPU load, memory operation, and API noise pics an efficient technique to increase the resilience of the centralized plane and stop DDoS control-plane assaults from spreading to the rest of the network [29].

The right resource dedication method, in which the SDN first authenticates each resource request before checking it against strict permission control criteria, can further increase resilience [30].

3.5.3 DEPENDABLE AUTHORIZATION AND AUTHENTICATION

The procedures used to recognize a non-identified source and then establish its access privileges are known as authentication and authorization as shown in Figure 3.9.

When properly implemented, these procedures can defend networks against particular attack types, including:

- False (statistical) feedback is given to the system in a number several as tricking it into thinking it is under attack, which causes unnecessary countermeasures to be deployed, wasting capitalizable resulting in suboptimal usage.

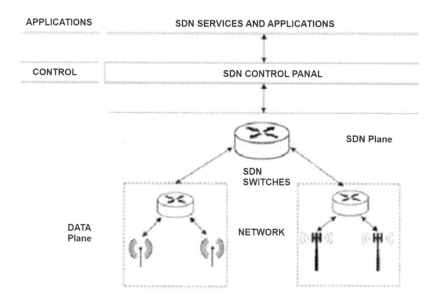

FIGURE 3.9 Dependable authorization and authentication.

- Altering a valid on-path request to cause a direct attack that changes network behavioral circulation that is not intended to be advanced or failing to forward circulation that must be forwarded, and breaching net isolates.

Isolates must be protected with enhanced security precautions because of their crucial nature. To avoid tampering with on-path communications, traffic must at the very least be integrity protected, but even this degree of security does not safeguard control data [31–33].

One method of avoiding the leak of control data is encryption. Encryption, especially when used in conjunction with integrity protection, is insufficient to thwart man-in-the-middle assaults. Therefore, reciprocal authentication is required for any communication within the control plane. Mutual authentication, as well as protection against replay attacks, secrecy, and integrity protection, are all possible with the help of security protocols like TLS and IPsec [34,35]. However, mutual authentication does have certain challenges, such as how to bootstrap safety into the scheme. Security certificates are one solution to this. So the key safety challenge is how these diplomas are generated, deployed, kept, and canceled. Without mutual authentication, encryption and integrity protection are less helpful in terms of security. The challenge with mutual authentication lies in the requirement for prior knowledge of the remote communicating endpoint, especially in the absence of a widely trusted third party. Mutual authentication may be manually done at a modest scale. To do this, administrators must install certificates or shared secrets on all endpoints. Manual implementation, however, could not be possible for complicated and physically distinct systems, particularly in nets anywhere various SDN mechanisms can be formed animatedly and managed by many gatherings. Tenants can utilize or subtilize to manage network behavior and the SDN provision of network configuration information via API calls to its services. Given the possibility of physical hardware resources being shared by competing tenants, this situation is fairly concerning. The SDN requires a strong authentication, authorization, and accountability architecture in addition to the usual security precautions, such as argument sanitization and validation, to safeguard the network against unwanted modifications. Additional security is provided by strong authentication and permission since they stop an attacker from pretending to be an SDN component, notably the SDN.

3.5.4 Multi-tenancy

The same physical network may be shared by numerous tenants in networks designed utilizing, each of whom may run their own virtue works. With multi-tenancy, network resources may be used more effectively, resulting in a lower total cost of ownership. By automatically scaling resources, for example, SDN helps tenants react more quickly to changing circumstances. Tenants shouldn't be able to interfere with one another's networks and don't even need to be aware that they are sharing network resources in order to have an acceptable degree of security.

A key component of the security of the SDN architecture is tenant isolation, which involves separating one tenant's operational capabilities from those of others.

3.5.5   Isolation of the Control Plane

One strategy for preventing the effects of one tenant's behavior tenants is isolation. This is a crucial part of the business that has to be strictly upheld. The SDN coordinates tenant isolation, which is carried out in SDN NEs by means using forwarding rules. While the SDN is responsible for ensuring secure isolation, tenants also contribute significantly to sharing that responsibility. Isolation on the network is mostly provided at the connection layer. Information leakage may occur if a tenant has lax network security protocols, leading to a loss of isolation at higher tiers. For instance, malicious SDN software with access to resources outside of the boundaries of isolation may hurt security by diverting traffic to a different location.

3.5.6   DataPlane Separation

SDN-created virtual networks may be vulnerable to the similar caring of the net-founded as conventional networks when used by tenants conducting business. However, because of the shared networking infrastructure, any or possibly all of these tenants may be affected by this assault. No entity needs to start a company vulnerable to assault; this is a new danger that might have an influence on me.

Using particular tenant keys, traffic may also be encrypted in addition to being isolated logically. In the event of a logical encapsulation failure, this ensures that data traffic will stay isolated and that no information will leak. Problems with isolation must be handled while considering resource use. Data leakage may be prevented through traffic isolation, but resource isolation is also necessary when using shared resources. As the issue overloads the underlying network hardware, the existence of a forwarding loop inside one tenant, for instance, may possibly effect all tenants. To address this issue, the SDN must impose resource separation and other techniques like rate restriction to reduce the potential negative effects that a tenant may have on the network.

3.5.7   Programmability

Programmability, or the capacity to quickly, securely, and effectively construct a network, is one of the major advantages brought forth by SDN. There are many levels of complexity and abstraction for SDN-programmed hand, SDN apps give users the ability to programmatically communicate network requirements to tenants. The SDN aggregates all requests and responds to higher-level queries using the resources available at lower levels. SDN program programs orthogonal (mutually exclusive/contradictory) requests, which makes this process more difficult. A section of the SDN network may then require dynamic reconfiguration by the automated solution.

3.5.8   Coherency in Configuration

Tenants' ability to make programmatic modifications to the network increases network agility by allowing networks to respond to shifting conditions. Practically speaking, programmability may, for instance, shorten the days or months it takes to build up a customer collaboration network to minutes.

Programmed programmability does away with the requirement for error-prone manual settings. As a result, it is possible to automatically reconfigure networks, giving the SDN a comprehensive perspective of the network and allowing it to quickly deploy new networks by doing regression testing and sanity checks.

3.5.9 DYNAMICITY

Networks constructed by utilizing methodology are reactive and dynamic, which creates new opportunities for defending against network threats. Some of the methods that can be used include black hole routing, honeypot forwarding, and automated network reconfigurations. Another method that takes advantage of SDN features is service chaining, which may be used to screen for malicious payload and start mitigating steps. When suspicious behavior is detected, the network can utilize its programmability characteristics to conduct further investigation into the issue or to initiate countermeasures. The feedback mechanism does have certain benefits in terms of security, but it also has some drawbacks. The core SDN principle of keeping these two planes separate is broken by the communication between the flat and the switch flat. As a result, the data plane may now be used as a stepping stone to attack the control plane. This interaction, like other feedback loops, has the potential to oscillate and eventually cause the network to become unstable if it is not properly controlled.

3.6 SDN SECURITY CONCERNS

The primary concerns with SDN Forwarding Device Attack: The flow of data over a network of malicious users perform denial of service (DoS) attacks when they are disturbed by access points or switches, which can cause network failure or interruption. SDN Security Concerns are shown in Table 3.2.

3.6.1 PERIL IN THE CONTROL PLANE

Any network issue resulting in the central controller's failure highlights the challenge of using hierarchical controller distributions to address this issue.

3.6.2 EXPOSURE OF THE COMMUNICATION CHANNEL

TLS is used by SDN southbound APIs like the Open Flow protocol to secure data-control channel connection, however, it is, frequently administratively deactivated and vulnerable to man-in-the-middle assaults, making it unsuitable.

3.6.3 FAKE TRAFFIC FLOWS

To disperse the DoS, an attacker or malfunctioning, non-malicious device resources in controllers or forwarding devices.

Authenticity is the characteristic ensuring that entities in SDN are indeed what they claim to be. Similar to the challenge of validity for forwarding devices in traditional networks, SDN networks can face hindrances in network performance due to this issue.

TABLE 3.2
SDN Security Concerns

Concern	Description
Unauthorized Access	Unauthorized users gaining access to the SDN network, potentially leading to data breaches.
Data interception	Intercepting sensitive data as it traverses the SDN, posing risks to data privacy and integrity.
Denial of service (DoS) attacks	Attacker flooding the SDN infrastructure with traffic, disrupting network operations and availability.
Controller vulnerabilities	Vulnerabilities in the SDN controller software, which could be exploited for unauthorized control.
Network slicing security	Ensuring isolation and security between network slices in multi-tenant SDN environments.
Flow table manipulation	Unauthorized modification of flow tables, redirecting traffic or causing network disruptions.
Identity spoofing	Attackers masquerading as legitimate users or devices within the SDN, potentially leading to breaches.
Policy violations	Violations of security policies or access control rules, compromising network security.
Malware and botnets	Infiltration of malware or botnets into the SDN, leading to malicious actions or data exfiltration.
Insider threats	Threats originating from within the organization, where authorized users abuse their privileges.

If confidentiality is not maintained, it can allow unauthorized access to network information or data. Confidentiality protects the exposure of information to unauthorized entities, ensuring that sensitive data remains inaccessible to those without proper authorization or clearance.

3.6.4 AVAILABILITY

This refers to the ability to authorized access to information, technology, and services at any time.

3.6.5 ACCESSIBLE PROGRAMMABLE API

Because APIs are open, attackers may see weaknesses more easily.

Changes and controllers are not directly linked for the transfer of information, enabling "man-in-the-middle" interceptions to compromise or utilize the information without being detected, potentially resulting in a black hole attack.

3.6.6 SECURITY ANALYSIS FOR SDN ENVIRONMENT

SDNs are replacing traditional networking technologies because of their utilization of centralized control, enabling more agile and programmable network management. Security Analysis for SDN Environment structure is shown in Figure 3.10.

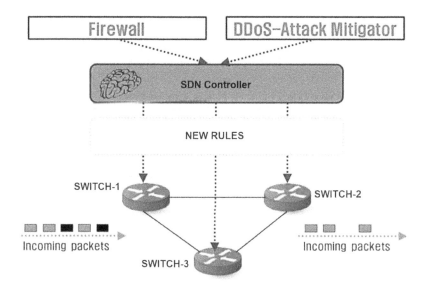

FIGURE 3.10   Security analysis for SDN environment.

Attacks on the system's vulnerabilities may have an impact on the privacy, integrity, and confidentiality of the system, which eventually affects the network's performance and efficiency. To address false positive alerts, this study provides a security analysis for implementing safety measures within SDN utilizing the CART (Classification and Regression Trees) model and an alert correlation model. Open programmable APIs, whose open nature makes the vulnerabilities more evident to attackers, is one of the security issues facing SDN. Unauthorized access to the central controller might seriously harm the data and introduce harmful codes into the system. Application layer attacks make up the majority of attacks against SDN. Attacks targeting the application coating comprise: Rubrics supplement: establishing and executing safety rules for SDN in diverse areas results in a variety of conflicts.

3.6.7   MALICIOUS CODE

Inserting malicious code into various programs can launch attacks that corrupt or destroy data.

The following attacks are included in the control layer:

3.6.8   DENIAL OF SERVICE ATTACKS

Denial of service attacks may target channels, controllers, or the connection between a supervisor and changes.

3.6.9   OCCURRENCES FROM REQUESTS

An assailant who gains to the request coating obtains subtle information about the net and uses that information to launch attacks on the control layer.

3.6.10 Infrastructure Layer Attacks Include the Following

Dos Attack: By sending out lots of mysteriously big packets on a regular basis, the attacker can dowse the flow table and the buffer flow, creating new rules that must be entered into the movement benches.

Man-in-the-middle Attack: Due to the lack of direct linkage between the changes and supervisors, "man-in-the-middle" attacks can intercept critical information without being detected, potentially leading to snooping and black hole attacks. Bout graph and alert correlation model analysis of security. The alert correlation model identifies the alerts, whilst the attack graph assesses the capacity to resist attacks.

3.7 CONCLUSION

The efficiency of SDN rests in its capacity as a skill to provide considerably more system autonomy, assure resource efficiency, and make networks adaptable. SDN should be treated carefully to prevent it from becoming an attack vector, just like any other emerging technology. However, SDN offers more visibility, programmability, and a centralized approach to network administration, opening up new options for the installation of enhanced security methods in the network. The necessity and need for safe, reliable, adaptable, and well-managed networks have been met by the development of the SDN. SDN is more open to attack than conventional networks, nevertheless, because of the separation of the two planes. This implies that network and control traffic's availability, consistency, authenticity, secrecy, and integrity may all be negatively impacted. This chapter analyses numerous solutions that have been proposed while outlining some of the fundamental risks to the SDN. Along with the problems brought on by employing wireless medium, WSDN also has security difficulties that are quite similar to the wireless SDN architecture. Furthermore, despite hazards or problems, real-time research utilizes the security advantages of a centralized SDN framework.

REFERENCES

[1] P. Whig, A. Velu and R. R. Naddikatu, "The economic impact of AI-enabled blockchain in 6G-based industry," In: Dutta Borah, M., Singh, P., Deka, G.C. (eds) *AI and Blockchain Technology in 6G Wireless Network*, Springer, Singapore, 2022, pp. 205–224.

[2] Y. Alkali, I. Routray and P. Whig, "Strategy for reliable, efficient and secure IoT using artificial intelligence," *IUP Journal of Computer Sciences*, vol. 16, no. 2, 2022, pp. 1–15.

[3] P. Whig, A. Velu and P. Sharma, "Demystifying federated learning for blockchain: A case study," in *Demystifying Federated Learning for Blockchain and Industrial Internet of Things*, IGI Global, 2022, pp. 143–165.

[4] P. Whig, S. Kouser, A. Velu and R. R. Nadikattu, "Fog-IoT-assisted-based smart agriculture application," in *Demystifying Federated Learning for Blockchain and Industrial Internet of Things*, IGI Global, 2022, pp. 74–93.

[5] P. Whig, A. Velu and R. Ready, "Demystifying federated learning in artificial intelligence with human-computer interaction," in *Demystifying Federated Learning for Blockchain and Industrial Internet of Things*, IGI Global, 2022, pp. 94–122.

[6] P. Whig, A. Velu and A. B. Bhatia, "Protect nature and reduce the carbon footprint with an application of blockchain for IIoT," in *Demystifying Federated Learning for Blockchain and Industrial Internet of Things*, IGI Global, 2022, pp. 123–142.

[7] P. Whig, A. Velu and R. R. Nadikattu, "Blockchain platform to resolve security issues in IoT and smart networks," in *AI-Enabled Agile Internet of Things for Sustainable FinTech Ecosystems*, IGI Global, 2022, pp. 46–65.

[8] H. Jupalle, S. Kouser, A. B. Bhatia, N. Alam, R. R. Nadikattu and P. Whig, "Automation of human behaviors and its prediction using machine learning," *Microsystem Technologies*, vol. 17, pp. 1–9, 2022.

[9] U. Tomar, N. Chakroborty, H. Sharma and P. Whig, "AI based smart agricuture system," *Transactions on Latest Trends in Artificial Intelligence*, vol. 2, no. 2, pp. 1–12, 2021.

[10] P. Whig, R. R. Nadikattu and A. Velu, "COVID-19 pandemic analysis using application of AI," *Healthcare Monitoring and Data Analysis Using IoT: Technologies and Applications*, pp. 1–12, 2022.

[11] M. Anand, A. Velu and P. Whig, "Prediction of loan behaviour with machine learning models for secure banking," *Journal of Computer Science and Engineering (JCSE)*, vol. 3, no. 1, pp. 1–13, 2022.

[12] G. Chopra and P. Whig, "A clustering approach based on support vectors," *International Journal of Machine Learning for Sustainable Development*, vol. 4, no. 1, pp. 21–30, 2022.

[13] M. Madhu and P. Whig, "A survey of machine learning and its applications," *International Journal of Machine Learning for Sustainable Development*, vol. 4, no. 1, pp. 11–20, 2022.

[14] G. Chopra and P. Whig, "Smart agriculture system using AI," *International Journal of Sustainable Development in Computing Science*, vol. 4, no. 1, pp. 1–10, 2022.

[15] G. Chopra and P. Whig, "Energy efficient scheduling for internet of vehicles," *International Journal of Sustainable Development in Computing Science*, vol. 4, no. 1, pp. 1–10, 2022.

[16] G. Chopra and P. Whig, "Using machine learning algorithms classified depressed patients and normal people," *International Journal of Machine Learning for Sustainable Development*, vol. 4, no. 1, pp. 31–40, 2022.

[17] A. Velu and P. Whig, "Studying the impact of the COVID vaccination on the world using data analytics," *Vivekananda Journal of Research*, vol. 10, no. 1, pp. 147–160, 2022.

[18] Y. Khera, P. Whig and A. Velu, "Efficient effective and secured electronic billing system using AI," *Vivekananda Journal of Research*, vol. 10, pp. 53–60, 2021.

[19] A. Velu and P. Whig, "Protect personal privacy and wasting time using NLP: A comparative approach using AI," *Vivekananda Journal of Research*, vol. 10, pp. 42–52, 2021.

[20] A. Rupani, P. Whig, G. Sujediya, and P. Vyas, "A robust technique for image processing based on interfacing of Raspberry-Pi and FPGA using IoT," in *2017 International Conference on Computer, Communications and Electronics (Comptelix)*, 2017, pp. 350–353.

[21] T. Bakhshi, "Securing wireless software-defined networks: Appraising threats, defenses & research challenges," in *In 2018 International Conference on Advancements in Computational Sciences (ICACS)*, 2018.

[22] I. F. Akyildiz, A. Lee, P. Wang, M. Luo and W. Chou. A roadmap for traffic engineering in SDN-OpenFlow networks. *Computer Networks*, vol. 71, pp. 1–30, 2014.

[23] K. Cabaj, J. Wytrebowicz, S. Kuklinski, P. Radziszewski and K. T. Dinh. SDN Architecture Impact on Network Security. In *FedCSIS (Position Papers)*, Position papers of the 2014 Federated Conference on Computer Science and Information Systems, pp. 143–148, 2014, September.

[24] D. Kreutz, F. M. Ramos, and P. Verissimo. Towards secure and dependable software-defined networks. In *Proceedings of the second ACM SIGCOMM workshop on Hot topics in software-defined networking*, pp. 55–60, 2013, August.

[25] Y. Zheng and P. Zhang, "A security and trust framework for virtualized networks and software-defined networking," *Security and Communication Networks*, pp. 3059–3069, 2016.

[26] D. Kreutz, F. M. Ramos, P. E.Verissimo, C. E. Rothenberg, S. Azodolmolky, and S. Uhlig, Software-defined networking: A comprehensive survey. *Proceedings of the IEEE*, vol. 103, no. 1, pp. 14–76, 2014.

[27] H. Daojing, S. Chan and M. Guizani, "Securing software-defined wireless networks," *IEEE Communications Magazine*, pp. 20–25, 2016.

[28] N. El Moussaid, A. Toumanariand M. El Azhari, "Security analysis as softwaredefined security for SDN environment," in *Fourth International Conference on IEEE*, 2017.

[29] A. Akhunzada, E. Ahmed, A. Gani, M. K. Khan, M. Imran, and Guizani, S, Securing software-defined networks: taxonomy, requirements, and open issues. *IEEE Communications Magazine*, vol. 53, no. 4, pp. 36–44, 2015.

[30] B. Agborubere and E. Sanchez-Velazquez, "openflow communications and TLS security in software-defined networks," in *IEEE International Conference on Internet of Things (iThings) and IEEE Green Computing and Communications (GreenCom) and IEEE Cyber, Physical and Social Computing (CPSCom) and IEEE Smart Data (SmartData)*, 2017.

[31] P. Porras, S. Shin and M. Fong, "A security enforcement Kernel for openflow networks," in *Proceedings of the First Workshop on Hot Topics in Software-Defined Networks*, 2012.

[32] S. T. Ali, V. Sivaraman, A. Radford, and S. Jha, A survey of securing networks using software-defined networking. *IEEE Transactions on Reliability*, vol. 64, no. 3, pp. 1086–1097, 2015.

[33] K. Kaynar, and F. Sivrikaya, Distributed attack graph generation. *IEEE Transactions on Dependable and Secure Computing*, vol. 13, no. 5, pp. 519–532, 2015.

[34] S. Scott-Hayward, S. Natarajan, and S. Sezer, A survey of security in software-defined networks. *IEEE Communications Surveys & Tutorials*, vol. 18, no. 1, pp. 623–654, 2015.

[35] J. Hizver, Taxonomic modeling of security threats in software-defined networking. In *BlackHat Conference* (pp. 1–16), 2015, August.

4 Importance of Dynamic Load Balancing and Virtualization Role in Dynamic Load Balancing

Daisy Sharmah, Kanak Chandra Bora,
Abdullah Saleh Alqahtani, and
Tahir Rashid Hakeem

4.1 INTRODUCTION

The emerging technology of cloud computing is booming in the industry, healthcare, agriculture, education sector, and government sector. People prefer to preserve data in the cloud rather than storing it in their computers or database. The huge use of the cloud is categorized under four deployment models that are stated below [1].

1.1 Public Model: This model is suitable for the general public.
1.2 Private Model: This model is available for multiple users.
1.3 Community Model: This model is best suited for a specific level of community.
1.4 Hybrid Cloud: This model is the mixture of 2 or more cloud models.

There are several uses of the cloud environment. Based on the delivery model, cloud computing is divided into three models [2] –

1.1 Infrastructure as a Cloud (IaaS): This service supplies framework-oriented materials as a service of cloud computing. For example, Amazon Web Services (AWS), Cisco Metacloud, etc.
1.2 Platform as a Service (PaaS): This model supplies the inbuilt configuration as an assistance to the users. For example, Google App Engine, Windows Azure, etc.
1.3 Software as a Service (SaaS): It provides a coordination of programs and data as guidance to the users. For example, Cisco Webex, Facebook, etc.

Load balancing is a methodology that offers methods to maximize throughput, optimized utilization of resources, and better implementation of the system. Load balancing creates a method to store the data for the users based on its availability.

DOI: 10.1201/9781003432869-4

One of the major objectives of load balancing is to equally synchronize the load in the entire cloud computing system. Balancing the load equivalently, administering the functions on virtual machines for the actual use of all the hardware and software systems used. There are different types of algorithms used built on various criteria. The load-balancer aims to help in resource assignment for resource uniformity and also to fulfil the need of the users at an optimum price that stimulates the users to discover the problems in balancing the load and to work on fixing them. As the use of cloud computing is increasing, the workload of this system is also affected and as a result, load balancing plays a vital role in this system. Therefore, based on obtainable investigation, the ongoing projects have been identified and encapsulated in a methodical approach to represent various problems [3].

The two versions are available for balancing the load [4]: Static and Dynamic. The static algorithm for balancing the load is suitable for well-structured environments with no modification further with a similar system. Dynamic algorithm for balancing the load is more flexible in nature and functional in both similar and similar environments [5].

The Distributed Load Imbalance System occurs when several users request access to the same server while other servers are sitting idle. To overcome this situation, Distributed Load Balance System is introduced for better performance of resource utilization and also can reduce the time limit of task execution.

4.2 RELATED WORKS

Afzal et al. [6] presented the problems of balancing the load that are investigated to propose better load-balancing methods in the future.

Aghdai et al. [7] described a scalable load-balancing architecture mentioned as 'Spotlight' to maintain the mapping between networks of the data centre. They have used Pre Connection Consistency (PCC) to improve the distribution of new services among load balancing. They also stated that PCC in load balancing has mainly two aspects maintaining PCC and flow dispatching. They mentioned Multipath Routing as a stateless flow dispatcher, which can be used for distributing an equal number of connections. They proposed their work as a stateful Adaptive Weighted Flow Dispatching (AWFD) algorithm. They suggested using their proposed algorithm to control the flow based on available capacity in each polling. They also mentioned that their proposed AWFD algorithm provides a platform as a spotlight for checking the available capacity. However, the distribution of load in multiple devices is a challenge for the proposed algorithm and the authors proposed a solution as consistent hashing that allows recovery of the system from the lost state and regenerates the PCC. Also, the authors discussed the stateful addressing in depth apart from mentioning only one stateless addressing which can be a focal point of research.

Ansar et al. [8] proposed a meta-heuristic load balancing algorithm. This algorithm is implemented using K-mean clustering of unsupervised learning.

Arunambika et al. [9] proposed a Replication and Migration Cost Minimization (RMCM) algorithm and an Optimal Cost Effective Technique (OCET) Selection Algorithm to reduce the cost of data placement. The RMCM is subdivided into three sub-algorithms. The sub-algorithms are the RMCM-PM Selection algorithm, RMCM-VM Selection algorithm, and RMCM-VM Placement and Migration Algorithm respectively. The first sub-algorithm RMCM-PM Selection algorithm finds the PM and their load patterns, and the second sub-algorithm RMCM-VM Selection algorithm finds the VMs and their coordination with the PMs based on load pattern and connection. The third sub-algorithm RMCM-VM Placement and Migration Algorithm discovers the new PMs to fill the necessities of the resources. The optimal Cost Effective Technique (OCET) is used to minimize the cost of cloud centres. The advantages of the proposed algorithms are less energy consumption migrating a minimum number of VMs, and saving lots of energy in data centres. However, the algorithms are executed using repetitive experiments. Only three CSPs are considered for the experiments.

Balaji et al. [1] mentioned the challenges and approaches of load balancing.

Belkhouraf et al. [10] illustrated a survey of some of its crucial problems. They proposed an algorithm using a scheme of multi-cluster. They suggested that their algorithm shows better performance in fault-tolerance rate.

Bhandari et al. [11] mentioned throttled load balancing algorithm with the availability of a virtual machine. A comparative study is made between another load-balancing algorithm with their proposed algorithm.

Chawla et al. [12] concentrated on the unavailability of virtual machine packets as per the requirement and described an algorithm to replicate the existing virtual machine packets. With the focus on minimizing the load of virtual machines, they also extended their concentration to minimize the overall price and the various time factors of load balancing.

Duan et al. [13] proposed a time prioritization-based Ensemble Resource Management and Ant-Colony Optimization (ECC-ACO) algorithm with the aim of effective resource allocation and scheduling mechanism. The authors explained the algorithm with the help of algorithmic and flowchart representation. They performed the simulation using six various nodes namely, one master node, four computer nodes, and one client. The performance is evaluated based on time-effective demand fulfillment rate, response time, and resource utilization time. The authors performed the comparisons between various mechanisms using a state-of-the-art method. After the calculation, the authors stated that the overall fitness of their proposed algorithm is 98%. However, they suggested extending the grouping mechanism for other algorithms since they have used only a group of two algorithms.

Ebadifard et al. [14] illustrated the honey bee algorithm to focus on task scheduling of load balancing. They observed that their proposed algorithm works better in minimizing make-span as compared with the round-robin algorithm.

Ghomi et al. [15] surveyed several metrics for load-balancing techniques that should be considered in future load-balancing strategies. In future works, they suggested the following: (1) Study and analyze more recent strategies in each of the proposed categories, (2) Evaluate each strategy in a simulation toolkit and compare them based on new metrics.

In this chapter, the authors Grover et al. [16] used Agent-Based Dynamic Load Balancing (ABDLB) approach in which a mobile agent plays a very important role, which is a software entity.

Gupta et al. [17], proposed Managed Server algorithm for load balancing with four virtual machines and two data centres. The cost efficiency of the proposed system is also mentioned in this chapter in a graphical representation.

Jena et al. [18] proposed load balancing for independent tasks in the cloud computing network.

Jenny et al. [19] considered the normal Particle Swarm Optimization (PSO) algorithm and Weight Improved Particle Swarm Optimization (WIPSO) algorithm. They observed that WIPSO results were better than Normal PSO. However, it was mentioned by the authors that a better range of parameters can provide a more efficient result.

Kalaivani et al. [20] proposed the Modified Bee Colony (MBC) and hybrid Modified Bee Colony-Bacterial Foraging Optimization (MBC-BFO) models with three classification techniques as Artificial Neural Networks (ANN), Recursive Neural Network (ReNN), and Recurrent Neural Network (RNNs). The author used nature-created optimization techniques and has the advantage of better detection frequency of errors. They considered True Positive (TP), True Negative (TN), False Positive (FP), and False Negative (FN) as the parameters and sensitivity, accuracy, false positive rate, and F-score as a matrix. However, the accuracy rate can be improved using other hybrid techniques. The execution time and complexity can be reduced further using modified techniques as suggested.

Kapoor et al. [21] mentioned that the traditional throttled load-balancing algorithm is a good approach for load balancing in cloud computing as it distributes the incoming jobs evenly among the VMs. Exploratory results have shown that the proposed approach gives better results than throttled and modified throttled algorithms when compared based on various criteria.

Kaur et al. [22] proposed an algorithm to check the performance of virtual machines. They suggested a paired tree load balancing algorithm to equalize the load of virtual machines.

The authors Kaur et al. [23] summarized the state of the art of various papers. They proposed an algorithm for task scheduling. They considered seven attributes in seven columns to check their performance for the four algorithms – FCFS, RR, SJF, & PSO. After their analysis, they conclude that task scheduling can be improved by lowering the makespan in every four algorithms. However, the authors analyzed only the basic algorithms to check the task scheduling. They suggested designing hybrid algorithms to improve performance. However, they have not considered the Ant Colony Organization (ACO) and Artificial Bee Colony (ABC) algorithms which are inspired by nature.

Kumar et al. [3] stated a comparative study among the various load-balancing algorithms in their paper. They suggested that many techniques can be used to balance the load of virtual machines and all of them have many factors with positive and negative aspects. They mainly focused on minimizing the response time. The authors also suggested many objectives of load balancing in cloud computing. However, they mentioned that there is a need for proper workload mapping and load-balancing techniques that consider different metrics.

Li et al. [24] describe a model of MHDNNL (Multiple Heterogeneous Deep Neural Networks Learning) for simultaneous scheduling decisions and uses more than one heterogeneous DNN to join the schedulers. Two key techniques are used in this model. The first technique is used to evaluate the scheduling decision and the second is to repay the memory. The model has the advantage of increasing the agent's capability to explore and improve the utilization of training samples. The validity and performance are verified in this model using a simulation technique in two parts. The model is compared with the other two algorithms – RR and MoPSO. They considered the parameters like QN (Number of Queues) and CN (Number of Clusters). However, the authors stated some of the challenges of this model as follows (1) Due to a fixed number of clusters, the model is not being able to predict the users' workload efficiently. (2) A multi-model collaborative scheduling is suggested for large data centres as this model uses only a single scheduling technique.

Mishra et al. [5] illustrated both homogeneous as well as heterogeneous load-balancing algorithms. They focused on the algorithms that reduce the energy consumption of the whole system.

Mukundha et al. [25] proposed a genetic load-balancing algorithm to use the resources with the focus of improving the throughput and lowering the response time.

Panwar et al. [26] proposed a dynamic load management algorithm for the spreading of the approaching demand among the virtual machines efficiently. The authors also suggested creating a hybrid model to upgrade the facilities.

Parida et al. [27] mentioned load balancing as the most dynamic problem in the cloud computing environment. They proposed the Salp Swarn Optimization technique as a meta-heuristic algorithm to solve this problem. The authors also proposed the binary version of the Salp Swarn Optimization algorithm to solve the problems in binary task assignments. However, the authors stated that the original Salp Swarn algorithm was a continuous process that could not be able to solve the binary problems.

Priyanka et al. [28] mentioned that balancing the load simultaneously avoids failure and reduces congestion which in turn improves elasticity and durability of resources, and it also reduces over-furnishing of Virtual Machines allotment and reduces resource utilization.

Pushpavati et al. [29] developed a paired-tree algorithm for load balancing. They performed implementation of the algorithm in CloudSim and they also found out the makespan of their proposed algorithm by comparing it with an enhanced bee colony algorithm using various cloudlet members. However, the authors have compared their proposed algorithm with only one algorithm which can be performed with further comparison with other algorithms also. They also suggested extending the mechanism of load balancing with augmented cloud architecture.

Ramegowda et al. [30] proposed an algorithm for multi-tenancy for resource allocation. However, the detection of virtual machines using reusable objects is kept for future use by the authors.

Rahman et al. [31] mentioned the importance of balancing the load. They provided a view of the load balancing facilities by major cloud players in the industry today. However, they stated that the technologies involved are still in their beginning and need to be matured.

Rani and Suri [32] proposed a model with a modified Ant Colony Optimization (ACO) technique with the Gravitational Search Algorithm (GSA) concept to resolve the problems of load balancing. The authors stated that their proposed model is used for searching distinct data from scheduling the task. They used the CloudSim toolkit to simulate their data and found that their proposed algorithm is working better in performance considering various parameters. The authors also mentioned that their proposed model can efficiently distribute the load by checking the capability of all the machines. They also described the CloudSim Toolkit, its characteristics, and its platform. However, only two models are compared with the proposed model and hence more algorithms are needed to be compared.

Rekha et al. [33] proposed an enhanced model named Artificial Bee Colony Optimization (ABC) to multi-line the tasks whenever they are at the initial state. They compared their proposed model with the other two algorithms. The over-used hosts are detected using Adaptive Neuro-Fuzzy Inference System (ANFIS) and virtual machines are migrated using Minimum Migration Time (MMT) technique. The authors achieved cloud data storage security by analyzing authorized key cryptography techniques called Elliptic Curve Cryptography. Their proposed model is checked using the factors like throughput and encryption time. However, intrusion detection is not considered in their proposed work.

Ren et al. [34] proposed a dynamic migration algorithm with a proposed method of fractal-based load-balancing trigger strategy.

Sagar et al. [35] proposed an algorithm to reduce the response time of the data centre for allotment of the latest appeal.

Salimi et al. [36] mainly focused on the virtual machines that are defined as the building blocks of cloud computing. The authors introduced the concept of virtual CPU co-scheduling for VM optimization. They mentioned the types of VM scheduling in this chapter and also explained the various advantages of VM scheduling. The authors used the CloudSim tool for simulating the results of performance. However, the authors mentioned that there are different techniques for parallel processing but they have tried to focus on the advantages and main aspects of VMs based on co-scheduling in this chapter.

Sarma et al. [37] illustrated different algorithms to balance the load. The simulation results of all the discussed algorithms are also shown in this chapter. The authors conclude that based on the results amongst the algorithms for cloud environment.

Shahapure et al. [38] first mentioned that the increased scalability of resources can decrease the performance level of cloud data centres. Therefore, focusing on these challenges, they have proposed an algorithm and explained the algorithm using mathematical hypothesis and flowchart representation. The proposed algorithm is analyzed using CloudSim and using Cloud Reports the reports are generated. However, the authors have considered limited parameters for measuring the various factors. They have not considered parameters like power consumption during peak hours. They have also mentioned migrating the algorithm further to the green cloud computing concept with a post-copy approach.

Sharma et al. [39] mentioned techniques to make a better make-span by distributing the load in many VMs. The reconstruction of their proposed algorithm is performed using MATLAB and their results are stated by the authors. They however suggested extending their work by considering criteria on multiple task allocation features.

Shifrin et al. [40] suggested a solution called Abstract Markov Decision Process (MDP) to combine multiple states into a single state. They stated that the virtual machine (VM) grows exponentially based on the memory needed. In this concept, they introduced aggregated MDP (aMDP) and detailed MDP (MDP). They subdivided an MDP to perform three operations virtual machine deployment, virtual machine termination, and load balancing. They used simulation techniques to accommodate five various tasks in both algorithms. The authors studied the feasibility of MDP in AWS (Amazon Web Services) infrastructure. However, this service is not allowing to access thresholds available through the AWS console. The authors suggested using MDP based orchestrator (MBO) combining load balancing and auto-scaling together to overcome the challenge.

Singh et al. [41] illustrated a virtual load-balancing algorithm with a pictorial characterization. They mentioned a comparison evaluation to calculate the response time and concluded that increasing the number of data centres can decrease the overall average response time.

Singh et al. [42] mentioned the reliability, some of the legal and compliant factors, security, ownership, performance, interoperability, multi-platform support, data management issues, and most importantly load balancing. However, the shortage of tools for the geographical distribution of servers and users is also mentioned in this chapter.

Singh et al. [43] as discussed, the CloudAnalyst tool used to determine the best among all the load-balancing algorithms. They mentioned that the response time of throttled is better than the round robin algorithm. Also, the processing time is considered to be in optimum level while the price issue is unchanged in all these algorithms. The authors concluded to concentrate their work on particle swarm optimization algorithms.

Srivastava et al. [44] proposed a model for balancing the load of cloud computing by dividing the model into different modules. Each module is described in this chapter. They have used 8 hosts and 10 VMs in the evaluation process. However, only one data centre is used for checking the performance of the load in this paper.

Sui et al. [45] proposed a technique using machine learning. They illustrated the K-means genetic algorithm to increase the power of searching local machines.

Tripathi et al. [2] mentioned designing a hybrid technique with a combination of ant and bee colony optimization techniques. They found the response time in greater outcome, showing the analysis results with the help of CloudAnalyst.

Tong et al. [46] illustrated virtual machine load and task rejection rate. They proposed an algorithm to focus on dynamic task-scheduling load-balancing and experimented with their proposed work using the CloudAnalyst technique.

Weinhardt et al. [47] discussed in this chapter the loopholes that have to be restrained to make the Cloud creativity into reality. They put a variance between Cloud and Grid Computing by classifying formulas. However, the authors mentioned that exchanging the idea of distinctive utilities needs a detailed comprehension of collective feature.

Wickremasinghe et al. [48] defined in their paper the CloudAnalyst as a Graphical user interface-based simulation tool with the enhancement of the CloudSim application.

4.3   MAJOR GOALS OF LOAD BALANCING

3.1 To build up the efficiency and performance of the system.
3.2 To set up a fault-tolerant system [49].
3.3 Provide support for the balancing of the system.
3.4 Making a better system using limited resources.
3.5 Provide better optimization of user satisfaction level.
3.6 Reducing the time of waiting and job execution.
3.7 Reducing energy consumption and carbon emission [50].

4.4   CHALLENGES OF LOAD BALANCING

4.1   Production: Calculating the execution time of process by CPU [15].
4.2   Overhead: Improved overhead at execution time.
4.3   Fault tolerance: Less number of faults for better production.
4.4   Relocation Time: Time taken by the processor to transfer one process.
4.5   Response time: Time consumed by the organization to the reaction to the process.
4.6   Resource utilization: Ability to efficiently utilize the resources.
4.7   Scalability: Load Balancing on a virtual machine with multiple clients.
4.8   Performance: Utilized to evaluate the carrying out of the processor [51].
4.9   Point of Failure: The entire system should not fail if one central node fails [25].
4.10 Geographically Located Nodes: The data centres are administered as per the geographical characteristics of an area for calculative reasons [1].

4.5   VIRTUALIZATION

Virtualization has the capacity to execute many VMs on a single device by distributing all the hardware resources [52]. The main objective of any migration technique should be to decrease the total relocation time and downtime. Virtualization is also accountable for balancing the load in the whole system, organizing, and synchronizing the allotment of resources [53].

The Virtual Machine Monitor (VMM) is the concept of using multiple operating systems in a single host [25]. The two types of virtualization techniques in cloud computing are:

Full Virtualization – The installation of one computer on another computer.

Para Virtualization – The running state of multiple operating systems on a single computer [25].

Virtualization is of two types: Client-installed and Hypervisor. In client-installed virtualization software, an operating system is installed on a section of hardware, and at the uppermost layer of it client virtualization software is installed [37]. The challenge of a VM is the live migration in optimum time from one host to another without interrupting the other hosts. In the case of hypervisor virtualization, there can be more than one VM to host the computers. In this type, every VM can execute its programs and multiple machines can use a single hardware at the same time.

4.6 TOOLS USED TO CHECK VIRTUALIZATION IN CLOUD COMPUTING

4.6.1 CLOUDANALYST

Cloud analysis is developed in Java for optimum performance. However, the cost is too high for the geographically distributed cloud system. Singh et al. [41] describes Cloud Analyst as a Graphical User Interface based software originated in CloudSim Architecture.

4.6.2 CLOUDSIM

There are different versions available of CloudSim as 1.0, 2.0, 3.0, etc. This simulating technique manages the load coming from the hosts.

4.7 ALGORITHMS USED IN LOAD BALANCING [41]

4.7.1 ROUND ROBIN ALGORITHM

There are two types of Round Robin algorithms used in load balancing and they are (i). Classic Round Robin Algorithm and (ii). Weighted Round Robin Algorithm.

4.7.1.1 Classic Round Robin Algorithm

The authors mentioned the steps of the Classic Round Robin Algorithm which are illustrated below [54]:

Step 1: Distribute the client information across a group of servers.
Step 2: Multiple servers and multiple clients can be involved.
Step 3: The servers are identical and configured to provide the same services to users.
Step 4: All are configured to use the same domain name with different IP Addresses.
Step 5: Load balancing has the list of all the IP Addresses with associated Internet Domain Names.
Step 6: When the request for the sessions is linked with the Domain Names, they are allocated in a circular sequential form.
Step 7: The first server is allocated the request as the client initiates the request and passes it to the server.
Step 8: The same process continues to the second and third servers.
Step 9: In the case of the fourth request, it is allocated to the first server again creating a ring of allocating resources.

4.7.1.2   Weighted Round Robin Algorithm

This algorithm has the following steps [55]:

Step 1: The network administrator assigns a fixed number of weights to each server in the pool.
Step 2: The most efficient and powerful server can be assigned as Weight = 100.
Step 3: The servers with a heavy weight can be assigned on more requests.
Step 4: The ring is formed based on the requests.
Step 5: It is considered by the system that the higher weightings are assigned on more requests in each cycle.

4.7.2   ACTIVE MONITORING ALGORITHM

This dynamic algorithm follows the steps as given below [56] (Prakash):

Step 1: The controllers maintain an index table.
Step 2: The servers are identified based on their loading at the current time.
Step 3: If any server is detected with the minimum load or in an idle state, then the load is allocated to that server.
Step 4: The index table is updated when the load is allocated to a server.
Step 5: The First Come First Served (FCFS) technique is used to allocate the load.
Step 6: The unique server id is used to assign tasks to every server.
Step 7: Every task completion allows the controllers to update the index table once again.
Step 8: Based on the request of the user on Internet usage, allocation of load to the particular server is performed by the load balancer by checking the index table.

4.7.3   THROTTLED LOAD BALANCING ALGORITHM

The Algorithm steps are given below [42]:

Step 1: It is dependent on the VM status.
Step 2: The VM allocation is in binary form as 'yes' or 'no' and it defines its status.
Step 3: The status information is stored in an index table at the load balancer.
Step 4: The index table consists of two parameters: ID of the VM and the status of whether the VM is available or busy.
Step 5: Initialize all the VM status is set to 'Available'.
Step 6: Once the Load balancer gets the forward request from the data centre, it searches for the available VM.
Step 7: If it gets the VM with the available status, then it sends the respective VM_ID (Virtual Machine ID) to the data centre.

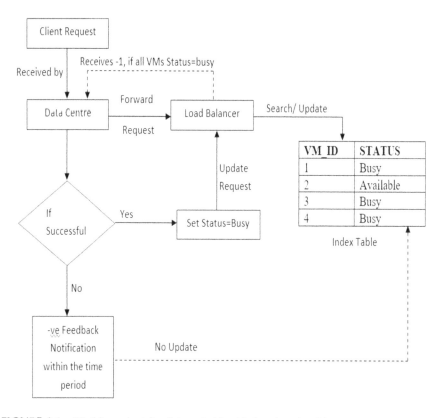

FIGURE 4.1   Working principle of throttled load balancing algorithm.

Step 8: The data centre makes the status of that VM as 'Busy' and sends the request of updating it to the Load balancer.

Step 9: The Load balancer updates the index table as it gets the update request.

Step 10: In case of all theVM's status is busy, the Load balancer sends a signal of -1 to the data centre.

Step 11: The data centre sends a negative feedback notification if it does not get any response from the Load balancer. At that time there will not be any update in the index table (Figure 4.1).

4.7.3.1   Limitations of Throttled Load Balancing Algorithm

4.7.3.1.1

Throttled Load Balancing Algorithm is hardware-dependent. The data centre of all the VMs should have the identical hardware arrangement for efficient working of the Throttled Load Balancing Algorithm [57].

4.7.3.1.2

The software environment is not a factor of Throttled Load Balancing Algorithm. It can be considered during the task selection of the VMs to improve the performance of Throttled Load Balancing Algorithm [58].

4.7.3.1.3

The cloud customer can enjoy the service of Throttled Load Balancing Algorithm more if the cost per request is calculated as per the environment demand [42].

4.7.3.1.4

The Throttled Load Balancing Algorithm can be improved by adding the following parameters [42].

4.7.3.1.4.1 Type of tasks

4.7.3.1.4.2 The software environment is needed if the task is dynamic.

4.8 CONCLUSION

The chapter substantiates the idea of load balancing, the importance of load balancing in virtualization, and its types. The basic techniques for dynamic load balancing are focused on in this chapter. The VMs utilized in these algorithms and how the virtualization concept is affecting these algorithms are mentioned here. For future use, more algorithms can be focused on the virtualization concept in dynamic load-balancing strategy.

REFERENCES

[1] K. Balaji et al., "Load balancing in cloud computing: Issues and challenges," *Turkish Journal of Computer Mathematics Education*, vol. 12, no. 2, pp. 3224–3231, 2021.

[2] A. Tripathi et al., "A hybrid optimization approach for load balancing in cloud computing," *Advances in Computer and Computational Sciences*. Springer Nature Singapore Pte Ltd, 2018, pp. 197–206, doi:10.1007/978–981-10-3773-3_19.

[3] P. Kumar and R. Kumar, "Issues and challenges of load balancing techniques in cloud computing: A survey," *ACM Computing Surveys*, vol. 51, no. 6, pp. 1–35, 2019, doi:10.1145/3281010.

[4] S. Kumar and D. S. Singh, "Various dynamic load balancing algorithms in cloud environment: A survey," *International Journal of Computing Application*, vol. 129, no. 6, pp. 14–19, 2015, doi:10.5120/ijca2015906927.

[5] S. K. Mishra et al., "Load balancing in cloud computing: A big picture," *Journal of King Saud University - Computer and Information Sciences*, vol. 32, no. 2, pp. 149–158, 2020, doi:10.1016/j.jksuci.2018.01.003.

[6] S. Afzal and G. Kavitha, "Load balancing in cloud computing – A hierarchical taxonomical classification," *Journal of Cloud Computing Advance System Application,* vol. 8, no. 1, pp. 1–24, 2019, doi:10.1186/s13677-019-0146–7.

[7] A. Aghdai et al., "Spotlight: Scalable transport layer load balancing for data center networks," *IEEE Transactions on Cloud Computer*, vol. 10, no. 3, pp. 2131–2145, 2020, doi:10.1109/TCC.2020.3024834.

[8] K. Ansar et al., "A hybrid HS-mean technique for efficient load balancing in cloud computing," *Springer Naure. Switzerland AG*, vol. 2019, pp. 40–48, 2019, doi:10.1007/978-3-030-02613-4_4.

[9] T. Arunambika and P. S. Vadivu, "Replication and migration cost minimization of cloud data center," *ICTACT Journal of Soft Computing*, vol. 11, no. 4, pp. 2449–2456, 2021, doi:10.21917/ijsc.2021.0350.

[10] Belkhouraf et al., "A secured load balancing architecture for cloud computing based on multiple clusters," *2015 IEEE*, 2015 International Conference on Cloud Technologies and Applications (CloudTech), https://doi.org/10.1109/CloudTech.2015.7336978.

[11] A. Bhandari and K. Kaur, "An enhanced post-migration algorithm for dynamic load balancing in cloud computing environment," *Advances in Intelligent Systems Computing*, vol. 811, pp. 59–73, 2019, doi:10.1007/978–981-13–1544-2_6.

[12] A. Chawla and N. S. Ghumman, "Package-based approach for load balancing in cloud computing," *Advances in Intelligent Systems Computing*, vol. 654, pp. 71–77, 2018, doi:10.1007/978–981-10–6620–7_9.

[13] J. Duan et al., "Time effective cloud resource scheduling method for data-intensive smart systems" [International journal], *International Journal of Information Technology and Web Engineering*, vol. 17, no. 1, pp. 1–15, 2022, doi:10.4018/IJITWE.306915.

[14] F. Ebadifard et al., "A dynamic task scheduling algorithm improved by load balancing in cloud computing," IEEE Explore 6th International Conference on Web Research (ICWR), vol. 2020, 2020, pp. 177–183, doi:10.1109/ICWR49608.2020.9122287.

[15] E. J. Ghomi et al., "Load-balancing algorithms in cloud computing: A survey," *Journal of Network and Computer Applications*, vol. 88, pp. 50–71, 2017, doi:10.1016/j.jnca.2017.04.007.

[16] J. Grover and S. Katiyar, "Agent based dynamic load balancing in cloud computing," *IEEE 2013 International Conference on Human Computer Interactions, Chennai, India, 2013 International Conference on Human Computer Interactions*, 1–6, 2013, doi:10.1109/ICHCI-IEEE.2013.6887799.

[17] A. Gupta, "Load balancing in cloud computing," *International Journal of Distributed Cloud Computing*, vol. 5, no. 2, pp. 22–28, 2017.

[18] U. K. Jena et al., "Hybridization of meta-heuristic algorithm for load balancing in cloud computing environment," *Journal of King Saud University – Computer and Information Sciences*, vol. 34, no. 6, Part A, pp. 1–11, 2020, doi:10.1016/j.jksuci.2020.01.012.

[19] L. J. Jenny and A. Paul, "QoS−aware web service composition using weight improved particle swarm optimization," *Science and Technology of Journal*, vol. 9, no. 2, pp. 65–70, 2021, doi:10.22232/stj.2021.09.02.07.

[20] S. Kalaivani and G. Gopinath, "Modified bee colony with bacterial foraging optimization based hybrid feature selection technique for intrusion detection system classifier model," *ICTACT Journal of Soft Computing*, vol. 10, no. 4, pp. 2146–2152, 2020, doi:10.21917/ijsc.2020.0305.

[21] S. Kapoor and C. Dabas, Cluster based load balancing in cloud computing, IEEE 2015 Eighth International Conference on Contemporary Computing (IC3) – Noida, India (2015.8.20-2015.8.22)] 2015 Eighth International Conference on Contemporary Computing (IC3) – Cluster based load balancing in cloud computing, 2015, pp. 76–81, doi:10.1109/IC3.2015.7346656.

[22] A. Kaur et al., "Meta-heuristic based framework for workflow load balancing in cloud environment," *International Journal of Information Technology*, vol. 11, no. 1, pp. 119–125, 2019, doi:10.1007/s41870-018-0231-z.

[23] R. Kaur et al., "Performance evaluation of task scheduling algorithms in virtual cloud environment to minimize makespan," *International Journal of Information Technology*, vol. 14, no. 1, pp. 79–93, 2022, doi:10.1007/s41870-021-00753-4.

[24] Q. Li et al., "MHDNNL: A batch task optimization scheduling algorithm in cloud computing," *International Journal of Information Technology and Web Engineering*, vol. 17, no. 1, pp. 1–17, 2022, doi:10.4018/IJITWE.310053.

[25] C. Mukundha et al., "A comprehensive study report on load balancing techniques in cloud computing," *International Journal of Engineering Research and Development*, vol. 13, no. 9, pp. 35–42, 2017.

[26] R. Panwar and B. Mallick, "Load balancing in cloud computing using dynamic load management algorithm" *International Conference on Green Computing and Internet of Things, Greater Noida, Delhi, India, 2015 International Conference on Green Computing and Internet of Things. IEEE*, 2015, pp. 773–778, doi:10.1109/ICGCIoT.2015.7380567.

[27] B. R. Parida et al., "Binary self-adaptive salp swarm optimization-based dynamic load balancing in cloud computing," *International Journal of Information Technology Web Engineering*, vol. 17, no. 1, pp. 1–25, 2022, doi:10.4018/IJITWE.295964.

[28] M. Priyanka and V. M. Sivagami, "A survey on load management techniques in cloud computing," *International Journal of Scientific Research in Computer Science, Engineering Information Technology*, vol. 2, no. 2, pp. 1115–1121, 2017.

[29] S. Pushpavati, U.K. D'Mello, "A tree based mechanism for the load balancing of virtual machines in cloud environments," *International Journal of Information Technology*, vol. 13, pp. 911–920, 2021, doi: https://doi.org/10.1007/s41870-020-00544-3

[30] A. Ramegowda et al., "Adaptive task scheduling method in multi-tenant cloud computing," *International Journal of Information Technology*, vol. 12, no. 4, pp. 1093–1102, 2020, doi:10.1007/s41870-019-00389-5.

[31] M. Rahman et al., "Load balancer as a service in cloud computing," *8th International Symposium on Service Oriented System Engineering- Oxford, United Kingdom 8th International Symposium on Service Oriented System Engineering*, vol. 2014. IEEE, 2014, pp. 204–211, doi:10.1109/SOSE.2014.31.

[32] S. Rani and P. K. Suri, "An efficient and scalable hybrid task scheduling approach for cloud environment," *International Journal of Information Technology*, vol. 12, no. 4, pp. 1451–1457, 2020, doi:10.1007/s41870-018-0175-3.

[33] S. Rekha and C. Kalaiselvi, "Secure and energy aware task scheduling in cloud using deep learning and cryptographic techniques," *ICTACT Journal of Communication Technology*, vol. 12, no. 02, pp. 2434–2441, 2021, doi:10.21917/ijct.2021.0360.

[34] H. Ren et al., "The load balancing algorithm in cloud computing environment," *IEEE 2012 2nd International Conference on Computer Science and Network Technology, Changchun, China, Proceedings of 2012 2nd International Conference on Computer Science and Network Technology*, pp. 925–928, 2012.

[35] J. Sagar and L. Bhambhu, "Algorithm of load balance in cloud computing," *International Journal of Computer Science Trends and Technology*, vol. 2, no. 5, pp. 40–43, 2014.

[36] H. Salimi et al., "Advantages, challenges and optimizations of virtual machine scheduling in cloud computing environments," *International Journal of Computer Theory and Engineering*, vol. 4, no. 2, pp. 189–193, 2012, doi:10.7763/IJCTE.2012.V4.448.

[37] P. Sarma et al., "A survey on load balancing algorithms in cloud computing," *International Journal of Computer Science and Engineering*, vol. 7, no. 6, pp. 169–176, 2019, doi:10.26438/ijcse/v7i6.169176.

[38] N. H. Shahapure and P. Jayarekha, "Virtual machine migration based load balancing for resource management and scalability in cloud environment," *International Journal of Information and Technology*, vol. 12, no. 4, pp. 1331–1342, 2020, doi:10.1007/s41870-018-0216-y.

[39] S. C. M. Sharma et al., "Efficient load balancing techniques for multi-datacenter cloud milieu," *International Journal of Information and Technology*, vol. 14, no. 2, pp. 979–989, 2022, doi:10.1007/s41870-020-00529-2.

[40] M. Shifrin et al., "VM scaling and load balancing via cost optimal MDP solution," *IEEE Transactions Cloud Computing*, vol. 10, no. 3, pp. 2219–2237, 2020, doi:10.1109/TCC.2020.3000956

[41] H. Singh and R. C. Gangwar, "Comparative study of load balancing algorithms in cloud environment," *International Journal of Recent Innovation Trends Computing and Communication*, vol. 2, no. 10, pp. 3195–3199, 2014, doi:10.17762/ijritcc.v2i10.3371.

[42] H. Singh and H. Kaur, "Optimised environment allocation for static and dynamic tasks based on throttle algorithm in cloud," *International Journal of Engineering Science and Research Technology*, vol. 7, no. 7, pp. 1–11, 2018, doi:10.5281/zenodo.1305803.

[43] S. P. Singh et al., "Analysis of load balancing algorithms using cloud analyst," *International Journal of Grid Distributed Computing*, vol. 9, no. 9, pp. 11–24, 2016, doi:10.14257/ijgdc.2016.9.9.02.

[44] P. Srivastava et al., "Load management model for cloud computing using Cloudsim," *International Journal of Computer Theory and Engineering*, vol. 9, no. 5, pp. 390–393, 2017, doi:10.7763/IJCTE.2017.V9.1172.

[45] X. Sui et al., "Virtual machine scheduling strategy based on machine learning algorithms for load balancing," *EURASIP Journal on Wireless Communications and Networking*, vol. 2019, no. 1, pp. 1–16, 2019, doi:10.1186/s13638-019-1454–9.

[46] Z. Tong et al., "DDMTS: A novel dynamic load balancing scheduling scheme under SLA constraints in cloud computing," *Journal of Parallel and Distributed Computing*, vol. 149, pp. 138–148, 2021, doi:10.1016/j.jpdc.2020.11.007.

[47] C. Weinhardt et al., "Cloud computing – A classification, business models, and research directions," *Business & Information Systems Engineering*, BISE, 391–399, 2009, doi:10.1007/s12599-009-0071–2.

[48] B. Wickremasinghe et al., 2010, "Project web". Available at: http://www.cloudbus.org/cloudsim/.

[49] M. B. Ansari and P. Sachin, "An efficient method for resource monitoring in cloud nodes using dynamic load balancing algorithm," *International Journal of Engineering Research & Technology*, vol. 4, no. 7, pp. 588–593, 2015, doi:10.17577/IJERTV4IS070323.

[50] A. P. Florence and V. Shanthi, "Energy aware load balancing for computational cloud," *IEEE International Conference on Computational Intelligence and Computing Research*, 2014.

[51] A. Garg and S. Dang, 2017, "Load balancing techniques, challenges & performance metrics," *Motherhood International Journal of Multidisciplinary Research & Development a Peer Reviewed Refereed International Research Journal*, vol. II, no. I, pp. 19–27.

[52] S. Arora and Sunanda, "Virtual machine availability and load balancing in cloud environment," *International Journal of Control Theory and Applications*, vol. 10, no. 4, pp. 183–190, 2017.

[53] D. A. Shafiq et al., "A load balancing algorithm for the data centres to optimize cloud computing applications," *IEEE Access*, vol. 9, pp. 41731–41744, 2021, doi:10.1109/ACCESS.2021.3065308.

[54] S. Shukla and R. S. Suryavanshi, 2019, "Survey on load balancing techniques," *International Conference of Emerging Trends in Technology and Application*.

[55] J. C. Villanueva, *Comparing Load Balancing Algorithms*, 2022 [Online]. Available: Comparing Load Balancing Algorithms | JSCAPE

[56] A. N. Singh and S. Prakash, "WAMLB: Weighted active monitoring load balancing in cloud computing," *Big Data Analytics. Advances in Intelligent Systems and Computing*, vol. 654.

[57] S. Agrawal and S. Nigam, "Performance testing of a hybrid algorithm based on throttled and ESCE load balancing algorithm," *International Journal for Research in Science Engineering*, vol. 2, no. 6, pp. 135–140, 2021.

[58] N. L. Hieu, C. T. Hung, "ITA: The improved throttled algorithm of load balancing on cloud computing," *International Journal of Computer Networks & Communications*, vol. 14, no. 1, pp. 25–39, 2022, doi: 10.5121/ijcnc.2022.14102

5 Predicting Consumer Behaviors with Data Analytics for Decision-Making

*Rupali Gill, Raj Gaurang Tiwari,
Ambuj Kumar Agarwal, and Vishal Jain*

5.1 INTRODUCTION

Predictive modeling is a statistical and mathematical process [1] that is used to predict future actions and results by investigating similar patterns for anticipating impending outcomes. This is also known as predictive analytics. The key question before starting the study is knowledge of past behavior and prediction of likely future trends. Companies nowadays are shifting towards predictive analysis [2,3]. The major reason for this trend is the larger amount of data, tough market and economic conditions, and the varied amount of software available. It helps the organizations solve various problems and find new opportunities. It helps in the detection of fraud by cyber security cells, predicting market analysis, and market trends to find new openings [4], inventory forecasting, managing resources, and calculating credit scores to assess a consumer's likelihood of known purchases.

The key feature and advantages of predictive modeling are as follow:

i) For improving the accuracy of new data [4] in prediction terms, new models are designed primarily. To achieve the prediction accuracy, the available data is used as a training set and its predictable performance is measured using a test sample when the model is built. This is the key distinction between [5], for instance, a model of descriptive regression and a model of predictive regression.

ii) To persuade a report about how the outcome of interest is linked to a collection of key-dependent variables, predictive models may include many more factors and variables that could be included in a descriptive model, which is typically more comprehensive [5]. Therefore, the predictive method uses all the available knowledge to improve predictive accuracy.

DOI: 10.1201/9781003432869-5

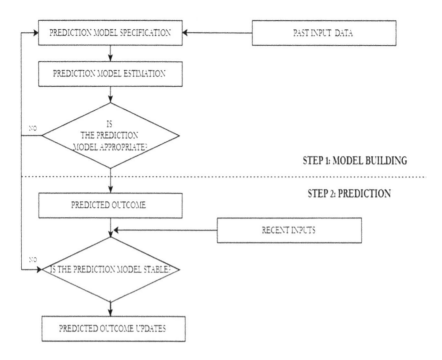

FIGURE 5.1   Steps for predictive modeling.

iii) Third, for each experimental stimulus [3,5], predictive models will generate a particular probability value. The probabilities are ranging from 0 to 1 and values can be continuous.

The steps to choosing a predictive model are a two-step process and it has been shown in Figure 5.1.

Step 1: Building a prediction model
Step 2: Prediction of the outcome

The major purpose of this chapter is to provide insight into predictive modeling in context to consumer behavior to find solutions that will help in decision-making. The chapter is organized into seven sections followed by the conclusion.

5.2   RELATED WORK

In this section, we are briefly explaining background terms, their importance, different factors influence, and real-life examples of consumer behavior which has been explained in Section 5.2.1–5.2.3 respectively.

5.2.1 Background Terms for Consumer Behavior: The Background Terms Have Been Explained As

i. Consumer behavior: It is a study of the intricate methods applied when people or groups of people are involved in marketing activities or group of activities like selecting [6], purchasing, using, or disposing goods, services, designs, or skills to satisfy desires and requirements.

ii. Consumer purchase: Consumer purchasing is a reaction to consumer behavior [3].

iii. Production of consumer decision (CD): Making CDs refers to decision-making regarding product and service selection [6]. It can be defined as a collection of statistics and analysis of information to evaluate and select the best way to solve a problem or make a purchase decision.

iv. Decision-making: It is characterized as the choice of different options for solving a problem [5] in a particular way, and the time and money needed to complete the purchase differ throughout purchase decisions.

v. Consumer buying decision models: Consumer buying decision models of consumer purchasing decisions apply to various identities and purchase perceptions from which customers view the market [7] and how/why they act as they do. They apply to how the purchasing decision process and overall buyer behavior are influenced by the various orientations. Various models were suggested by some researchers [6–8] with their most acceptable customer purchase decision model for all forms of products/services.

5.2.2 Importance of Customer Behavior Analytics

There are three major reasons to study consumer behavior analytics:

i. Gain insight: The division of the customer site by group analysis to identify market segments.

ii. Entice and interact by evaluating past sales and demographics, approaching the consumer group with correct offers.

iii. Improve retention: This helps businesses to assess consumer value and to attract customers with a constructive retention approach

5.2.3 Different Factors Influencing Consumer Behavior

Consumer purchases are strongly influenced by cultural, social, personal, and psychological factors.

Figure 5.2 shows the factors for influence-buying.

i. When and when to sell/buy?
   Figure 5.3 shows the percentage of where to showcase a product.

ii. How to sell or showcase to influence the consumer market?
   Figure 5.4 shows how to showcase a product.

Percentage of factors that influence buying

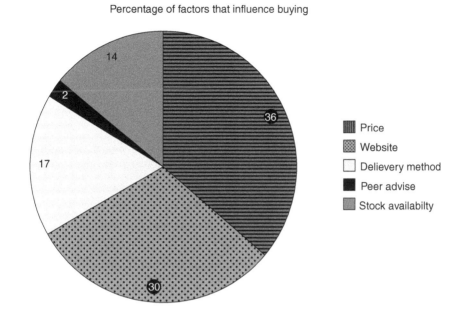

- Price
- Website
- Delievery method
- Peer advise
- Stock availabilty

FIGURE 5.2   Factors that influence buying.

Percentage of where to showcase

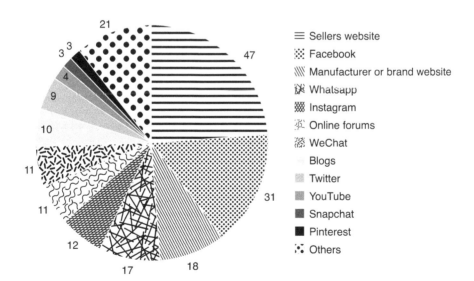

≡ Sellers website
Facebook
\\\\ Manufacturer or brand website
Whatsapp
Instagram
Online forums
WeChat
Blogs
Twitter
YouTube
Snapchat
Pinterest
Others

FIGURE 5.3   Percentage of showcases.

How to Showcase ?

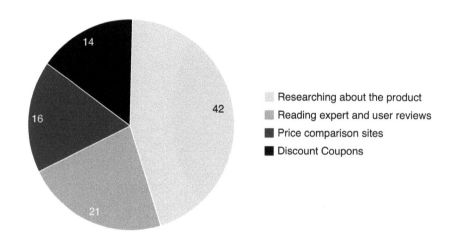

FIGURE 5.4   How to showcase.

5.2.4   REAL-LIFE EXAMPLES OF CONSUMER BEHAVIOR
APPLYING PREDICTIVE ANALYTICS

According to previous studies, different types of online shoppers are projected to reach 224 million in 2019 [9] in the US and M-commerce will reach $284 billion by 2020 [10]. Consumer behavior examples have been explained in the following section:

i. Financial services and credit card, banking:
   Companies can detect, measure, and reduce any fraudulent activity that can take place before it happens. Hence, helping them in maximizing sales [10], measuring risk, and customer satisfaction and retention. For instance, a bank named Commonwealth Bank is using predictive analysis to detect such activity.
ii. Governments and the public sector:
   The government and public sectors are using predictive analysis to detect and prevent any fake payments, improper usage of funds [11], address public activities and complaints, or any criminal activity. The Hong Kong government is using predictive modeling to detect and prevent such actions and activities.
iii. Health care providers and insurers:
   Health care providers are using predictive analytics to predict symptoms of diseases [11], check effectively to find new medical experiments. Taipei Medical University uses predictive modeling to analyze and monitor

performance in its medical system. The Blue Cross and Blue Shield of North Carolina are developing a more accurate predictor of hospital delivery and deploying nurse case managers to assist high-risk patients.

iv. Insurance-based companies:

Insurance companies use predictive analytics to check and detect premium rates, and fraud claims and speed up claim payments to help in customer retention and improve marketing strategies [11,12]. For example, Farmers Mutual Group, which used predictive modeling assessed the most risked policyholders within two hours of an earthquake.

v. Manufacturers and retailers

Manufacturers and retailers use predictive modeling [7,12] to identify marketing trends, brand loyalty, and possible areas of improvement for product distribution and supply. For example, Lenovo has detected a product problem by 30% and the warranty has been reduced by 10 to 15% on problems that were previously difficult to identify. Macy has increased its use of predictable statistics and reduced email subscriptions by 20%.

vi. Media, entertainment, and telecommunication companies:

Media, entertainment and telecommunication companies use predictive modeling to get insight into trends, driving factors, and potential audiences [13]. Foxwoods Resort Casino and T-Mobile are plying predictive modeling to meet up to the marketing trends.

5.3 MODELS OF CONSUMER BUYING BEHAVIOR PROCESS

With the emergence of customer-biased approach, there is more need to understand consumer behavior.

Consumers are the key focus of development and the decline of marketing-based strategies. The techniques range from the introduction of new products and services to the distribution and purchase of these products and services. Consumer behavior defines [13,14] how people make decisions about how to use their available resources, such as time, money, and effort to purchase various goods and services. It includes what they buy, why they buy it, when they buy it, where they buy it, how often they buy it, and how often they use it. Consumer behavior is an action taken by a person in the purchase and use of goods and services, including psychological and social processes that precede and follow these actions.

Consumer behavior is a broad and complex issue. Understanding consumer behavior and "knowing customers" is not so simple [15]. It is almost impossible to accurately predict how customers will participate in decision-making. The efforts of all advertisers are to influence the actions of customers desirably. Performance or weakness throughout the process determines the best of a bad marketing campaign or even the company itself.

Consumer behavior models can be classified into two types:

5.3.1 Traditional
5.3.2 Contemporary

5.3.1 TRADITIONAL MODELS ARE FURTHER CLASSIFIED INTO FOUR TYPES

i. Economic model: In the economic model, the consumer behavior focuses on the concept that the consumers' purchasing pattern is built on the concept of making [16] and it is one of the most profitable factors while reducing expenses. Consumer behavior can therefore be predicted [16] based on economic factors such as the purchasing behavior of the consumer and the price of competitive goods. An economic model is based on the following effects:
   • Price effect: Price is inversely proposal to quantity.
   • Substitution Effect: The price of the competent product is directly proportional to the original purchase value of the product.
   • Income effect: Whether more revenue is gained or more money is available, the quantity consumed will be greater.

ii. Learning model: A learning model is made on the presumption that the need to meet basic and learned needs determines consumer behavior [17]. Food, clothing, and shelter include basic needs, while anxiety and shame are learned needs. Therefore, a customer will prefer to buy stuff that will suit their needs and provide satisfaction. This model suggests that human decisions are based on certain core principles as mentioned below:
   • Drive: A powerful internal stimuli that motivate behavior [16].
   • Stimuli: The stimuli are inputs and it is capable of stimulating drives or motives [8].
   • Cues: The cues are signals that are serving as a stimulus to a certain drive [10].
   • Response: It is how the stimuli are responded to an individual [8].

iii. Psychoanalytic model: This model [13] takes into the idea on an account basis and checks whether consumer behavior is affected by both the conscious and subconscious mind.

iv. Sociological model: The sociological model is largely focused on the assumption that the purchasing behavior of the consumer is focused on its role and societal [11] influence. The actions of the customer can also be affected by the people she interacts with and the community that her society exhibits.

5.3.2 CONTEMPORARY MODELS

In this section, the consumer behavior models have been explained. There are three types which are as follows:

   i. Howard-Sheth Model
   ii. Engel-Kollat-Blackwell Model
   iii. Nicosia Model
   iv. Stimulus-Response Model

i. Howard-Sheth model (1969): The model was developed in 1969 [15] and used the concept of response from stimuli to understand consumer buying patterns as shown in Figure 5.5. Phases of Howard-Sheth model:
   • Extensive problem solving (EPS)
   • Limited problem solving (LPS)
   • Routinized response behavior (RRB)

ii. Engel-Kollat-Blackwell model: The model was developed in 1978 [16] and was based on an informed customer behavior problem analysis and learning model. This model offers a clear overview of customer active knowledge search and assessment process. This model demonstrates the decision-making elements and their relationships and experiences [16]. The diagram of Engel-Kollat Blackwell model has been shown in Figure 5.6. They see consumer behavior as a decision process in their consumer model and

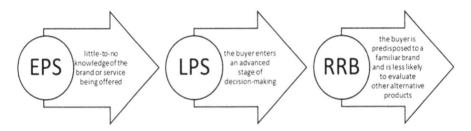

FIGURE 5.5   Howard-Sheth model.

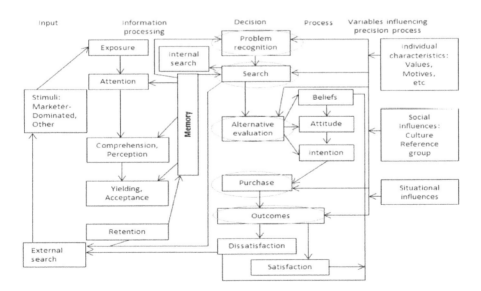

FIGURE 5.6   Engel-Kollat-Blackwell model.

define five behaviors during the process of decision-making over a different
era that are as follows:
- Problem recognition/Need recognition
- Information search
- Evaluation of alternatives
- Choice
- Post-purchase evaluation

iii. Nicosia model: This model was developed in 1966 [17], by Francesco
Nicosia. The Nicosia model tries to establish a connection between the customer and the organization to understand consumer behavior. The model
suggests that communication from a company first influences customer bias
toward a product or service [13]. The customer will have a certain attitude
towards the product based on the factory connection. Attitude leads to the
product search and evaluation of the product features by the customer. The
satisfaction level of the customer leads to a positive response and leads to
a decision to buy a product [17]. The descriptive way of Nicosia model has
been shown in Figure 5.7.

iv. Stimuli response Model: The model was proposed by Middleton in 1994
[18]. The stimuli response model was also known as an adapted model of
consumer behavior decision-making. Marketers must figure out the change
in stimuli response by understanding the customer needs. Marketing stimuli
can be of different types such as product, price, place, and promotion and
economic, technological, political, and cultural factors. The buyer under-
stands these factors [13] which are later converted to buyers' response
towards a choice of brand, choice of brand, choice of dealer, and timing
and quantity of purchase. The marketer must understand the change in

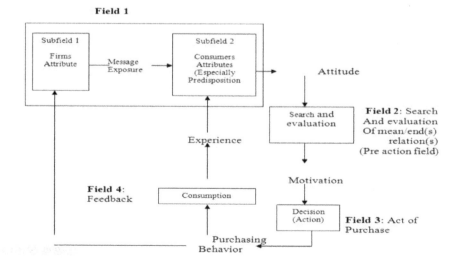

FIGURE 5.7 Nicosia model (Nicosia Model of Consumer Decision Process).

marketing behavior based on changing stimuli. The characteristics of buyers are based on the buyers' perseverance and decision-making process and it has been shown in Figure 5.8.

5.4   PREDICTIVE MODELING

With the increase of the broader concepts of big data, predictive modeling became more popular. With the increase of big data, there was a need for interpretation for better decision-making. In this section, the prediction modeling usage terms such as 'where', 'why', and types of predictive models have been described. Predictive modeling follows an 8-step process which has been shown in Figure 5.9.

Statistical algorithms and machine-learning techniques collect and analyze data but predictive modeling uses a large volume of data. The outcome of this helps in making a decision. To achieve this, predictive models are trained to predict the

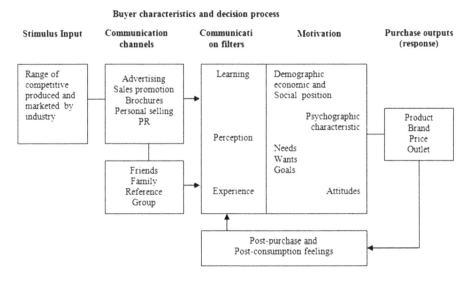

FIGURE 5.8   Stimuli response Model.

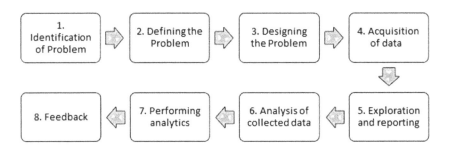

FIGURE 5.9   Predictive modeling process.

According to SPSS:

" Organizations that incorporate **predictive analytics** into their daily
operations in this way improve their business processes, enhancing decision
making and gaining the ability to direct, optimize, and automate decisions, on
demand, to meet defined business goals.

And, based on survey data, Forbes says:

" A vast majority of executives who have been overseeing predictive marketing
efforts for at least two years (86%) report increased return on investment (ROI)
as a result of their predictive marketing.

Only 5% say they've not experienced an improvement in ROI or a decline in ROI from
their efforts at predictive analytics.

FIGURE 5.10   Statistics about predictive modeling.

values. Many organizations are switching to predictive modeling to help increase
return on investment (ROI) as shown in Figure 5.10.

5.4.1   WHY USE PREDICTIVE MODELING?

    i. A large volume of data and to effectively use it
   ii. More facilities available to make up with outcomes
  iii. Current market trends, demanding prior information

5.4.2   WHAT ARE PREDICTIVE MODELS?

Predictive Models are the models intended to assess, discover, observe, and analyze
patterns and trends on the collected data to draw useful information [10,12,14].

   a) *Types of predictive models*
      i. *Forecast models*

The forecast model is one of the most widely used speculative models. It manages
metric value predictions by estimating new data values based on historical data read-
ings. Features of forecast models include:

   • Used for numerical values in historical data
   • Can input multiple parameters
      ii. *Classification models*

The categorization of information is based on historical data and is an extension of
forecast models.

Features of classification models:

- Can be easily retrained with new data
- provide a broad analysis
  iii. *Outliers models*

This model works on the analysis of outliers and works with anomalous data entries within a dataset.
Features of outliers' model:

- identifies unusual data, either in isolation or concerning different categories and numbers
- effective in detecting fraud because of the capability of finding anomalies
  iv. *Time series model*

The time series model works with time as the input value [19]. The model uses time series at different points of time from the historical data for trend prediction analysis.
Features of the time series model:

- Trend prediction over the years
- Can calculate progress or forecast for multiple projects and regions
- Can take into account extraneous factors
  v. *Clustering model*

The model works on the collection of data and clustering the data into groups [18] with commonalities.
Features of clustering model:

- Dividing the data into clusters leads to categorization based on the type of customers/product/need
- Identify the most relevant features that contribute to the formation of consumer clusters
- Clustering results should be interpretable, allowing marketers and decision-makers to understand the characteristics of each cluster.
- The clustering model should be robust to variations in the data and outliers.
- Provide visualizations of consumer clusters for better communication and understanding.

5.5 STATISTICAL ANALYSIS AND MARKET RESEARCH TOOLS

5.5.1 Decision Tree (DT)

The DT is a tree-like model that reports decisions and their possible consequences [1]. Consequences can be the result of events, the cost of services, or services. In its tree-like structure, each branch represents a choice between some alternatives and each leaf represents a decision. According to input variables [5,7,11], it divides data into smaller sets. It helps people analyze decisions. Freedom of understanding and interpretation make log trees popular for use. The DT important algorithm is used to represent decisions and it is a predictive model for appearance. It uses the branching method [12,15] to show all possible effects in certain conditions. In DT, the internal node represents the attribute test, the branch shows the result. Thus, the leaf represents the decision made as shown in Figure 5.11.

5.5.2 REGRESSION

Regression is one of the most well-known mathematical methods that measure the relationship between variables. The regression model finds the communication between dependent variables and one or more independent variables.

However, this model analyzes a number of dependent variables that vary in the change in the values of independent variables in a regression model relationship [2,19] in a different way. This modelled relationship among dependent and independent relationships has been shown in Figure 5.12:

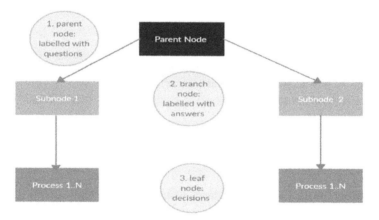

FIGURE 5.11   Decision tree.

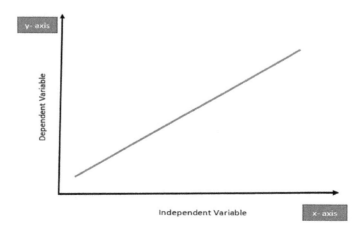

FIGURE 5.12   Regression model.

Regression models can be classified into three types, Simple linear regression (SLR), Multiple linear regression (MLR), and polynomial regression (PR) [8,10–12,20]. SR is a statistical method to find the relationship between two continuous variables. MLR is the method to find the relationship among more than two continuous variables. PR is a special case of linear regression.

5.5.3 Support Vector Machine

It is a machine learning module that is widely used in predicted classification and simulation. With the help of integrated learning algorithms, the data is analyzed to determine the divisive and positive values [3,4]. It is a very popular separation algorithm. It is a discriminatory category defined by the hyperplane to classify examples. It uses the representation of the samples in the plane so that the samples are subdivided into hyperplane segments. The new samples were then classified as belonging to the hyperplane side. Support Vector Regression (SVR) is similar to SVM in that it is subdivided, with some minor differences. Figure 5.13 represents the SVM representation:

5.5.4 Bayesian Theorem

It is a statistical technique in which parameters are taken from the probability with well-defined variables through "degree of belief" [5]. It is based on Bayes' theorem and it uses priori and posteriori property terms. Bayes' theorem works [6,15] on the reverse principle of conditional probability. It states to find the prior probability of an event when posteriori probability is an event that has already occurred been shown in Figure 5.14. The Bayesian theorem has an edged advantage in predictive modeling for understanding marketing trends, fraud and risk prevention, understanding consumer behavior.

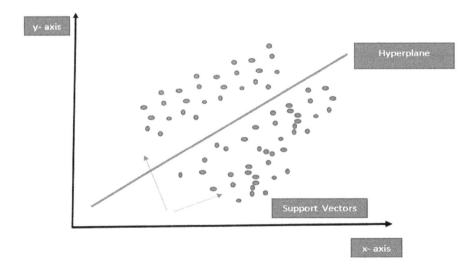

FIGURE 5.13 Support vector machine model.

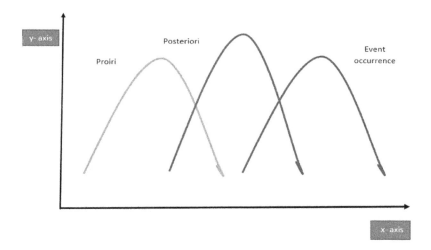

FIGURE 5.14 Bayesian model.

5.6 OTHER METHODS

5.6.1 ENSEMBLE LEARNING

A supervised machine learning algorithm trains similar types of models and finally combines their results of predicting the outcomes. The use of this model improved accuracy [9,10]. The bias and variance are reduced. Also, it helps identify the best model which can be used for prediction and forecasting [8].

5.6.2 GRADIENT BOOST MODEL

Gradient Boost model is a classification and regression machine learning technique that is being commonly used in predictive modeling. It uses the concept of ensemble learning where similar weak types of prediction models are ensembled in the form of decision trees [6]. Then applying boosting techniques, the accuracy of the weak model is improved. The same is done by training and re-training the dataset. The model is less prone to overfitting.

5.6.3 ARTIFICIAL NEURAL NETWORK (ANN)

ANN is a network of physiological artificial neurons based and simulates the functions of the central nervous system to interpret input signals and generate outputs [7]. ANN is a dynamic model that would be capable of simulating highly complicated relations.

5.6.4 Time Series Analysis (TMA)

TMA is a statistical method that uses data from a time series that is obtained at a given interval over some time. It combines the conventional techniques of data mining with forecasting [9]. Time series is categorized into two-frequency and time domains. The major application areas in stock market prediction and weather forecasting.

5.6.5 k-Nearest Neighbours (k-NN)

K-nearest neighbour is a classification and regression machine learning technique and it is a non-parametric method. The input in this approach includes the nearest neighbour training samples in the feature space [10]. What excludes class membership in editorial problems and output is the structure of the object in retrospective problems.

5.6.6 Principle Component Analysis (PCA)

The PCA is based on mathematical techniques and it is used for data visualization which has been used for prediction. This model is firmly related to the multiple regression used to solve a matrix's eigenvectors. It is commonly used in defining the variance in a dataset [11].

5.7 STATISTICAL TESTS

5.7.1 Discrete Independent Variable

The value is obtained by counting through a variable is a discrete variable.

  i. *Z-test:* It is the mean of a distribution.
 ii. *One Sample t-test:* It can compare only a single sample mean to a specified constant and it is a parametric test.
iii. *Independent Sample t-tests:* It compares the means of two groups.
 iv. *Repeated t-tests (paired t-tests):* The test is known as a paired sample t-test and is sometimes called the dependent sample t-test. This is the statistical procedure and it finds whether the mean difference between two sets of observations is zero or not.
  v. *Repeated measure ANOVA:* It is a one-way model and it is similar to the ANOVA test.
 vi. *Mixed Model ANOVA:* This model is the two-way model. Also, this model is a combination of a between-unit ANOVA and a within-unit ANOVA.
vii. *One-way ANOVA:* This test determines whether there are any statistically significant differences between the means of two or more independent (unrelated) groups.

viii. *Multivariate ANOVA (MANOVA):* It is used when there are two or more dependent variables and it is a multivariate procedure.

ix. Factorial ANOVA(F-Anova): The f-ANOVA inspects the variance test with more than one independent variable. It can also be used for more than one level of Independent Variable.

5.7.2 CONTINUOUS INDEPENDENT VARIABLE

The value obtained by measuring a variable is known as the continuous independent variable.

i. *Pearson's r correlation:* Measure the power of the connection between the two variables.

ii. *Spearman's correlation:* This variation is partial and measures the relative correlation (the dependence of the calculations between the measurements of the two variations). It determines whether it also defines how well the relationship between the two differences can best be defined by monotonic activity.

iii. *Simple Regression (SR):* SR is a statistical process and it estimates the relationships between a dependent variable and one or more independent variables.

iv. *Multiple Regression (MR):* In MR, different independent variables or functions of independent variables have been used.

v. *Multivariate Regression:* It is a method that only estimates one retrospective model with more than one variable effect. Even if there is more than one predictor variant in the multivariate regression model, the model is called multiple multivariate regression.

vi. *Kappa's regression:* The regression happens when your data raters (or collectors) give the same score to the same data item.

5.8 DECISION-MAKING MODELS

These models are the basic ones to develop a convergent approach to the decision-making paradigms of any organization or firm. Crucial assumptions are the benchmark to emphasize during the process and are explained below:

5.8.1 THE CLASSICAL MODEL

The basic approach to the decision-making process could be achieved by understanding the classical model. The rational model is another name for a classical model as the decision makers keep their emotions aside and think logically [19]. Some salient features of the classical model are as follows:

- The clarity in the problem statement
- A clear view of the objective to be achieved

- Weights and criteria are agreed upon by the people
- Well-known alternatives
- Foresighted results
- Rational decision makers

The classical model can be considered for decision-making as it has the below-mentioned benefits:

 i. Unbiased known problems
 ii. Efficiently processing of related information
 iii. Foreseeing present and futuristic effects of decisions
 iv. Prominent search for alternatives to yield best-known results

5.8.2 BOUNDED RATIONALITY MODEL

The ultimate result of decision-making is to accomplish the desired goal. Rationality attempts to perform the decision-making with well-defined courses of action to attain the specified goals. The decision maker should have the required knowledge and capability to access all possible alternative plans of action to reach the optimum goal. The best of the alternatives should be picked to accomplish the desired goal. This course of action might not be achieved if the decision maker settles for much less than the desired goal [15]. This process of settling for a less aspired goal is discussed under the Bounded Rationality model, which was conceptualized by Herbert Simon.

The reason for this solution may seem to be a lack of knowledge, time, or even inability to achieve goals. They agree with limited understanding or rationality in decisions.

Different concepts regarding the Bounded Rationality model are as follows:

 i. Sequential Attention to an alternative solution:

In general, people seek an attainable solution one at a time for their problems in place of searching for all probable solutions and getting one to settle for. It is not mandatory to go with the best one but to search for all solutions and then settle for one to get a satisfying goal.

 ii. Heuristic:

The assumptions that help the decision maker to find all probable solutions that could yield success are termed under the heuristic approach.

5.8.3 RETROSPECTIVE DECISION MODEL

To justify the decisions made by the decision makers, they rely on providing rationalized choices for their decisions once the decision has already been made.

The authors developed a model that conceptualizes such behavior of decision makers. He observed the graduating business students regarding their job choices. The process is intended to validate instinctive decision-making by trying to make logical and reasonable decisions on crucial topics.

i. Challenges of predictive modeling for decision-making

According to the infographic, 43% of those surveyed said that access to data was a major problem that hampered their ability to use any data. Much of the information is processed in different functional silos, organizational categories, or across national borders, making it difficult to fully understand how consumers respond to marketing efforts. Another 39% of respondent problems were reported by entering information in the various areas where it is being processed. Just 37% of respondents are stated to be generating actionable insights from the data [14]. Figure 5.15 shows the statistics of important skills required for applying predictive modeling for decision-making.

Just 37% of respondents report generating actionable perspectives from the results. The mindless use of data mining methods may not produce information and may confuse real relationships hidden in the data. Instead, consumer behavioral awareness helps to examine and recognize the component that causes significant behaviors.

FIGURE 5.15   Statistics of important skills.

5.9 CONCLUSION

Guessing analysis is a continuous branch of data engineering that often makes predictions of any presence or probability of data. Guessing statistics use data mining methods to make predictions about future events and to make recommendations for these predictions. The current chapter provides details of various predictive analysis models, consumer behavior models, and decision-making models. The role of these models is different. The summary of the sections discussed in this chapter is that predictive modeling has a great future for making decisions in consumer behavior.

REFERENCES

[1] B. Kaminski, M. Jakubczyk and P. Szufel, 2018, "A framework for sensitivity analysis of decision trees", *Central European Journal of Operations Research*, Vol-26, Issue-1, Pages-135–159.

[2] J. S. Armstrong, 2012, "Illusions in regression analysis", *International Journal of Forecasting*, Vol-28, Issue-3, Pages-689–694.

[3] C. Cortes, 1995, "Support-vector networks", *Machine Learning*, Vol-20, Issue-3, Pages-273–297.

[4] Ben Hur et al., 2001, "Support vector clustering", *Journal of Machine Learning Research*, Vol-2, Pages-125–137.

[5] Peter M. Lee, 2012, *Bayesian Statistics: An Introduction*, 4th Edition, John Willey and Sons Ltd.

[6] Friedman, Jerome H., 2001, "Greedy function approximation: a gradient boosting machine", *Annals of Statistic*, Vol-29, Issue-5, Pages-1189–1232.

[7] W. S. McCulloch and Walter Pitts, 1943, "A logical calculus of the ideas immanent in nervous activities", *The Bulletin of Mathematical Biophysics*, Vol-5, Issue-4, Pages-115–133.

[8] T. R. Ramesh, U. K. Lilhore, M. Poongodi, S. Simaiya, A. Kaur and M. Hamdi, 2022, "Predictive analysis of heart diseases with machine learning approaches", *Malaysian Journal of Computer Science,* Vol. 1, Pages-132–148.

[9] J. Lin, E. Keogh, S. Lonardi and C. Chiu, 2003, "A symbolic representation of time series, with implications for streaming algorithms", *Proceedings of the 8th ACM SIGMOD Workshop on Research Issues in Data Mining and Knowledge Discovery*, Pages-2–11.

[10] N. S. Altman, 1992, "An introduction to Kernel and nearest-neighbor nonparametric regression", *The American Statistician*, Vol-46, Issue-3, Pages-175–185.

[11] H. Abdi and L. J. Williams, 2010, "Principal component analysis", *WIREs: Computational Statistics*, Vol-2, Issue-4, Pages-433–459.

[12] U. K. Lilhore, M. Poongodi, A. Kaur, S. Simaiya, A. D. Algarni, H. Elmannai, V. Vijayakumar, G. B. Tunze and M. Hamdi, 2022. "Hybrid model for detection of cervical cancer using causal analysis and machine learning techniques", *Computational and Mathematical Methods in Medicine*, Vol-, Pages-1–17.

[13] H. Han, 2021, "Consumer behavior and environmental sustainability in tourism and hospitality: A review of theories, concepts, and latest research", *Journal of Sustainable Tourism,* Vol-29, Issue-7, Pages-1021–1042.

[14] R. Hadi, S. Melumad and E. S. Park, 2023, "The Metaverse: A new digital frontier for consumer behavior", *Journal of Consumer Psychology*, Vol-33, Pages-1–25.

[15] J. A. Howard and J. N. Sheth, 2001, "A theory of buyer behavior", *Marketing: Critical Perspectives on Business and Management,* Vol-3, Pages-81.

[16] T. K. Jisana, 2014, "Consumer behaviour models: An overview", *Sai Om Journal of Commerce & Management* Vol-1, Issue-5, Pages-34–43.

[17] T. Milner and D. Rosenstreich, 2013, "A review of consumer decision-making models and development of a new model for financial services", *Journal of Financial Services Marketing,* Vol-18, Issue-2, Pages-106–120.

[18] N. B. Kanagal, 2016, "An extended model of behavioural process in consumer decision making", *International Journal of Marketing Studies,* Vol-8, Issue-4, Pages-87–93.

[19] L. Zhao, Z. G. Fang and S. Liu, "Study on the damping equilibrium of duopoly strategy output-making based on bounded rationality and knowledge", *International Conference on Grey Systems and Intelligent Services, IEEE,* 2007

[20] Z. Fang, S. Liu and A. Ruan, "Study on a new duopoly strategy output-making model based on the experienced ideal output and the best strategy decision-making coefficient", *IEEE International Conference on Systems, Man and Cybernetics, IEEE,* 2007

6 Software-Defined Networking (SDN)
Revolutionizing Network Infrastructure for the Future

Parth Mukul Gupta

6.1 INTRODUCTION TO SDN: A BRIEF OVERVIEW OF SDN AND ITS EVOLUTION OVER THE YEARS

Software-Defined Networking (SDN) is a network architecture approach that separates the control plane from the data plane, allowing for dynamic network management and programmability. In traditional networking, network devices such as switches and routers are responsible for both forwarding data packets and making decisions about how those packets should be routed. In an SDN architecture, the control plane is separated and moved to a centralized controller, which is responsible for managing and directing the flow of network traffic. This allows for more flexibility, agility, and scalability in network management.

SDN has its roots in research work at UC Berkeley and Stanford University in the mid-2000s, where researchers explored the idea of decoupling the control and data planes in network devices. This led to the development of the Open Flow protocol, which allowed for the centralized management of network devices through a standardized protocol. The Open Networking Foundation (ONF) was formed in 2011 to promote the adoption of SDN and Open Flow, and a number of commercial and open-source SDN solutions were developed in the years that followed.

Over time, the concept of SDN has evolved to encompass a broader range of network management and automation capabilities. This has led to the development of software-defined WAN (SD-WAN) solutions, which use SDN principles to manage wide-area networks, as well as software-defined security (SDS) solutions, which use SDN to provide more dynamic and adaptive security controls.

In traditional networking, network devices such as routers and switches are responsible for both forwarding and controlling network traffic. The control plane and data plane are tightly integrated, meaning that decisions about how to handle network traffic are made by each device in real-time, based on the rules programmed into the device. This architecture is sometimes referred to as a "distributed" model, because the control and data planes are distributed across many different devices.

In contrast, SDN programmable networks separate the control plane and data plane into two distinct layers. The data plane remains on the network devices and is

DOI: 10.1201/9781003432869-6

responsible for forwarding network traffic, but the control plane is centralized in a separate controller. This controller uses a software-based "brain" to make decisions about how to handle network traffic, and then communicates those decisions to the individual network devices through a standardized protocol such as OpenFlow. This architecture is sometimes referred to as a "centralized" model, because the control plane is centralized in a single device (Figure 6.1).

The architecture of traditional networking and SDN programmable networks differ in how they separate the control plane and data plane, and how they make decisions about how to handle network traffic. Traditional networking devices make these decisions individually in real-time, whereas SDN programmable networks use a centralized controller to make decisions and communicate them to the individual devices.

One of the key benefits of SDN is its ability to provide network programmability and automation, allowing for more efficient and streamlined network management. This can lead to significant cost savings, as well as improved network reliability and performance. Additionally, SDN can facilitate the deployment of new network services and applications, as network administrators can quickly and easily configure and manage the network to support these new use cases.

In short, SDN is an innovative approach to network architecture that has evolved over the years to encompass a broad range of network management and automation capabilities. With its ability to provide programmability and flexibility, SDN is poised to play a key role in the future of network management and automation.

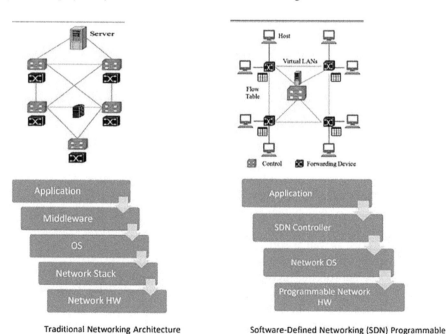

FIGURE 6.1 The architecture of traditional networking and software-defined networking (SDN) programmable networks.

6.1.1 LITERATURE REVIEW

Alchalabi, Adhami, Ja'afreh, et al. (2022) investigate the viability of current network designs, solutions, and study in integrating SDN applied via edge computing with the IoT architecture. The technological difficulties of deploying IoT apps have also been addressed, along with the crucial theories and algorithms pertinent to this situation. We intend to give the reader guidance on how to apply those networks and make progress in overcoming their challenges, in contrast to other papers that present concepts and predictions of SDN and IoT.

SDN is a promising and groundbreaking technology that is widely used in the realm of digitalization. Decoupling the control component from the forwarding plane was made possible by the main SDN features (Chaudhary, et al. 2022). A programmable SDN network is used to automate network administration. As the network demand increases, SDN is a dynamic method of changing the topology of the network. Scalability, dependability, and flexibility are the main advantages of implementing SDN.

The management of networks is highly difficult. It takes a lot of labor to maintain, run, and provide a secure communication network (Neeraja, Reddy, and Mukund 2014). To apply the intricate high-level network policies, network administrators must deal with low-level vendor-specific configurations. Since network devices are typically closed and vertically integrated, there are few opportunities for development or innovation due to the rigidity of the underlying infrastructure. The network switches in the data plane are reduced to being simple packet forwarding devices as a result of this separation, leaving a conceptually centralized software program to manage the operation of the entire network.

Improvements in network function virtualization (NFV) and SDN technology have the potential to lower costs and increase the flexibility of Internet protocol (IP) networks. Conceptually, SDN isolates the hardware that powers network management logic from that hardware, giving network managers more control over how the network functions and a unified view of the complete network. It might be feasible to reduce the issues with legacy networks, though, by merging SDN and NFV. Data centers, data center networks, and network as a service offerings are just a few of the contexts in which Jammal et al. (2014) address the benefits of utilizing SDN.

Due to the rapidly growing problem of cybercrime, these associations' resources, knowledge, and reputation are at risk (Rajvanshi, Singh, Gupta, and Gupta 2022). To launch their attacks online, cybercriminals are using more sophisticated techniques. Before any evidence was gathered, it was expected that digital protection would change how security was conducted. Organizations are increasingly considering digital security as part of their overall threat to the executive system. Transporters frequently rely on arbitrary procedures determined by master judgments due to the special characteristics of digital assaults. Hence, this area of network security and information security is essential specifically in the security sector.

SDN has various benefits over traditional networking, including network programmability, easier configuration management, greater security, and improved performance. By isolating the control plane from the data plane and networking devices, SDN is able to attain the performance. More research opportunities are also encouraged by network programmability. Because SDN is still developing, academics and technocrats need to pay attention to it. Manani and Prajapati (2019) had conducted a survey on numerous fundamental facets of SDN, including its history, definition, and architecture. It also discusses the uses and benefits of SDN in comparison to traditional networks. Also, this survey report highlights the numerous future research fields of this groundbreaking network design for prospective researchers.

As we see in Singh, Gupta, and Gupta (2022), the study of remote computer agents connected to one another by middle hardware is known as a distributed approximate dynamic programming (ADP) system which is a distributed computing system (DCS). It includes a system where computer networks are used to connect hardware or software components, which are then controlled by simple message transmission. This ADP program is crucial to many applications that place a high priority on high-speed real-time simulation. One of the most crucial methods for leveraging the special resources available in the real-world environment is the methodical deployment of workers between processing nodes. If we don't execute this phase properly, the system will completely collapse due to the increase of processing nodes.

6.1.2 Cases and Applications of SDN in Different Domains

SDN has emerged as a new paradigm for network architecture that separates the control plane from the data plane. This enables network administrators to dynamically manage network traffic flows and implement network policies without relying on the manual configuration of individual network devices. Here are some cases and applications of SDN in different domains:

1. Data Centers: In data center networks, SDN can be used to simplify network management, improve network scalability, and provide better traffic engineering capabilities. SDN can be used to dynamically allocate network resources to different applications, and provide fine-grained traffic management and QoS policies.
2. Wide Area Networks (WAN): In WANs, SDN can be used to optimize traffic flows, reduce latency, and improve network performance. SDN can provide centralized control and management of WANs, allowing network administrators to dynamically allocate bandwidth to different applications and optimize traffic routing.
3. Telecommunications Networks: SDN can be used in telecommunications networks to improve network efficiency and enable faster service delivery. SDN can be used to automate network provisioning, enable service chaining, and provide end-to-end network visibility.
4. Internet of Things (IoT): In IoT networks, SDN can be used to manage network traffic flows, optimize device connectivity, and provide better security. SDN can be used to dynamically configure network policies based on IoT device characteristics and network conditions, and to provide fine-grained access control to IoT devices.

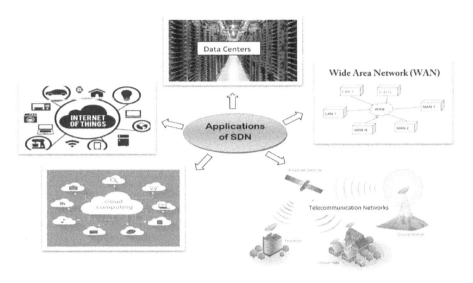

FIGURE 6.2   Applications of SDN in different domains.

5. Cloud Computing: In cloud computing networks, SDN can be used to improve network agility, reduce network complexity, and provide better security. SDN can be used to automate network provisioning, enable network virtualization, and provide better visibility into network traffic flows (Figure 6.2).

Overall, SDN has a wide range of applications in various domains, and it has the potential to revolutionize network management and operations.

6.2   SDN IN THE CURRENT LANDSCAPE: A REVIEW OF THE CURRENT STATE OF SDN AND HOW IT IS BEING USED IN VARIOUS INDUSTRIES

SDN is a network architecture that allows network administrators to manage network services through the abstraction of lower-level functionality. With SDN, network managers can centralize and simplify the management of their network resources, allowing them to be more agile and responsive to changing business needs.

In the current landscape, SDN is being used in various industries, including telecommunications, data centers, cloud computing, and internet service providers (ISPs).

In the telecommunications industry, SDN is being used to build next-generation networks that are more agile, flexible, and efficient. Telecommunications companies are using SDN to virtualize their network functions, which allows them to offer new services and applications more quickly and cost-effectively. SDN is also being used to optimize network traffic, ensuring that critical applications receive the necessary bandwidth and prioritization.

Data centers are another area where SDN is being widely adopted. SDN is being used to automate the management of network resources, which can reduce the complexity of managing large data centers. It also enables network administrators to manage network resources more effectively, allocate bandwidth dynamically, and ensure that resources are available when they are needed.

Cloud computing providers are also using SDN to improve the performance and reliability of their services. By using SDN, cloud providers can optimize the routing of traffic between their data centers and their customers, ensuring that traffic is always flowing through the most efficient path.

In the ISP industry, SDN is being used to provide more flexible and cost-effective network services. ISPs are using SDN to virtualize their network functions, which allows them to offer customized services to their customers. SDN is also being used to optimize network traffic, ensuring that critical applications receive the necessary bandwidth and prioritization.

In short, SDN is being widely adopted in various industries, including telecommunications, data centers, cloud computing, and ISPs. SDN enables network administrators to centralize and simplify the management of their network resources, making their networks more agile, flexible, and efficient.

6.3   EMERGING TRENDS IN SDN: A DISCUSSION OF THE LATEST TRENDS AND INNOVATIONS IN SDN, SUCH AS INTENT-BASED NETWORKING, NETWORK SLICING, AND NETWORK AUTOMATION

SDN is a rapidly evolving field, with several emerging trends and innovations that are transforming the way networks are designed, deployed, and managed. Some of the latest trends and innovations in SDN, including intent-based networking, network slicing, and network automation are:

1. Intent-based Networking
   Intent-based networking (IBN) is a new approach to network management that uses high-level business policies to automate network configuration and management. IBN enables network administrators to define business goals, objectives, and policies, and then relies on artificial intelligence (AI) and machine learning (ML) algorithms to translate these policies into network configurations. IBN allows network administrators to focus on business outcomes rather than network configurations, making network management more intuitive, efficient, and effective. Instead of manually configuring network devices, IBN allows network administrators to define high-level business policies and objectives, which are then translated into network configuration and operational instructions.

   IBN uses analytics and automation to monitor network traffic and performance, detect anomalies, and make real-time adjustments to network policies and configurations to ensure that they align with the intended business outcomes. This approach enables faster, more accurate, and more reliable network management, as well as greater agility and responsiveness to changing business needs.

IBN is becoming increasingly popular in enterprise networking, as it allows organizations to better align their network infrastructure with their business objectives, improve network performance and reliability, and reduce the burden on network administrators.

2. Network Slicing

Network slicing is a technique that enables network operators to create multiple virtual networks on top of a single physical network infrastructure. The idea is to divide a single physical network into multiple logical networks, each with its own set of resources and characteristics, such as bandwidth, latency, and security. Network slicing allows network operators to allocate network resources to different applications, services, and customers based on their specific needs. It also enables operators to provide a more customized and flexible network service to customers and is an essential technology for supporting emerging use cases such as 5G and the Internet of Things (IoT).

With network slicing, network operators can provide different levels of service to different users based on their requirements. For example, a virtual network slice could be created for a hospital to ensure low latency and high reliability for critical medical applications, while another virtual network slice could be created for a streaming service to provide high bandwidth and low latency for streaming video.

Network slicing is made possible by SDN and network function virtualization (NFV) technologies, which allow network operators to dynamically configure and manage the virtual networks. It is expected to play a critical role in enabling the next generation of 5G networks, which require greater flexibility and scalability to support a wide range of new applications and services.

3. Network Automation

Network automation is the use of software and automation tools to streamline and simplify network management tasks. It involves using programming languages, scripts, and other automation tools to streamline network operations and reduce manual intervention. Network automation enables network administrators to perform repetitive and time-consuming tasks automatically, reducing the risk of errors and freeing up resources to focus on more critical tasks. Network automation can also improve network security by enforcing consistent security policies across the network.

With network automation, tasks that were previously performed manually, such as network provisioning, configuration, and monitoring, can be performed automatically. This not only saves time and effort but also minimizes the risk of human errors that can result in network downtime or security breaches.

There are several benefits to implementing network automation, including increased efficiency, reduced network downtime, faster deployment of network services, improved network security, and lower operational costs.

Network automation can be implemented in various ways, including using SDN and NFV technologies, creating scripts to automate repetitive tasks, and using automation tools such as Ansible, Chef, and Puppet.

Overall, network automation is becoming increasingly important as organizations seek to optimize their network operations and keep up with the demands of the rapidly evolving technology landscape.

In summary, these emerging trends in SDN, including intent-based networking, network slicing, and network automation, are transforming the way networks are designed, deployed, and managed. These technologies enable network operators to provide more flexible, customizable, and secure network services to their customers while also simplifying network management and reducing costs. As the demand for faster, more reliable, and more secure network services continues to grow, these trends are likely to become even more critical in the years to come.

6.4   INTEGRATION WITH CLOUD COMPUTING: AN ANALYSIS OF HOW SDN CAN BE INTEGRATED WITH CLOUD COMPUTING AND HOW IT CAN ENHANCE THE PERFORMANCE AND SECURITY OF CLOUD-BASED APPLICATIONS

SDN can be integrated with cloud computing to enhance the performance and security of cloud-based applications. In a traditional network, network policies are defined by the hardware devices themselves, which makes it difficult to manage and scale the network infrastructure. In contrast, SDN allows network administrators to manage the network infrastructure centrally through software. This approach provides greater flexibility, scalability, and agility to the network infrastructure.

One of the primary benefits of SDN is that it can enhance the security of cloud-based applications. SDN enables network administrators to create security policies that are centrally managed and applied across the network. This approach ensures that security policies are consistently enforced across the entire network, reducing the risk of security breaches.

Another benefit of integrating SDN with cloud computing is that it can enhance the performance of cloud-based applications. SDN allows network administrators to prioritize network traffic and allocate network resources dynamically based on the specific needs of the application. This approach ensures that critical applications receive the necessary resources to perform optimally, while less important applications are given fewer resources.

SDN can also help to reduce the complexity and cost of managing a cloud-based network infrastructure. Because network policies are managed centrally through software, network administrators can make changes to the network infrastructure more quickly and easily than with a traditional network. This approach can also help to reduce the cost of managing the network infrastructure because it requires fewer hardware devices.

In short, integrating SDN with cloud computing can enhance the performance and security of cloud-based applications. This approach provides network administrators with greater flexibility, scalability, and agility to manage the network infrastructure. As cloud computing continues to grow in popularity, SDN is likely to play an increasingly important role in managing and securing cloud-based applications.

6.4.1 INTEGRATION OF SDN WITH CLOUD COMPUTING TO ENHANCE THE PERFORMANCE AND SECURITY OF CLOUD-BASED APPLICATIONS

SDN and cloud computing are two powerful technologies that, when combined, can significantly improve the performance and security of cloud-based applications. SDN allows for the centralized management and control of network resources, while cloud computing provides a scalable and flexible infrastructure for hosting applications.

SDN is a network architecture that separates the control and data planes of the network, enabling centralized control of network traffic flow. When integrated with cloud computing, SDN can enhance the performance and security of cloud-based applications by providing dynamic and flexible network management capabilities.

Here are some ways in which SDN can be integrated with cloud computing and enhance the performance and security of cloud-based applications:

1. Network Virtualization: SDN can enable network virtualization, which enables multiple virtual networks to be created on a single physical network infrastructure. This can enhance the security of cloud-based applications by isolating traffic and preventing unauthorized access to sensitive data.
2. Automated Provisioning: SDN can automate the provisioning of network resources, enabling faster deployment of cloud-based applications. This can enhance the performance of cloud-based applications by providing the necessary resources on demand.
3. Dynamic Traffic Management: SDN can dynamically manage network traffic flow based on application needs, enabling efficient use of network resources. This can enhance the performance of cloud-based applications by ensuring that they receive the necessary network resources when needed.
4. Network Security: SDN can provide enhanced network security by enabling centralized management of security policies and protocols. This can enhance the security of cloud-based applications by providing a unified and consistent security framework.
5. Scalability: SDN can enable scalability of network resources, enabling cloud-based applications to easily scale up or down based on demand. This can enhance the performance of cloud-based applications by providing the necessary resources when needed.
6. Dynamic Network Configuration: SDN allows for the dynamic configuration of network resources based on application needs. This means that network resources can be provisioned and de-provisioned on demand, in response to changes in application traffic or user demand. This can help to ensure that the network is always optimized for the needs of the applications running in the cloud.

7. Network Segmentation: SDN can also be used to create secure network segments within a cloud environment. This can help to prevent unauthorized access to sensitive data or applications. By segmenting the network, it's possible to limit the attack surface and reduce the risk of data breaches.

8. Application-Aware Networking: SDN can also be used to create application-aware networks. This means that the network can be configured to prioritize traffic from specific applications, ensuring that they receive the bandwidth and network resources they need to perform optimally. This can help to improve the performance and responsiveness of cloud-based applications.

9. Centralized Management and Control: With SDN, network resources can be managed and controlled from a centralized location. This can help to simplify network administration and reduce the risk of errors or misconfigurations. It can also help to ensure that network policies are enforced consistently across the cloud environment.

Overall, the integration of SDN with cloud computing can enhance the performance and security of cloud-based applications by providing dynamic and flexible network management capabilities.

6.5   SECURITY AND PRIVACY IN SDN

SDN is a network architecture that separates the control plane from the data plane, allowing for greater network programmability, flexibility, and scalability. While SDN offers many benefits, including enhanced network security, it also presents new security and privacy challenges that need to be addressed.

6.5.1   CONSIDERATIONS FOR SECURITY AND PRIVACY IN SDN

1. Authentication and Authorization: One of the most important security concerns in SDN is ensuring that only authorized users and devices can access the network. Authentication and authorization mechanisms need to be implemented to prevent unauthorized access, particularly to the controller, which controls the network. Strong passwords, multi-factor authentication, and role-based access control (RBAC) can all help to ensure that only authorized users have access to the network.

2. Encryption: To protect sensitive data transmitted over the network, encryption should be implemented at multiple levels, including the data plane, control plane, and management plane. This can help prevent eavesdropping and tampering.

3. Monitoring and Logging: Monitoring and logging tools can help to detect and mitigate security incidents in real-time. Network administrators should monitor the network for unusual activity, such as unusual traffic patterns or unauthorized access attempts. Logs should be kept for all network activity, including user activity, network configuration changes, and security events.

4. SDN Security Standards: Security standards, such as the Open Networking Foundation's (ONF) Security Technical Advisory Group (STAG) guidelines, can help to ensure that SDN deployments are secure. Network administrators should follow these guidelines when deploying SDN networks.

5. Network Segmentation: Network segmentation can help to limit the impact of a security breach by isolating affected network segments. For example, traffic from different departments or user groups can be kept separate to prevent unauthorized access to sensitive data.

6. Privacy: Privacy is also an important concern in SDN, particularly in environments where sensitive data is transmitted over the network. Network administrators should ensure that data is protected during transmission and that only authorized users have access to it.

Overall, security and privacy in SDN require a multi-faceted approach that includes authentication and authorization, encryption, monitoring and logging, adherence to security standards, network segmentation, and privacy protection measures.

SDN has emerged as a promising approach to network management, offering increased flexibility and agility. However, with this increased flexibility and programmability comes the challenge of ensuring security and privacy. In this discussion, we will explore some of the challenges and solutions related to security and privacy in SDN.

6.5.2 CHALLENGES RELATED TO SECURITY AND PRIVACY IN SDN

1. Centralized control plane: SDN's centralized control plane can be a single point of failure and an attractive target for attackers. If the control plane is compromised, the entire network can be brought down.

2. Vulnerabilities in software and hardware: SDN relies on software and hardware components that can be vulnerable to attacks. These vulnerabilities can be exploited to gain unauthorized access to the network or to launch attacks on other systems.

3. Lack of standardization: There is currently no widely accepted standard for SDN security, which can lead to inconsistent and incomplete security implementations across different networks.

4. Privacy concerns: SDN's centralized architecture can raise privacy concerns since it can potentially enable network operators to monitor and control all network traffic.

6.5.3 SOLUTIONS RELATED TO SECURITY AND PRIVACY IN SDN

1. Distributed control planes: Distributed control planes can provide redundancy and reduce the impact of a single point of failure. This approach can be used to increase the resilience of the network and prevent complete network shutdown.

2. Secure software and hardware: Security must be integrated into all components of the SDN stack, from the hardware to the software. This can be achieved by using secure development practices, regularly patching and updating software and hardware, and conducting regular security audits.
3. Standardization: Standardization can help promote consistent security implementations across different networks. Standards bodies and industry groups can work together to develop and promote SDN security standards.
4. Data privacy: To address privacy concerns, network operators can implement encryption, access controls, and other measures to protect sensitive data. Additionally, network operators can provide transparency about their data collection and use practices to build trust with users.

In brief, security and privacy are critical concerns for SDN. To address these challenges, a combination of technical solutions and industry collaboration is needed to develop secure and privacy-preserving SDN systems.

6.6 SDN AND 5G NETWORKS: AN EXPLORATION OF THE POTENTIAL BENEFITS OF SDN IN 5G NETWORKS, SUCH AS NETWORK SLICING AND DYNAMIC RESOURCE ALLOCATION

SDN and 5G networks are two related but distinct technologies that are transforming the way networks are designed, deployed, and managed. SDN is a networking architecture that separates the control plane (which determines how data is routed) from the data plane (which moves the data). This separation allows network administrators to centrally manage network traffic and configure network devices using software-based controllers, rather than manually configuring individual switches and routers. By decoupling the control and data planes, SDN can improve network scalability, flexibility, and agility.

5G, on the other hand, is the next generation of cellular wireless technology, which promises to deliver faster data speeds, lower latency, and greater connectivity. Unlike previous generations of cellular technology, which focused primarily on consumer use cases (such as voice and data services), 5G is also designed to support a wide range of industrial and enterprise use cases, such as IoT, autonomous vehicles, and smart cities.

SDN and 5G are closely related because they both rely on network virtualization, which allows network resources to be abstracted from the underlying hardware and managed programmatically. SDN can provide the network orchestration and automation needed to support 5G use cases, while 5G can provide the high-speed connectivity needed to support SDN deployments. Overall, SDN and 5G represent two key technology trends that are transforming the way networks are designed, deployed, and managed, and are likely to continue to shape the future of networking for years to come.

6.6.1   Potential Benefits of Using SDN in 5G Networks

SDN is a networking architecture that separates the control plane from the data plane, allowing for centralized control and management of network resources. Meanwhile, 5G networks are the fifth generation of wireless networks that offer faster speeds, lower latency, and increased network capacity compared to previous generations.

There are several potential benefits of using SDN in 5G networks, including:

1. Network slicing: Network slicing is the ability to create virtual networks on a single physical network infrastructure. This allows network operators to create customized network slices for different use cases, such as IoT, autonomous vehicles, and mobile broadband. SDN provides the necessary programmability and control to create and manage these network slices dynamically.
2. Dynamic resource allocation: SDN allows for dynamic resource allocation, which means that network resources can be allocated on an as-needed basis. This allows for more efficient use of network resources and can help to reduce network congestion and improve network performance.
3. Network automation: SDN can automate many network management tasks, such as provisioning, configuration, and monitoring. This can help to reduce the time and effort required to manage the network, and can also help to improve network reliability and availability.
4. Flexibility and scalability: SDN provides greater flexibility and scalability compared to traditional networking architectures. This means that network operators can easily add or remove network resources as needed, without having to make significant changes to the network infrastructure.
5. Simplified Network Management: SDN can simplify network management in 5G networks. With SDN, network administrators can centrally manage and configure the network from a single location, rather than managing individual network elements. This can lead to significant cost savings and improved network performance.
6. Improved Security: SDN can also improve security in 5G networks. By separating the control and data planes, SDN can provide better visibility into network traffic and help identify potential security threats. Additionally, SDN can enable operators to quickly deploy security policies and enforce them across the network.

Overall, SDN has the potential to significantly improve the performance, flexibility, and scalability of 5G networks. By enabling network slicing, dynamic resource allocation, and network automation, SDN can help to create a more efficient and adaptable network infrastructure that can meet the diverse needs of different applications and use cases.

6.7   SDN IN THE INTERNET OF THINGS (IOT): A REVIEW OF HOW SDN CAN BE USED TO MANAGE AND SECURE IOT DEVICES AND NETWORKS

SDN can play a significant role in the IoT by providing a flexible and efficient way to manage network traffic, enhance security, and improve overall network performance.

The IoT involves connecting a wide range of devices, sensors, and other objects to the Internet, which requires a robust and scalable network infrastructure. SDN can help manage the complexity of such networks by separating the control plane from the data plane, allowing for centralized control and management of network traffic. This allows for greater flexibility and agility in adapting to changing network conditions and traffic patterns.

In addition, SDN can improve security in IoT networks by enabling network administrators to implement granular access controls and monitor traffic in real-time. This is particularly important in IoT networks, where the large number of connected devices and the diversity of their capabilities and security requirements can make it difficult to manage security effectively.

Furthermore, SDN can enable the efficient allocation of network resources in IoT networks, by dynamically adjusting network traffic flows and prioritizing certain types of traffic. This can help improve network performance and reduce latency, which is particularly important for real-time applications such as those found in industrial control systems or health care.

In short, SDN can help address many of the challenges associated with managing IoT networks, by providing greater flexibility, security, and efficiency. As the IoT continues to grow, SDN is likely to become an increasingly important tool for managing the complex networks that underpin this rapidly evolving ecosystem.

6.7.1   Ways SDN Can Be Used for IoT Security

SDN can be used to manage and secure IoT devices and networks by providing a centralized and programmable control plane that can dynamically manage network traffic and enforce security policies. Here are some ways SDN can be used for IoT security:

1. Segmentation: IoT devices can be segmented into separate virtual networks based on their function or security requirements. This enables the network administrator to enforce policies that restrict traffic between segments, reducing the attack surface.
2. Traffic Management: SDN controllers can dynamically route IoT traffic based on network conditions and policies. For example, IoT devices that require low latency, such as real-time sensors, can be given priority over other traffic.
3. Policy Enforcement: SDN controllers can enforce security policies such as access control, encryption, and intrusion detection and prevention (IDS/ IPS). Policies can be applied dynamically and at scale across the entire network, reducing the burden on individual devices.

4. Visibility: SDN provides visibility into IoT network traffic, allowing administrators to monitor and analyze device behavior. This can help identify anomalous behavior or potential security threats.
5. Automation: SDN can be used to automate network management tasks, reducing the risk of human error and freeing up IT resources. For example, if an IoT device is compromised, SDN can automatically quarantine the device and alert the administrator.

In summary, SDN can help manage and secure IoT devices and networks by providing a centralized control plane, segmentation, traffic management, policy enforcement, visibility, and automation.

6.8 THE FUTURE OF SDN: A GLIMPSE INTO THE FUTURE OF SDN AND HOW IT COULD REVOLUTIONIZE THE NETWORKING INDUSTRY, SUCH AS ENABLING AUTONOMOUS NETWORKS, ENHANCING NETWORK AGILITY, AND SUPPORTING NEW APPLICATIONS AND SERVICES

SDN is a technology that separates the control plane from the data plane in network infrastructure, allowing for more efficient management, greater flexibility, and easier automation of network operations. The future of SDN is promising, as it continues to evolve and grow in importance in the networking industry.

6.8.1 TRENDS AND DEVELOPMENTS SHAPING THE FUTURE OF SDN

1. Increased adoption: SDN is becoming more mainstream as more organizations see the benefits of this technology. As a result, we can expect to see more SDN deployments across different industries, including healthcare, finance, and transportation.
2. Expansion of SD-WAN: SD-WAN (Software-Defined Wide Area Network) is a type of SDN that enables organizations to connect remote sites and branch offices over a wide geographic area. With the increasing demand for remote work and the need for more reliable and secure connectivity, we can expect to see more organizations adopting SD-WAN solutions.
3. Integration with cloud computing: With the rise of cloud computing, there is a growing need for networking solutions that can seamlessly connect on-premises networks with cloud-based resources. SDN is well-positioned to meet this need, and we can expect to see greater integration between SDN and cloud computing platforms in the future.
4. Emphasis on security: As network security threats continue to evolve and become more sophisticated, SDN will play an increasingly important role in securing network infrastructure. We can expect to see more emphasis on security features and capabilities in SDN solutions.

5. Continued innovation: The networking industry is constantly evolving, and we can expect to see continued innovation in the SDN space. New technologies and standards will emerge, and existing SDN solutions will continue to improve and evolve.

Overall, the future of SDN looks bright. With its ability to improve network efficiency, flexibility, and automation, SDN will continue to play an important role in shaping the future of networking.

6.8.2 Some Ways in Which SDN Could Shape the Future of Networking

SDN has the potential to revolutionize the networking industry by enabling more efficient, scalable, and flexible network architectures. Here are some ways in which SDN could shape the future of networking:

1. Autonomous networks: SDN can enable the creation of self-managing, autonomous networks that can adapt to changing network conditions and traffic patterns. By using machine learning and artificial intelligence algorithms, SDN controllers can make automated decisions about network routing, traffic prioritization, and other network functions, reducing the need for manual configuration and intervention.
2. Enhanced network agility: SDN enables network administrators to quickly adapt to changing business requirements and network traffic patterns by dynamically provisioning and configuring network resources. This can lead to increased network agility, improved performance, and lower operational costs.
3. Support for new applications and services: SDN can enable the development and deployment of new applications and services that require high levels of network flexibility and programmability. For example, SDN can support the deployment of virtual networks, enabling service providers to create customized network services for their customers.
4. Improved security: SDN can enable the creation of more secure network architectures by providing centralized control and visibility over network traffic. This can help network administrators to detect and respond to security threats more quickly and effectively.
5. Simplified network management: SDN can simplify network management by providing a unified, programmable interface for configuring and managing network resources. This can reduce the complexity of network operations, reduce the risk of configuration errors, and improve overall network efficiency.

Overall, SDN is expected to play a significant role in shaping the future of networking, enabling more efficient, scalable, and flexible network architectures that can support the growing demands of modern applications and services.

6.8.3   SDN Implications for Research and Innovation

SDN has significant implications for research and innovation in the field of networking. Here are a few ways in which SDN can impact research and innovation:

1. Enabling New Networking Architectures: SDN enables the separation of the control plane and data plane in network devices. This separation allows for the creation of new network architectures that were previously not possible. Researchers and innovators can use this flexibility to develop new and more efficient networking architectures.
2. Facilitating Network Virtualization: SDN can facilitate network virtualization, which allows multiple virtual networks to coexist on a single physical network infrastructure. This capability can enable new applications and services that were not possible with traditional networking.
3. Supporting Network Programmability: SDN allows network administrators to program network devices through APIs, enabling more efficient network management and automation. Researchers and innovators can leverage this programmability to develop new network services and applications.
4. Advancing Network Security: SDN enables more granular control over network traffic, which can help enhance network security. This capability can facilitate the development of new security applications and services.
5. Enhancing Network Monitoring: SDN can provide more visibility into network traffic, allowing for better monitoring and analysis. This capability can enable researchers and innovators to develop new monitoring and analysis tools that can help optimize network performance.

Hence, SDN has significant implications for research and innovation in the networking field. The flexibility and programmability of SDN can enable the development of new networking architectures, services, and applications, and can facilitate network virtualization, security, and monitoring.

6.8.4   Potential Novel Application of Open SDN

SDN technology is transforming the way networks are designed, deployed, and managed. SDN decouples the network's control plane from the data plane, allowing administrators to manage the network centrally from a single control point, rather than configuring each network device separately. This centralization makes network management more efficient and flexible, enabling organizations to respond quickly to changes in network demand.

One potential novel application of Open SDN is in the health care industry. Health care organizations rely on network infrastructure to deliver critical patient care services, including telemedicine, electronic health records (EHRs), and medical imaging. Open SDN could provide health care providers with a more flexible, secure, and scalable network infrastructure that can adapt to changing patient care demands.

For example, Open SDN could be used to prioritize network traffic for critical patient care services, ensuring that these applications receive the network resources they need to function reliably. SDN could also enable health care providers to segment their networks to isolate sensitive patient data and prevent unauthorized access. Additionally, Open SDN could provide health care organizations with a scalable and flexible network infrastructure that can adapt to changing patient care demands, such as spikes in network traffic during peak periods.

Overall, Open SDN has the potential to transform the healthcare industry by providing a more efficient, secure, and flexible network infrastructure that can support critical patient care services.

6.9   A SUMMARY AND A CALL TO ACTION FOR FURTHER RESEARCH AND DEVELOPMENT IN THE FIELD OF SDN

This chapter on the future of SDN highlights the potential of SDN to revolutionize networking and provides insights into the direction in which the technology is heading. The following are some of the key points discussed in the chapter:

1. The shift towards a software-centric approach to networking is accelerating, and SDN is at the forefront of this shift. With SDN, network administrators can programmatically control and manage the network, allowing for greater flexibility, automation, and efficiency.
2. The deployment of 5G networks and the increasing demand for IoT devices will require more agile and scalable networking solutions, making SDN a crucial technology for the future.
3. The convergence of networking and cloud computing is also driving the adoption of SDN. As more organizations move their workloads to the cloud, they require a more dynamic and flexible networking infrastructure to support these workloads.
4. The rise of Artificial Intelligence (AI) and Machine Learning (ML) is expected to play a significant role in the future of SDN. These technologies can be used to optimize network performance, predict network failures, and automate network operations.
5. The chapter also discusses the challenges and limitations of SDN, such as the lack of standardization and interoperability, security concerns, and the need for skilled personnel.

To further advance the field of SDN, there is a need for continued research and development in the following areas:

1. Standardization and interoperability: There is a need for industry-wide standardization to ensure that SDN solutions can work seamlessly across different vendors and platforms.
2. Security: With the increasing importance of networking in critical infrastructure, there is a need for more robust security measures to protect against cyber-attacks.

3. Automation: The automation of network operations can greatly improve efficiency and reduce the risk of human error. Research into the use of AI and ML for network automation is therefore essential.
4. Scalability: With the growing demand for networking solutions, there is a need for SDN solutions that can scale to meet the needs of large organizations.

In conclusion, the future of SDN is bright, but there is a need for continued research and development to overcome the challenges and limitations of the technology. By addressing these challenges and investing in further research, we can unlock the full potential of SDN and create a more efficient, secure, and scalable networking infrastructure for the future.

REFERENCES

Benzekki, K., Fergougui, A. E., and Elbelrhiti Elalaoui, A., (2016) Software-defined networking (SDN): A survey. *Security and Communication Networks*, 9(18), pp. 5803–5833.

Campbell, A. T., Katzela, I., Miki, K., and Vicente, J., (1999) Open signaling for ATM, internet and mobile networks (opensig'98). *ACM SIGCOMM Computer Communication Review*, 29(1), pp. 97–108.

Chaudhary, R., Aujla, G. S., Kumar, N., and Chouhan, P. K., (2022) A comprehensive survey on software-defined networking for smart communities. *International Journal of Communication Systems*, e5296. ISSN1074-5351; eISSN1099-1131. doi:10.1002/dac.5296

Farhady, H., Lee, H., and Nakao, A., (2015) Software-defined networking: A survey. *Computer Networks*, 81, pp. 79–95.

Hu, F., Hao, Q., and Bao, K., (2014) A survey on software-defined network and OpenFlow: From concept to implementation. *IEEE Communications Surveys & Tutorials*, 16(4), pp. 2181–2206.

Ja'afreh, M., Adhami, H., Alchalabi, A. E. et al. (2022) Toward integrating software-defined networks with the Internet of Things: A review. *Cluster Computing*, 25, pp. 1619–1636. https://doi.org/10.1007/s10586-021-03402-4

Jammal, M., Singh, T., Shami, A., Asal, R., and Li, Y., (2014) Software-defined networking: State of the art and research challenges. *Computer Networks*, 72, pp. 74–98, ISSN 1389-1286, https://doi.org/10.1016/j.comnet.2014.07.004.

Kreutz, D., Ramos, F. M. V., Verissimo, P., Rothenberg, C. E., Azodolmolky, S., and Uhlig, S., (2015) Software-defined networking: A comprehensive survey. *Proceedings of the IEEE*, 103(1), pp. 14–76.

Limoncelli, T. A. (2012) Openflow: A radical new idea in networking. *Communications of the ACM*, 55(8), pp. 42–47.

Manani, M., and Prajapati, N., (2019) A survey of software-defined network: The rise of future network. *Journal of Emerging Technologies and Innovative Research*, 6(4), pp. 439–452, ISSN-2349–5162

Masoudi, R., and Ghaffari, A., (2016) Software-defined networks: A survey. *Journal of Network and Computer Applications*, 67, pp. 1–25.

McKeown, N., Anderson, T., Balakrishnan, H., Parulkar, G., Peterson, L., Rexford, J., Shenker, S., and Turner, J., (2008) Openflow: Enabling innovation in campus networks. *ACM SIGCOMM Computer Communication Review*, 38(2), pp. 69–74.

Namal, S., Ahmad, I., Ylianttila, M., and Gurtov, A., (2015) Security in software-defined networks: A survey. *IEEE Communications Surveys & Tutorials*, 17(4), pp. 2317–2346.

Neeraja, A., Reddy, N.C.S., and Mukund, (2014) Improving network management with software-defined networking. *International Journal of Science and Research (IJSR)*, 3(7), pp. 659–662.

Rajvanshi, P. R., Singh, T., Gupta, D., and Gupta, M. (2022) Cybersecurity and data privacy in the insurance market. In Sood, K., Balusamy, B., Grima, S. and Marano, P. (Eds.) *Big Data Analytics in the Insurance Market* (*Emerald Studies in Finance, Insurance, and Risk Management*), Emerald Publishing Limited, Bingley, pp. 1–20. https://doi.org/10.1108/978-1-80262-637-720221001

Singh S., Gupta D., and Gupta M., (2022) Optimized task allocation technique using mathematical fuzzy logic in heterogeneous distributed computational system. In *2022 International Conference on Computational Intelligence and Sustainable Engineering Solutions (CISES)*, Greater Noida, India, pp. 37–45, doi: 10.1109/CISES54857.2022.9844410.

Tennenhouse, D.L., and Wetherall, D.J., (2002) Towards an active network architecture. In *DARPA Active NEtworks Conference and Exposition, 2002. Proceedings*. IEEE, pp. 2–15.

7 Software-Defined Network
Security Solutions, Applications, and Future

Himani Mittal

7.1 INTRODUCTION

SDNs are extremely flexible computer networks where the role of the machine doesn't decide the physical configuration. The software on the node can change the role of the machine and all the devices on the network can have a similar architecture. There are no devices devoted to routers and gateways, but the same machine can take any function as decided by the administrator. Lantz, Heller, and McKeown [1] in their research paper discuss the Mininet where the simulator has nodes that can be configured for any role through virtualization. SDNs are the application of the same to real networks.

Network operators now have additional programming freedom because of SDN [2,3]. SDN shifts the focus of network administration from making device configurations from scratch (setting up the links and the routers individually) in order to control network functionality to creating software that takes care of all such settings and makes managing the network and troubleshooting easier. SDN helps to manage the persistent issues of network and route management along with making access-control and security a primary objective. This is achieved by splitting the state distribution and network specification as separate functions. Separating the control and data plane makes switches and routers into forwarding devices, which is a fundamental feature of SDN-based networks. There is a centralized controller for the implementation of the control plane. This centralized controller is logically centralized but physically distributed. The centralized controller manages the network behavior. Having a network operating system software in SDN has manifold advantages. Firstly, changing network policies through software is easier and less prone to mistakes than changing configurations for each device manually. Second, a control program can instantly respond to erroneous network state changes and preserve the high-level network policies in place. Third, the creation of more complex network functions is made simpler by the centralized controller providing instant and comprehensive knowledge of network status. The core value proposition of SDN is its ability to program the network and control the data plane.

SDNs are an inexpensive way to build cloud services, intelligent services, and networking that is both energy-efficient and highly secure [4]. SDN emphasizes four main characteristics: split the network into control and data plane, centralized controller with network state perspective, open interfaces between controllers and data plane devices, and network configuration/programming through external software applications. In a conventional network, the network node contains both data and control planes. The node's configuration and the programming of the data flow channels are the responsibility of the control plane. These pathways are then transferred to the data plane after being established. At a physical level, data forwarding is based on the configurations made earlier. Any type of change to the configuration is possible only after the forwarding policy is established. Network providers desiring to scale their networks in response to different peak-lean traffic demands, rising mobile device attached to network, and "big data" based applications, point to this as a problem. SDN has developed from these service-oriented requirements of network providers. Control is transferred from the many network nodes to the distinct, central controller. A network operating system (NOS) that manages SDN switches takes data through their forwarding plane and modifies it, giving the SDN controller hosting the applications an abstract description of the network topology. As a result, the controller may take advantage of entire network knowledge to enhance flow management and fulfil service-user demands for scalability and flexibility. For instance, the application may be able to dynamically distribute bandwidth into the data plane. Performance and flexibility, scalability, security, and interoperability are the main problems with SDN implementation.

Due to the inherent network complexity, proprietary and perimeter-based security solutions that are challenging to manage, and the flimsy concepts of identity in IP networks, security has proven to be a challenge in communication networks [5]. Similar to this, the Internet architecture, which establishes guidelines for using the underlying infrastructure, inherits the issues brought on by the infrastructure, is rife with security issues, and is unreceptive to innovation. As a result, numerous ideas for (re)architecting the Internet have been put up to reduce its fundamental constraints, as well as its complexity and security flaws.

The chapter is organized as follows: Section 7.2 discusses the security issues in the SDN environment. Here, both the traditional solutions that added components to the network, proposed multi-domain SDN controllers, the addition of additional extensions to open flow-based SDNs. Then the new-age solutions for SDN security based on entropy and machine learning techniques are discussed. In Section 7.3, the applications of SDN are discussed. The modern IoT networks and cloud computing that we see are based on the concepts of SDN. The farther areas where SDN can help are also reported in the chapter. Section 7.4 includes the future directions of SDN.

7.2 SECURITY ISSUES IN SDN

The author of [2] discusses SDN's concern of security and dependability. He claims that conventional networks were safer. This is because of the vendor-specific network equipment, relatively static design, the availability of several software, and the decentralized structure of the control plane. This was the case since each device (or group of devices) came from a separate vendor, necessitating the attacker's knowledge of the unique characteristics of each type of device as well as any design defects to connect to the network. Only a small portion of the network was exposed as a result. However, this benefit is not present in SDN. Since only the functionality of each device is described in terms of software, their basic designs are all identical. The author identifies two significant dangers· First, the network can be controlled via software and is subject to bugs and loopholes in the software design. Second, the concentration of all power at a central point in the centralized controller. The network could theoretically be controlled by anyone if the controller was compromised. The author discusses potential threats and remedies based on these weaknesses.

- Traffic flow that has been forged or artificially created by a malicious person after gaining access to the control server. An intrusion detection system is a potential fix.
- An attack on a switch's vulnerability to cause traffic to be diverted, slowed down or faked. A device with an autonomous trust management system based on SDN principles may be the answer.
- Attacks on the insecure TLS/SSL-controlled control-device communication. This assault may be utilized as a DoS assault. The use of encryption and controller trust methods are potential options.
- Attack on the controller, as a compromised controller compromises the entire network. Possible remedies include diversifying protocols, limiting interfaces, utilizing cryptography, replicating devices, and updating the controller's state (from time to time).
- Attack involving application trust concerns and controller vulnerabilities. To authenticate the application, a method is required. Automatic trust management programs could be the answer.
- Administrative stations, which have a single point of control, are vulnerable. Several user authentications involving multiple users and guaranteed recovery to ensure that the device reboots in a secure state are potential solutions.
- The absence of reliable sources for forensics and remediation to learn what inspired the creation of the device and what steps the attacker took, data is required. Undeletable logs and traces could be a potential option (Immutability).
- Replication, Diversity, Dynamic Switch Association, Trust between Controllers & Devices, and Self-Healing are some of the SDN capabilities that are necessary to address the risks listed above. Secure components, Security domains, and Trust between Controllers and Apps Patching and updating on time.

The author discusses several problems similar to [2] and points out that SDN is well suited for network forensics, security policy alteration, and service security insertion [4]. **Network forensics**: provides for identification of the network threats in a fast way and updates the network policies on the go and reprogram the network to optimize the experience. **Security policy alteration**: it facilitates defining the security policies and spreads the policy across the network thereby reducing the errors in the configuration of policies in network elements. **Security service insertion**: it provides for targeted application of firewall and intrusion detection system according to the network provider's policies.

The author takes a closer look at security concerns and the remedies. He mentions, that in SDN architecture, the network is divided into three planes – the Data plane, the Control plane, and the Application plane [5]. The first one is concerned with network elements (NE) that forward user data according to the configurations given in the centralized controller. The control plane contains the NOS, representation of NE, and high-level topology of the network. The application plane is for network management, policy management, and security management. The chapter discusses the challenges and limitations of SDN in terms of security, size, and debuggability. Security is crucial, as there is a central controller responsible for managing the entire network. If the security of the controller is at threat, then the whole network is in danger. Another point of failure is the controller and data communication, which if compromised can lead to the illegal use of the network. There are pros and cons to SDN. On the pro side, SDN has the advantage of hassle-free management of network. Whereas the cons are that security is very crucial due to the central point of failure. The chapter lays down the security issues and possible solutions in several programmable networks namely, Active networking, 4D approach, Sane, and Ethane. It describes OpenFlow as the most widely used SDN software. The security issues in different planes discussed are:

a) Application Plane:
   - Lack of authentication & authorization
   - Fraudulent flow rules insertion
   - Lack of access control & accountability
b) Control Plane
   - DoS attacks
   - Unauthorized controller access
   - Scalability & availability challenges.
c) Data Plane
   - Fraudulent flow rules
   - Flooding attacks
   - Controller hijacking or compromise
   - TCP-Level attacks
   - Man-in-the-middle attack

The chapter discusses several SDN security platforms that help in overcoming these security issues. These are listed below with citations to the latest implementations of these tools.

- FRESCO [6] is an OpenFlow framework created to make it easier to quickly design and modularly assemble detection and mitigation modules that are compatible with OF. A click-inspired programming framework is provided by FRESCO, an OpenFlow application in and of itself, to let security researchers to create, exchange, and combine various vulnerability detection and mitigation modules. The various testing outcomes of FRESCO with OpenFlow in managing security threats are covered in the study. FRESCO enables quick prevention and identification of network issues. Components for identification and prevention are coded and connected as modularized libraries to offer a network defense. The FRESCO prevention module provides forwarding rules to prevent an attack after an identification module detects the error in the network. The core of FRESCO contains a security module for applications included in the framework's application layer, which is used to develop apps. The Python-developed application layer modules for the FRESCO operate over the NOX OpenFlow controller. The NOX OpenFlow controller and the Security Enforcement Kernel (SEK) are interconnected, and SEK provides capabilities that FRESCO uses to enforce the regulations.

- VeriFlow [7] is a layer between the SDN controller and NE. It performs checks on a running network for policy violations when each forwarding rule is added. The author tested that VeriFlow can complete thorough inspection within microseconds of rule insertion.
- An open-source OpenFlow controller built on Erlang is called flowER. Its goal is to offer an easier environment for creating Erlang network control applications [8]. Traveling (http://www.travelping.com), the company that created FlowER, is already utilizing it in its for-profit products even though it is still in development. Each Erlang application is packaged as an RPM or DEB package in the deployment model for which the flowER is designed.
- SE-FloodLight [9], sometimes known as Floodlight, is a Java OpenFlow controller that was created by the community and is open-source. It supports OpenFlow protocols 1.0 through 1.5.
- DDoS detection [10–13], in which the most recent techniques for DDOS detection in SDN systems are covered.
- HyperFlow [14], is an OpenFlow control plane for distributed SDN. HyperFlow is scalable and has all the benefits of SDN. HyperFlow localizes policy-making to specific controllers by passively synchronizing views of controllers across the network. This reduces the time it takes for the control plane to respond to forwarding requests for user data. In the event of component failure and network partitioning, HyperFlow is resilient. A crucial component lacking in existing OpenFlow deployments is the ability to join separately managed OpenFlow networks.
- FortressNox [15] The open-source NOX OpenFlow controller is enhanced by FortNOX. It automatically determines if the new flow rules are against security regulations. Even in the presence of dynamic flow tunneling, FortNOX may identify rule inconsistencies using predetermined action rules.

In an SDN-enabled centralized network, which was the predominant trend for early suggested SDN designs, employing a single controller, three essential conditions cannot be met: First, single point of failure and efficiency [16,17]. Second, scalability is reduced by a single controller and third, high availability is not possible with single controller. Efficiency is not sufficiently established with just one centralized controller. One of the most important elements of any design is redundancy. Any controller could experience a failure at any time, leaving the network without a control plane. Security is seen as a crucial component. If an attacker takes control of the controller, the network's whole management is lost. It is obvious that if we have numerous controllers, we can lessen the problem since they will cooperate to determine when another controller is acting inappropriately and, as a result, isolate the attacker from the network. The author proposes DISCO, a DIstributed SDN COntrol plane for WAN and overlay networks [16]. Each SDN controller in this scenario has intra-domain functionality (inside its own network) and inter-domain functionality. The network is partitioned into different domains (the network of all SDN controllers). Agents support the inter-domain functionality. Four primary agents are implemented by the system. Sharing information about neighboring links with all domains is the responsibility of the connectivity agent. This aids in the discovery of novel domains. Monitoring agent delivers the information about the working links (bandwidth and latency) between all neighboring links from time to time. The reachability agent promotes hosts' existence in domains on an event basis so that they can be reached. Like RSVP, the reservation agent handles the setup and breakdown of the inter-domain flow. DISCO works well with heterogeneous network topologies and is resilient to disruptions.

The new-age security mechanism reported in a survey by Sahay [18] reports use of entropy and machine learning for intrusion detection. The previous efforts tried to fix the SDN security issues by change in network elements behavior and policy-making. These measures based on entropy and machine learning methods namely, KNN, study the traffic of the network and try to categorize the packets as malicious or regular. The vulnerability detection in the network is reported to be dealt with using test cases to match the traffic against openflow specifications and other researcher reported in the survey uses finite state machines for the vulnerability detection. There are papers included in the survey that aim at attacking mitigation by the user willingly registering for attack mitigation and the ISP then managing the customer for possible attack using traffic engineering methods. The use of big data analysis is reported in the survey. Several SDN controllers function simultaneously in large-scale networks as a cluster. Cluster management architecture based on big data analysis is required to manage the physically scattered and logically centralized controllers. The security of this cluster is another difficulty. The chapter includes an authentication mechanism required for data sources at the controller. In addition, the control plane is optimized for big data analysis using an ant colony optimization technique. The survey discusses a framework for network intelligence that makes use of large data and SDN's network programmability. To administer the entire network, the big-data based setup offers an error-resilient, resizable, and real-time platform for data extraction. In the work of Song [19], use of machine learning methods for dealing with SDN security issues is reported.

7.3   APPLICATIONS OF SDN

Due to the design of the SDN, many applications are easily available. These are listed in [20,21] and are discussed below:

Monitoring and Measurement Applications: Zhang [22] in his paper talks at length about the metrics that are used in SDNs for monitoring and measurement of network. The author investigates two performance indicators in SDN, namely, link delay and bandwidth. He suggests intra- and inter-domain discovery as a parameter for measuring topology performance indicator in SDN. The author points out the difficulty in security and measurement in SDN network. The foremost is scale and size of the network. Second, network measurement alone is not sufficient to realize all the problems in the network. Better techniques are needed that can find the yet undiscovered security issues on its own. Lastly, he says that performance and resources wasted due to unmatched measurement thresholds is a key issue. The measurement threshold must be designed keeping this in mind.

In the work of Sharma and Gawade [23], a trust-based mechanism is used for network monitoring in multiple planes of SDN. So monitoring and measurement methods in SDN architecture are inherent to SDN and can be used in other types of networks as an application of SDN.

Security and Virtualization: As already discussed in the paper, the SDN network solves many problems of security that were present in traditional network. The main security issues in SDN are controller-related and hardware-based. These are also being dealt with using machine learning methods. Similarly, virtualization is inherent to SDN Definition and all the applications of SDN inherit this feature.

Cloud computing: Distributed Application Control and Cloud Integration: According to Azodolmolky [24], private or hybrid cloud can be managed with several advantages by using OpenFlow-based SDN. A logically centralized control plane offers a comprehensive view of the cloud resources and network availability. This will guarantee that cloud federation is routed to data centers with suitable resources, over lines with adequate bandwidth, and at service levels. Services for bandwidth-on-demand with SDN support offer automated and intelligent service provisioning that is guided by client needs and cloud service orchestration logic.

In network, orchestration is automating the management of connections and operations in the network. Mayoral [25], in his work, used the orchestration of SDN controller in Cloud architecture and compares several orchestration methods.

In work performed by Son [26], discusses the SDN-based cloud architecture in detail. The chapter discusses the use of SDN for cloud computing with focus on data center power optimization, traffic engineering, network virtualization, and security. The author also presents, simulation and empirical evaluation methods developed for SDN-enabled clouds.

BigData: According to Wang's work [27], an SDN controller-based BigData architecture has a lot of advantages. A master node, or application controller, is a common feature of large data applications like Hadoop, Dryad, Spark, and HBase that handles all incoming job requests. The SDN controller was interfaced to the master node for each specific application, such as the Hadoop scheduler or HBase master, to allow cross-layer network control. It is connected to larger coordination frameworks, like Mesos, that control numerous concurrent applications using the same data center. The SDN controller offers a universal interface to configure devices and manage network forwarding because it may be shared by several applications. Additionally, it offers a query interface so that applications can access reliable network data. The SDN controller offers an interface for BigData applications that accepts traffic demand matrices in a common format from application controllers.

Cui [28] mentions that SDN benefits big-data applications concerning data processing, data delivery, programming, big data architectures, and scheduling.

In scientific applications of big data, there is a need for high-performance, sizable, and programmable networks to support data transfer in a fast and efficient manner [29]. The author suggests the Ameabanet as a solution that is based on SDN and guarantees QoS.

Optical Network: Cevijetic [30] in his work discusses that for 5G mobile applications, optical network evolution should offer more than just transmission speed improvements. It ought to pave the way from the present "cell-centric" networking paradigm to a future "device-centric" one. Key 5G mobile technologies, such as massive MIMO, extremely high network densities, D2D communication, and an environment with a growing number of diverse and unpredictable bring-your-own-device networks, must be considered in this evolution. In his chapter, strategies for addressing these 5G mobile challenges in the context of next-generation optical front haul networks have been proposed. These strategies include moving past raw CPRI signalling, supporting arbitrary WDM optics types, evolving the dynamic topology toward a mesh architecture, and using SDN-based network control. The proposed methods are expected to not only improve user-side quality-of-experience but also significantly aid in monetizing the underlying optical network infrastructure.

Yan [31], in his work, mentions that SDN facilitates the implementation of user-defined and application-specific data collection, monitoring techniques, and the employment of emerging data analytics and machine-learning techniques on top of network management.

To simplify the coordinated virtualization of optical and Ethernet networks supported by optical virtualizable transceivers, he proposes real-time multi-technology transport layer monitoring (V-BVT) [32]. The hardware monitoring in both the Ethernet and optical layers is included in a monitoring and network resource configuration approach that is suggested. In addition to the application that analyses the monitored data acquired from the database and the SDN background, the scheme shows the data and control interactions among various network levels.

Wireless Network: According to Wang [33], the volume of traffic in communication networks has grown exponentially over the last ten years as a result of the proliferation of new devices and applications. It is generally accepted that NWNs must be multi-tiered with overlay coverage and tiny cell deployment to obtain natural evolution and satisfy evolving requirements. Small cell deployment in congested areas, however, presents a number of difficulties, including erratic interfaces, frequent handovers, and substantial backhauling. SDN provides a fresh approach to tackle the aforementioned difficulties by dissecting the control plane and data plane. The author presented an intelligent wireless network architecture for NWNs in his article introducing SDNC. His architecture emphasizes the use of interface sets in the creation of virtual RATs to enable a variety of services. Low handover latency between heterogeneous networks is accomplished along with the handover strategy.

The architecture and implementation of SDN aided TCP for wireless networks are presented in [34]. His method intelligently addresses mobility-induced packet losses to prevent a drop in transmitting rate. Additionally, during mobility, the moment the receiver is reassigned to the network, data transfer begins right away. His SDN-assisted TCP does not break end-to-end semantics, in contrast to existing methods, and the TCP protocol running at the end hosts does not need to be changed. He used the Mininet Wi-fi emulation platform to put this strategy into practice and assess it. The outcomes demonstrate the approach's usefulness.

7.4   FUTURE DIRECTIONS

Artificial Intelligence has entered everywhere. And so is the SDN. Latah [35] discusses the use of Artificial intelligence in SDN and defines the cognitive SDN, which is the future direction of SDN. Routing, traffic categorization, flow clustering, intrusion detection, load balancing, fault detection, QoS and QoE optimization, admission control, and resource allocation are just a few of the issues that have been solved using AI and ML methodologies. However, in the SDN era, AI's function was greatly expanded thanks to the significant efforts made by the business sector and the research community. Recent studies have revealed a significant trend in the scientific community's application of AI methods in SDNs. It is important to note that the most popular methods for resolving various networking-related issues were ML, metaheuristics, and FSs. In his study, Latah reviewed a number of works. AI, Neural networks, classification method SVM and decision trees are some methods to overcome SDN security issues.

Ayoubi [36], in his work, mentions the efforts of the research community to automate the networks. For making the network autonomous, it must think and make decisions. And this is possible with the help of AI and specifically machine learning techniques. Using ML for managing the network is not easy. AI is being used for fault management, configuration management, accounting management, performance management and security management. Techniques namely, Neural Networks, K-Nearest Neighbor, Decision trees, SVM are used for fault prediction, fault localization, prevention of attack, service configuration in particular and intrusion detection at large.

[37–39] are works of different authors who have used machine learning for network issues like DDoS. [40] is another review paper that covers the use of AI in Cognitive SDN.

The future direction is the development of a network that manages itself intelligently without human intervention and offers services and applications that further use AI to solve people's problems. And this statement is really powerful.

REFERENCES

[1] Lantz, B., Heller, B., & McKeown, N. (2010). A network in a laptop: Rapid prototyping for software-defined networks. *Proceedings of the 9th ACM SIGCOMM Workshop on Hot Topics in Networks.*

[2] Kreutz, D., Ramos, F. M. V., & Verissimo, P. (2013). Towards secure and dependable software-defined networks. *Proceedings of the Second ACM SIGCOMM Workshop on Hot Topics in Software-Defined Networking.*

[3] Monsanto, C., Reich, J., Foster, N., Rexford, J., Walker, D., & Cornell, P. (2013). Composing software-defined networks. *10th USENIX Symposium on Networked Systems Design and Implementation (NSDI 13).*

[4] Sezer, S., Scott-Hayward, S., Chouhan, P. K., Fraser, B., Lake, D., Finnegan, J., Viljoen, N., Miller, M., & Rao, N. (2013). Are we ready for SDN? Implementation challenges for software-defined networks. *IEEE Communications Magazine 51*(7), 36–43.

[5] Ahmad, I., Namal, S., & Ylianttila, M. (2015). Security in software-defined networks: A survey. *IEEE Communications Surveys & Tutorials 17*(4), 2317–2346.

[6] Shin, S. W., Porras, P., Yegneswara, V., Fong, M., Gu, G., & Tyson, M. (2013, February). Fresco: Modular composable security services for software-defined networks. In *20th Annual Network & Distributed System Security Symposium.* NDSS.

[7] Khurshid, A., Zhou, W., Caesar, M., & Godfrey, P. B. (2012, August). Veriflow: Verifying network-wide invariants in real-time. In *Proceedings of the First Workshop on Hot Topics in Software-Defined Networks* (pp. 49–54).

[8] FlowEr: https://www.oreilly.com/library/view/software-defined-networking-with/97817 83984282/05477cfd-40c4-451d-9fe7-199571170bad.xhtml (last accessed on 5 December 2022).

[9] FloodLight: https://www.sciencedirect.com/topics/computer-science/floodlight-controller (last accessed on 5 December 2022).

[10] DDOS: https://www.kentik.com/kentipedia/ddos-detection/ (last accessed on 5 December 2022).

[11] Jia, K., Liu, C., Liu, Q. Wang, J., Liu, J., & Liu, F. (2022). A lightweight DDoS detection scheme under SDN context. *Cybersecurity 5*, 27. https://doi.org/10.1186/s42400-022-00128-7

[12] Neethu, S., & Aradhya, H. R. (2022). Detection of DDoS attacks in SDN. *ECS Transactions 107*(1), 18305.

[13] Kokila, R. T., Selvi, S. T., & Govindarajan, K. (2014, December). DDoS detection and analysis in SDN-based environment using support vector machine classifier. In *2014 Sixth International Conference on Advanced Computing (ICoAC)* (pp. 205–210). IEEE.

[14] Tootoonchian, A., & Ganjali, Y. (2010, April). Hyperflow: A distributed control plane for OpenFlow. In *Proceedings of the 2010 Internet Network Management Conference on Research on Enterprise Networking* (Vol. 3, pp. 10–5555).

[15] FortNox: https://www.oreilly.com/library/view/software-defined-networking-with/ 9781783984282/ea8b7e7e-f80d-4e82-88b4-7a4cc311c40f.xhtml (last accessed on 5 December, 2022)

[16] Phemius, K., Bouet, M., & Leguay, J. (2014, May). Disco: Distributed multi-domain sdn controllers. In *2014 IEEE Network Operations and Management Symposium (NOMS)* (pp. 1–4). IEEE.

[17] Blial, O., Ben Mamoun, M., & Benaini, R. (2016). An overview on SDN architectures with multiple controllers. *Journal of Computer Networks and Communications, 2016,* Article ID 9396525, 8 pages, 2016. https://doi.org/10.1155/2016/9396525

[18] Sahay, R., Meng, W., & Jensen, C. D. (2019). The application of software-defined networking on securing computer networks: A survey. *Journal of Network and Computer Applications 131*, 89–108.

[19] Song, C., Park, Y., Golani, K., Kim, Y., Bhatt, K., & Goswami, K. (2017, July). Machine-learning based threat-aware system in software-defined networks. In *2017 26th International Conference on Computer Communication and Networks (ICCCN)* (pp. 1–9). IEEE.

[20] SDN Applications: https://opennetworking.org/sdn-resources/sdn-reading-list/sdn-applications/ (last accessed on 5 December, 2022)

[21] SDN Applications: https://www.datacenterknowledge.com/archives/2016/03/31/top-five-apps-and-services-that-can-benefit-from-sdn (last accessed on 5 December, 2022)

[22] Zhang, H., Cai, Z., Liu, Q., Xiao, Q., Li, Y., & Cheang, C. F. (2018). A survey on security-aware measurement in SDN. *Security and Communication Networks* 2018, Article ID 2459154, 14 pages. https://doi.org/10.1155/2018/2459154

[23] Sharma, G., & Gawade, S. (2022). Exploring trust in SDN along with network monitoring. In: Singh, P. K., Singh, Y., Chhabra, J. K., Illés, Z., & Verma, C. (eds) *Recent Innovations in Computing. Lecture Notes in Electrical Engineering*, vol. 855. Springer, Singapore. https://doi.org/10.1007/978-981-16-8892-8_20

[24] Azodolmolky, S., Wieder, P., & Yahyapour, R. (2013). SDN-based cloud computing networking. *2013 15th International Conference on Transparent Optical Networks (ICTON)*. https://doi.org/10.1109/icton.2013.6602678

[25] Mayoral, A., Vilalta, R., Muñoz, R., Casellas, R., & Martínez, R. (2017). SDN orchestration architectures and their integration with Cloud Computing applications. *Optical Switching and Networking 26*, 2–13. https://doi.org/10.1016/j.osn.2015.09.007

[26] Son, J., & Buyya, R. (2018). A taxonomy of software-defined networking (SDN)-enabled cloud computing. *ACM Computing Surveys 51*(3), 1–36. https://doi.org/10.1145/3190617

[27] Wang, G., Ng, T. S. E., & Shaikh, A. (2012). Programming your network at run-time for big data applications. *Proceedings of the First Workshop on Hot Topics in Software-Defined Networks - HotSDN '12*. https://doi.org/10.1145/2342441.2342462

[28] Cui, L., Yu, F. R., & Yan, Q. (2016). When big data meets software-defined networking: SDN for big data and big data for SDN. *IEEE Network 30*(1), 58–65. https://doi.org/10.1109/mnet.2016.7389832

[29] Shah, S. A. R., Wu, W., Lu, Q., Zhang, L., Sasidharan, S., DeMar, P., … Noh, S.-Y. (2018). AmoebaNet: An SDN-enabled network service for big data science. *Journal of Network and Computer Applications 119*, 70–82. https://doi.org/10.1016/j.jnca.2018.06.015

[30] Cvijetic, N. (2014). Optical network evolution for 5G mobile applications and SDN-based control. *2014 16th International Telecommunications Network Strategy and Planning Symposium (Networks)*. https://doi.org/10.1109/netwks.2014.6958537

[31] Yan, S., Khan, F. N., Mavromatis, A., Gkounis, D., Fan, Q., Ntavou, F., … Simeonidou, D. (2017). Field trial of machine-learning-assisted and SDN-based optical network planning with network-scale monitoring database. *2017 European Conference on Optical Communication (ECOC)*. https://doi.org/10.1109/ecoc.2017.8346091

[32] Ou, Y., Davis, M., Aguado, A., Meng, F., Nejabati, R., & Simeonidou, D. (2018). Optical network virtualisation using multitechnology monitoring and SDN-enabled optical transceiver. *Journal of Lightwave Technology 36*(10), 1890–1898. https://doi.org/10.1109/jlt.2018.2794600

[33] Wang, K., Wang, Y., Zeng, D., & Guo, S. (2017). An SDN-based architecture for next-generation wireless networks. *IEEE Wireless Communications 24*(1), 25–31. https://doi.org/10.1109/mwc.2017.1600187wc

[34] Singh, K. V., Gupta, S., Verma, S., & Pandey, M. (2019). Improving performance of TCP for wireless network using SDN. *Proceedings of the 20th International Conference on Distributed Computing and Networking - ICDCN '19*. https://doi.org/10.1145/3288599.3288626

[35] Latah, M., & Toker, L. (2019). Artificial intelligence enabled software-defined networking: A comprehensive overview. *IET Networks 8*(2), 79–99.

[36] Ayoubi, S., Limam, N., Salahuddin, M. A., Shahriar, N., Boutaba, R., Estrada-Solano, F., & Caicedo, O. M. (2018). Machine learning for cognitive network management. *IEEE Communications Magazine 56*(1), 158–165. https://doi.org/10.1109/mcom.2018.1700560

[37] Restuccia, F., D'Oro, S., & Melodia, T. (2018). Securing the internet of things in the age of machine learning and software-defined networking. *IEEE Internet of Things Journal 5*(6), 4829–4842.

[38] Cui, J., Wang, M., Luo, Y., & Zhong, H. (2019). DDoS detection and defense mechanism based on cognitive-inspired computing in SDN. *Future Generation Computer Systems 97*, 275–283.

[39] Dong, S., & Sarem, M. (2019). DDoS attack detection method based on improved KNN with the degree of DDoS attack in software-defined networks. *IEEE Access 8*, 5039–5048.

[40] Xie, J., Yu, F. R., Huang, T., Xie, R., Liu, J., Wang, C., & Liu, Y. (2018). A survey of machine learning techniques applied to software-defined networking (SDN): Research issues and challenges. *IEEE Communications Surveys & Tutorials 21*(1), 393–430.

8 Multi-Hop Routing Protocol in SDN-Based Wireless Sensor Network
A Comprehensive Survey

Mandeep Singh and Aruna Malik

8.1 INTRODUCTION

Wireless sensor networks (WSNs) are regarded as one of the most significant 21st-century technologies due to advancements in the creation of smart and micro-sensors. A wireless small network of sensors and agents (WSAN) is another name for WSN [1]. The device is made up of independent sensors. To track environmental or physical variables like temperature, humidity, noise, pressure, etc., they are dispersed spatially. These less expensive and more compact sensors are made possible by small batteries, constrained memory space, and computing power. These sensors function by sensing and gathering information from their surroundings, then transmitting it to the central location. WSN was initially required for military purposes, but it is now used in many different areas, including border control surveillance, water surveillance, process management in industry, monitoring of the health care system, etc. Many protocols and algorithms designed for MANET are suitable for ad-hoc networks but not for WSNs. Ad-hoc wireless networking approaches are necessary for applications that use WSNs [2]. The following properties set wireless sensor networks apart from mobile ad hoc networks:

- Global identity: Due to the vast number of applications, global identity is not favored in WSN (which boosts runtime overhead). MANET demands inter-node communication.
- Data-centric: In WSN, redundancy is necessary, although this concept is ignored in MANET until the need for file sharing arises.
- Scalability: The majority of applications call for the installation of billions of nodes. to make the network denser and set it apart from MANET.
- When it comes to quality of service (QoS) and dependability, MANET outperforms the Internet. Both WSN and per-node trustworthiness are required, but WSN standards are more stringent. Because programs using WSN must be more adaptable, QoS measurements vary. Sensor nodes are energy-efficient because their cells are non-replaceable.

DOI: 10.1201/9781003432869-8

- Fault-tolerant: Due to the limited battery life of sensors, WSN is projected to continue operating even when a significant number of nodes fail. So, To make a WSN more fault-tolerant than a LAN, special consideration must be given to conventional network.
- Size of the network: Varied types of WSN applications will result in different network sizes. It was designed to their needs, which resulted in the creation of many MANETS that requires fewer protocols for dissimilar applications compared to other networks.
- Operating software: Because WSNs have constrained memory and computing power, their software must take the network into consideration. Although operating software must be straightforward, MANET's intricacy necessitates heavy software, which can be used with weight protocols for routing.

Internet transmission patterns are less common than those of MANET. Unlike WSNs, MSNs frequently experience sporadic spurts of slow data rates that last for a long time. Most of the time, data flows and fast data rates are the norm. The above-mentioned distinctions between MANET and WSN prevent the use of existing protocols and MANET algorithms in WSN. The development and implementation of WSNs are thought to have advanced as a result of the numerous research methods that have been put into practice on a global scale to address a variety of application and design issues. A better quality of service (QoS) and fast connectivity access to a range of digital media apps are user demands that current 4G networks are unable to satisfy. This is brought on by factors such as constrained spectrum, constrained scalability, proprietary interfaces, device-centric design, complex protocols, pricey facilities, and the existence of diverse networks [3].

A number of remedies have been proposed [4] for some of the aforementioned issues. It is anticipated that 5G networks will offer network connectivity wherever and whenever it is needed. Compared to current 4G networks, 5G networks are expected to perform significantly better, with 1000 times more network capacity, 10–100 numerous times greater speed of data, more than 90% savings on electricity, less than one millisecond of end-to-end delay, and 99% accessibility to service [5]. New approaches and technologies are being developed to satisfy the needs of 5G networks and get around their challenges. Some positive aspects of 5G include massive antenna designs and millimetre-wave technologies. MIMO (multiple-input multiple-output) technology, also known as a large antenna, allows reliable, secure, and energy-efficient communications [6].

Numerous advantages of integrating MD2D collaboration with mobile networks include expanded cellular coverage, enhanced quality of service and quality of experience, reduced communication delay, enhanced load balancing by outsourcing, mobile data traffic, raised assets, and power distribution [7]. Additionally, when telecommunications infrastructure is unavailable, it is required for disaster recovery apps. Different methods have been suggested to combine MD2D messaging with cellular networks. One of the suggested options is to build MANETs close to cell boundaries or crowded areas so that devices can create one-hop or multi-hop links to get to the base stations (BS) or other nodes that are near [8]. Several nodes or equipment linked effortlessly in a self-configuring and organized themselves way without a fixed framework make up a MANET. Devices can travel around the network freely thanks to MANETs, which can also create multi-hop links to provide communication. Each node performs the role of a router, sending data to one or more particular locations. Due to the lack of centralized control, MANETs aren't expandable as the number of routes and nodes grows. Therefore, by combining the best aspects of MANETs and mobile phones, the new hybrid design can improve overall efficiency and do away with their limitations. Despite these advancements, MANETs in mobile networks encounter the following challenges: Device-to-device (D2D) or mobile data choosing a mode for optimal performance, effective radio allocation of resources, and other neighbor searches are among them, Security issues, pricing regulations for relaying devices, and interference control in in-band telecommunications where D2D and mobile communication share the same telecom spectrum [9].

In D2D overlay wireless networks, various methods [10] are outlined for reducing interference, improving resource allocation, and maximizing spectrum use. Although several approaches and solutions have been put forth for mobile communication, there are a number of limitations that merit mentioning, including the lack of computerization, expensive of network upgrades, inadequate flexibility, the difficulty of service deployment, the close coupling between the control layer and data layer, the lack of fine-grained resource control in mobile networks, and scalability issues caused by centralized the data layer operations on long-term evolution. (LTE). One solution to the aforementioned issues is to incorporate the software-defined networking (SDN) idea into mobile networks. By creating a novel, flexible infrastructure with open interfaces where control layer operations are logically managed centrally under one or more control entities and isolated from transferring devices, SDN seeks to address these issues. Network functions are programs that run on top of the controller and allow for quicker and more flexible network innovation and upgrade via firmware upgrades as opposed to costly and exhausting equipment or framework upgrading.

8.1.1 WSN CHALLENGES

Several study challenges, such as secure system operation, secrecy, transparency and diversity, real-time management and operations, and from raw data to knowledge, can be overcome in order to create realistic WSN. A hostile, unsteady, and expanding environment must be overcome by the debut. The following list of design problems caused by the distinctive features of WSN is provided:

1. Node deployment that is ad hoc and random thousands, tens of thousands, or even more nodes make up many WSNs. Statically (manually) or randomly distributed nodes are both options. These nodes must organize themselves independently in order to communicate because they are haphazardly positioned throughout the hostile area. Prior to sharing information, a network must be created.
2. Dynamic and unsupervised environment: Sensor points are dispersed at random in this environment. Due to early energy depletion or other

environmental variables, some sensor nodes in this scenario may cause a network failure. Fault tolerance must be considered when creating protocols for WSN apps.

3. Limited capacity and computing power: Battery-powered sensor nodes have a somewhat constrained battery capacity. Developers of hardware and software now confront a number of new challenges as a result of this functionality. New study is required not only in the design of transmission protocols and networks, but also in devices, to address the limited energy potential of sensor nodes.

4. Different application requirements: Every day, a large number of WSN apps are developed, and each one has different requirements. They must use various network builds, methods of communication, and techniques because their requirements are different.

5. Untrustworthy Transmission: Interference messages affect wireless networks. (c.g., SNR). These signals cause communication between the wireless sensor units to become unstable. It can also be broken at any moment. It also has a range restriction. For WSN, this creates a new challenge that will call for more complex answers.

8.2 LITERATURE REVIEW

8.2.1 SDN

SDN is a promising choice for network technologies of the next generation [11]. It offers flexibility by establishing network capabilities via software as opposed to hardware. Despite questions regarding its viability and efficacy [12], SDN is a potential alternative for future networks through real-world implementation. This section introduces SDN technology and associated developments.

8.2.1.1 Architecture SDN

The separation of the packet forwarding layer and network management plane is a core premise of software-defined networking. Each typical network component is a distinct system responsible for both data transmission and routing, as shown in Figure 8.1(a). The division of the control and data planes in Figure 8.1(b) simplifies

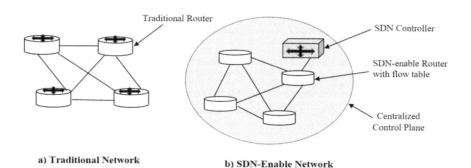

FIGURE 8.1   Traditional vs software-defined networking.

the network elements of an SDN-enabled network. By achieving central management and adapting routing based on the present network perspective, the SDN controller achieves control. The SDN-enabled router merely forwards data at the data plane level in accordance with the informed pathways that are listed in the flow table. As a result, networking can be changed quickly and flexibly.

OpenFlow [13] is the most widely used SDN paradigm at present. OpenFlow has grown into a market standard, especially in data centers and corporate networks, despite the fact that its developers originally recommended its use with test procedures or designs. Several attempts were made to establish a customizable infrastructure before Open Flow's success. The Ethane [14] protocol, that can be seen as a VLAN [15] method from a certain angle, serves as the foundation for OpenFlow. OpenFlow uses Ethernet switches and implies a wired communicating infrastructure. To strike a balance between universality and adaptability, it makes use of the notion that "the majority of Internet switches and routers today consist of routing tables" [16]. The network is made up of controllers and switches that can support OpenFlow underneath the SDN design. A routing table, a safe connection, and the OpenFlow system are required to be present in a switch for it to enable OpenFlow. The control layer is a remote device that establishes a safe channel connection with an OpenFlow-enabled switch. The software program controls inputs while the flow tables manage to physically advance. The controller(s) modifies the routing table of an OpenFlow-enabled switch using the OpenFlow protocol over a secure channel in order to implement software-defined management. The original OpenFlow standard serves as the foundation for all SDN research described in this thesis, unless otherwise stated. There are many SDN implementations already in place in corporate networks, including those at Google's data centers [17]. The SDN framework has undergone extensive study since the Open-Flow release to be completed. Numerous exhaustive studies, such as [18], continue to review and summarize modern works. Network management [19], security [20], network function virtualization [21], service quality [22], cloud computing [23], and network state [24] are some research fields. The change in the physical medium also presents new research challenges, making the application of the SDN idea to optical and wireless networks distinctive [25].

8.2.1.2 SDN Control Plane

The north layout, south layout, and possible east/west layout are the four separate parts that make up the SDN control plane.

- A network's management system is the controller.
- The network shows make use of the north interface.

For contact between the controller and the forwarding device, the south layout is used. If the south functionality is provided by a separate, specialized network, the control channel is defined by [26, 27] as "off to," otherwise it is defined as "in-band."

Communication between controllers is enhanced by the east–west link. Notably, the majority of SDN systems in use today lack east–west linkage because multiple managers are frequently unnecessary. When using SDN controllers like NOx, there are two different control options available [28]. A controller that works reactively reacts passively to device requests. The passive insertion of rules in this reactive control style could result in a significant delay in the delivery of the first packet. Proactively administered rules increase new flow throughput while reducing new flow latency by pushing rules out in preparation. Even though a device operating in anticipatory control mode can decrease the first-packet delay, the unpredictable nature of connection failure can have a negative impact on performance [29]. Responsiveness, robustness, and scalability continue to be significant issues for SDN controllers [30].

Furthermore, the decentralization of the SDN data and control planes is a crucial area of study. Considering scalability, dependability, and durability, it has been stated [31] that the physically distributed SDN controller must be logically centralized. Flowvisor [32] is a proxy controller for logical decentralization that divides network resources amongst many controllers. Hyperflow [33] and Onix [34] are other suggested distributed control planes. Although it has been proven that architectural outsourcing can reduce lookup overhead and increase reaction speed, the appropriate level of decentralization [35] remains unanswered. Kandoo [36] presents a hybrid approach to achieve controllable diversity.

8.2.1.3   Deployment of Wireless Network SDN

SDN advancement in wireless communications is significantly less compared to SDN's rising popularity in data centers and business networks [27]. Even while SDN research generates new issues with the mobile network and portable devices, SDN has the possibility of addressing many of the issues that wireless communication networks have faced since their inception [27].

8.2.1.3.1   SDN Implementation in Wireless Infrastructure Networks

To facilitate networking, network architectures must deploy specialized network equipment, including ground stations in WMANs and wireless connections in wireless local area networks (WLANs). Infrastructure-based wireless networks are made up of WCNs and WLANs because they use the infrastructure of the network.

Infrastructure-less wireless technologies, in contrast, lack a specialized network infrastructure [37]. SDN deployment in WCNs lowers hardware costs while boosting network management and scalability. Bell Labs, for instance, provides "software-defined mobile networks" [38] to enhance the design and management of mobile network systems. Another illustration of a fifth-generation (5G) wireless system design is SoftAir [39]. The centralized control plane of SDN improves the efficiency of WLAN device coordination. The Stanford Open Roads deployment [40] is an important test that presents a flexible architecture for describing resource requirements as slices [41] and demonstrates the idea of a lightweight virtualized entry point for numerous access points so that the network can be managed globally. An SDN-based load balancing method that takes into account gateway traffic in a network of connections is provided in [42]. In case the main controller malfunctions, [43] incorporates a local controller that acts as failsafe control system. Additionally, SDN incorporates wireless communication technologies by default, which may improve the network's wireless ability, usability, and use of resources

[44] by offering a systematic approach for enhancing and improving a number of protocols, such as WiFi, 3rd Gen, and 4th Gen [45]. It proposes an SDN architecture that allows for smooth mobility between WiMAX, WiFi, and LTE. With the following attempts to integrate Quality of Service (QoS) and other functionalities, SDN architecture becomes more comprehensive [46].

8.2.2 Wireless Sensor Networks (WSNs)

This section describes WSNs, an essential component of infrastructure-free wireless communication applications. As stated in Section 8.2.1, determining how to implement SDN in an infrastructure-free scenario remains problematic. Beginning with the structure and characteristics of the WSN, this section discusses how habitat monitoring apps are created and what must be considered when doing so.

8.2.2.1 Structure of WSN

A WSN is usually made up of distributed sensor devices that are used to keep an eye on a specific place. Wireless sensors can be directly traced to the Cold War period [47], when their initial military uses were proposed. By the end of the 1990s, cheaper sensors made it possible to employ them for a broader range of functions, including environmental sensing, tracking vehicles, protecting perimeters, monitoring habitats, and controlling battlefields [47].

Two perspectives can be used to study the layout of a WSN: the connected network and sensor devices. Typically, a sensor gadget serves multiple purposes. Noting the fact that terminals can be heterogeneous—that is, they can have different sensing, computing capacities, storage facilities, and persistence,—is important. Figure 8.2 shows the skeleton of a WSN's communication mechanism. Data is collected by nodes that gather data and subsequently converge at the sinking point, as shown in the image, where it may be accessed by the end user. Notably, with this WSN architecture, which is easily compatible with the SDN idea, the sink can act as a centered controller to direct sensor nodes on packet forwarding. According to [48], WSNs require cross-layer control of movement, power, and responsibilities.

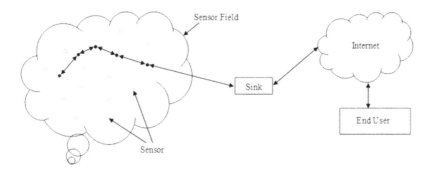

FIGURE 8.2   WSN architecture.

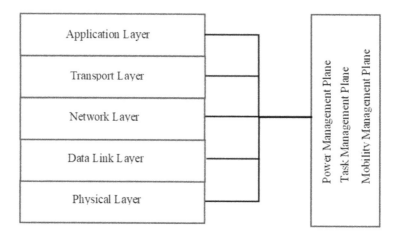

FIGURE 8.3 WSN protocol stack.

The protocol hierarchy used by sensor nodes is summarized in Figure 8.3. Only conceptual links between the three management planes and the five-layer network protocols are shown in Figure 8.3. Because the management planes must be set up to handle a variety of circumstances, this is still a rich area of study even though the five-layered model is comparable to a typical computer network. It might be simpler to satisfy the requirements of specific applications because SDN makes network management more customizable.

8.2.3   MULTI-HOP NETWORKING

As discussed in previous sections, multi-hop networks of communications are widely used by WSNs. Effective control structure development for wireless multi-hop connectivity is still a challenge. To analyze efficient SDN control for WSNs, this section examines significant studies on multi-hop wireless communications.

8.2.3.1   Networking with Multiple Hops Wireless Connectivity

Cellular devices can communicate with non-radio-range devices using a technique called ad hoc communication. For this form of multi-hop communication to work, packets must be transmitted from the starting point to the recipient by intermediary wireless devices. These nodes that intermediate between nodes are more flexible than in conventional computer networks like Ethernet because they are wireless devices with node mobility, constrained resources, efficiency, and a wireless channel. Many studies have been done in the last few decades to find solutions to the problems brought on by a constantly shifting topology.

The SCF method is supported by a more contemporary conception of DTN that permits irregular connectivity in ad hoc networking. In DTN, a node can convey a message until it reaches its intended recipient(s) or an intermediary node that is more suitable. DTN enables forwarding, which increases the adaptability of message delivery by capitalizing on the encounter possibilities presented by the movement of nodes. Opportunistic forwarding's ability to meet predetermined delivery circumstances is still up for debate [49] due to the complicated nature of node movement and buffer control. In multi-hop information networks, routing is essential. To reach numbers of end nodes, the multicast routing issue necessitates the determination of suitable intermediary nodes. Multicast routing, which takes into consideration multiple destinations as opposed to unicast routing, which only has one, enables the best use of network resources. Multiple locations exacerbate the routing issue and add to the routing costs. Multicast routing's effectiveness and reliability are much more important in wireless ad hoc networks.

8.2.3.2   Overview of Multi-Hop Forwarding

Flooding and a pandemic transmission are two main transfer approaches used in multi-hop communications. The information spreads throughout the network as a consequence of each node retransmitting the data packet to its nearby neighbors. Numerous improved flooding strategies, including distance-based, statistical, counter-based, cluster-based, and position-based ones, have been recommended [50] to enhance dependability and prevent the broadcast storm problem. Proposed forwarding techniques are based on node encounters and intermittent connectivity. When one node comes within the communication range of another node, a node encounter takes place.

Although mailing based on pandemic transmission doesn't call for additional traffic data, the node must be able to store and forward the received message, making buffering and delay tolerance is the most significant drawbacks of encounter-based approaches [51]. To improve the performance of approaches based on epidemics, research has been conducted to prevent message duplication and make use of node-to-node contact information [52]. Multicast and unicast routing play significant roles in enhancing forwarding performance. A forwarding table specifies the next hop towards the destination(s) to direct packet forwarding throughout the routing mechanism. This enables the construction of more effective routes between nodes by reducing pointless transmissions. Routing methods are divided into three categories: reactive source-initiated ad-hoc, pre-emptive table-driven, and hybrid [53]. The performance of unicast forwarding will decline as the number of locations rises. Therefore, multicast solutions are provided to optimize the use of communications with numerous recipients. Multicast techniques can be categorized as Mesh approach, flooding-based, grouping approach, or tree-based depending on their dissemination structure. Group membership management is a critical part of multicast routing, as the accompanying maintenance costs can be considerable. Stateless multicast protocols do not require all participating nodes to store multicast forwarding states.

8.3   SDN ARCHITECTURE

In addition to providing the initial conceptual approach in the form of the SDN, [54] provided a novel way for utilizing OpenFlow technology for tackling dependability issues in wireless sensor networks. In [55], the Sensor Network was first mentioned. Here are some significant suggestions for integrating SDN with WSN.

a) Software-Defined Networking in Wireless Sensor networks (SDN-WISE)
b) Software-Defined Wireless Sensor Network (SD-WSN)
c) Tiny SDN
d) Service-centric networking for Urban-scale Feedback Systems (SURF)

8.3.1 IMPLEMENTATION OF SDN IN WIRELESS SENSOR NETWORKS (SDN-WISE)

Although it has been shown that the aforementioned configurations have several benefits over traditional WSNs without SDN [56], there certainly are also some drawbacks.

a) The network cannot function properly without key protocol information.
b) There haven't been any evaluations of the suggested fixes' efficacy because the designs haven't been put to use. The first deployment of an OpenFlow SDN architecture designed specifically for WSNs is SDN-WISE, which was created in [56].

In contrast to current systems, the SDN-WISE architecture seeks to allow direct programming of sensor nodes while limiting the sharing data between nodes and the controller. SDN-WISE also makes it easier to build SDN controller code. This is a big advance over previously proposed alternatives since it increases the flexibility and simplicity of network programming. In addition, SDN-WISE offers the capability to operate its regulator in a virtual environment. Its functioning can be examined using simulation tools such as OMNET++ and COOJA. SDN-WISE attempts to deploy sensor assets wisely, regardless of the fact that this might lead to a lower data transfer rate. It suggests implementing a scheduling cycle to regularly switch the broadcasting component from on to off in order to save energy and increase energy efficiency. Additionally, SDN-WISE raises the system's awareness of the package information because WSNs are inherently pertinent data. Based on the information contained in the packet's preamble and payload, nodes can handle packets. In addition, flow tables introduce relational operators with more complex functionality.

The FlowVisor divides the system's resources into manageable parts in OpenFlow. Each component is only associated with a single controller at any given moment.

In addition, in a WSN, the same piece of data may be significant to a different application operating on a different controller. SDN-WISE permits several controllers to declare distinct rules for a single packet based on their respective requirements.

8.3.1.1 SDN-WISE Protocol

Each of the sensing nodes contains a Micro Control Unit (MCU) and an IEEE 802.15.4 transmitter. The MCU manages the transmitting component and decides how to move forward using the WISE flow chart. In accordance with the controller's setup instructions, it also consistently modifies the WISE flow table. The In-Network Packet Processing (INPP) plane is positioned above the Forwarding (FWD) layer in the network structure. It is in charge of gathering data and analyzing it further. Through the merging of small packets travelling the same route, the INPP layer in SDN-WISE lowers network overhead [56].

Network coding is currently being developed as part of INPP and will be proven to be highly effective in a variety of WSN applications. This will be demonstrated. On the Topology Discovery layer, you'll have access to all of the layers. It controls the behavior of nodes at every level. A WISE-VISOR directs the network's control logic. It consists of a topology management (TM) component that handles the network resource abstraction. This enables various logical networks to operate over the same collection of physical devices while following various management rules. Different managers are in charge of deciding these rules. Signals received from the sink must be formatted by the adaptation layer in order for WISE-VISOR to handle them [57].

8.3.1.2   Topological Revelation

The topology management solution of WISE-Visor generates a coherent representation of the whole system by gathering local structure information from the sensor nodes via TD messages. For example, when a node S sends a TD packet to a random sensor node R, R will do the following:

a) In the list of neighbors that Node A maintains, Node B's ID, as well as its current RSSI and battery level, will be included.
b) Node R will determine whether the newly received TD packet from node S is closer to the sink than previously enrolled packets. If the requirement is met, node A will set its next node in the controller's path to be the same as node B's and update its value to be equal to the current value incremented by one.
c) The energy capacity of Node R will be set in the TD packet's corresponding field.
d) Node R will use wireless technology to send its updated TD packet.
e) In order to communicate with the WISE-Visor, each sensor node creates a packet that includes an up-to-date list of the other nodes in its vicinity and periodically transmits it to the monitor. Also regularly eliminated is the list of neighbors. A node will send a packet to the node designated as the next hop on the path to the controller if it gets one meant for the WISE-Visor. Figure 8.4 depicts the many fields that can be found in an SDN-WISE packet's header.

8.3.2   Software-Defined Wireless Sensor Network (SD-WSN)

The first effort to combine SDN and WSNs is represented by SD-WSN. The SD-WSN architecture aims to solve the problems with network management, counter-productivity, rigid policy change, and resource underutilization in WSNs [18]. The OpenFlow algorithm presumptively uses extremely sophisticated networking hardware in the underlying network. WSN networks, on the other hand, are made up of low-power and low-spec devices. Direct implementation of OpenFlow in the WSN realm would not be beneficial because it was primarily intended to be a wired protocol. A novel WSN-compatible protocol is presented by SD-WSN along with a number of modifications. The SD-WSN's main element is the Sensor OpenFlow (SOF) interface. Between the data layer and the control layer, it serves as a common

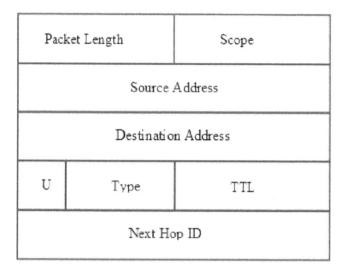

Packet Length	Scope
Source Address	
Destination Address	

U	Type	TTL

Next Hop ID

FIGURE 8.4   Packet header for SDN-WISE.

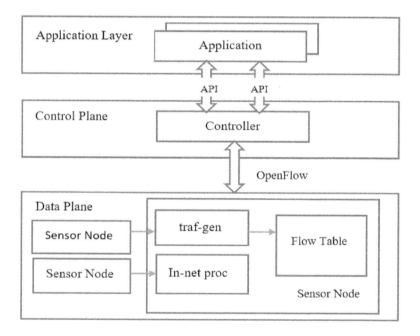

FIGURE 8.5   SD-WSN architecture.

transmission mechanism. The goal is to increase the programmability of the base network by using user-configurable flow tables. According to Figure 8.5 [54], the SD-WSN design provides the following features:

8.3.2.1   Data Plane

It is important to keep in mind that wireless sensor networks are largely data-centric, meaning that the actual data itself is valued more than the source. As a result, they employ a one-of-a-kind addressing technique that includes qualities. For example, "nodes with a temperature greater than 30." It is imperative that this be taken into consideration before moving on with the design of flow tables. WSNs implement addressing systems on the Class 1 and Class 2 levels. Class 1 is made up of addresses that are 16 bits long and are one of a kind, but Class 2 is made up of pairs of concatenation attributes, also known as CAVs. There are two methods for generating a flow:

(a) Redefinition of the routing table: Class 1 addressing schemes are managed by SD-WSN. In order to generate flow matches, it uses a syntax that is analogous to OpenFlow eXtensible Match, or OXM for short.

(b) IP Enhancement: The second technique for enhancing WSN is to employ IP. Two commercial IP stacks, uIP/uIPv6 and Blip, are recommended.

8.3.2.2   Control Plane

It ensures the timely delivery of communications and permits dependable TCP/IP connectivity. Each participant is recognized by their IP addresses. Typically, these identifiers are not accessible in WSN. If the system administrator chooses the first non-IP routing technique indicated in the previous section, a Sensor OpenFlow (SOF) link can be launched quickly on the WSN using SD-WSN. Because IP stacks by default include TCP versions, SOF channels will still be able to function independently if the network operator decides to integrate WSN with IP. The same WSN must provide service to the SOF channel. Problematic because the extra control interaction among the control unit and sensor network must be transported, which is problematic for a WSN with limited energy resources. In addition, the WSN contains a great deal of control traffic, which, if not handled properly, will cause the network to become overloaded.

Messages that are sent and received in packets make up the bulk of traffic control packets. A packet-in is the controller's response to a node's request for guidance on how to manage an unmatched packet. The controller's answer describing how the packet should be handled is known as a "packet-out." The controller in a WSN gets a lot of requests, and the control flow is frequently bursty. The network will become overloaded if many sensors simultaneously send the controller numerous requests for flow setup. It will also happen frequently because every flow has an expiry timer. Therefore, data bottlenecks will be prevented.

WSN nodes generate their own data packets as opposed to just transmitting those of other nodes, which is how conventional networks function. Each sensor component on the SD-WSN is given an entirely novel traffic-gen module to create traffic. The WSN also needs to periodically aggregate data to get rid of information that is redundant. SDN, however, does not provide this feature. To solve this issue, the SD-WSN model includes an in-network protocol module. If processing is not necessary, the data will be delivered straight to the flow table. OTA technology can be used to modify algorithm modifications [58].

8.3.3 TinySDN

Built on TinyOS, TinySDN is an SDN system. Sensor node and the SDN controller node are the two main components of TinySDN, which brings numerous controllers into WSN. The architecture of TinySDN gives attention to issues with energy supply, transmission delay, and link layer frame size. The majority of these issues were not properly addressed by the previous SDN in WSN designs that were presented. Additionally, this system is the initial SDN-based one for TinyOS devices. In a typical WSN device, sending and receiving signals are handled by the same radio module at any given moment. Therefore, the transmission channel and bandwidth for the data and control layers must be shared. The network has been slowed by this in-band control. Control and data flows need to be segregated. The IEEE 802.15.4 norms have an extremely constrained bandwidth, which causes an average increase in latency of 250 kbps with each additional hop until it hits the controller, claims [60]. The node configuration enables a substantial reduction in latency when the controller is placed immediately on the washbasin. With the help of the cutting-edge idea of tinySDN, it is clear that a WSN may employ a number of controllers, one of which may be situated close to the end node (Figure 8.6).

8.3.3.1 SDN-Enabled Sensor Node

OpenFlow does not address end devices because they are seen as supplementary to SDN. As opposed to end devices, sensing nodes in a WSN produce data packets. As a result, TinySDN can configure a node with SDN capabilities that can serve as both an SDN switch and an SDN endpoint device. To connect and obtain route characteristics, each node with SDN support must find an SDN controller node.

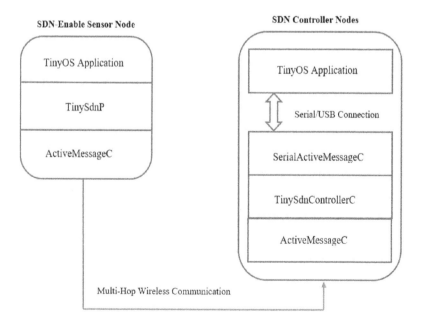

FIGURE 8.6 TinySDN framework.

8.3.3.2 Controller Node for SDN

The following are the two elements of the SDN control system that generate network patterns:

a) Sensor Module: The module that communicates with sensor nodes that support SDN by means of ActiveMessageC and runs on the sensor mote. Between the controller server element and the network, it acts as a bridge. Messages are received from the network via the server-controlling module, which then sends them to the controller server.

b) Network flow and topology data are managed by the control plane logic using the controller server module, which also runs controller applications.

8.3.3.3 Tiny SDN Flows and Actions Specification

Acts are referred to as forward and drop in TinySDN. The forward action sends packets to the following hop as opposed to the elimination action, which tells a packet to be discarded. The two types of flows that TinySDN offers are control flows and data flows. While flow controls are designed for control communication between SDN management nodes and SDN sensor nodes, data flows are meant for application data traffic. Flows are organized using flow entries, which each include four fields. For control flow tables, the identifying field is referred to as "Destination Node ID," whereas it is referred to as "Flow ID" for data flow tables.

An SDN-enabled sensor node's initial task after network starting is to find and join a single SDN controller node. TinySDN use the collections Tree Protocol for this search. This kind of communication is commonly used in multi-hop TinyOS-based architectures because it provides two key advantages: hardware freedom and a high number of SDN controllers. Information collecting about network topology involves two steps: The TinySDN functionality of each sensor node first identifies its neighbors and evaluates the connectivity of those neighbors. In the second phase, a CTP channel or control flow is used to transmit the link state data to the TinySDN controller node.

Services-Centric Networking for Urban Feedback Systems for Large-Scale (SURF) is a type of SDN Architecture. Sensing applications are seen as being more important in WSNs than traditional network applications like the firewall. The difference between a normal SDN and WSNs is acknowledged by the SURF design. It acknowledges that, unlike in typical OpenFlow SDN networks, nodes incorporate switches in addition to one or more application components. The problem of people using a large infrastructure while having varying needs is also addressed [59]. The following features are available on the SURF controller:

a) It creates and oversees network-wide data flows that ensure the necessary QoS level.

b) In terms of sensing and communication quality, the ideal set of nodes whose can meet a distant sensing request are found.

c) It moves flows or applications to accommodate external reallocation requests or modifications in order to dynamically alter data flow and sense application assignments.

The following are the layers of the SURF architecture:

8.3.3.3.1 Applications for Network

This layer manages the network and corporate apps that manage a group of resources that one or more SDN controllers are in charge of managing. Apps running at this plane get events and announcements on the state of the virtual networks (VNs) when many entities use the same virtualized WSN infrastructure, and they can then change their QoS and bandwidth as appropriate.

8.3.3.3.2 SDN Controller

Responding to requests provided across northbound interfaces by users is the controller's primary responsibility. These programs, which are connected to the Network Information Base (NIB), give the networking control system instructions on how to carry out tasks like managing resources and re-optimization, reacting to and producing events as a result of changes in the underpinning network, and analysing a set of forwarding packets guidelines. The southbound API is then used to deploy these rules on the WSN nodes. Making network virtualization possible was one of the main motivations behind the creation of SURF. The SURF SDN concept for control offers four distinct entities within the control system to enable this feature. A few of these are:

a) A network function virtualization (NFV) or virtual network (VN) request's ability to be accommodated by the network is determined by the resource allocator. The function of the resource allocator will cooperate with the virtualizer to distribute the actual resources needed to create the VN if the service request is feasible.

b) The virtualizer: This part is in charge of building a VN agent that represents the equipment using a portion of the NIB's view and actions that the application can employ.

c) Orchestrator: The orchestrator makes sure that the service function chains that carry out network services are flexible in how they combine network operations and may operate independently according to service-based notions.

d) Management: The controller's management plane consists of an operational supporting service, a service manager, a tenant manager, and a physical network management model that keeps track of the physical framework. The tenant manager is responsible for managing the database of tenant functions, the service manager is responsible for managing the database of VN applications and functions, and the network model is responsible for managing the database of network dynamics [61].

8.3.3.3.3 Virtual and Physical Wireless Sensor Networks

The decisions that were taken at the controller layer are implemented at this tier by the virtual or physical network devices, which connect through the southbound interface. WSNs may benefit from the addition of the well-known Constrained Application Protocol (CoAP). It is expected that the controller's southbound plane will support various protocols that have been developed with the infrastructure's constraints in mind. Additionally, a topology manager that modifies the NIB of the SDN control logic is located within this plane of the controller. It also examines the adjustments that must be made to the sensor node's protocol stack for it to communicate with the controller via the southbound API.

8.4   FUTURE RESEARCH AND SCOPE

In order to improve multi-hop communication in SDWN, strategic packet forwarding is examined in this chapter. Modern dissemination strategies are looked into as the relevant literature is reviewed. As an application case, an SDMSN system for habitat monitoring is taken into consideration. The practical use of direction movement in pathless mobility is looked at and evaluated in light of the limitations of current strategies for spreading information. It is crucial to note that this study provides an analytical framework that, at a simplified core level, can be expanded to more fantastical scenarios when mobile nodes move in directions that are associated, like in the case of animals in their natural environment surveillance system, for instance. Animals in the wild occasionally move at different speeds or even halt altogether, but when they have a clear objective in mind, like traveling to a particular location, they normally move continually.

Additional research can be done in the following areas:

- Additional variables, such as storage requirements, transmission delay, residual energy, and contact time, could be taken into account to more accurately reflect real-world network conditions. Different bandwidth requirements for delivery result in harder optimization challenges that are currently unsolved.
- A variety of mobility-related information, including time, place, and social barriers and linkages, can be taken into consideration. It is possible to conduct more research on the frequency and precision of information regarding mobility as well as how to effectively transmit this data to the process of making decisions.
- To characterize animal movements more realistically and for other purposes, it is necessary to conduct more research on actual movement traces. One such analysis can involve estimating directional deviation based on recent or previous data. This research may be useful for broader use cases involving path-unrestricted mobility.

8.5   CONCLUSION

Reviewing the various capabilities provided by an SDN controller makes it clear that the SDN is a perfect replacement for the traditional connectivity paradigm and that it is able to address some of the most prevalent problems in the current connectivity environment, like data overload. Expandable servers and cellular connectivity are ideal applications for the SDN since they simplify managing networks. Conventional SDN models provide a flexible administrator but fail to consider the constraints of a WSN. As a consequence of this, they cannot be quickly implemented in a WSN that possesses only a limited amount of resources. SDN has been found to give richer programmatic interfaces in addition to simpler network management and increased control over network devices.

This benefit comes in addition to the fact that SDN makes network management easier. It is particularly useful for VoIP and multimedia communications when data flow can be molded and managed since it ensures content delivery. The substantial use of WSNs and SDNs has been shown to be the networking technologies of the future. In the next ten years, there will be millions of nodes of wireless sensors connected to the Internet, making WSNs essential components of the IoT. More research into this cutting-edge strategy is recommended because only the SDN can effectively control a design's smooth functionality to address this issue. The security of the whole network is seriously compromised by the SDN controller's centralized design, making a catastrophic network collapse more likely. SDN is an emerging concept in the networking industry. Despite this, there is no doubt that fresh breakthroughs in this field are going to be brought about as a direct result of the growing need for WSN deployments.

REFERENCES

[1] F. Akyildiz and I. H. Kasimoglu. Wireless sensor and actor networks: Research challenges. *Ad-Hoc Network* 2(4): 351–367, 2004.

[2] H. Karl and W. Andreas. *Protocols and architectures for wireless sensor networks.* Wiley, New York, 2007.

[3] A. Gupta and R. K. Jha. A survey of 5G network: Architecture and emerging technologies. *IEEE Access* 3: 1206–1232, 2015.

[4] M. Shafi, A. F. Molisch, P. J. Smith, T. Haustein, P. Zhu, P. De Silva, F. Tufvesson, A. Benjebbour and G. Wunder. 5G: A tutorial overview of standards, trials, challenges, deployment, and practice. *IEEE Journal on Selected Areas Communications* 35(6): 1201–1221, 2017.

[5] A. A. Barakabitze, A. Ahmad, R. Mijumbi and A. Hines. 5G network slicing using SDN and NFV: A survey of taxonomy, architectures and future challenges. *Computer Network* 167: 106984, 2020.

[6] M. Agiwal, A. Roy and N. Saxena. Next generation 5G wireless networks: A comprehensive survey. *IEEE Communication Surveys Tutorials* 18(3): 1617–1655, 2016.

[7] A. Asadi, Q. Wang and V. Mancuso. A survey on device-to-device communication in cellular networks. *IEEE Communications Surveys Tutorials* 16(4): 1801–1819, 2014.

[8] M. N. Tehrani, M. Uysal and H. Yanikomeroglu. Device-to-device communication in 5G cellular networks: Challenges, solutions, and future directions. *IEEE Communication Magazine* 52(5): 86–92, 2014.

[9] U. N. Kar and D. K. Sanyal. An overview of device-to-device communication in cellular networks. *ICT Express* 4(4): 203–208, 2018.

[10] R. Zhang, X. Cheng, L.Yang and B. Jiao. Interference-aware graph based resource sharing for device-to-device communications underlaying cellular networks. In *2013 IEEE Wireless Communications and Networking Conference (WCNC)*. IEEE, 2013, pp. 140–145.

[11] B. A. A. Nunes, M. Mendonca, X. N. Nguyen, K. Obraczka and T. Turletti. A survey of software-defined networking: Past, present, and future of programmable networks. *IEEE Communications Surveys Tutorials* 16(3): 1617–1634, 2014.

[12] S. J. Vaughan-Nichols. Openflow: The next generation of the network. *Computer* 44(8): 13–15, Aug. 2011.

[13] N. McKeown, T. Anderson, H. Balakrishnan, G. Parulkar, L. Peterson, J. Rexford, S. Shenker and J. Turner. Openflow: Enabling innovation in campus networks. *SIGCOMM Computer Communication Review* 38(2): 69–74, 2008.

[14] M. Casado, M. J. Freedman, J. Pettit, J. Luo, N. McKeown and S. Shenker. Ethane: Taking control of the enterprise. *SIGCOMM Computer Communication Review* 37(4): 1–12, 2007.

[15] B. A. A. Nunes, M. Mendonca, X. N. Nguyen, K. Obraczka and T. Turletti. A survey of software-defined networking: Past, present, and future of programmable networks. *IEEE Communications Surveys Tutorials* 16(3): 1617–1634, 2014.

[16] N. McKeown, T. Anderson, H. Balakrishnan, G. Parulkar, L. Peterson, J. Rexford, S. Shenker and J. Turner. Openflow: Enabling innovation in campus networks. *SIGCOMM Computer Communication Review* 38(2): 69–74, 2008.

[17] S. Jain, A. Kumar, S. Mandal, J. Ong, L. Poutievski, A. Singh, S. Venkata, J. Wanderer, J. Zhou, M. Zhu, J. Zolla, U. Hˇolzle, S. Stuart and A. Vahdat. B4: Experience with a globally-deployed software-defined wan. *SIGCOMM Computer Communication Review* 43(4): 3–14, 2013.

[18] D. Kreutz, F. M. V. Ramos, P. E. Veríssimo, C. E. Rothenberg, S. Azodolmolky and S. Uhlig. Software-defined networking: A comprehensive survey. *Proceedings of the IEEE* 103(1): 14–76, 2015.

[19] H. Kim and N. Feamster. Improving network management with software-defined networking. *IEEE Communications Magazine* 51(2): 114–119, 2013.

[20] S. Scott-Hayward, S. Natarajan and S. Sezer. A survey of security in software-defined networks. *IEEE Communications Surveys Tutorials* 18(1): 623–654, 2016.

[21] J. Matias, J. Garay, N. Toledo, J. Unzilla and E. Jacob. Toward an sdnenabled nfv architecture. *IEEE Communications Magazine* 53(4): 187–193, 2015.

[22] A. Kassler, L. Skorin-Kapov, O. Dobrijevic, M. Matijasevic and P. Dely. Towards qoe-driven multimedia service negotiation and path optimization with software-defined networking. In *Software, Telecommunications and Computer Networks (SoftCOM), 2012 20th International Conference on*, September 2012, pp. 1–5.

[23] T. C. Yen and C. S. Su. An sdn-based cloud computing architecture and its mathematical model. In Information Science, Electronics and Electrical Engineering (ISEEE), 2014 International Conference on, volume 3, April 2014, pp. 1728–1731.

[24] T. Parker, J. Johnson, M. Tummala, J. McEachen and J. Scrofani. Dynamic state determination of a software-defined network via dual basis representation. In Signal Processing and Communication Systems (ICSPCS), 2014 8th International Conference on, December 2014, pp. 1–7.

[25] J. R. A. Amazonas, G. Santos-Boada and J. Sol'e-Pareta. A critical review of openflow/sdn-based networks. In 2014 16th International Conference on Transparent Optical Networks (ICTON), July 2014, pp. 1–5.

[26] T. Luo, H. P. Tan and T. Q. S. Quek. Sensor openflow: Enabling software-defined wireless sensor networks. *IEEE Communications Letters* 16(11):1896–1899, 2012.

[27] I. T. Haque and N. Abu-Ghazaleh. Wireless software-defined networking: A survey and taxonomy. *IEEE Communications Surveys Tutorials* PP(99): 1–1, 2016.

[28] N. Gude, T. Koponen, J. Pettit, B. Pfaff, M. Casado, N. McKeown and S. Shenker. Nox: Towards an operating system for networks. *SIGCOMM Computer Communication Review* 38(3): 105–110, 2008.

[29] V. Muthumanikandan and C. Valliyammai. A survey on link failures in software-defined networks. In *2015 Seventh International Conference on Advanced Computing (ICoAC), December 2015*, pp. 1–5.

[30] N. Kapoor and M. Sood. A survey on issues of concern in software-defined networks. In *2015 Third International Conference on Image Information Processing (ICIIP)*, December 2015, pp. 295–300.

[31] B. A. A. Nunes, M. Mendonca, X. N. Nguyen, K. Obraczka and T. Turletti. A survey of software-defined networking: Past, present, and future of programmable networks. *IEEE Communications Surveys Tutorials* 16(3): 1617–1634, 2014.

[32] R. Sherwood, M. Chan, A. Covington, G. Gibb, M. Flajslik, N. Handigol, T.-Y. Huang, P. Kazemian, M. Kobayashi, J. Naous, S. Seetharaman, D. Underhill, T. Yabe, K. Yap, Y. Yiakoumis, H. Zeng, G. Appenzeller, R. Johari, N. McKeown and G. Parulkar. Carving research slices out of your production networks with openflow. *SIGCOMM Computer Communication Review* 40(1): 129–130, 2010.

[33] A. Tootoonchian and Y. Ganjali. Hyperflow: A distributed control plane for openflow. In Proceedings of the 2010 Internet Network Management Conference on Research on Enterprise Networking, INM/WREN'10, Berkeley, CA, 2010, pp. 3–3. USENIX Association.

[34] T. Koponen, M. Casado, N. Gude, J. Stribling, L. Poutievski, M. Zhu, R. Ramanathan, Y. Iwata, H. Inoue, T. Hama, and S. Shenker. Onix: A distributed control platform for large-scale production networks. In *Proceedings of the 9th USENIX Conference on Operating Systems Design and Implementation*, OSDI'10, Berkeley, CA, 2010, pp. 351–364. USENIX Association.

[35] D. Levin, A. Wundsam, B. Heller, N. Handigol and A. Feldmann. Logically centralized?: State distribution trade-offs in software-defined networks. In *Proceedings of the First Workshop on Hot Topics in Software-Defined Networks*. ACM, 2012, pp. 1–6.

[36] S. H. Yeganeh and Y. Ganjali. Kandoo: A framework for efficient and scalable offloading of control applications. In *Proceedings of the First Workshop on Hot Topics in Software-Defined Networks*, HotSDN '12, New York, 2012, pp. 19–24. ACM.SSSSSSS

[37] R. N. B. Rais, M. Mendonca, T. Turletti and K. Obraczka. Towards truly heterogeneous internets: Bridging infrastructure-based and infrastructureless networks. In *2011 Third International Conference on Communication Systems and Networks (COMSNETS 2011)*, January 2011, pp. 1–10.

[38] L. E. Li, Z. M. Mao and J. Rexford. Toward software-defined cellular networks. In *2012 European Workshop on Software-Defined Networking*, October 2012, pp. 7–12.

[39] I. F. Akyildiz, P. Wang and S.-C. Lin. Softair: A software-defined networking architecture for 5g wireless systems. *Computer Networks,* 85, 1–18, 2015.

[40] K.-K. Yap, M. Kobayashi, D. Underhill, S. Seetharaman, P. Kazemian and N. McKeown. The Stanford Openroads deployment. In *Proceedings of the 4th ACM International Workshop on Experimental Evaluation and Characterization*, WINTECH'09, New York, 2009, pp. 59–66. ACM.

[41] L. Suresh, J. Schulz-Zander, R. Merz, A. Feldmann and T. Vazao. Towards programmable enterprise WLANS with ODIN. In *Proceedings of the First Workshop on Hot Topics in Software-Defined Networks*, HotSDN'12, New York, 2012, pp. 115–120. ACM.

[42] F. Yang, V. Gondi, J. O. Hallstrom, K. C. Wang and G. Eidson. Openflowbased load balancing for wireless mesh infrastructure. In *2014 IEEE 11th Consumer Communications and Networking Conference (CCNC)*, Jan 2014, pp. 444–449.

[43] A. Detti, C. Pisa, S. Salsano and N. Blefari-Melazzi. Wireless mesh software-defined networks (wmsdn). In *2013 IEEE 9th International Conference on Wireless and Mobile Computing, Networking and Communications* (WiMob), October 2013, pp. 89–95.

[44] M. Bansal, J. Mehlman, S. Katti and P. Levis. Openradio: A programmable wireless dataplane. In *Proceedings of the First Workshop on Hot Topics in Software-Defined Networks*, HotSDN '12, New York, 2012, pp. 109–114. ACM.

[45] K.-K. Yap, M. Kobayashi, R. Sherwood, T.-Y. Huang, M. Chan, N. Handigol and N. McKeown. Openroads: Empowering research in mobile networks. *SIGCOMM Computer Communication Review* 40(1): 125–126, 2010.

[46] M. Yang, M. Li, D. Jin, L. Su, S. Ma and L. Zeng. Openran: A software-defined ran architecture via virtualization. In *Proceedings of the ACM SIGCOMM 2013 Conference on SIGCOMM*, SIGCOMM'13, New York, 2013, pp. 549–550. ACM.

[47] K. Sohraby, D. Minoli and T. Znati. *Wireless sensor networks: Technology, protocols, and applications.* John Wiley & Sons, 2007.

[48] I. F. Akyildiz, W. Su, Y. Sankarasubramaniam and E. Cayirci. Wireless sensor networks: A survey. *Computer Networking* 38(4): 393–422, 2002.

[49] C. C. Sobin, V. Raychoudhury, G. Marfia and A. Singla. A survey of routing and data dissemination in delay tolerant networks. *Journal of Network and Computer Applications* 67: 128–146, 2016.

[50] S.-Y. Ni, Y.-C. Tseng, Y.-S. Chen and J.-P. Sheu. The broadcast storm problem in a mobile ad hoc network. In *Proceedings of the 5th Annual ACM/IEEE International Conference on Mobile Computing and Networking*, MobiCom '99, New York, 1999, pp. 151–162. ACM.

[51] P. Chaudhary, S. Goel, P. Jain, M. Singh, P. K. Aggarwal and Anupam. The astounding relationship: Middleware, frameworks, and API. In *2021 9th International Conference on Reliability, Infocom Technologies and Optimization (Trends and Future Directions) (ICRITO)*, 2021, pp. 1–4, https://doi.org/10.1109/ICRITO51393.2021.9596088.

[52] Y. Cao, N. Wang, Z. Sun and H. Cruickshank. A reliable and efficient encounter-based routing framework for delay/disruption tolerant networks. *IEEE Sensors Journal* 15(7): 4004–4018, 2015.

[53] S. Mishra, A. Shukla, S. Arora, H. Kathuria and M. Singh. Controlling weather dependent tasks using random forest algorithm. In *2020 Third International Conference on Advances in Electronics, Computers and Communications (ICAECC)*, 2020, pp. 1–8, https://doi.org/10.1109/ICAECC50550.2020.9339508.

[54] A. Mahmud and R. Rahmani. Exploitation of OpenFlow in wireless sensor networks. In *Proceedings of 2011 International Conference on Computer Science and Network Technology*, Harbin, 2011, pp. 594–600.

[55] T. Luo, H. P. Tan and T. Q. S. Quek. Sensor openflow: Enabling software-defined wireless sensor networks. *IEEE Communications Letters* 16(11): 1896–1899, 2012.

[56] L. Galluccio, S. Milardo, G. Morabito and S. Palazzo. SDN-WISE: Design, prototyping and experimentation of a stateful SDN solution for WIreless SEnsor networks. In *2015 IEEE Conference on Computer Communications (INFOCOM)*, Kowloon, 2015, pp. 513–521.

[57] A. De Gante, M. Aslan and A. Matrawy. Smart wireless sensor network management based on software-defined networking. In *2014 27th Biennial Symposium on Communications (QBSC)*, Kingston, ON, 2014, pp. 71–75.

[58] H. Garg, M. Singh, V. Sharma and M. Agarwal. Decentralized Application (DAPP) to enable E-voting system using Blockchain Technology. In *2022 Second International Conference on Computer Science, Engineering and Applications (ICCSEA)*, Gunupur, India, 2022, pp. 1–6, https://doi.org/10.1109/ICCSEA54677.2022.9936413.

[59] A. Sharma, M. Singh, M. Gupta, N. Sukhija, and P. K. Aggarwal. IoT and blockchain technology in 5G smart healthcare. *Blockchain Applications for Healthcare Informatics*, 1: 137–161, 2022. https://doi.org/10.1016/b978-0-323-90615-9.00004-9

[60] M. Singh, N. Sukhija, A. Sharma, M. Gupta and P. K. Aggarwal. Security and privacy requirements for IoMT-based smart healthcare system. *Big Data Analysis for Green Computing*, 1: 17–37, 2021.

[61] B. Trevizan de Oliveira, L. Batista Gabriel and C. Borges Margi. TinySDN: Enabling multiple controllers for software-defined wireless sensor networks. *IEEE Latin America Transactions* 13(11): 3690–3696, 2015.

9 Performance Analysis of Load Balancing Algorithm with Cloud Computing

A Survey

Manish Bhardwaj, Vishal Jain, Jyoti Sharma, and Alok Mishra

9.1 INTRODUCTION

Cloud computing services have become commonplace because of the widespread availability of the Internet. According to NIST, using cloud computing, you can access a shared pool of computer resources such as networks, servers, storage, and applications whenever and wherever you need them. They can be assigned and released with minimum management or service provider involvement [1]. As a cloud-based service provider (CSP), it offers three services: SaaS, PaaS, and Infrastructure (IaaS). Users have access to a variety of on-demand physical and virtual resources.

Virtualization is used in cloud computing to provide access to the resource [2]. Virtualization is a way to simulate real-world machines without having to buy them. It is possible to run apps on a virtual machine as if they were running on a real machine. Virtualization mimics the capabilities of a real computer [3]. Virtualization enables us to scale down the number of servers we need to run, thereby saving money on both space and power. The virtualization technique allows for quick scaling of cloud resources [4].

Users have instant access to the resources they need in the cloud since they are dynamically allocated. As the number of users grows, so does the amount of available resources [5].

The difficulty of load balancing arises when cloud resources are allocated to customers on demand. Some nodes in the cloud will be overworked, while others will be underworked if the workload is not divided adequately. Users will experience service interruptions if resources offered by the cloud are not allocated efficiently [6].

A system bottleneck might be caused by an unbalanced load. The allocation of resources must be done in an effective manner in order to maximize usage and avoid delays in providing service [7–10].

It is possible to group the system's nodes into clusters, and each cluster performs the work of load balancing independently. There will be nodes assigned to each cluster that will be responsible for distributing the load [11–13]. A hierarchical structure can be used for this.

DOI: 10.1201/9781003432869-9

A variety of load-balancing techniques have been used to distribute the workload across the available machines in a cloud environment. Load-balancing techniques like Round Robin, Throttled, Min-Min, and Min-Max, as well as behavior-based approaches like Honey Bee and Ant Colony load balancing, are just a few examples [14]. A single load-balancing algorithm is insufficient for effective load balancing. As a result, a load-balancing algorithm that incorporates the best aspects of multiple algorithms is necessary.

Computing resources have been more widely available thanks to the Internet's popularity in recent years, allowing for the development of cloud computing [15]. As a result, cloud computing forces traditional service providers to have two distinct methods of delivering services. These companies provide both the infrastructure and the services. Arrangement of cloud platforms and resources leased by infrastructure providers according to consumption. In order to provide customers, service providers rely on resources provided by the infrastructure providers [16]. Cloud computing has tempted the likes of Google, Amazon, and Microsoft, and is now seen as having a significant impact on today's IT firms.

9.2   CLOUD COMPUTING OVERVIEW

Cloud computing is a technique that uses the Internet and central remote servers to keep applications and data running on a shared infrastructure. Without having to install anything, cloud computing allows users to access their personal files from any computer with an Internet connection [17]. Because of the centralization of storage, memory, computation, and bandwidth, this technology allows for inefficient computing.

Instead of running on a local computer, such as a laptop, tablet, or smartphone, a software or application is hosted on a network of connected servers. A user connects to a server, just like in the conservative client-server model, to carry out a task [18]. Because of the notion of virtualization, computation in the cloud can be distributed over multiple connected computers.

One or more physical servers can be configured and separated into numerous unconnected "virtual servers," all of which work independently and appear to the user as a single physical device, using virtualization [19].

The end user is unaffected by the ups and downs of these virtual servers because they do not have a physical structure [20]. End-user and operator benefits include broad access to many devices, resource pooling, on-demand service, fast flexibility, and service surveying capacity as a result of coarse computing resources.

As a method of disseminating computer resources, cloud computing allows anybody with an Internet connection and an interest in virtualized hardware and software to access shared resources. Involved in this are virtualized distributed computing, networking, web services, and web-developed software.

In today's world, the concept of cloud computing has piqued the interest of consumers in parallel, distributed, and virtualized computing architectures [21]. As a cost-effective and convenient method of accessing IT resources, it looks to be widely used. Because of virtualization in cloud computing, a large number of users with a wide range of computational requirements can share a single physical infrastructure. Concerns about data security are on the rise due to the rapid expansion of cloud computing services. Cloud computing adoption has been stymied by a lack of security [22].

9.3 BASICS OF LOAD BALANCING IN CLOUD COMPUTING

The distribution of a system's load among its many resources is known as load balancing [2]. As a result, in a cloud-based design, the workload must be divided across the resources so that each resource performs roughly the same amount of work at any one moment. Some approaches for balancing requests are a must in order to give a rapid response solution for requests [23]. Distributing work over a number of servers and resources is how Cloud Load Balancers keep the web flowing smoothly. They increase productivity, reduce response time, and avoid overload.

Some algorithms aim to maximize output, while others aim to minimize response time, while still, others aim to maximize resource utilization, while others aim to strike a balance between all of these measures [24]. In a cloud computing context, multiple load-balancing methods operate inside the framework shown in Figure 9.1.

The term "load balancing" refers to the practice of allocating a larger portion of a system's processing load to a smaller number of nodes in order to improve overall system performance. A distributed system environment is one in which load is transferred to other nodes in order to increase both the usage of resources and the response time of a job.

The ideal load-balancing method should ensure that no node is overloaded or under loaded [25]. However, in a cloud computing context, the selection of a load

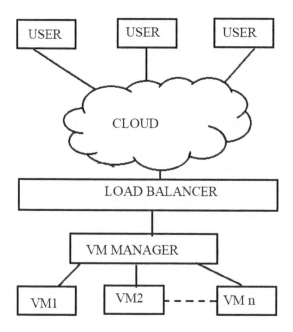

FIGURE 9.1   Basic layered architecture of load balancing.

balancing technique is more difficult because of additional constraints, such as security, dependability, throughput, and so on.

It is therefore essential to increase job response time by dispersing the system's overall load in a cloud computing environment using a load-balancing technique. In addition, the algorithm must make certain that no one node is overloaded [26].

Using a load balancer cooperatively or non-cooperatively is one of two options. Nodes work together in a cooperative network to achieve the shared aim of reducing response time [27]. For the sake of improving the reaction time of local tasks, tasks are conducted independently in noncooperative mode.

Static and dynamic load-balancing algorithms are the two most common types of load balancing algorithms. In the process of distributing the load, a static load balancing algorithm makes no consideration for the prior state or activity of a node [28].

A dynamic load balancing method, on the other hand, keeps track of a node's past state as it distributes the load. Non-distributed and distributed implementations of the dynamic load balancing algorithm are available [29]. The advantage of dynamic load balancing is that if any node fails, it will not stop the system; rather, it will just impair the performance of the entire system. There are more messages in a distributed system than in a non-distributed setting since the nodes may communicate with one another.

As a result, the quantity of messages in the network increases as a result of the necessity to select a suitable server in real-time. Policies are used by dynamic load balancers to keep track of newly updated information [30].

9.3.1 Measurement Parameter for Load Balancing

To determine whether or not a load-balancing strategy is effective, certain measuring factors must be taken into consideration.

Time of Response: If the user requests something and waits for an answer, that is what is known as the response time.

Fault tolerance: The ability of the load-balancing algorithm to allow the system to work in certain failure situations of the system.

Throughput: The amount of work that can be completed in a particular period is referred to as the throughput.

Utilization: Utilization of various resources is monitored with the help of this tool.

Output: In terms of performance, accuracy, cost, and speed are all taken into account while evaluating an algorithm.

Scalability: The algorithm's ability to scale up or down in response to changing conditions is referred to as scalability.

9.3.2 Methods for Distributing Traffic Among Multiple Servers

Load-balancing algorithms are numerous. Based on the current condition of the system, load balancing methods are divided into two categories:

Fixed algorithm: When working in a steady and homogeneous environment, a Static Algorithm is ideal.

Randomize Algorithm: When working in a diverse setting, Dynamic Algorithms can be a useful tool.

Static algorithms work best in contexts with high levels of uniformity and consistency. Static algorithms, on the other hand, are rigid and unable to adapt to changes in the attributes [31]. Static load-balancing techniques do not check the condition and functionality of the node in previous tasks when assigning tasks to the nodes. Static Algorithms include:

i) **Load Balancing Round Robin Algorithm**
   This algorithm allocates a set amount of quantum time to each task. In a circular approach, it allots jobs to all of the nodes. There is no famine since processors are assigned in a circular order [32]. When the burden is evenly distributed among the processes, this technique delivers a faster response time. But there may be instances where certain nodes are overloaded, while others stay idle and underutilized. Figure 9.2 shows the pattern followed in the method of round robin process.

ii) **Algorithm for Load Balancing using MIN-MIN**
   There is a list of tasks and the shortest possible completion time is determined for each of the available nodes. The machine is given a task with a short completion time. As a result, the algorithm's name is min-min. Update the machine's list and running time. When there are more than a few tiny tasks, it works well [33].

iii) **Load Balancing Algorithm using MIN-MAX**
   There is a list of tasks and the shortest possible completion time is determined for each of the available nodes. The machine is given a task that must be completed in the shortest amount of time. As a result, the algorithm's name is min-max. Refresh the machine's list and running time [8].

In dynamic and heterogeneous situations, dynamic algorithms deliver better results. It's easier to customize these algorithms. Algorithms that can adapt to changing input parameters are known as dynamic algorithms. These algorithms, on the other

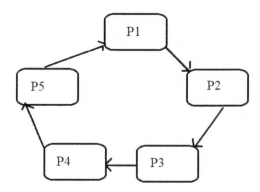

FIGURE 9.2   Pattern of round Robin method.

hand, are more difficult to understand. Due to this, the system's performance will be improved as tasks are prioritized according to their present status, which is a major benefit. [9] There are two ways to build dynamic algorithms:

All of the nodes in the system communicate with one another, and a load-balancing algorithm is run across them all. All of the nodes share the burden of load balancing. Cooperative or non-cooperative interactions among nodes are possible [34]. Even if a node in the system fails, the system will continue to function. In a distributed cooperative system, every node collaborates [35]. There is no cooperation among the nodes in a non-cooperative distributed system [36].

Centralized or semi-distributed non-distributed systems are both possible. Central node in a centralized system is responsible for balancing the system's workload. They all communicate with this core node. The functionality will be halted if the central node fails. In the event of a failure, it will be difficult to recover [37]. Clusters of nodes are formed in a semi-distributed system. It is the core node of each cluster that distributes the system's load. Failure of the cluster's single central node will put an end to its operation [38]. Load balancing is handled by multiple central nodes. As a result, load balancing is more precise [39].

9.3.3 Honey Bee Algorithm

Based on the behavior of honey bees in finding food, this algorithm was created. The honey bees return to the hive to tell the colony about the new food sources they've discovered. They accomplish this by moving together as a group [40]. To describe this dance, it's known as "waggle dancing." In order to let other bees know exactly where the food supply is, they do a waggle dance. Waggle dances are a way for bees to communicate information about the quality, quantity, and distance of the food supply from their colony.

9.3.4 Throttled Balancing Algorithm

For virtual machines, throttled load balancing techniques are the ideal choice. The list of all virtual machines in the system is kept up to date by the load balancer. The indexing table is scanned whenever a request is received by the load balancer [41]. Whenever a virtual machine becomes available, the work is then assigned to that particular virtual machine for execution. Each time a resource is allocated or de-allocated, the load balancer updates the indexing table. Figure 9.3 shows the complete structure of throttled balancing process in the form of request and response.

9.3.5 Equally Spread Current Execution Algorithm

A load balancer keeps track of all of the virtual computers and jobs that are running on them. The list of VMs is scanned by the load balancer when it receives a request. VMs that can handle the client's request are allocated to those VMs when they are found. There is an equitable distribution of the load among all VMs using this approach.

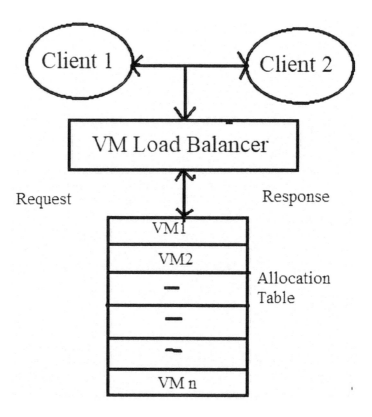

FIGURE 9.3   Structure of throttled balancing.

9.3.6   ALGORITHM BASED ON ANT COLONY OPTIMIZATION

An ant's natural instinct is to take the quickest route to food. This method is based on genuine ant behavior. An ant's movement begins when a request is made. Ants constantly check to see if the node is under or overloaded. If the ant encounters an overburdened node, it returns to its nest. And if an ant discovers a node that is underutilized, it moves on. To gather data from various nodes, ant activity is exploited in this way [42].

9.3.7   RANDOMLY BIASED SAMPLING

Random sampling of the system domain is used to balance the load in this approach. To visualize the system, a virtual graph is created. An in-degree is an indicator of the amount of resources available to each of the nodes of a directed graph. Nodes with at least one degree of in-degree are assigned jobs by the load balancer. When a job is done, the node's in-degree is incremented and decremented, correspondingly. Using a technique known as random sampling, this can be accomplished [43].

9.3.8 Modified Algorithm for Balancing the Load

This method is concerned with intelligently allocating jobs to the available VMs. This algorithm keeps track of the number of virtual machines (VMs) and their current status (BUSY/AVAILABLE). First, this algorithm selects a VM based on the VM's current state. It is decided which VM should be used for the request. The return value is −1 if the VM isn't readily available for use. According to the state of VM [44] when new requests come in, the previous VM index + 1 is selected.

9.3.9 Load Balancing in Hierarchical Format

Load-balancing decisions are made at several levels in Hierarchical Load Balancing. The parent node is in charge of keeping the other nodes in check [45]. Load distribution is the responsibility of the parent node. Even in a diverse setting, hierarchical load balancing can be applied [46]. Hierarchical load balancing can also benefit from Cluster [47–50]. Clustering is the process of putting together groupings of objects that are similar in nature. The logical grouping of VMs is based on their shared properties [51–53]. VMs have reached their highest level yet. Level 1 receives jobs and routes them to level 2 based on the resources that each job requires (Table 9.1). VM is selected and the job is assigned to a VM for execution by Level 2. Figure 9.4 shows the hierarchical structure of the load-balancing method.

9.4 LOAD-BALANCING COMPARISON

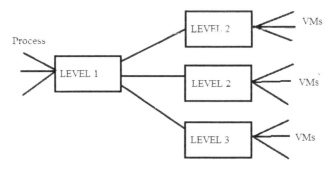

FIGURE 9.4 Structure of hierarchical balancing.

TABLE 9.1

Advantages and Disadvantages of Load Balancing Algorithms

Name of Algorithm	Disadvantage	Advantage
Load balancing using round robin	1. A time slice is used to fix each node. 2. It isn't scalable or adaptable, either. 3. It's possible that some nodes are under tremendous stress, while others are completely idle. 4. The prior allocation of a virtual machine is not saved. 5. There must be some sort of pre-emption.	1. Fairness and simplicity are the primary goals of this method. 2. It's a cyclical process. 3. When the workload is evenly distributed, the reaction time is quick. 4. There is no starvation in our country.
Load Balancing using MIN-MAX	1. Chooses the work that will take the longest to complete. 2. As a result, people are starving to death. The larger chores will take precedence over the minor ones. 3. Uneven distribution of weight.	1. The algorithm is straightforward. 2. It concurrently does a number of smaller tasks.
Load Balancing using MIN-MIN	1. Choose the assignment that can be completed in the shortest amount of time possible. 2. Login engagement of single process. Priority will be given to smaller jobs, which will be completed before larger ones. 3. Load-balancing issues 4. Doesn't take into account the current demand on the resource.	1. Because of its simplicity and speed. 2. It is best suited for modest tasks.
Load Balancing using Throttled	1. To begin, it scans over the whole list of virtual machines (VMs). 2. VM's current load is not taken into account.	1. Each VM's state is recorded in the list of VMs. 2. Excellent performance 3. Better utilization of resources.
Load Balancing using Honeybee Behavior	1. The overall throughput will not be impacted by an increase in resources.	1. Algorithm inspired by nature that self-organizes. 2. Increasing the size of the system will lead to better performance. 3. In a multi-cultural setting, this product is ideal.

9.5   CONCLUSION

Users of cloud computing can access scalable, virtualized, and distributed hardware and software resources via the Internet. One of the most critical issues in cloud computing is load balancing. All nodes in the cloud are equitably burdened with work, thanks to this method. The output of this research can reach a high level of customer satisfaction and resource utilization through efficient load balancing. Thus, the system's overall performance and resource utilization will be enhanced as a result. As a result of efficient load balancing, energy consumption, and carbon emissions can be reduced even more. The performance of the system will be improved by using a hierarchical structure.

REFERENCES

[1] M. Armbrust, A. Fox, R. Griffith, A. D. Joseph, R. Katz, A. Konwinski, and G. Lee et al. "A View of Cloud Computing." *Communications of the ACM* Vol. 53, no. 4 (2010): 50–58.

[2] A. Rao, K. Lakshminarayanan, S. Surana, R. Karp, and I. Stoica. "Load Balancing in Structured P2P Systems." In: Kaashoek, M.F., Stoica, I. (eds) *Peer-to-Peer Systems II*, pp. 68–79. Springer, Berlin Heidelberg, 2003.https://doi.org/10.1007/978-3-540-45172-3_6

[3] N. Ajith Singh, and M. Hemalatha. "An Approach on Semi Distributed Load Balancing Algorithm for Cloud Computing Systems." *International Journal of Computer Applications* Vol. 56, no. 12 (2012): 1–21.

[4] H. Mehta, P. Kanungo, and M. Chandwani. "Decentralized Content Aware Load Balancing Algorithm for Distributed Computing Environments." In *Proceedings of the International Conference & Workshop on Emerging Trends in Technology*, pp. 370–375. ACM, 2011.

[5] A. M. Nakai, E. Madeira, and L. E. Buzato. "Load Balancing for Internet Distributed Services Using Limited Redirection Rates." In *Dependable Computing (LADC), 2011 5th Latin-American Symposium on*, pp. 156–165. IEEE, 2011.

[6] Y. Lu, Q. Xie, G. Kliot, A. Geller, J. R. Larus, and A. Greenberg. "JoinIdle-Queue: A Novel Load Balancing Algorithm for Dynamically Scalable Web Services." *Performance Evaluation* Vol. 68, no. 11 (2011): 1056–1071.

[7] X. Liu, L. Pan, C.-J. Wang, and J.-Y. Xie. "A Lock-Free Solution for Load Balancing in Multi-Core Environment." In *Intelligent Systems and Applications (ISA), 2011 3rd International Workshop on*, pp. 1–4. IEEE, 2011.

[8] J. Hu, J. Gu, G. Sun, and T. Zhao. "A Scheduling Strategy on Load Balancing of Virtual Machine Resources in Cloud Computing Environment." In *Parallel Architectures, Algorithms and Programming (PAAP), 2010 Third International Symposium on*, pp. 89–96. IEEE, 2010.

[9] A. Bhadani, and S. Chaudhary. "Performance Evaluation of Web Servers Using Central Load Balancing Policy Over Virtual Machines on Cloud." In *Proceedings of the Third Annual ACM Bangalore Conference*, p. 16. ACM, 2010.

[10] H. Liu, S. Liu, X. Meng, C. Yang, and Y. Zhang. "Lbvs: A Load Balancing Strategy for Virtual Storage." In *Service Sciences (ICSS), 2010 International Conference on*, pp. 257–262. IEEE, 2010.

[11] J. Wu, S. A. Haider, M. Bhardwaj, A. Sharma, and P. Singhal. "Blockchain-Based Data Audit Mechanism for Integrity over Big Data Environments." *Security and Communication Networks* Vol. 2022, (2022): Article ID 8165653, 9 pages.

[12] M. Raveret Richter. "Social Wasp (Hymenoptera: Vespidae) Foraging Behavior." *Annual Review of Entomology* Vol. 45, no. 1 (2000): 121–150.

[13] O. A. Rahmeh, P. Johnson, and A. Taleb-Bendiab. "A Dynamic Biased Random Sampling Scheme for Scalable and Reliable Grid Networks." *INFOCOMP Journal of Computer Science* Vol. 7, no. 4 (2008): 1–10.

[14] N. S. Pourush, and M. Bhardwaj. "Enhanced Privacy-Preserving Multi-Keyword Ranked Search over Encrypted Cloud Data." *American Journal of Networks and Communications* Vol. 4, no. 3 (2015): 25–31.

[15] Z. Zhang, and X. Zhang. "A Load Balancing Mechanism Based on Ant Colony and Complex Network Theory in Open Cloud Computing Federation." In *Industrial Mechatronics and Automation (ICIMA), 2010 2nd International Conference on*, Vol. 2, pp. 240–243. IEEE, 2010.

[16] S.-C. Wang, K.-Q. Yan, W.-P. Liao, and S.-S. Wang. "Towards a Load Balancing in a Three-Level Cloud Computing Network." In *Computer Science and Information Technology (ICCSIT), 2010 3rd IEEE International Conference on*, Vol. 1, pp. 108–113. IEEE, 2010.

[17] A. Kumar, S. Rohilla, and M. Bhardwaj. "Analysis of Cloud Computing Load Balancing Algorithms." *International Journal of Computer Sciences and Engineering* Vol. 7 (2019): 359–362.

[18] R. Stanojević, and R. Shorten. "Load Balancing Vs. Distributed Rate Limiting: An Unifying Framework for Cloud Control." In *Communications, 2009. ICC'09. IEEE International Conference on*, pp. 1–6. IEEE, 2009.

[19] Y. Zhao, and W. Huang. "Adaptive Distributed Load Balancing Algorithm Based on Live Migration of Virtual Machines in Cloud." In *INC, IMS and IDC, 2009. NCM'09. Fifth International Joint Conference on*, pp. 170–175. IEEE, 2009.

[20] A. Singh, M. Korupolu, and D. Mohapatra. "Server-Storage Virtualization: Integration and Load Balancing in Data Centers." In *Proceedings of the 2008 ACM/IEEE conference on Supercomputing*, p. 53. IEEE Press, 2008.

[21] Nidhi Jain, and I. Chana. "Cloud Load Balancing Techniques: A Step Towards Green Computing." *IJCSI International Journal of Computer Science Issues* Vol. 9, no. 1 (2012): 238–246.

[22] R. P. Padhy. "Load Balancing in Cloud Computing Systems." PhD diss., National Institute of Technology, Rourkela, 2011.

[23] M. Bhardwaj. "7 Research on IoT Governance, Security, and Privacy Issues of Internet of Things." *Privacy Vulnerabilities and Data Security Challenges in the IoT* Vol. 115 (2020): 115–128.

[24] R. D. Williams. "Performance of Dynamic Load Balancing Algorithms for Unstructured Mesh Calculations." *Concurrency: Practice and Experience* Vol. 3, no. 5 (1991): 457–481.

[25] M. Shreedhar, and G. Varghese. "Efficient Fair Queuing Using Deficit RoundRobin." *Networking, IEEE/ACM Transactions on* Vol. 4, no. 3 (1996): 375–385.

[26] M.-Y. Wu, W. Shu, and H. Zhang. "Segmented Min-Min: A Static Mapping Algorithm for Meta-Tasks on Heterogeneous Computing Systems." In *HCW*, p. 375. IEEE, 2000.

[27] A. Sharma, A. Tyagi, and M. Bhardwaj. "Analysis of Techniques and Attacking Pattern in Cyber Security Approach: A Survey." *International Journal of Health Sciences* Vol. 6, no. S2 (2022): 13779–13798. https://doi.org/10.53730/ijhs.v6nS2.8625

[28] T. Kokilavani, and D.I. George Amalarethinam. "Load Balanced Min-Min Algorithm for Static Meta-Task Scheduling in Grid Computing." *International Journal of Computer Applications* Vol. 20, no. 2 (2011): 43–49.

[29] G. Ritchie, and J. Levine. *A Fast Effective Local Search for Scheduling Independent Jobs in Heterogeneous Computing Environments*. Center for Intelligent Systems and their Applications School of Informatics University of Edinburg.

[30] S. Nitika, and G. Raj. "Comparative Analysis of Load Balancing Algorithms in Cloud Computing." *International Journal of Advanced Research in Computer Engineering & Technology (IJARCET)* Vol. 1, no. 3 (2012): 120.

[31] Q. Zhang, L. Cheng, and R. Boutaba. "Cloud Computing: State-Of-The-Art and Research Challenges." *Journal of Internet Services and Applications* Vol. 1, no. 1 (2010): 7–18.

[32] S. Nitika, and G. Raj. "Comparative Analysis of Load Balancing Algorithms in Cloud Computing." *International Journal of Advanced Research in Computer Engineering and Technology* Vol 1, no. 3 (May 2012).

[33] Z. Chaczko, V. Mahadevan, S. Aslanazadeh, and Christopher, *IPCSIT* Vol. 14, IACSIT Press, Singapore, 2011.

[34] C.-L. Hung, H.-H. Wang, and Y.- C. Hu. "Efficient Load Balancing Algorithm for Cloud Computing Network." *International conference on information science and technology* (IST 2012), 2012, 28–30.

[35] Y. Sahu and M. K. Pateriya. "Cloud Computing Overview and Load Balancing Algorithms." *Internal Journal of Computer Application* Vol. 65, no. 24 (2013): 101–108.

[36] N. Sran and N. Kaur. "Comparative Analysis of Existing Load Balancing Techniques in Cloud Computing." *International Journal of Engineering Science Invention* Vol. 2, no. 1 (2013): 1–4.

[37] F. Mohammadi, S. Jamali, and M. Bekravi. "Survey on Job Scheduling Algorithms in Cloud Computing." *International Journal of Emerging Trends & Technology in Computer Science (IJETTCS)* Vol. 3, no. 2 (March–April 2014): 151–154.

[38] B. Yuce, M. S. Packianather, E. Mastrocinque, D. T. Pham, and A. Lambiase. "Honey Bees Inspired Optimization Method: The Bees Algorithm." *Insects* Vol. 4, no. 4 (2013 Nov 6): 646–662. doi: 10.3390/insects4040646. PMID: 26462528; PMCID: PMC4553508 2013.

[39] B. Sahoo, S. Mohapatra, and S. K. Jena. "A Genetic Algorithm Based Dynamic Load Balancing Scheme for Heterogeneous Distributed Systems." In *Proceedings of the International Conference on Parallel and Distributed Processing Techniques and Applications*, PDPTA 2008, Las Vegas, Nevada, USA, 14–17 July 2008, 2 Volumes. CSREA Press, 2008.

[40] K. Dasguptaa, B. Mandalb, P. Duttac, J. K. Mondald, S. Dame. "A Genetic Algorithm (GA) based Load Balancing Strategy for Cloud Computing." In *International Conference on Computational Intelligence: Modeling Techniques and Applications (CIMTA)*, Vol. 10, 2013.

[41] S. V. Pius and T. S. Shilpa "Survey on Load Balancing in Cloud Computing." In *International Conference on Computing, Communication and Energy Systems (ICCCES2014)*.

[42] J. Uma, V. Ramasamy, and A. Kaleeswaran. "Load Balancing Algorithms in Cloud Computing Environment - A Methodical Comparison." *International Journal of Advanced Research in Computer Engineering & Technology (IJARCET)* Vol. 3, no. 2 (February 2014): 79–82.

[43] B. Mondala, K. Dasgupta, and P. Dutta. "Load Balancing in Cloud Computing using Stochastic Hill Climbing - A Soft Computing Approach." *Procedia Technology* Vol. 4 (2012): 783–789. doi: 10.1016/j.protcy.2012.05.128 C3IT-2012.

[44] A. Y. Zomaya. and Y.-H. Teh "Observations on Using Genetic Algorithms for Dynamic Load Balancing." *IEEE Transactions on Parallel and Distributed Systems* Vol. 12, no. 9 (September 2001): 899–911.

[45] N. S. Raghava and D. Singh. "Comparative Study on Load Balancing Techniques in Cloud Computing." *Open Journal of Mobile Computing and Cloud Computing* Vol. 1, no. 1 (August 2014): 18–25.

[46] B. Suri. "Implementing Ant Colony Optimization for Test Case Selection and Prioritization." *International Journal on Computer Science and Engineering (IJCSE)* Vol. 3, no. 5, 1–7.

[47] Shiny. "Load Balancing in Cloud Computing: A Review." *IOSR Journal of Computer Engineering (IOSR -JCE)* Vol. 15, no. 2 (November–December 2013): 22–29.

[48] M. Ahmed, A. Sina, R. Chowdhury, M. Ahmed, and M. H. Rafee. "An Advanced Survey on Cloud Computing and State-of-the-art Research Issues." *IJCSI International Journal of Computer Science Issues* Vol. 9, no. 1 (January 2012): 201–207.

[49] T. Desai, and J. Prajapati. "A Survey of Various Load Balancing Techniques and Challenges in Cloud Computing." *International Journal of Scientific & Technology Research* Vol. 2, no. 11 (November 2013): 158–161.

[50] O. M. Elzeki, and M. Z. Reshad. "Improved Max-Min Algorithm in Cloud Computing." *International Journal of Computer Applications* Vol. 50, no. 12 (July 2012): 22–27.

[51] Z. Chaczko, V. Mahadevan, S. Aslanzadeh, and C. Mcdermid. "Availabity and Load Balancing in Cloud Computing." In *International Conference on Computer and Software Modeling*, IPCSIT, Vol. 14, IACSIT Press, Singapore 2011.

[52] R. K. Mondal, E. Nandi, and D. Sarddar. "Load Balancing Scheduling with Shortest Load First." *International Journal of Grid and Distributed Computing* Vol. 8, no. 4 (2015): 171–178.

[53] R. K. Mondal, and D. Sarddar. "Load Balancing with Task Subtraction of Same Nodes." *International Journal of Computer Science and Information Technology Research* Vol. 3, no. 4 (October–December 2015): 162–166.

10 Comprehensive Survey of Implementing Multiple Controllers in a Software-Defined Network (SDN)

*K. Bavani, P. Deepalakshmi,
and Ezhil Kalaimannan*

10.1 INTRODUCTION

The demand for internet-based services are the platforms for Internet of Things [1–3] is only going up, straining old networks to their breaking point. The network sector is forced to alter its traditional design due to the unprecedented rapid expansion of these internet services. The Software-Defined Network (SDN) has been introduced [4] by Open Networking Foundation (ONF). SDN comes with a complete programmability system and the operations done in this network are completely automated. SDN has emerged as a transformative technology that has redefined the way we approach and manage computer networks. In the realm of networking, where agility, scalability, and adaptability are paramount, SDN offers a revolutionary approach that deviates from traditional network architectures. SDN fundamentally changes how we control and manage networks by separating the control plane from the data plane. In traditional networks, network devices such as routers and switches handle both control and data forwarding. SDN introduces the concept of centralized control, where a dedicated SDN controller becomes the nerve center of the network. This separation enhances network programmability and dynamic adaptability. At the core of SDN lies the SDN controller, which acts as the orchestrator of network traffic. It communicates with network devices through southbound APIs, such as OpenFlow, to convey instructions regarding traffic routing and forwarding. The controller maintains a comprehensive view of the network topology and uses this information to make real-time decisions, optimizing traffic flow and ensuring efficient resource utilization.

The introduction of northbound APIs allows applications and services to interact with the SDN controller. This programmability empowers organizations to create custom network applications tailored to their specific requirements. Whether it's implementing Quality of Service (QoS) policies, traffic optimization, or security measures, SDN's northbound APIs provide the flexibility to customize the network to suit the needs of the applications running on it. SDN's network abstraction simplifies network management by providing a unified view of the infrastructure, abstracting the underlying complexity of individual network devices. This abstraction layer streamlines network administration, making it more intuitive and efficient. Network administrators can now define policies and configurations in software, alleviating the need for manual device-by-device configuration. The dynamism of SDN is a hallmark feature. Network adaptation in real-time to changing conditions, such as network congestion or traffic spikes, is a reality. The SDN controller can respond promptly by rerouting traffic or adjusting network policies, ensuring optimal network performance and responsiveness to application demands. Moreover, security in SDN benefits from fine-grained control over traffic flows. The control plane enables the implementation of security policies that filter, isolate, or inspect traffic for potential threats. In the face of security events or breaches, SDN can swiftly implement access controls and firewall rules, enhancing network security. SDN's impact extends beyond data centers and corporate networks. It plays a pivotal role in the deployment and management of 5G networks and the Internet of Things (IoT), where the need for dynamic network control and optimization is paramount. Therefore, SDN is represented as a paradigm shift in the networking landscape. It introduces centralized control, programmability, abstraction, and dynamic adaptability, all of which empower organizations to build networks that are more agile, responsive, and efficient. As we continue to embrace the digital age and witness the proliferation of data-intensive applications and emerging technologies, SDN is poised to play an increasingly crucial role in shaping the future of networking. The distinctive feature of this network is the physical separation of the forwarding data plane from the control plane. The control plane in SDN is responsible for making decisions [5] about how network traffic should be routed and managed. It operates independently of the data plane, allowing for centralized control and dynamic adaptation. The control plane uses SDN controllers to maintain a global view of the network, implement network policies, and update flow tables in network devices. It also facilitates interactions with network applications through northbound APIs, enabling customization and programmability. Overall, the control plane is a key component that enhances network management and responsiveness in SDN. The network switches that are present in the data plane checks and directs the incoming traffic packets. These switches do the checking of traffic packets from the flow rules that is sent by the centralized controller. The forwarding plane in SDN is responsible for the actual forwarding of network traffic. It operates in network devices like switches and routers, carrying out instructions provided by the centralized SDN controller. The forwarding plane processes incoming packets and determines how to forward them based on pre-configured flow entries in the device's flow table. It plays a crucial role in executing the routing and forwarding decisions made by the control plane, ensuring that data packets are efficiently directed through the network. The southbound interface [6,7] in (SDN is a communication interface that allows the SDN controller to interact with network devices in the data plane. It serves as the channel through which the controller sends instructions and updates to these devices, enabling centralized network control. Common southbound protocols, such as OpenFlow, facilitate the programming of flow tables in network devices, allowing for dynamic control of traffic forwarding and network policies. The southbound interface plays a crucial role in the separation of the control and data planes in SDN, enhancing network flexibility and programmability. The southbound interface is a skeptical interface that is present between the control plane and the data plane. OpenFlow interface is the most widely used southbound interface.

To develop the control plane, many different architectures of centralized controllers are represented among which any one of the architectures can be used. The other two interfaces are the eastbound and westbound interfaces. The eastbound interface lies between the two controllers of SDN [8] and the westbound interface. This interface is used to interchange the information between the two controllers. The application layer consists of SDN applications such as firewalls, load balancing, traffic engineering, etc. These applications are intended to execute certain control and management policies. To communicate with the control plane, northbound interface is used by these applications. The logically centralized SDN controller provides the benefit of allowing network managers to automatically control the traffic flows to manage [9] shifting traffic needs in next-generation networks. Many controllers make use of several methods to offer a scalable, coherent, fault-tolerant, and secure platform. Several SDN controllers are evaluated with the help of the four-performance metrics such as scalability, reliability, consistency, and security. Based on the requirements of application and dynamic networks in today's world, the network administrators feel more complex to manage the traditional network architecture. This was the motive behind the emergence of SDN [10,11]. SDN has a logically centralized controller architecture in which the controller is separated from the forwarding data plane and acts a centralization thereby controlling and managing the entire network devices and its functions. This network is a complete programmable network. The SDN controller plays a vital role, as it provides the network operators to modify the flexibility of the network and also to implement new functions to the network. This process is possible as the SDN can gather the global information of the entire network [12]. This network allows the network administrators to implement new policies malleable as the controller delivers APIs to the upper applications.

The SDN controller is of different types, which can be either centralized or distributed architecture. The centralized architecture is the network consisting of a single network and the distributed architecture is the network consisting of multiple controllers. From the survey done in [13], it can be understood that for medium-sized networks, implementation of a single controller is much better. But according to [14–16], when considering the parameters of scalability, availability, security, and efficiency of the network, implementation of multiple controllers is essential. The implementation of multiple controllers utilizes load balancing and therefore helps in lowering the response latency of requests and also avoids the controllers to overload [17]. The controller failure can be avoided if the security of the control plane can be progressed, if the multiple controllers are deployed in SDN as it offers a redundancy mechanism [18–20]. In [21], a survey has been done comparing both the centralized and distributed network architectures of SDN. In [20], it can be understood that for implementing the distributed architecture, four important parameters must be considered: Scalability, consistency, robustness, and security. In [22], a detailed survey has been done by comparing the centralized and distributed controllers of SDN and examines various challenges that take place in the distributed controller architecture of SDN.

The architecture, placement, scheduling and design principles are the four important aspects of multiple controllers that outline the performance of multiple controllers. The features of design principles such as the availability, consistency, and fault tolerance must be considered if the multiple controllers are to be implemented in SDN architecture. To enhance the communication from one controller to another, effective consistency solutions must be provided. For placing the multiple controllers in SDN architecture, some design principle features of fault tolerance, availability and reliability must be considered. Scheduling strategies are to be considered for effective load balancing, for the purpose of dynamic traffic taking place in networks. The response time and communications can also be reduced.

10.2 SDN ARCHITECTURE AND OPENFLOW

10.2.1 SOFTWARE-DEFINED NETWORK

As concepts in the technical areas improve, there is a dynamic shift in the networking sectors in this period. As a result, programmable networks are required to address these networking notions. This network is completely software-based. SDN establishes network programmability [23]. The control plane in this network serves as the network's controller, also known as the SDN controller. The overview structure of the SDN is represented in Figure 10.1. This controller uses the OpenFlow protocol for communication (also known as the OpenFlow controller) to interact with

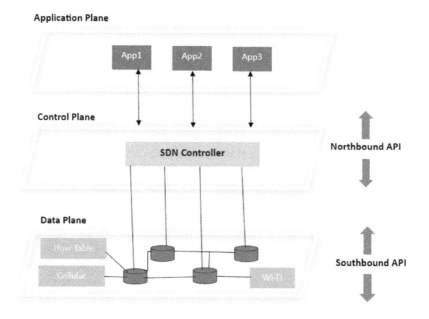

FIGURE 10.1   Overview of software-defined network [4].

various networking devices in the network. To allow the controller to connect with other networking devices, the southbound interface (OpenFlow) controls these networking devices, makes them still and uses them to forward data packets. SDN is quickly expanding in the industry and scientific communities. Although it is more beneficial in today's society, it has a number of problems that must be overcome.

10.2.2 OVERVIEW OF SDN FRAMEWORK AND ITS INTEGRANTS

This network's structure is entirely software-based, allowing for complete network programmability. It enables the controller to govern the network's behaviour dynamically using open interfaces. In SDN, the controller exerts centralized control over the whole network, where the data plane, also known as the forwarding plane, joins networking devices to bring forth all active data route elements. The control plane makes it easier for users and network administrators to allocate resources at the virtual level. As a result, this network has been perfectly virtualized. The architecture of SDN is shown in Figure 10.1. It consists of three primary layers known as the data plane, control plane and the application plane SDN deployment parts include the SDN controller, southbound API, northbound API, and network applications. The comparison of SDN with Traditional and Conventional networks is shown in Table 10.1.

10.2.2.1 Data Plane

The data plane in SDN is the operational heart of the network, responsible for the actual forwarding of data packets. It consists of network devices such as switches and routers, which process and forward incoming data packets based on predefined rules and flow entries. In SDN, the data plane operates under the control and instructions provided by the centralized SDN controller in the control plane. This separation of the data plane from the control plane enables network flexibility and adaptability, allowing for dynamic traffic routing, optimization, and customization. The data plane contains packet-forwarding devices. These devices indicate data packets to the specified destination; they are not authorized to make decisions on their own. They use the OpenFlow APIs to interact with the controller as necessary. This interface is enabled by forwarding devices, which provide a forwarding table containing three

TABLE 10.1
Disparity of SDN with Traditional and Conventional Networks

Characteristics	Conventional Network	Traditional Network	SDN
Network Management	Difficult	Difficult	Easy
Performance	Static	Static	Dynamic
Configuration	Manual	Manual	Automatic
Innovation	Limited in design and operations	Limited in design and operations	Improved design and operation with software upgrade
Programmable Network	No	No	Yes

fields that provide rules, actions, counters, or metrics. The rule determines if there is a match in the data packet. When a match is found, the matching packets' actions are carried out, such as forwarding them to outgoing ports or the controller, dropping them, or changing them.

10.2.2.2   Southbound API

The Southbound API in SDN serves as the communication link between the SDN controller and network devices in the data plane. It enables the controller to send instructions and updates to network switches, routers, and other hardware, facilitating centralized network control. This interface standardizes communication, abstracts device-specific details, and empowers the controller to customize network behavior, enhancing the flexibility and efficiency of SDN. The controller can control network behavior and monitor the flow table entries of incoming traffic packets for all switches using this API. They feature several mutual interfaces that link the controller. These interfaces include OpenFlow, OpFlex, and OpenState. The OpenFlow protocol interface is preferred by the southbound API. This OpenFlow protocol provides information about the Packet-In message, Event-based messages, and measurements of flow to the SDN controller's networking operating system.

10.2.2.3   Controller

In SDN, the controller is a centralized software component that serves as the brain of the network. It is responsible for making decisions about how network traffic should be routed and managed, based on policies and network conditions. The controller communicates with both network devices in the data plane and applications in the application layer, translating high-level network objectives into low-level network configurations. This separation of control from the data plane allows for centralized network management and dynamic adaptation, making SDN networks more flexible, programmable, and responsive. A distinct collection of controllers is offered, each with its own underlying architecture. To identify which controller for SDN is best for you, look at whether it has a centralized or distributed design. The controller has limits, one of which is that when the controller overloads and so offloads, the entire network fails. This is mostly due to the controller's role as the network's centralization.

10.2.2.4   Northbound API

The northbound API is used to create a variety of applications. The northbound API retrieves the low-level information of the southbound API to set the instructions in the forwarding network devices. The creation of these applications guarantees that the intended features, such as data management, data path computation, and security, are met. The controller supports a variety of northbound APIs for application development, however there is no ideal or standard northbound API. The reason for this is that every northbound APIs have had a unique prioritizing factor of apps that will be linked to the application plane to execute specialized duties up to this point.

10.2.2.5   Application Plane

The application plane in SDN is the layer where network applications and services operate. These applications interact with the SDN controller through northbound APIs, enabling them to request specific network behaviors and services. The application plane plays a crucial role in customizing network functionality, implementing services like traffic engineering, security, load balancing, and network optimization. It leverages the flexibility and programmability of SDN to cater to the specific needs of organizations and applications, making network management more adaptable and responsive. The application plane contains high-level instructions that are sent to the controller, and these instructions are the flow rules that are performed on the forwarding devices.

10.2.3   OpenFlow Protocol and Its Function

The realm of networking has experienced a profound transformation with the advent of SDN. At the core of this transformation is the OpenFlow protocol, a revolutionary communication standard that empowers SDN by providing a standardized and flexible way to control network devices and traffic flows. OpenFlow's emergence marked a significant departure from traditional networking paradigms, and it has since become a linchpin in the SDN landscape, enabling network innovation and dynamic control. OpenFlow Protocol, developed at Stanford University, functions as the bridge between the centralized SDN controller and the network devices in the data plane. In essence, it serves as the language that the controller and switches speak to communicate and coordinate network management and traffic forwarding. Its primary role is to program flow tables within network switches and routers, defining how incoming packets should be processed and forwarded. The fundamental function of the OpenFlow Protocol can be summarized as follows:

10.2.3.1   Flow Table Programming

OpenFlow's core function is to program flow tables residing within network devices. These flow tables are akin to a network device's decision-making engine, dictating how packets should be handled based on rules, matching criteria, and actions. The protocol allows the SDN controller to dynamically populate these flow tables with rules and actions, enabling fine-grained control over packet forwarding.

10.2.3.2   Centralized Control

OpenFlow's most compelling feature is its support for centralized network control. It aligns with SDN's principle of separating the control plane from the data plane. By centralizing control in the SDN controller, network administrators can make network-wide decisions, optimize traffic, and enforce policies in a unified manner, fostering agility and adaptability.

10.2.3.3   Real-Time Adaptation

One of OpenFlow's strengths lies in its real-time adaptability. As network conditions change or new policies are required, the SDN controller can send immediate updates to the flow tables in network devices. This dynamic adaptation ensures that the network can respond swiftly to varying traffic patterns and evolving requirements.

10.2.3.4   Standardization

OpenFlow standardizes the communication interface between the SDN controller and network devices. This standardization enhances interoperability and simplifies network management, as it eliminates the need for proprietary protocols and device-specific configurations.

10.2.3.5 Abstraction of Network Devices

The protocol abstracts the complexities of network device configurations, allowing the SDN controller to focus on high-level network policies and behaviors. This abstraction layer streamlines network management, making it more intuitive and efficient.

OpenFlow Protocol has catalyzed a wave of innovation in SDN. It has opened the door to advanced network functions and services, including traffic engineering, load balancing, Quality of Service (QoS) provisioning, and security enforcement. Moreover, it has been instrumental in the deployment of SDN in diverse networking environments, from data centers and campus networks to wide-area networks and telecommunications infrastructure. The OpenFlow protocol versions are represented in Table 10.2. This Protocol stands as a testament to the power of standardization [24] and centralized control in SDN. It has redefined network management, enabling networks to be more flexible, responsive, and adaptable to the demands of modern applications and services. OpenFlow's role as a foundational element in SDN underscores its importance in shaping the future of networking and driving continued innovation in the field.

TABLE 10.2
Versions of OpenFlow Protocol [24]

OpenFlow version	Features
OpenFlow 1.0.0 [25]	– Basic flow-based forwarding control. – Flow table entries with match-action rules. – Packet-in and packet-out messages. – Minimal forwarding and filtering capabilities.
OpenFlow 1.1.0 [26]	– Improved flow table entries with multiple tables. – Support for IPv6. – Group table for multi-cast and multi-path handling. – QoS improvements with rate limiting. – Better support for statistics collection.
OpenFlow 1.2.0 [27]	– IPv6 extension headers support. – Vendor-specific extensions for custom functionality. – Port and queue statistics. – Multiple flow tables with table-miss entries.
OpenFlow 1.3.0 [28]	– Quality of Service (QoS) improvements. – IPv6 prefix matching. – Enhanced metering and statistics.
OpenFlow 1.4.0 [29]	– Improved IPv6 support and header matching. – Multiple auxiliary connections for asynchronous messages. – Flow entry lifespan and eviction policies. – Controller role negotiation for redundancy.
OpenFlow 1.5.0 [30]	– Resilience enhancements with group and meter features. – Packet modification capabilities. – Table features for flow table information. – Support for connection tracking and connection reuse.

10.2.4   SDN SECURITY

Security is a paramount concern in the world of networking, and its importance only grows as networks become more dynamic and adaptable. SDN represents a transformative approach to network management, one that promises greater flexibility, agility, and efficiency. However, as organizations embrace SDN, it's crucial to understand the unique security challenges and opportunities that this paradigm shift presents. At the heart of SDN lies the concept of centralized control. Instead of distributed decision-making in individual network devices, SDN centralizes control in an SDN controller. This centralization offers several security advantages. First, it allows for uniform policy enforcement across the entire network, making it easier to implement security measures consistently. Second, it simplifies network segmentation and isolation, which are critical for containing and mitigating security breaches. Third, the centralized controller can detect and respond to security threats more effectively, as it has a holistic view of network traffic. However, centralization also introduces new attack surfaces.

If the SDN controller is compromised, an attacker can gain control over the entire network, potentially causing widespread damage. Therefore, securing the controller itself is paramount. This involves measures such as strong authentication, access controls, and encryption to protect controller communications. Moreover, the Southbound API, which enables communication between the SDN controller and network devices in the data plane, must be secured. Unauthorized access to this API could allow attackers to manipulate network devices and traffic flows. Encryption and secure authentication mechanisms are vital here as well. SDN's programmability, while a powerful feature, also brings security considerations. Applications that interact with the SDN controller through northbound APIs can potentially introduce vulnerabilities. Therefore, careful vetting of applications and code review processes are essential to ensure that applications do not compromise the network's security.

Traffic engineering, one of SDN's key advantages, can be leveraged for security. By directing traffic through specific paths and applying security policies in real-time, SDN can mitigate Distributed Denial of Service (DDoS) attacks, isolate compromised network segments, and detect unusual traffic patterns indicative of cyber threats. Furthermore, SDN facilitates granular network segmentation and micro-segmentation, allowing organizations to create security zones and isolate critical assets. This reduces the attack surface and limits lateral movement in case of a breach.

Monitoring and analytics capabilities are enhanced in SDN, providing better visibility into network traffic and potential security threats. Machine learning and artificial intelligence can be integrated to identify anomalous behavior and trigger automated responses to security incidents. Intrusion detection and prevention systems (IDPS) can be seamlessly integrated into SDN environments. These systems can analyze traffic in real-time and take immediate actions to block or divert malicious traffic flows. Therefore, security in SDN is a multifaceted challenge and opportunity. While centralization can simplify security policy enforcement and threat detection, it also introduces new risks. Therefore, a comprehensive security strategy in SDN must encompass secure controller and API access, rigorous application vetting, traffic engineering for security, granular segmentation, monitoring, and adaptive response mechanisms. As organizations navigate the evolving landscape of network security, SDN provides a dynamic framework that can be harnessed to address modern cybersecurity challenges effectively.

10.2.5 The Control Plane and Its Functionality in SDN

In the ever-evolving landscape of networking, SDN has emerged as a transformative paradigm that redefines how networks are controlled and managed. At the core of SDN lies the control plane, a fundamental component responsible for orchestrating network behavior and ensuring its responsiveness to dynamic demands. The control plane's functionality in SDN represents a pivotal departure from traditional networking approaches, offering unparalleled agility, flexibility, and programmability. The primary role of the control plane in SDN is to serve as the brain of the network. It is the decision-making center, responsible for determining how network traffic should be handled, routed, and forwarded. Unlike traditional networks, where individual network devices make autonomous decisions, SDN centralizes control, allowing a single entity – the SDN controller – to make network-wide decisions. This centralization forms the bedrock upon which SDN's transformative capabilities are built.

The control plane operates through a set of sophisticated algorithms and logic that leverage a holistic view of the network's topology and traffic flows. It continuously analyzes network conditions, monitors traffic patterns, and assesses performance metrics. Armed with this comprehensive understanding, the control plane can make real-time decisions, optimizing the flow of traffic, ensuring efficient resource utilization, and responding to changing network conditions promptly. One of the core functions of the control plane is the programming of flow tables within network devices, such as switches and routers, in the data plane. These flow tables define how incoming packets should be processed and forwarded. The control plane populates these tables with rules, actions, and matching criteria, effectively instructing network devices on how to handle specific traffic flows. This fine-grained control empowers organizations to tailor network behavior to their specific needs, whether it's implementing Quality of Service (QoS) policies, traffic optimization, or security measures.

Additionally, the control plane in SDN supports network virtualization and abstraction. It abstracts the underlying network infrastructure, presenting a unified and simplified view of the network to administrators. This abstraction layer streamlines network management by eliminating the need for manual configuration of individual devices. Administrators can define network policies and configurations in software, dramatically reducing the complexity associated with traditional network management. The dynamism of SDN is another hallmark feature facilitated by the control plane. The ability to adapt and respond to changing network conditions is a defining characteristic of SDN. The control plane can swiftly reroute traffic, adjust network policies, or redistribute resources in real-time, ensuring optimal network performance and responsiveness to the demands of applications and services.

Furthermore, the control plane plays a pivotal role in enhancing network security within SDN. It can implement security policies that filter, isolate, or inspect traffic for potential threats by having centralized visibility and control over traffic flows. In the event of security incidents or breaches, the control plane can respond promptly, implementing access controls, firewall rules, or threat mitigation measures. The functionality of the control plane in SDN represents a paradigm shift in the networking landscape. It embodies centralization, programmability, abstraction, and dynamic adaptability, all of which empower organizations to build networks that are more agile, responsive, and efficient. As we navigate the complexities of the digital age and witness the proliferation of data-intensive applications and emerging technologies, the control plane in SDN stands as a beacon of innovation and transformation in the world of networking.

10.3   ADVANTAGES OF DEPLOYING MULTIPLE CONTROLLERS IN SDN

A single controller SDN provides the benefits of managing and controlling the entire network devices and its operations and also it abstracts the network infrastructure. Scalability and reliability are the two main issues that occur in SDN to bring the controller down, leading it to a failure. Deploying multiple controllers in SDN environments provides several advantages. This approach enhances fault tolerance, scalability, and load balancing. It allows for geographic distribution, improves security, enables policy and traffic isolation, supports customization, ensures resource isolation, and facilitates fault isolation, all contributing to a more resilient and flexible SDN infrastructure.

10.3.1   Robustness

Robustness aims at providing a backup controller in SDN. In case one controller fails due to overloading or some faults, then another controller takes the load of the failed controller and continues the network to operate without any issues. This helps the network to maintain performance and stability. Also, it lowers network failures and controller faults.

10.3.2   Administration

The administration capability is very much limited in single controller SDN. For a large-scale network with various domains [31], it's impossible for the single controller to administrate the network efficiently. But the multiple controllers implemented in various domains can be able to efficiently manage the administration process [32].

10.3.3   Scalability

For a single controller SDN, the OpenFlow approach causes heavy load and therefore lowers the scalability of the network. Adding and removing the controllers dynamically is enhanced in multiple controllers of SDN. Also, the response requests which cause a bottleneck at single controller SDN architecture [33], are managed efficiently by the multiple controllers in SDN. Implementing multiple controllers in SDN architecture supports huge number of tenants [34] which is not possible in a single controller environment.

10.3.4 Latency Reduction

The single controller has to deal with all the latency-sensitive applications and so if it responds to every event of it, then the controller overloads and offloads and also increases the response latency. To prevent this from occurring, multiple controllers are installed and either the requests are load-balanced or the most appropriate request will be progressed to that particular controller. This is implemented to lower the traffic processing latency in SDN.

10.4 CHALLENGES OF MULTIPLE CONTROLLERS IN SDN ARCHITECTURE

Even though the multiple controllers act as a good replacement strategy for the single controller environment in SDN, it comes out with certain challenges that have to be addressed.

10.4.1 CONSISTENCY

The controller consensus problem [35,36] is a major drawback in deploying multiple controllers in SDN architecture. That is, while implementing the multiple controllers in SDN architecture, obtaining the network state information between multiple controllers is a major issue. So, many of the multiple controllers of this architecture completely depend on the consensus algorithm to coordinate the network state information within the controllers.

10.4.2 PLACEMENT

The Placement challenge addresses the NP-hard problems such as the number of controllers required as well as their topology details (like where they should be placed). Latency and load are the other two placement challenges in multiple controller SDN environments.

10.4.3 SCHEDULING

Scheduling is one of the challenges in deploying multiple controllers in SDN architecture. The issues outlined here are described as:

- When one controller overloads, at which point the other controller must be scheduled to protect the network from failing.
- And if the controller gets overloaded, then how to balance it as quickly as possible.

10.5 ARCHITECTURE OF MULTIPLE CONTROLLERS IN SDN

An innovative design in the controller architecture of SDN is done to break down the single point of failure. The OpenFlow in SDN acts as a communication protocol. With the help of OpenFlow, the SDN controller gathers the information and alters that information to flow entries which is later forwarded to the switches. Advancing from the development of OpenFlow 1.2, it has introduced the advantage that the switches can be connected to two different controllers which includes master, slaves, or equal controllers. This strategy presents the evolution of multi-controller architecture thereby preventing the single point of failure in SDN. In a multi-controller SDN, routing the data packets, there are two controllers that manage the network efficiently. Both the controllers will be in a synchronized state (logically centralized) where whenever a data packet enters the switch, both the controllers install the forwarding paths in all the switches of the entire network. Therefore, even if the network traffic flow increases, the controllers will act as a backup for each other and also manage the SDN network effectively by preventing failure. When a multi-controller architecture is preferred, it is very important to focus on the design of a multi-controller in SDN. The design of multi-controller architecture can be of flat, hierarchical, and hybrid design. In the hierarchical model, the network consists of one controller which is otherwise called a super controller, where this controller relates to several other controllers which are otherwise called child controllers. It gives adequate information to the child controllers so that, according to the network status information, even if there's any change in the network topology, the child controllers can respond to it dynamically. In this design, the child controllers are placed at the last layer and their connected parents are placed at the higher layer. So, the child controllers can manage only the OpenFlow switches that are present in their layer and are able to report to the parent controller which are connected to them. The multi-controller architecture in SDN which represents the hierarchical design is shown in Figure 10.2.

Here, the communications are disabled for the controllers that are present in the same layer. In this case, if a controller needs [37] to communicate with the other controller of the same layer, then it can be done with the help of the root controller. This model is said to improve the performance of SDN.

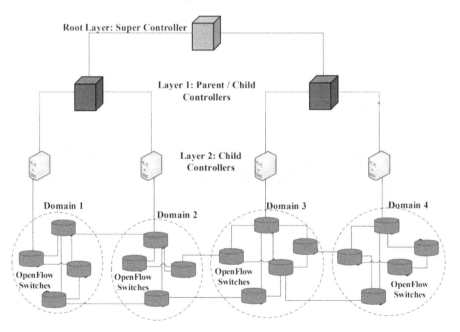

FIGURE 10.2 Multi-controller architecture of SDN which represents the hierarchical model [38].

The next design is the flat model. The architecture of this model is not a layered structure. Here, in this model the network topology is partitioned into sub domains where each sub domain is separately monitored and controlled by each controller. Here, to maintain the entire view of the network topology of SDN, the controller of each part actively communicates with each other. The multi-controller architecture in SDN which represents the flat design is shown in Figure 10.3.

In this design, there is no presence of a supercontroller, so intricate programs [39] are necessary to make sure that all the controllers present in each part of the network topology can efficiently take necessary actions to maintain and manage the network efficiently. These controllers must be capable of addressing the issues that are arising in the SDN and providing the solutions for the issues effectively. In this case, a major disadvantage takes place where a heavy traffic exchange occurs in between the controllers. If any additional network part is added, then the installation and configuration for that domain is done quickly and also the connectivity with the controllers are also done efficiently.

The next model is the Hybrid model which is the combination of both the hierarchical model and the flat model. The entire network is partitioned into two parts in which one part represents the hierarchical model, and the other part represents the flat model. The first partitioned network part which represents the hierarchical model consists of one controller which is otherwise called a super controller, where

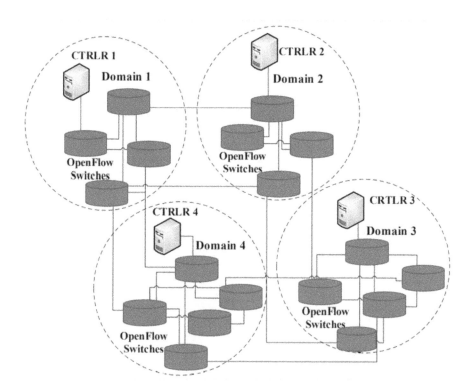

FIGURE 10.3 Multi-controller architecture of SDN which represents the flat model [38].

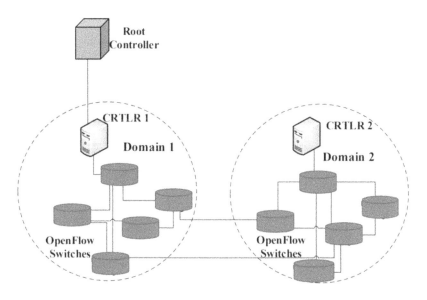

FIGURE 10.4   Multi controller architecture of SDN which represents the hybrid model [38].

this controller relates to several other controllers which are otherwise called child controllers. The super controller provides the entire view of that partitioned network topology. It gives adequate information to the child controllers so that, according to the network status information even if there's any change in that part of network topology, the child controllers can respond to it dynamically. The second partitioned network part, which represents the flat model where this model further divides the partitioned network into further parts where each part is separately monitored and controlled by each controller. Here, to maintain the entire view of the partitioned network topology of SDN, the controller of each part actively communicates with each other.

Here, there is no presence of a super controller, so intricate programs are necessary to make sure that all the controllers present in each part of the particular partitioned network topology can efficiently take necessary actions to maintain and manage the network efficiently. The multiple controller architecture in SDN which represents the flat design is shown in Figure 10.4. This model is said to solve the large complex problems that arise in the flat model and hierarchical model of large scale [40] SDN-enabled networks.

10.6   EXISTING MULTIPLE CONTROLLERS IN SDN

There are various multiple controllers in SDN, each with its own features. Existing multiple controllers are compared based on the aspects of their baseline controller, development languages, features, and Open source in Table 10.3.

The POX [41] controller plays a vital role in deploying OpenFlow protocol in the SDN. OpenFlow protocol paves way for both the controller and the switches to communicate efficiently. Different applications like firewall, switch etc., can be run using POX controllers.

TABLE 10.3

Comparison of Existing Multiple Controllers Based on the Aspects of Their Baseline Controller

Name	Language	Baseline Controller Platform	Open source	Features
POX [41]	Python	NOX	Yes	Can be used in large scale networks and for enhancing the flow management.
ONOS [47]	Java	Floodlight	Yes	Fault tolerance
Onix [43]	Python, C++, Java	–	No	Can be used in large scale networks
Kandoo [44]	C, C++, Python	–	Yes	Enhances to process the network events more efficiently.
Flowvisor [45]	C	–	Yes	Switch level virtualization
Hydra [49]	Java	–	No	Functional slicing
ElastiCon [51]	Java	Floodlight	No	Switch migration
Disttm [50]	Java	Floodlight	No	Collaborative traffic matrix estimation
Pratyaastha [48]	Java	–	No	Switch assignment
IRIS [53]	Java	Floodlight	Yes	Distributed control plane for carrier-grade large networks
Fleet [52]	Python	–	No	Malicious administrator problem detection and elimination
NVP [54]	Python, C++	Onix	No	Network Virtualization
OpenDaylight [55]	Java	–	Yes	Clustering, scalability, and availability
PANE [56]	Java	–	No	Fine-grained allocation mechanism
YANC [57]	C++ Python	–	No	File system design
Smartlight [58]	C++ Java	Floodlight	No	Fault tolerance

HyperFlow [42] controller is another type of distributed controller. This controller, therefore, supports OpenFlow protocol. The Onix [43] controller is used mainly for the purpose of making the network to achieve better reliability and scalability. It uses the NIB and consists of three parts which are Network connection infrastructure, Physical network infrastructure and the network control logic to maintain the state of the network efficiently.

Kandoo [44] is a type of hierarchical distributed SDN control plane. This controller handles networking events from the provincial applications where it does not require global information as the root controller handles the non- provincial controller. As both of these provincial and non-provincial applications are handled separately by this controller, it can avoid the prospective blockage that occurs mostly in scalability of the network.

FlowVisor [45] is an OpenFlow controller, which is an inline proxy, where the server intercepts the connection between OpenFlow-based network devices and multiple controllers. The inline proxy here refers to the transparent proxy as the connection interception is done without modifying the responses and requests.

DISCO [46] is a type of distributed SDN control plane that govern their own partitioned subdomain of the network and efficiently interacts with each other.

ONOS [47] is an open network operating system that provides control and layout of the network. So, it is not necessary to implement the routing and switching protocols in the network.

Pratyaastha [48] enhances both latency and cost. It is shown that, if the pratyaastha controller is implemented in SDN, then it provides 42% reduction in operating cost and 44% decrease in the flow setup.

Hydra [49] is a novel SDN controller that selects partitions using convergence time as its major measure, but it also considers the account communication between programs inside a partition and to minimize the response time, application instances are placed across the partitioned network domain.

Disttm [50] focuses on optimizing traffic flows across multiple networks controlled by various SDN controllers. DistTM aims to minimize congestion, improve network performance, and enhance resource utilization by intelligently managing the distribution of traffic across these networks.

ElastiCon [51] estimates the flow traffic conditions in every network and then dynamically assigns the controllers accordingly. In addition, some protocol based on switch migration and the algorithms of load balance are introduced to make the multiple controller network function flexibly.

With the help of the threshold voting system and independently produced settings, Fleet [52] solves the problem of malevolent administrators on numerous controllers.

To improve scalability and availability, IRIS [53] suggests a multi-controller architecture that uses hierarchical SDN network.

NVP controller [54] provides a network virtualization platform that captures the messages that has been exchanged between the controllers and the switches [43].

OpenDaylight [55] enhances both scalability and availability of the network. Various instances of this controller support clustering and also work together as a unit for improving the network performance.

PANE [56] focuses on providing a pulverized allocation of network resources to various controllers and also with a solution to solve the unavoidable struggles that arise due to various requests from multiple controllers.

Yanc [57] builds a file system that makes the network to operate more flexibly by storing the network configuration and state.

Smartlight [58] is the first controller that focuses on the design and execution of fault tolerant architecture of the software-defined network.

10.7   DESIGN PRINCIPLES OF MULTIPLE CONTROLLERS

Consistency, fault-tolerance, and availability are the three main design principles that are to be focused on whenever the distributed controllers are implemented.

10.7.1 CONSISTENCY

The logic rules in switches become inconsistent when the distributed controllers are implemented in SDNs. This brings out the instability in the network. When the controllers exchange messages between them, it becomes asynchronous. This occurs due to inconsistency. Many proposed methods help the network from reaching the inconsistency state. In [59], multi-level consistency models have been proposed so that multiple application-specific models can be implemented. In [60], clustering techniques are used to deploy a better consistent model. In [61], the traffic flow between the controllers is examined due to adopted consistency protocols. In [62], an adaptive consistency model has been proposed for SDN controllers. In the case of two controllers, this model protects the network from being inconsistent. But when many controllers are being implemented in the SDN, then the consistency becomes a major issue. Many studies have shown that if inconsistency occurs, it affects the performance of the SDN [63].

The below mentioned are the three main sections of consistency.

10.7.1.1 State Consistency

State consistency helps for the requirement of an identical global view of all the controllers as the cluster members of the distributed state are replicated here. It is of two types: Strong consistency and weak consistency.

When a controller changes its network state from old to new, the other controllers also read that network state and gets updated to a newest value. This process is called strong consistency. If the network state is not changed in a controller, then all the other controllers will get a concluding value in order to maintain the eventuality of the state, which is otherwise called as "eventual consistency." Some of the existing multiple controllers that achieve state consistency are shown in Table 10.4.

10.7.1.2 Version Update Consistency

In this consistency, surveys have shown that the inconsistent state in a controller can be detected. Frameworks like Header Space Analysis [64] and VeriFlow [65] are used to detect the inconsistency in controllers by examining the network configuration

TABLE 10.4
Multiple Controllers Achieving State Consistency

Controllers	Techniques	Consistency
DISCO [46]	Messenger, agent	Strong
OpenDaylight [55]	Raft	Strong
ElastiCon [51]	Hazelcast	Strong
HyperFlow [42]	Event-based	Weak
Onix [43]	Replicated transaction database	Strong
	DHT	Weak
ONOS [47]	Cassandra database	Weak
	Raft	Strong

and the data plane. Some solutions not only detect the inconsistency but also help to solve this problem. In [66], transactional semantics are used to recognize consistent message processing. The OFRewind [67] makes use of the hypervisor and repeats the network events by archiving the work of the controller domain. The HotSwap [68] annals the past network events of the old controller and produces it in the new controllers.

10.7.1.3   Rules Update Consistency

In general, the rules which are modernized are always in a consistent state, but if these rules are distributed, then they result in an asynchronous process [69] which leads to an inconsistent state. For example, when the flow entries are forwarded, asynchronous updates take place. Asynchronous updates state that some switches will get updated again and again repeatedly while some switches have not yet been updated [70]. If this continues, then updating the rules becomes a challenge. In [71], to overcome this challenge, consistency of rules in SDN has been proposed where it includes the consistency for both the packets and the flow in order to avoid the asynchronous updation of rules. This consistency policy checks for the correctness of rules in getting updated [72]. In [73], a protocol has been proposed which is based on OpenFlow safety rules update, that ensures consistency in packet rules. This lowers the forwarding entries from getting occupied during the process of updating.

10.7.2   Fault-Tolerance

When a network fault occurs due to the failure of the centralized controller, fault tolerance takes place which helps the network to operate normally without any intervention [74]. It is an approach where it helps the controller to increase its consistency, to function the network safely and also improve the network performance [75]. So, it is mandatory that whenever a controller is designed to install in the SDN, it must be ensured that it achieves fault tolerance. In SDN, fault tolerance is also associated with the distributed control plane [76].

10.7.2.1   Passive Replication

Every switch in the network is able to communicate only with its own parent controller. Only if that parent controller fails, any one of the other controllers that is acting as a backup controller comes into existence and establishes communication to all those switches and protects the network from failure.

10.7.2.2   Active Replication

Active Replication is a repetitive technique where every switch in the network can able to communicate with multiple controllers at the same time, and also the other controllers can manage the switches without any fault when the actual controller fails.

As the controller controls and monitors the entire network, when a network fault occurs, it affects the flow of data in the network as well as causes the data flow interruption between the controllers and the switches. Only through the failover mechanism, this issue can be solved [77]. When a fault occurs in a switch, the switch informs the controller about the malfunction. The controller will then reconfigure the appropriate switches after recalculating in accordance with the message or selecting an open route from the backup route list that was previously computed. Protection techniques are required to lessen the detrimental effects of separating the control plane and data plane to satisfy operators' requirements for fault tolerance. Algorithms are proposed [78] to provide a fast recovery whenever a network failure occurs. To handle the network failure taking place in OpenFlow, monitoring functions and protection mechanisms are proposed in [79].

There are several mechanisms available that can be used to solve various network faults. These mechanisms come up with both advantages and disadvantages. Among these mechanisms, the failover mechanism is the common mechanism. It leads to a computation burden on the controllers as well as taking a long time for recovery as the interaction takes place between the switches and the controllers. This mechanism is of two categories: Preventive protection mechanism and Recovery after fault mechanism. The preventive protection mechanism takes a short recovery time by recovering the mutual fault messages. The recovery after fault mechanism gives computational burden to the controller as well as takes a long recovery time. These mechanisms are used together in order to recover from faults.

10.7.3 AVAILABILITY

Availability describes the amount of time the SDN functions. If there is no determination in multiple controllers of SDN, then it may lead to danger. To ensure the availability of SDN controllers, three factors must be improved. Rules backup, controller load, switch requests are the three important factors that are to be considered to ensure the availability of SDN controllers.

In [80], a solution has been proposed to increase the availability of SDN by targeting the rules backup factor. Also, many requests from switches are sent to the controller, where it should deal with them. Even if the controller deals with it, the availability of the SDN will be affected by the overweight load [81]. To balance this load, Distributed architecture can be opted. But also, if the network traffic is distributed unevenly, then it results in lowering the availability of SDN controllers. In [82], the network traffic can be adjusted among the controllers by intermittently checking the load. If any deviation is found in the load window, it will accordingly increase or decrease the controller pool to adapt to the current request. In this checking process, if the load window is higher than the controller pool, then a new controller comes into existence to ensure the availability of the SDN.

By modifying controller load, availability may actually be improved by both lowering the switch requests and simultaneously altering the traffic in the network. By transferring the load to switches, the former lowers controller load. The latter does so by increasing the maximum controller load. Additionally, availability also depends on security. Even without the availability of numerous controllers, the SDN network will be at risk if several controllers are in egregiously unsafe circumstances. Therefore, in addition to the aforementioned three factors, controller security should be taken into account to increase availability. When deployed at scale, SDN may lose availability if security issues cannot be resolved [83,84].

10.8 CONCLUSION

SDN increases the effectiveness of network use and achieves programmability. However, the scalability and dependability of SDN networks are constrained by a single controller. Future SDN development will require a multiple controller architecture. A detailed survey has been done in this paper about the development of multi controllers in SDN. The introduction and summary of existing multi controllers, such as design principles and architectures are discussed in detail. Additionally, the advantages and disadvantages of current, pertinent study findings are analyzed. In future, a survey will be done in the aspects of scheduling and placement of multiple controllers in Software-defined networks.

REFERENCES

1. Zhang, Q., L. Cheng, and R. Boutaba. "Cloud computing: State-of-the-art and research challenges." *Journal of Internet Services and Applications* 1 (2010): 7–18.
2. Rossi, F. D., G. D. C. Rodrigues, R. N. Calheiros, and M. D. S. Conterato. "Dynamic network bandwidth resizing for big data applications." In *Proceedings of Thirteenth IEEE International Conference on eScience*, 2017.
3. Samaan, N., and A. Karmouch. "Towards autonomic network management: An analysis of current and future research directions." *IEEE Communications Surveys & Tutorials* 11, no. 3 (2009): 22–36.
4. Cabaj, K., J. Wytrebowicz, S. Kuklinski, P. Radziszewski, and K. T. Dinh. "SDN architecture impact on network security." In *FedCSIS (Position Papers)*, 2014, pp. 143–148.
5. "Software-Defined Networking: The New Norm for Networks", *ONF White Paper*, April 13, (2012).
6. McKeown, N., T. Anderson, H. Balakrishnan, G. Parulkar, L. Peterson, J. Rexford, S. Shenker, and J. Turner. "OpenFlow: Enabling innovation in campus networks." *ACM SIGCOMM Computer Communication Review* 38, no. 2 (2008): 69–74.
7. Limoncelli, T. A. "OpenFlow: A radical new idea in networking: An open standard that enables software-defined networking." *Queue* 10, no. 6 (2012): 40–46.
8. Yu, Y., X. Li, X. Leng, L. Song, K. Bu, Y. Chen, J. Yang, L. Zhang, K. Cheng, and X. Xiao. "Fault management in software-defined networking: A survey." *IEEE Communications Surveys & Tutorials* 21, no. 1 (2018): 349–392.
9. Xia, W., Y. Wen, C. H. Foh, D. Niyato, and H. Xie. "A survey on software-defined networking." *IEEE Communications Surveys & Tutorials* 17, no. 1 (2014): 27–51.
10. Farhady, Hamid, HyunYong Lee, and Akihiro Nakao. "Software-defined networking: A survey." *Computer Networks* 81 (2015): 79–95.
11. Li, W., W. Meng, and L. F. Kwok. "A survey on openflow-based software-defined networks: Security challenges and countermeasures." *Journal of Network and Computer Applications* 68 (2016): 126–139.
12. Lopes, F. A., M. Santos, R. Fidalgo, and S. Fernandes. "A software engineering perspective on SDN programmability." *IEEE Communications Surveys Tutorials* 18, no. 2 (2016): 1255–1272.
13. Heller, B., R. Sherwood, and N. Mckeown. "The controller placement problem." *ACM SIGCOMM Computer Communication Review* 42 no. 4 (2012): 473–478.

14. Jain, S., A. Kumar, S. Mandal, J. Ong, L. Poutievski, A. Singh, S. Venkata, J. Wanderer, J. Zhou, and M. Zhu, et al. "B4: Experience with a globally-deployed software-defined WAN." *ACM SIGCOMM Computer Communication Review* 43, no. 4 (2013): 3–14.

15. Berman, M., J. S. Chase, L. Landweber, A. Nakao, M. Ott, D. Raychaudhuri, R. Ricci, and I. Seskar Geni. "A federated testbed for innovative network experiments." *Computer Networks* 61 (2014): 5–23.

16. Al-Fares, M., S. Radhakrishnan, B. Raghavan, N. Huang, A. Vahdat, and Hedera. "Dynamic flow scheduling for data center networks." In *Proceedings of the 7th USENIX Conference on Networked Systems Design and Implementation*, 2010, pp. 19–19.

17. Karakus, M., and A. Durresi. "Quality of service (qos) in software-defined networking (SDN): A survey." *Journal of Network and Computer Applications* 80 (2017): 200–218.

18. Shalimov, A., D. Zuikov, D. Zimarina, V. Pashkov, and R. Smeliansky. "Advanced study of SDN/OpenFlow controllers." In *Proceedings of the 9th Central & Eastern European Software Engineering Conference in Russia*, 2013, pp. 1–6.

19. Yan, Q., F. R. Yu, Q. Gong, and J. Li. "Software-defined networking (SDN) and distributed denial of service (DDoS) attacks in cloud computing environments: A survey, some research issues, and challenges." *IEEE Communications Surveys & Tutorials* 18, no. 1 (2015): 602–622.

20. Oktian, Y. E., S. G. Lee, H. J. Lee, and J. H. Lam. "Distributed SDN controller system: A survey on design choice." *Computer Networks* 121 (2017): 100–111.

21. Nunes, A., M. Mendonca, X. N. Nguyen, and K. Obraczka. "A survey of software-defined networking: Past, present, and future of programmable networks." *Communications Surveys Tutorials IEEE* 16, no. 3 (2014): 1617–1634.

22. Kreutz, D., F. M. V. Ramos, P. Esteves Verissimo, C. Esteve Rothenberg, S. Azodolmolky, and S. Uhlig. "Software-defined networking: A comprehensive survey." *Proceedings of the IEEE* 103 no. 1 (2014): 10–13.

23. Bavani, K., M. P. Ramkumar, and G.S.R. Emil Selvan. "Statistical approach based detection of distributed denial of service attack in a software-defined network." In *2020 6th International Conference on Advanced Computing and Communication Systems (ICACCS)*, IEEE, 2020, pp. 380–385.

24. Zhang, Y., L. Cui, W. Wang, and Y. Zhang. "A survey on software-defined networking with multiple controllers." *Journal of Network and Computer Applications* 103 (2018): 101–118.

25. OpenFlow Specification 1.0. http://www.openflow.org/documents/ openflow-spec-v1.0.0.pdf. (Accessed: 2017/04/05) (2009).

26. OpenFlow Specification 1.1.0. http://www.openflow.org/ documents/openflow-spec-v1.1.0.pdf. (Accessed: 2017/04/05) (2011).

27. OpenFlow Specification 1.2.0. https://www.opennetworking.org/ images/stories/downloads/specification/openflow-specv1.2. pdf. (Accessed: 2017/04/05) (2011).

28. OpenFlow Specification 1.3.0. https://www.opennetworking.org/ images/stories/downloads/specification/openflow-spec-v1.3.0.pdf. (Accessed: 2017/04/05) (2012).

29. OpenFlow Specification 1.4.0. https://www.opennetworking.org/ images/stories/downloads/sdn-resources/onf-specifications/ openflow/openflow-spec-v1.4.0.pdf. (Accessed: 2017/04/07) (2013).

30. OpenFlow Specification 1.5.0. https://www.opennetworking.org/ images/stories/downloads/sdn-resources/onf-specifications/ openflow/openflow-switch-v1.5.0.noipr.pdf. (Accessed: 2017/04/07) (2014).

31. Hong, C.-Y., S. Kandula, R. Mahajan, M. Zhang, V. Gill, M. Nanduri, R. Wattenhofer. "Achieving high utilization with software-driven WAN." *ACM SIGCOMM Computer Communication Review ACM* 43 (2013): 15–26.

32. Fratczak, T., M. Broadbent, P. Georgopoulos, and N. Race. "Homevisor: Adapting home network environments." In *2013 Second European Workshop on Software-Defined Networks*, IEEE, 2013, pp. 32–37.

33. Yeganeh, S. H., A. Tootoonchian, and Y. Ganjali. "On scalability of software-defined networking." *IEEE Communications Magazine* 51, no. 2 (2013): 136–141.
34. Bozakov, Z., and P. Papadimitriou. "Autoslice: Automated and scalable slicing for software-defined networks." In *Proceedings of the 2012 ACM Conference on CoNEXT Student Workshop, ACM*, 2012, pp. 3–4.
35. Zhang, T., P. Giaccone, A. Bianco, and S. De Domenico. "The role of the inter-controller consensus in the placement of distributed SDN controllers." *Computer Communications* 113 (2017): 1–13.
36. Liu, W., R. B. Bobba, S. Mohan, and R. H. Campbell. "Inter-flow consistency: A novel SDN update abstraction for supporting inter-flow constraints." In *Communications and Network Security (CNS), 2015 IEEE Conference on*, IEEE, 2015, pp. 469–478.
37. Huang, J.-J., Y.-Y. Chen, C. Chen, and Y. H. Chu. "Weighted routing in hierarchical multi-domain SDN controllers." In *2015 17th Asia-Pacific Network Operations and Management Symposium (APNOMS)*, IEEE, 2015, pp. 356–359.
38. Hossein, A., M. Watts, and K. Ahmadi. "An overview of multi-controller architecture in software-defined networking." In *CITRENZ Conference (2019)*, 2019.
39. Duan, Q., N. Ansari, and M. Toy. "Software-defined network virtualization: An architectural framework for integrating SDN and NFV for service provisioning in future networks." *IEEE Network* 30, no. 5 (2016): 10–16.
40. Hu, Y., W. Wang, X. Gong, X. Que, and S. Cheng. "On reliability-optimized controller placement for software-defined networks." *China Communications* 11, no. 2 (2014): 38–54.
41. Narisetty, R.R., L. Dane, A. Malishevskiy, D. Gurkan, S. Bailey, S. Narayan, and S. Mysore. "OpenFlow configuration protocol: Implementation for the of management plane." In *2013 Second GENI Research and Educational Experiment Workshop*, IEEE, 2013, pp. 66–67.
42. Tootoonchian, A., and Y. Ganjali. "Hyperflow: A distributed control plane for openflow." In *Proceedings of the 2010 Internet Network Management Conference on Research on Enterprise Networking*, Vol. 3, 2010, pp. 10–5555.
43. Koponen, T., M. Casado, N. Gude, J. Stribling, L. Poutievski, M. Zhu, R. Ramanathan, Y. Iwata, H. Inoue, and T. Hama, et al. "Onix: A distributed control platform for large-scale production networks." *OSDI* 10 (2010): 1– 6.
44. Hassas Yeganeh, S., and Y. Ganjali. "Kandoo: A framework for efficient and scalable offloading of control applications." *The Workshop on Hot Topics in Software-Defined Networks* (2012): 19–24.
45. Sherwood, R., G. Gibb, K.-K. Yap, G. Appenzeller, M. Casado, N. McKeown, and G. Parulkar. "Flowvisor: A network virtualization layer." *OpenFlow Switch Consortium, Technical Reports* 1 (2009): 132.
46. Phemius, K., M. Bouet, and J. Leguay. "Disco: Distributed multi-domain SDN controllers." *Network Operations and Management Symposium* (2013): 1–4.
47. Berde, P., M. Gerola, J. Hart, Y. Higuchi, M. Kobayashi, T. Koide, B. Lantz, B. O'Connor, P. Radoslavov, and W. Snow. "Onos: Towards an open, distributed SDN os." *The Workshop on Hot Topics in Software-Defined Networking* (2014): 1–6.
48. Krishnamurthy, A., S. P. Chandrabose, and A. Gember-Jacobson. "Pratyaastha: An efficient elastic distributed SDN control plane." In *Proceedings of the Third Workshop on Hot Topics in Software-Defined Networking*, ACM, 2014, pp. 133–138.
49. Chang, Y., A. Rezaei, B. Vamanan, J. Hasan, S. Rao, and T. N. Vijaykumar. "Hydra: Leveraging functional slicing for efficient distributed SDN controllers." In *2017 9th International Conference on Communication Systems and Networks (COMSNETS)*, IEEE, 2017, pp. 251–258.
50. Hark, R., D. Stingl, N. Richerzhagen, K. Nahrstedt, and R. Steinmetz. "Disttm: Collaborative traffic matrix estimation in distributed SDN control planes." In *IFIP Networking Conference (IFIP Networking) and Workshops, 2016*, IEEE, 2016, pp. 82–90.

51. Dixit, A., F. Hao, S. Mukherjee, T. Lakshman, and R. R. Kompella. "Elasticon; an elastic distributed SDN controller." In *Architectures for Networking and Communications Systems (ANCS), 2014 ACM/IEEE Symposium on*, IEEE, 2014, pp. 17–27.

52. Matsumoto, S., S. Hitz, and A. Perrig. "Fleet: Defending SDNs from malicious administrators." In *Proceedings of the Third Workshop on Hot Topics in Software-Defined Networking*, ACM, 2014, pp. 103–108.

53. Lee, B., S. H. Park, J. Shin, and S. Yang. "Iris: the OpenFlow-based recursive SDN controller." In *Advanced Communication Technology (ICACT), 2014 16th International Conference on, IEEE*, 2014, pp. 1227–1231.

54. Koponen, T., K. Amidon, P. Balland, M. Casado, A. Chanda, B. Fulton, and I. Ganichev et al. "Network virtualization in multi-tenant datacenters." In *11th USENIX Symposium on Networked Systems Design and Implementation (NSDI 14)*, 2014, pp. 203–216.

55. Medved, J., R. Varga, A. Tkacik, and K. Gray. "Opendaylight: Towards a model-driven sdn controller architecture." In *Proceeding of IEEE International Symposium on a World of Wireless, Mobile and Multimedia Networks 2014*, IEEE, 2014, pp. 1–6.

56. Ferguson, A. D., A. Guha, C. Liang, R. Fonseca, and S. Krishnamurthi. "Participatory networking: An API for application control of SDNs." In *ACM SIGCOMM Computer Communication Review* 43, no. 4 (2013): 327–338.

57. Guha, A., M. Reitblatt, and N. Foster. "Machine-verified network controllers." *ACM SIGPLAN Notices* 48 (2013): 483–494.

58. Botelho, F., A. Bessani, F. Ramos, and P. Ferreira. "Smartlight: A practical fault-tolerant SDN controller." *arXiv preprint arXiv* 1407.6062 (2014): 1–7.

59. Bannour, F., S. Souihi, and A. Mellouk. "Software-defined networking: A self-adaptive consistency model for distributed SDN controllers." *RESCOM* 2017 (2017): 7–8.

60. Aslan, M., and A. Matrawy. "A clustering-based consistency adaptation strategy for distributed SDN controllers." In *2018 4th IEEE Conference on Network Softwarization and Workshops (NETSOFT)*, IEEE, 2018, pp. 441–448.

61. Muqaddas, A. S., P. Giaccone, A. Bianco, and G. Maier. "Inter-controller traffic to support consistency in ONOS clusters." *IEEE Transactions on Network and Service Management* 14, no. 4 (2017): 1018–1031.

62. Sakic, E., F. Sardis, J. W. Guck, and W. Kellerer. "Towards adaptive state consistency in distributed SDN control plane." In *Communications (ICC), 2017 IEEE International Conference on*, IEEE, 2017, pp. 1–7.

63. Dan, L., A. Wundsam, B. Heller, N. Handigol, and A. Feldmann. "Logically centralized: State distribution trade-offs in software-defined networks." (2012): 1–6.

64. Kazemian, P., G. Varghese, and N. McKeown. "Header space analysis: Static checking for networks." *NSDI* 12 (2012): 113–126.

65. Khurshid, A., W. Zhou, M. Caesar, and P. Brighten Godfrey. "Veriflow: Verifying network-wide invariants in real time." In *Proceedings of the First Workshop on Hot Topics in Software-Defined Networks*, 2012, pp. 49–54.

66. Peresini, P., M. Kuzniar, N. Vasi c, M. Canini, and D. Kostiu. "Of CPP: Consistent packet processing for OpenFlow." In *Proceedings of the Second ACM SIGCOMM Workshop on Hot Topics in Software-Defined Networking*, ACM, 2013, pp. 97–102.

67. Wundsam, A., D. Levin, S. Seetharaman, A. Feldmann, et al. "Ofrewind: Enabling record and replay troubleshooting for networks." In *USENIX Annual Technical Conference*, 2011, pp. 15–17.

68. Vanbever, L., J. Reich, T. Benson, N. Foster, and J. Rexford. "Hotswap: Correct and efficient controller upgrades for software-defined networks." In *Proceedings of the Second ACM SIGCOMM Workshop on Hot Topics in Software-Defined Networking*, ACM, 2013, pp. 133–138.

69. Forster, K.-T., R. Mahajan, and R. Wattenhofer. "Consistent updates in software-defined networks: on dependencies, loop freedom, and blackholes." In *IFIP Networking Conference (IFIP Networking) and Workshops, 2016*, IEEE, 2016, pp. 1–9.

70. Panda, A., W. Zheng, X. Hu, A. Krishnamurthy, and S. Shenker. "SCL: Simplifying distributed SDN control planes." In *14th USENIX Symposium on Networked Systems Design and Implementation (NSDI 17)*, USENIX Association, 2017, pp. 329–345.
71. Reitblatt, M., N. Foster, J. Rexford, and D. Walker. "Consistent updates for software-defined networks: Change you can believe in!" In *Proceedings of the 10th ACM Workshop on Hot Topics in Networks*, 2011, pp. 1–6.
72. Reitblatt, M., N. Foster, J. Rexford, C. Schlesinger, and D. Walker. "Abstractions for network update." *ACM SIGCOMM Computer Communication Review* 42, no. 4 (2012): 323–334.
73. Mcgeer, R. "A safe, efficient update protocol for OpenFlow networks." In *The Workshop on Hot Topics in Software-Defined Networks*, 2012, pp. 61–66.
74. Schiff, L., S. Schmid, and M. Canini. "Ground control to major faults: Towards a fault tolerant and adaptive SDN control network." In *Dependable Systems and Networks Workshop, 2016 46th Annual IEEE/IFIP International Conference on*, IEEE, 2016, pp. 90–96.
75. Botelho, F., F. M. Valente Ramos, D. Kreutz, and A. Bessani. "On the feasibility of a consistent and fault-tolerant data store for SDNs." In *Second European Workshop on Software-Defined Networks*, 2013, pp. 38–43.
76. Sridharan, V., M. Gurusamy, and T. Truong-Huu. "On multiple controller mapping in software-defined networks with resilience constraints." *IEEE Communications Letters* 21, no. 8 (2017): 1763–1766.
77. Sharma, S., D. Staessens, D. Colle, M. Pickavet, and P. Demeester. "OpenFlow: Meeting carrier-grade recovery requirements." *Computer Communications* 36, no. 6 (2013): 656–665.
78. Beheshti, N., and Y. Zhang. "Fast failover for control traffic in software-defined networks." In *Global Communications Conference*, 2012, pp. 2665–2670.
79. Kempf, J., E. Bellagamba, A. Kern, and D. Jocha. "Scalable fault management for openflow." In *IEEE International Conference on Communications*, 2012, pp. 6606–6610.
80. Williams, D., and H. Jamjoom. "Cementing high availability in OpenFlow with rule-bricks." In *Proceedings of the Second ACM SIGCOMM Workshop on Hot Topics in Software-Defined Networking*, ACM, 2013, pp. 139–144.
81. Toumi, K., M. S. Idrees, F. Charmet, R. Yaich, and G. Blanc. "Usage control policy enforcement in sdn-based clouds: A dynamic availability service use case." In *High Performance Computing and Communications; IEEE 14th International Conference on Smart City; IEEE 2nd International Conference on Data Science and Systems (HPCC/SmartCity/DSS), 2016 IEEE 18th International Conference on*, IEEE, 2016, pp. 578–585.
82. Dixit, A., F. Hao, S. Mukherjee, T. V. Lakshman, and R. Kompella. "Towards an elastic distributed SDN controller." *ACM SIGCOMM Computer Communication Review* 43, no. 4 (2013): 7–12.
83. Qi, C., J. Wu, H. Hu, G. Cheng, W. Liu, J. Ai, and C. Yang. "An intensive security architecture with multi-controller for SDN." In *Computer Communications Workshops (INFOCOM WKSHPS), 2016 IEEE Conference on*, IEEE, 2016, pp. 401–402.
84. Dacier, M. C., H. König, R. Cwalinski, F. Kargl, and S. Dietrich. "Security challenges and opportunities of software-defined networking." *IEEE Security & Privacy* 15, no. 2 (2017): 96–100.

11 Control Plane Security Issues in Software-Defined Networking
A Comprehensive Review

Krishnaraj Rao, K. Bhavya, K. R. Raghunandan,
Radhakrishna Dodmane Surendra Shetty,
and Sardar M. N. Islam

11.1 INTRODUCTION

SDN is another network technology that gives a more adaptable and versatile network design equipped for answering rapidly to changes in business and end-client needs through improved network management [1]. SDN's power has been shown step by step, stretching out from little neighborhood to public cloud models. Generally speaking, SDN shows its extraordinary accomplishment by giving more prominent unwavering quality, viability, straightforwardness, and adaptability at a lower cost [2]. In any case, notwithstanding its various benefits, SDN security remains a wellspring of worry among research networks. SDN is a new networking technology that takes out the limits of customary networks. Conventional network bottlenecks incorporated the intricacy of customary networks, the design of individual gadgets utilizing seller-explicit dialects, an absence of a worldwide perspective on the network, and a brought-together controlling point [3]. The evolution of network security is a competition between attackers and security networks to see who can break and steal the network first. Security analysts and experts have worked hard and made significant progress in combating the threats posed by their adversaries. Regardless, the rapid advancement of data and communication breakthroughs, such as cell phones and distributed computing virtualization, places an additional burden on network executives in terms of network security [4]. As technology advances, so do new threats, assault techniques, and attack channels. As a result of increased industry interest and the rise of cloud advantages, the complex traditional model, which is so dependent on each provider and has competing tactics, has become unscalable and unadopted. As a result, network configuration experts promoted another network technology called as programming-defined networking (SDN). Figure 11.1 depicts a real-world SDN network.

DOI: 10.1201/9781003432869-11

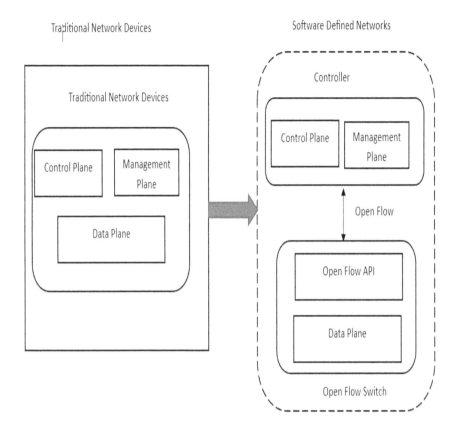

FIGURE 11.1   Depicts a real-world SDN network.

Cloud administrations are becoming increasingly popular, and large organizations are migrating to SDN-based network executions. These virtual innovations
improve sensibility, consistency, and management quality. The significance of safety
arrangement is relevant for joined supervised networks and has become one of the
concerns. Consider a combined virtual server acting as a controller, initiating and
managing streams in the data plane utilizing the OpenFlow correspondence standard. Because of the use of OpenFlow, the controller becomes an important target
for the attacker for the following reasons.

- There is no norm for security execution in the OpenFlow convention, so
  product designers utilize their own exclusive techniques.
- Since SDNs are programmable, they are significantly more defenseless
  against a wide scope of noxious attacks and code takes advantage.
- Disavowal of administration and side channel attacks can be aimed at the
  southward point of interaction.
- SDN arrangement mistakes can be more not kidding than customary network blunders.
- Critical to establish trust.

11.2 BACKGROUND OF SOFTWARE-DEFINED NETWORKS

SDN is a network technique that enables network administrators to powerfully implement, adjust, oversee, and regulate network behaviour using convention. OpenFlow. IT network frameworks are changing due to SDN in terms of how they are managed, organized, and controlled [5]. The SDN viewpoint is based on separating the control plane from the information plane, with one deciding on information sending options and the other carrying them out. The non-control plane, like the SDN concept, is overseen by a combined controller in charge of stream control. To communicate between the two planes, the Open Networking Foundation's (ONF) OpenFlow protocol is used [6]. The SDN engineering is divided into three planes, as shown in Figure 11.2.

The control plane in the SDN design is made up of an SDN controller, which is a separate work from the information plane. The information plane is made up of the equipment used to transmit packages, such as switches, switches, and middlebox machines (Intrusion discovery frameworks, load balancers, and firewalls). Open-source protocols like OpenFlow are used by the SDN controller to connect

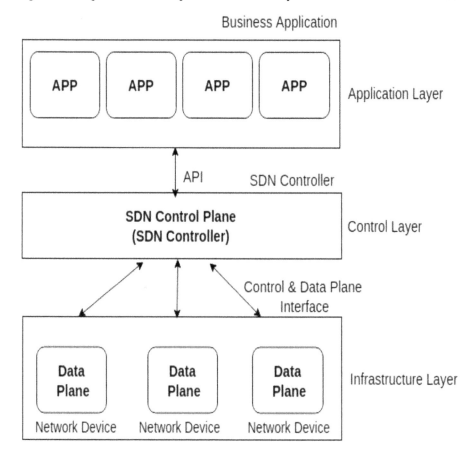

FIGURE 11.2 SDN architecture.

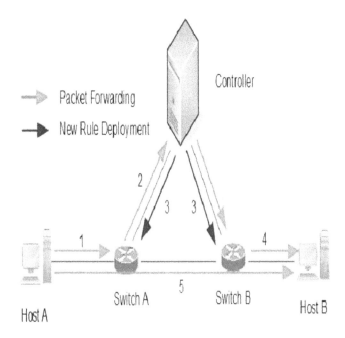

FIGURE 11.3   SDN tasks.

to the switches that transmit bundles. According to [7], the SDN application plane includes applications designed to carry out network logic and control procedures. This high-level aircraft communicates with the control plane using a Northbound API. The most evident particular characteristic of the product-described network is the free connection of the control and information planes (SDN). As a result, SDN transitions from vertical to flat network part coordination and provides distinct working layers for strategy development, requirement, and implementation. The control plane, on the other hand, is regarded as the most important layer in the SDN design; it consists of a combined programming controller that handles correspondences across applications and network devices via open connection points [7]. It also provides focused management capabilities such as geography disclosure, state synchronization, and device management with the outsider projects establishment [8]. The control SDN currently upholds network control rationale and gives the application layer a theoretical perspective on the global network [9,10]. The OpenFlow convention is widely used in the ongoing SDN.

Figure 11.3 shows an explanation of the SDN tasks. The primary SDN activity is to transport traffic in the network for a parcel. For each new parcel, it searches stream tables for matching data.

11.3   SECURITY ISSUES IN SDN

SDN and personal, national, and hybrid cloud networks exist here, and web operations teams are distributed. Companies in all industries are at various stages of researching, evaluating, and implementing current system technologies. SDN provides the equipment required for on- premises and cloud network speed, scale, and self-service. Organizations that want to shift from reactive to preventive system management must use performance monitoring. According to the article, a standard measure is required to see when resources are over or underutilized, and setting lower thresholds on the standard identifies potential problems before they impact the system. One of the most prominent data security issues of the day is web safety, especially as it relates to the biggest system on the planet, the internet. Some educational institutions have already linked their technology resources into a single system, while others are in the process of doing so. The next step for these organizations is to assess the costs and advantages of connecting their private networks—with their reliable users—and the anonymous users and networks of the internet. Let's take a look at SDN security. Regardless of the deployment model, whether classic hybrid or virtual overlay, or the controller agent communication protocol, such as open flow versus vendor-specific API's or I2RS SDN, an organization's perimeter security is provided. SDN has altered the definition of the network perimeter. In situations where any IP-based device connected to a network may pose a threat, each network element must be secured in its own right. SDN security is the requirement for SDN components to protect the functionality of the SDN by establishing secure boundaries around services and access.

A. Security for the SDN

The goals of security and SDNs are as follows when it comes to SDN and security. Instead of acting as an overlay, the SDN design enables security to be embedded into the network. It does not rely on the SDN model. As previously noted, regardless of the model used, security is a concern. Design needs for security can be incorporated.

Centralized policy administration, automatic provisioning, real-time mitigation, and the ability to execute security checks on configurations as they are implemented on the network are all advantages. These are all benefits of SDN, and they are all built in from the ground up and from the start. Another consideration is that many common network attacks will have varying effects on an SDN system. Because in today's networks, we have things like DDoS attacks and well-known attacks, and some of them will influence the network in an SDN network in a somewhat different way. The process for putting them in place will change as well. There is a bit of a learning curve when it comes to knowing how some of these dangers will be applied and arise in an SDN network. In a normal DDoS attack, an attacker will often target numerous devices in the first step of a DoS at-tack. By focusing on each device individually, they will develop invalid flows for each of them or perhaps they will try to slow down the CPU on a single device in order to influence the throughput and service provided by that device. In general, they will try to attack as many devices as they can. However, this occurs on a per-device basis, and in most circumstances, it is limited to that unique device. The modified flow information will then be sent back to the controller via the SDN agent.

If the information forwarded by the agent is faulty in some way, this can cause the controller CPU to spike. Another scenario is that the controller will use the incorrect information to communicate the improper network flows to other agents in the network, harming more than one agent. Even by concentrating on and attacking just one agent, we can see how the SDN DoS attack spreads. The success of this method, however, is reliant on how well the SDN is protected. An SDN is composed of numerous levels and interactions, each of which necessitates a different level of security. Multi-layered security is required for multi-layer, multi- component models. SDN security brings new potential threats and weaknesses, with DoS attack since SDN is a layered design, each layer needs its own security. The easiest method to ensure this is to identify each of the levels and then apply appropriate mitigation requirements and security techniques to aid in layer protection management. The control of an SDN network is its beating heart. It connects network devices on one end and applications on the other. Any interaction between devices must go through the controller. Controllers employ open flow protocols to configure network devices. Approaches to controller hardening aim to protect the control from access-based attacks and misconfigurations. Furthermore, any operating system running on the controller must be patched and maintained appropriately. Management security includes always ensuring that when you contact the controller and configure anything on the controller, you utilize secure protocols such as SSH or HTTPS.

In many cases, the controller can provide individual host-based firewalling to protect the device from unauthorized access and services. There is also security by design in terms of control-specific hardening. Let's have a look at device hardening for agents and controllers, SDN agents, and other network devices that receive commands from the controller, such as routers, switches, and fire-walls. Many strategies that are currently employed in non-SDN installations are used to harden SDN devices. Some of the important ways include implementing routing plane security elements such as authentication as well as routing protocol-specific characteristics such as BGP TTL security. Control plane policing is another option for ensuring predictable CPU activity. Control plane and management plane protection are used to adjust and limit device resources, as are data plane security approaches that try to reject undesired traffic as soon as feasible rather than forward it to other network devices.

Some of the hardening strategies you may wish to apply here include control plane protection, routing protocol security, first hop routing protocol security, and control plane protection. Consider how to manage ICMP traffic by turning off ICMP redirection. In addition, both ICMP unreachable calls and proxies are secure routing methods. The goal of control plane policing is not necessarily to prevent attacks, but rather to ensure that the services that do require network bandwidth and operations. On the management plane, secure protocols are utilized to manage your infrastructure. As a result, SSH, SCP, HTTPS, and SNMP v3 are no longer supported. Because the fundamental point of safeguarding the data plane is to be able to reject content as quickly as possible before sending it on to other destinations.

To secure any network, the services provided on that network must be specified, as well as the needs based on the network security policy. The idea is to allow only what is required while denying everything else. Closing ports, removing unused services, and managing network access points are simple things to do to reduce certain potential vulnerability areas. This is also an excellent opportunity to safeguard critical traffic by ensuring bandwidth and prioritizing specific services. Using traffic policing and shaping to reduce the use of new and undiscovered risks is an effective way to do so. Disabling unnecessary ports, protocols, and services, as well as employing an infrastructure access list to identify your necessary flows and only allow those to access the device, are some of the approaches to adopt for network service security. Firewall protection can be used to secure network services, police traffic, and prioritize key flows.

In SDN deployments, the next layer is applications and APIs. Many network devices operate on closed operating systems with few or no API interfaces to external-to-external applications for data collection, management, or provisioning. To extract and convey information to other applications, well-known protocols such as Syslog, SNMP, and SSL are employed. SDN enables the development of applications with direct access to the controller, allowing them to directly modify network aspects. It is vital to utilize secure coding methods while designing apps to preserve the controller's integrity from unstable and insecure code. In SDN installations, many network devices run closed operating systems with limited or no API interfaces to external applications for statistics collection, management, or provisioning. To extract and convey information to other applications, well-known protocols such as Syslog, SNMP, and SSL are employed. SDN enables the development of applications with direct access to the controller, allowing them to directly modify network aspects. When designing applications, it is vital to employ secure coding methods. Because the controller's integrity must be safeguarded from unstable and insecure conditions. Threat mitigation solutions should be implemented on and around agents, and threat management protocols should be in place. One of the most effective agent threat management processes is the capacity to identify certain attack types, such as denial of service attacks, spoofing attacks, fragmentation attacks. It is invaluable to be able to connect them to specific attack mitigation measures, which frequently include detecting attack patterns and comprehending multiple attack pathways. Securing the SDN controller becomes critical to ensuring the network's normal operation. SDN controller security must be deployed in multiple dimensions and must cover all possible entry points for hackers. The main threat vectors affecting the SDN architecture integration points are summarized below, starting with the individual planes, and are used to examine the security of the SDN controller.

B. **Security by the SDN**

SDN agents and controllers can be configured to act as a perimeter for a specific device or service. Content inspection, identity management, and threat defense, can all be applied to connections and forms via security services linked with agent systems. Controllers are allocated to attacks and anomalies in order to enforce network-wide containment and disseminate protection upgrades. After deployment, issues are handled, and performance monitoring becomes automated and centralized. Agent systems incorporate security services. When configuring a feature, you can check for correct policy, correct configuration, and correct configuration syntax. Implementing a route, prohibiting a routing protocol recall, and then trying to secure that route protocol is an example of an implausible situation. It is critical to be able to perform a configuration check to guarantee that the configuration is right before it is passed down to an agent. Because, once again, attacks or service disruptions are not always the result of external users attacking the network and it can also be the result of simple configuration issues. By automatically protecting the agents as soon as it detects an attack, may restrict or eliminate distributed DDoS type attacks and the effects they have on the network. The most essential aspect of SDN security is that it is embedded into the deployment from the outset. It's no longer an overlay. Security is an essential component of core technology and notice the layered approach to the system in this typical SDN implementation. After that, the containment and mitigation strategy can be transmitted to the SDN layer, and therefore to other agents in the network. When this is completed, we will have enterprise-wide protection, with policy updates distributed to all network agents.

SDN confronts two significant security problems. One strategy is to use SDN to address traditional network security issues. Another goal is to secure SDN and strengthen SDN-enabled infrastructure. SDN is subject to seven key threat vectors in terms of the latter.

The following are the threat vectors:

- Fake traffic flow
- Attack on control plane
- Attack on switch and controller weaknesses
- Vulnerabilities in administrative stations
  - Lack of reliable sources for network recovery
- Lack of trust between management and control applications

A DDoS attack on controllers is the most devastating attack on the entire network.

11.4   CONTROL PLANE SECURITY

Since the SDN controller is a novel entity in conventional networks, special attention must be paid to its security. With regard to SDN control plane security, it is asserted that many of the same arguments that make SDN data plane protection challenging, such as the incompatibility of existing solutions and the control plane's unproven reliance on the info plane, also apply [11].

DDoS attacks on the SDN control layer seek to disrupt networks by overloading the controller with traffic from multiple sources [12,13]. Based on the flow rules, the controller determines how to forward packets. When a new network packet is discovered in the data plane by the switch and no flow rules match the existing flow information in the flow table, the entire packet or a portion of the header is sent to the controller to resolve the query. The attacker's first step is to identify the SDN network. It should be noted that traditional networks typically have a forwarding table that is preconfigured. As a result, there is no additional time required to process and create a flow input for a new incoming packet.

In contrast, the controller in SDNs requires some time to create a new flow input for a new incoming packet. Furthermore, the driver takes longer to process the first packet than the subsequent packages. Attackers use this knowledge to determine whether a network is SDN or not, using network scanning tools to see if there is a difference between the response times of the first and subsequent packets.

Figure 11.4 depicts how a DDoS attack on the SDN controller is carried out. It is observed when an attacker infects other devices to become a part of the infected

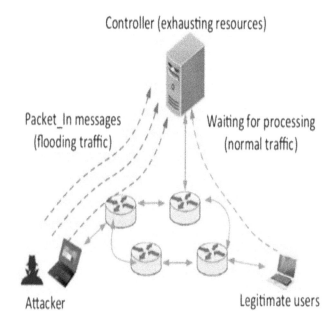

FIGURE 11.5   Attack on SDN controller [11].

machines. When the bots are ready to attack, they are given a command to attack for a set period of time. When a data packet does not match the flow table, the OpenFlow switch sends a message to the controller and loads messages Packet into the exceeding controller's processing capacity. The controller's resources will be depleted as a result of this type of attack, and legitimate traffic will be restricted access to the controller.

The control layer termed as brain of SDN manages the entire network by controlling all switches. To communicate between the SDN controller and switches, a standard southbound API is used (Figure 11.5). The controllers in the SDN architecture are a particularly appealing target for DDoS attacks because they could be thought of as the network's "single point of failure."

11.5 COMPARATIVE STUDY

Attacks on an SDN, have the potential to be devastating, as previously discussed. Attack risks have increased, particularly when compared to traditional networks. The most serious vulnerabilities are those affecting access control and availability [14,20]. Many researches have studied these vulnerabilities and presented several survey papers. Table 11.1 gives the comparative study of various works carried out to study the vulnerabilities in SDN networks and what are the focused area of study (Figure 11.6).

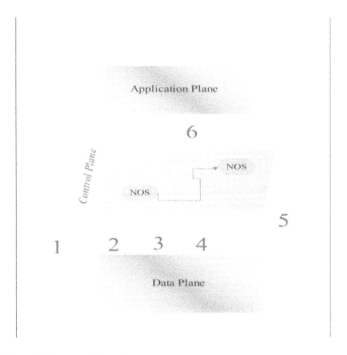

FIGURE 11.6 SDN control plane threats.

TABLE 11.1
Comparison of Our Work with Other Similar Survey Papers

	Baway et al. [14]	Joelle et al. [15]	Don g et al. [16]	Fajar et al. [17]	Xu et al. [18]	Kalkan et al. [19]	Our work [2]
Architecture of SDN	X	X	X	X	X	X	✓
SDN security issues	X	X	X	X	X	✓	✓ [3]
Security by the SDN	X	X	X	X	X	X	✓
Security for the SDN	✓	✓	X	X	✓	X	✓
ControlPlane security	X	X	X	✓	X	X	✓
Comparative study	X	X	X	X	X	X	✓
Research gaps	X	X	X	X	X	X	✓

11.6 CONCLUSION

This chapter provides overview of SDN and its security. SDN architecture and security of it has been studied and investigated by identifying the numerous danger vectors available to an attacker when attacking a software-defined network. Furthermore, the taxonomy of potential assaults in relation to the main components of SDN is presented. Following that, the primary challenges confronting SDN data and control plane protection are highlighted as well as reviewed available solutions in the literature. A classification for SDN-based security services is presented in detail, which has lately gained traction in the literature. Because the network data plane is decoupled from the control plane in the SDN environment, centralized network management and programmable network control are available. A significant and rapid spike in incoming traffic from many sources at varying rates, on the other hand, could overburden the SDN controller, resulting in resource exhaustion. As a result, attackers might use specific SDN functionalities to perform DDoS attacks against the controller. DDoS assaults could have a significant impact on the controller's operation, resulting in decreased performance or the failure of the entire SDN network. As a result, developing an efficient detection method for DDoS assaults based on traffic flow statistics must be addressed. Unfortunately, most existing detection techniques for DDoS assaults against the controller with single or many targets struggle to detect low- and high-rate attacks with good accuracy and a low false-positive rate. As a result, there is a need for an effective approach to identify both low-rate and high-rate DDoS attacks on the SDN controller with high accuracy and a low false-positive rate, regardless of the number of targets and attackers. Finally, a series of comparisons for future study possibilities in these areas are discussed.

REFERENCES

1. B. Mladenov, "Studying the DDoS attack effect over SDN controller southbound channel", in: *10th IEEE National Conference with International Participation (ELECTRONICA)*, pp. 1–4, 2019.
2. R. Kandoi, and M. Antikainen, "Denial-of-service attacks in OpenFlow SDN networks", in: *IEEE International Symposium on Integrated Network Management (IM)*, pp. 1322–1326, 2015.
3. S. Jose, L. R. Nair, and V. Paul, "Towards detecting flooding DDOS attacks over software-defined networks using machine learning techniques", *Revista Geintec-Gestao Inovacao e Tecnologias*, vol. 11, no. 4, pp. 3837–3865, 2021.
4. W. Stallings, *Foundations of Modern Networking: SDN, NFV, QoE, IoT, and Cloud*. Addison-Wesley Professional, 2015.
5. B. H. Lawal, and A. Nuray, "Real-time detection and mitigation of distributed denial of service (DDoS) attacks in software-defined networking (SDN)", in: *26th IEEE Signal Processing and Communications Applications Conference (SIU)*, pp. 1–4, 2018.
6. C. Kodzai, *Impact of Network Security on SDN Controller Performance*. University of Cape Town, 2020.
7. F. Bannour, S. Souihi, and A. Mellouk, "Distributed SDN control: Survey, taxonomy, and challenges", *IEEE Communications Surveys & Tutorials*, vol. 20, no. 1, pp. 333–354, 2017.
8. D. Li, C. Yu, Q. Zhou, and J. Yu, "Using SVM to detect DDoS attack in SDN network," *IOP Conference Series: Materials Science and Engineering*, vol. 466, no. 1, pp. 012003, 2018.
9. D. Glăvan, C. Răcuciu, R. Moinescu, and N.-F. Antonie, "Detecting the DDoS attack for SDN controller", *Scientific Bulletin MirceacelBatran Naval Academy*, vol. 22, no. 1, pp. 1–8, 2019.
10. J. Singh and S. Behal, "Detection and mitigation of DDoS attacks in SDN: A comprehensive review, research challenges and future directions", *Computer Science Review*, vol. 37, p. 100279, 2020.
11. B. B. Gupta, G. M. Perez, D. P. Agrawal, and D. Gupta, *Handbook of Computer Networks and Cyber Security*. Springer, vol. 10, pp. 978–973, 2020.
12. M. Nenova, G. Iliev, S. Javed, K. S. Bhosale, "New techniques for DDoS attacks mitigation in resource-constrained networks", in: *Distributed Denial of Service Attacks (Concepts, Mathematical and Cryptographic Solutions)*, De Gruyter Publication, vol. 6, p. 83, 2021.
13. J. R. Shaikh, and G. Iliev, "A technique for DoS attack detection in e-commerce transactions based on ECC and optimized support vector neural network", *Control and Cybernetics Journal*, vol. 47, no. 4, pp. 439–463, 2018.
14. N. Z. Bawany, and J. A. Shamsi, "SEAL: SDN based secure and agile framework for protecting smart city applications from DDoS attacks", *Journal of Network and Computer Applications*, vol. 145, pp. 102381, 2019.
15. M. M. Joëlle, and Y.-H. Park, "Strategies for detecting and mitigating DDoS attacks in SDN: A survey", *Journal of Intelligent & Fuzzy Systems*, vol. 35, no. 6, pp. 5913–5925, 2018.
16. S. Dong, K. Abbas, and R. Jain, "A survey on distributed denial of service (DDoS) attacks in SDN and cloud computing environments", *IEEE Access*, vol. 7, pp. 80813–80828, 2019.
17. A. P. Fajar, and T. W. Purboyo, "A survey paper of distributed denial- of-service attack in software-defined networking (SDN)", *International Journal of Applied Engineering Research*, vol. 13, no. 1, pp. 476–482, 2018.

18. S. Shin, L. Xu, S. Hong, and G. Gu, "Enhancing network security through software-defined networking (SDN)," in *2016 25th International Conference on Computer Communication and Networks (ICCCN), 2016*, IEEE, pp. 1–9.

19. K. Kalkan, L. Altay, G. Gür, and F. Alagöz, "JESS: Joint entropy- based DDoS defense scheme in SDN", *IEEE Journal on Selected Areas in Communications*, vol. 36, no. 10, pp. 2358–2372, 2018.

20. K. R. Raghunandan, R. Dodmane, K. Bhavya, N. S. K. Rao and A. K. Sahu, "Chaotic-map based encryption for 3D point and 3D Mesh Fog data in edge computing," *IEEE Access*, vol. 11, pp. 3545–3554, 2023, doi: 10.1109/ACCESS.2022.3232461.

12 Assessment of the Role of IoT in Electronic Banking Industry

Rashi Rastogi

12.1 INTRODUCTION

Data is one of the most valuable assets in the management of automation systems, and it has been increasingly accessible in the age of innovation thanks to the development of information technology [1]. This means that financial markets and banking are all examples of technological advancements made by humans in recent decades. IoT is now widely used in the banking and financial sector. Every single one of these offerings produces hundreds of daily records [2]. As a result, the management of data has emerged as a crucial component of IoT services. IoT is an expanding global data infrastructure. Alternative data is increasingly used by financial and banking professionals today [3]. The banking and finance sectors also make use of IoT by doing forecasting research and discovering new patterns with which to create comprehensive decision-making frameworks. There are millions of records that are shared between banks and other financial institutions [4]. This is especially true in the banking and finance industry, where the success of production agents is heavily reliant on data, and so the IoT has a greater impact there. This function is becoming more and more crucial to the comprehension of the banking and financial markets. Messages, decisions, service providers, and future predictions are all aspects of daily life that are made easier thanks to the IoT, a widely adopted communication paradigm [5]. The IoT has evolved into a useful tool for enhancing the retail experience due to the proliferation of mobile phones and wireless devices like sensors [6,7]. The layered architecture of the IoT-based financial services system is depicted in Figure 12.1. Customers can be given personalized recommendations based on a statistical analysis of their financial data such as their earnings, account balances, and available funds, all within a broad framework [8].

The layers used in this architecture are:

- Device Management layer: Many kinds of IoT devices, such as those that use Ethernet or Wi-Fi, or those that rely on mobile phones or low-power radios, are part of this layer.
- Communication layer: This layer serves the same purpose as the network layer in classic Internet architecture.

DOI: 10.1201/9781003432869-12

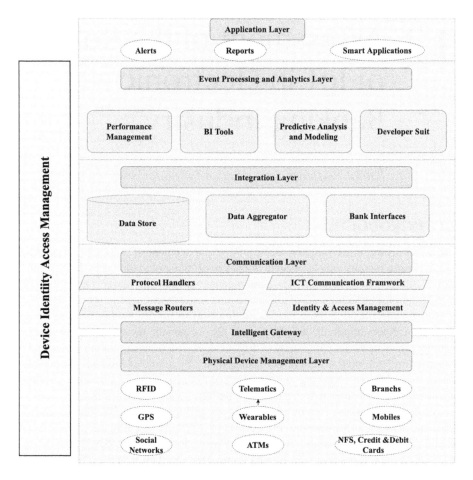

FIGURE 12.1   Layered architecture of IoT used for financial industries.

- Integration layer: Structured and unstructured data are combined at this layer.
- Event analysis and processing layer: This layer monitors the combined data and regulates the recounting events.
- Application layer: The application layer connects the apps to the underlying system.

12.2   MOTIVATION

Banks and businesses now have access to a wider range of financial services because of innovations in digital transfer. This method can be emphasized as a cutting-edge improvement for financial and banking access, reflecting the influence of IoT on finance and banking and its services [9]. For instance, millions of data are produced every day by online transactions, banking applications, and Internet banking.

Since the management of these financial services and Internet banking has significant effects on the financial and banking markets, doing so effectively is a pressing concern [10].

12.3   ADVANTAGES OF IOT IN BANKING

- Real-time Feedback: IoT devices in a bank can monitor customer behavior to learn useful insights. This information can be useful for the management team in assessing the monetary requirements of various businesses.
- Identifying Fraudulent Activity: The banking industry is stunned by rampant fraud. The rate of these kinds of events has increased intensely during the previous decade. IoT in banking is one strategy to prevent this type of scam. The biometric technology has the potential to significantly reduce the impact of fraud. But there are always those who manage to bypass the system altogether. By alerting users with every transaction, IoT management serves to keep customers aware of any forthcoming problems. When a user reports a transaction as fake, the transaction is immediately stopped and their account is locked until further investigation is completed. The instantaneous feedback and coordination provided by the automated IoT system makes such rapid responses possible.
- Customer Service: The provision of customer service is a key application area for IoT technology. The IoT collects information on its users and tracks their digital activities. For customer care purposes, that's priceless information. It will document the customer and their monetary wants and needs. Financial institutions can utilize this information to provide budgeting advice.
- Data Analytics: The IoT most significant impact on any sector is the enhancement of analytical capacity. When talking about the IoT, data is key. The amount of information that can be collected by an IoT network is truly stunning. The data is processed by specialized automated algorithms into illegal intelligence for the sector. The banking industry can utilize this to learn more about their customers. In terms of financing, that's quite useful. The banking sector, like the real estate industry, can employ an IoT network to keep tabs on the financial health of prospective customers. Financial IoT may access a wide range of trade data feeds. The issuance and trading volume of private and government bonds aid financial institutions in making more informed management decisions.
- Improved Security: In the banking industry, safety is dominant. The foundation of this system is the faith that customers have in banks to protect their money. An institution's security system's initial infrastructure can benefit from the IoT.
- Automation: The banking industry stands to gain enormously from the implementation of automated technology. The IoT allows financial institutions to automate routine tasks with custom-built software. With the help of IoT technologies, smart devices can also perform better. The basis of self-checkout systems is also the IoT infrastructure.

12.4   CHALLENGES OF IOT IN THE BANKING SECTOR

Many challenges remain in applying IoT technology [15]. These are as follows:

- Security Issue: On the client side, security is reinforced by IoT systems. For financial institutions, though, things seem different. Due to its novelty, the IoT has yet to be standardized. The most fundamental part, though, is just collecting information from a variety of sources. The IoT network is vulnerable to skilled hackers who can exploit the devices' poor security measures. Though they might not take sensitive data, they could potentially cause the system to provide inaccurate results. There's a wide variety of devices in this list. It may also refer to people equipped with a variety of devices, such as smart security cameras, automated teller machines, and so on. The major flaw of this method is that it is difficult to ensure the security of each and every one of these devices to the same degree. It's simple for malicious attacker to interfere with feedback devices, thereby feeding the IoT network with false information.
- Redundancy: The IoT generates a massive amount of data. This feature is common in most industries, and it's not surprising to find it in the financial sector. Unfortunately, 90% of such data is meaningless. The majority of the information collected will not be useful to the financial institutions. Therefore, a large amount of data processing is required to extract the relevant information.
- The Trouble with Uniformity: As a field of study, IoT has only recently emerged. Currently, there are no globally adopted standards for ensuring a consistent and compatible system interface.

This chapter is divided into sections. In section I, the introduction of banking system and the role of IoT in banking have been discussed. Furthermore, benefits and challenges of IoT have been presented. In Section 12.2 background of financial services of banking and IoT has been presented. Section 12.3 presents the literature review of various papers that considered role of IoT in banking management. Furthermore, in Section 12.4 the assessment of IoT in banking system has been presented. At last, in Section 12.5 the conclusion and future directions have been presented.

The objective of this chapter is to investigate the current state of IoT in banking and monetary services. This research focuses on how the IoT is changing the face of finance and banking, namely in the areas of electronic banking, financial markets, financial services, and banking management. In light of this, the purpose of this research is to provide a description of the present-day state of macro data technology and the IoT in the banking and finance sectors.

12.5   BACKGROUND

The purpose of the IoT is to increase knowledge and provide service to system end-users. Processing raw data and building up massive amounts of it to derive renewed insights is where the real money is spent on data acquisition. However, this kind of behavior can cause privacy concerns for users [11]. Through the IoT, devices and people are able to exchange data and information with each other and the wider world at any time, from any location, and using any available network or service. Between 50 and 100 billion devices are expected to be online by 2020 [12].

Many IoT applications are made with a single user in mind [13]. By applying cloud computing and IT, big data can affect the market based credit system of businesses and consumers. Offline banking and financial transactions are now possible because of mobile Internet technologies, cloud computing, and big data services [14].

12.6　LITERATURE REVIEW

Khanboubi et al. [16], The next step in the digital revolution that will affect people's daily lives is the IoT. Connected items signify the expansion of the Internet beyond the digital realm and into the physical world. The goals of this chapter are to (1) introduce the various applications of IoT in the financial sector, and (2) examine how digital developments and IoT have altered the conventional bank's operational model. It would be fascinating to compile the various digital trends that have an equivalent effect on banking procedures.

Bansal et al. [17] We all know that the banking and finance industries are extremely intricate, and that many changes are coming to these fields right now. Data in the form of information is processed and collected at unprecedented rates every day. As the volume of data grows, it becomes more challenging for financial institutions to effectively manage it alongside their other operations. This chapter outlines the possible impact of the IoT on the banking industry and how its many transformations may usher in paradigm-shifting changes to the status quo. Financial institutions can improve their market share by catering their services to individual customers' requirements using real-time data analysis provided by IoT. The IoT will one day be able to develop such technologies that can link actual objects, allowing them to make rational decisions on their own.

According to Mohaghar et al. [18], the rapid development of the IoT has resulted in the appearance of new banking services. The IoT is still a relatively new concept in Iran, but it has already proven useful in a number of industries, including banking, where it has allowed for more efficient and timely responses to consumers' inquiries regardless of their location. The study's goal is to catalog and rank IoT applications in Iran's banking sector using resiliency metrics. The first step is to identify banking-related IoT applications based on a thorough literature analysis and real-world experiences. Next, the Grey Decision-making Trial and Evaluation Laboratory was used to assign relative importance to each indicator. Finally, the multi-attribute utility theory has been prioritized in IoT-based applications in Iran's banking sector (MAUT). In this investigation, they use business continuity indicators to account for the financial sector's vulnerability to market fluctuations. Using MAUT also takes into account the value of banking specialists when executing IoT banking services. Results show that Iranian banks have access to IoT-based services as transmitting immediate reports, smart ATMs, contactless electronic payments, and electronic checks. Then, Iranian banks prioritize providing these necessary services within their resources.

According to Boumlik and Bahaj [19], the banking industry is extremely dynamic and highly sensitive. Data management and real-time monitoring of fraud issues are even greater hurdles in this industry than they are for many others due to the massive volume of data, arriving at lightning speed from a variety of sources in both organized and unstructured formats and requiring immediate attention. Typically, banks and other financial institutions may test new payment methods that present greater challenges and security risks in an effort to push their customers to develop their digital competence.

According to Suseendran et al. [20] financial institutions have been pushing for the development of innovative FinTech (financial technology) solutions in tandem with the IoT for the better part of a decade IoT. The new business environment must accommodate the needs of FinTech and IoT. A number of businesses are impacted by the investments at the monetary level. Therefore, it is essential to enhance the company's future trajectory. With the help of the internet of services that supply ideas linked online, FinTech can introduce a new service of tools and products for emerging enterprises. More and more organizations are seeing value in implementing IoT initiatives today. Current monetary authorities in direct society are terrible when it comes to adopting new financial practices. New invention achieves social advancement. Combining FinTech and IoT helps to generate fresh, groundbreaking ideas that may be included into a business's strategic strategy and operations.

According to Almugari et al. [21], the research team behind this study hopes to learn how factors including public perception, fear of security breaches, perceived value of convenience, social pressure, and established routines affect the rate of IoT adoption within India's banking sector. In total, 467 Indian consumers were used as the study's sample. To ensure the questionnaire's validity, accuracy, and applicability for the study at hand, a Confirmatory Factor Analysis (CFA) is performed. When compared to the specified values, the indices for both the CFA model fit and the SEM model fit are determined to be good, therefore the Structural Equation Modeling (SEM) model is utilized to evaluate the study's hypotheses. The findings show that the use of the IoT in Indian banks is significantly affected by factors including ease of use, social influence, privacy and security, and general knowledge. However, the findings demonstrate that neither price nor routines play a significant role in the spread of IoT. This research aims to analyze how Indian financial institutions are utilizing IoT. In light of India's aspirations to join the ranks of the world's developed nations, the IoT has vast potential in a variety of industries; without a doubt, such technology in the banking industry can serve as a foundation for this goal. The purpose of this article is to provide guidance to policymakers and manufacturers of IoT objects so that they may facilitate the development of such an easily adopted and publicly useful service in financial institutions.

H. Ramalingam and V. Venkatesan [22] writes, as a part of smart infrastructure, the IoT presents a great opportunity for the financial sector. ATMs, POS terminals, and mobile banking apps are currently the banking industry's cutting edge. To fulfil the expanding needs of the financial services industry, digital banks must implement intelligent banking edge systems, and the IoT is a key component of this type of infrastructure.

According to Lande et al. [23] Everything nowadays is either wirelessly connected or hardwired. As time progresses, it becomes necessary to update conventional methods of operation. An increase in IoT data has resulted from consumers' elevated trust in connected devices and the web. The IoT alters people's daily routines and the way businesses are approached. This article discusses the impact of the IoT in the banking and finance industry. In order to improve their market share and deliver better services to their customers, banks need to transform IoT data into profitable information. Topics including financial fraud and IoT-based fraud detection in its early stages are intended to be covered in this research.

Research by El-Aziz et al. [24], Even if IoT appears to be the next big thing, its implementation is still in its early stages, notably in the financial sector. It is obvious that there is a lack of research on facilitating and moderating factors, as only a small number of studies identify factors affecting preparedness to IoT applications in banks in general. Therefore, the purpose of this study is to identify the primary factors influencing employee awareness to IoT applications in the Egyptian banking sector and to emphasize the mediating and moderating elements. Egypt's population is among the world's largest, and the country is also making steady progress toward technological adoption. Among bank HR personnel, 479 valid surveys were sent out. Regression and SEM were used for statistical analysis on the data gathered. Readiness for IoT applications was shown to be significantly affected by the factors "Security," "Networking," "Software Development," and "Regulations." That's why there's a lot of consensuses on how ready we are to go. Although 'Efficiency' was shown to play a moderating function, 'Security' and 'User Intention' were found to fully mediate the association between research factors and readiness to IoT applications. This research not only helps to close a knowledge gap in the Egyptian banking sector, but also adds to the growing literature on IoT applications overall. Finally, it presents guidance to bank management on how to best promote IoT applications among staff.

Patel et al. [25] IoT is one component of the interconnected, intelligent environment in which modern humans exist. Because of this, reducing the amount of power required by various IoT technologies is the primary obstacle researchers must overcome. You can't stop or limit the digital world because of how quickly and powerfully it's evolving. A GIoT is offered as a means to realize IoT with low power usage. On the other hand, because of front-line innovations like AI and ML, businesses may improve their bottom lines, cut expenses, and deliver a better service to their customers. This chapter's goal is to provide a high-level overview of the banking industry's use of GIoT and its life cycle. Additionally, they discussed the potential applications of AI and ML in the financial sector. Furthermore, this chapter has examined the critical function of AI and ML in the financial sector and uncovered frontline technologies that can be implemented to lessen the impact on the environment caused by the IoT.

Khanboubi and Boulmakoul [26] Modern forms of communication have a deep effect on the management of financial operations and significantly outline their ecosystem. The IoT social media, digital money, blockchain, and artificial intelligence (AI) are also important developments. In many cases, one technology cannot exist without another. The IoT refers to the connecting of individually identifiable computing devices within the framework of a surrounding network of such systems. Those pieces of linked machinery working together should make it possible to automate a number of time-consuming, manual procedures in the banking industry. As the IoT-driven digital transformation takes hold, new business models and products are being developed to accommodate it. They also examined the way in which IoT-based digital threats affect conventional banking procedures. It would be beneficial to group together the various forms of digital risk that have analogous effects on banking operations. They examined these tools so that may put up novel procedures for realizing the digital transition.

Li et al. [27] Workflow and prediction performance is crucial for business process automation. It's beneficial because it allows banks to be more adaptable in how they carry out their businesses, which in turn boosts efficiency across the board. The distributed IT system used by retail bank branches. Branch banking is vulnerable by the inability of legacy operating systems to accommodate a wide variety of innovative end-user services. The inability to communicate with other banking systems or electronic devices is a major obstacle. This study proposes a solution that utilizes AI and dynamic workflow technology. As a result, banking user services become more adaptable and competitive in their pursuit of pleased clients. To reduce the amount of time spent developing and maintaining banking systems and the number of errors

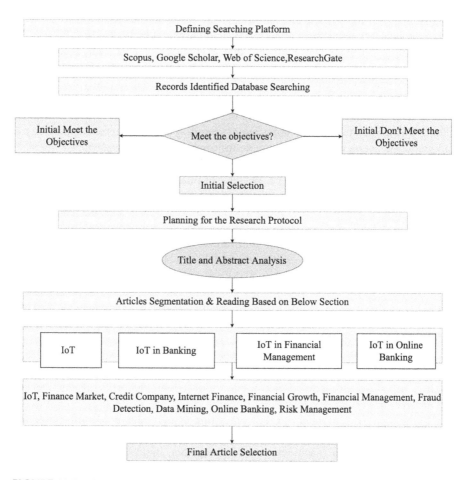

FIGURE 12.2   Assessment process.

that occur within them, they designed a unified process control module to aid end users in implementing adaptable financial transaction procedures.

12.7 ASSESSMENT OF IOT IN BANKING INDUSTRIES

In this section, a detailed assessment of electronic banking industry with IoT has been discussed. Figure 12.2 depicts the detailed assessment process. Data from the stock market (price, volume traded, interest rates, etc.), social media, and other online resources are all cited as sources of knowledge about the financial markets (e.g., Facebook, Twitter, newspapers). The financial market relies heavily on this information for a wide variety of purposes, including but not limited to forecasting future returns and fluctuations, assessing market position, detecting oversupply, assessing market risk, tracking stock turnover, and so on. The comprehensive theoretical framework is shown in Figure 12.3.

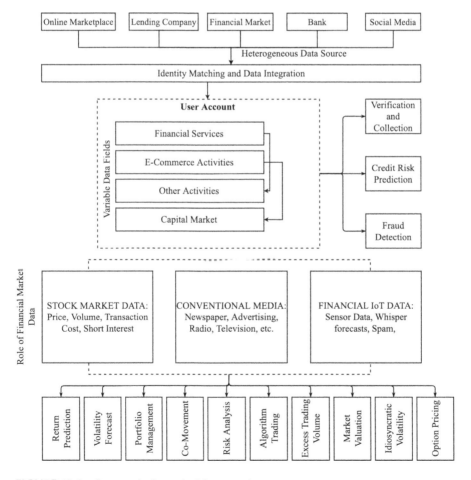

FIGURE 12.3 Systematic theoretical framework.

Figure 12.2, illustrates the assessment process for the study. It is a stepwise process for article selection for particular topics. Here, this study mainly emphasizes on IoT approach applied for banking services. All steps such as searching platform definition, record identification, analysis of title and abstract, etc., are included in Figure 12.2, and must be fulfilled in order to get the preferred article.

The sources depending on financial market information are mentioned in Figure 12.3, including information collected from various related sources such as lending company, online marketplace, banks, financial market, and social media (e.g., Twitter, Linkedin, Facebook). An important role played by these data in financial market such as market fluctuations prediction, market position assessment, oversupply identification, market risk analysis, market returns predictions, and so on. Figure 12.3 illustrates an effective framework for this study.

Elsevier, Springer, Taylor & Francis, Willie, Emerald, Sage, etc. were among the most heavily prioritized publishers for this study's data collection. With 31%, Springer is in the lead, followed by IEEE with 25%. Figure 12.4 displays the breakdown of each database's percentage share. Figure 12.5 depicts the average yearly growth rate of IoT-related journal articles. Research on IoT appears to have accelerated after 2018, and there is area for both Big data and IoT in the emerging subject of IoT for Electronic Banking. It's not a new idea to use Big data for communication, but it wasn't until after 2011 that Big data in IoT was introduced and examined in depth. Future academics may benefit from looking at the rate of publication growth in IoT to better understand the direction of research and adjust their efforts accordingly. Table 12.1 depicts the number of papers published during a particular year by various publishers. It shows publication data from 2018 to 2022.

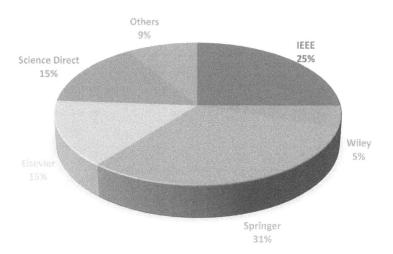

PUBLICATIONS

FIGURE 12.4 Pie chart representation of research papers sources.

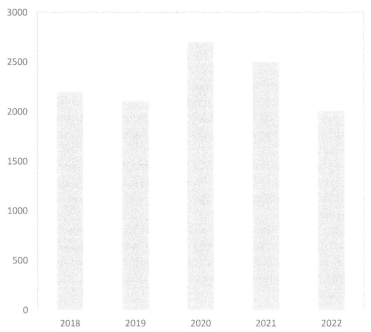

PUBLICATIONS RELATED TO IoT IN BANKING
AND FINANCIAL FIELD

FIGURE 12.5   Analysis of papers based on years.

TABLE 12.1
Publication Related to IoT in Banking and Finance

Publisher	2018	2019	2020	2021	2022	Publications
Springer	823	617	910	713	545	3608
Elsevier	213	403	368	310	498	1792
Science Direct	367	287	290	437	317	1698
IEEE	548	488	718	721	378	2853
Wiley	98	167	115	140	85	605
Others	138	197	341	225	198	1099

12.8   CONCLUSION AND FUTURE WORK

Banking provides the basis for the modern business era, and the incorporation of
crucial points such as IoT devices improves data quality in real-time, allowing for
more effective decision processing and greater scalability. Growing demand for
banking services has led to an expansion of banking products as well as retail and
branch locations. At the edge, digital banking infrastructure plays a crucial role

in supporting the IoT by providing integrated and real-time services. In the future, IoT banking will serve as the foundation upon which all other banking services and products are built. However, digitalization is being driven in the IoT financial and banking sector. Businesses of all sizes are excited to use these innovations to begin their digital transformations, which will lead to more efficiency, higher revenues, and a better ability to satisfy customers. While it's true that many businesses keep track of important new data, it's fair to wonder what this information can tell us about the banking and finance sectors. Every banking and financial service, from this point of view, is frontline in terms of technology and treats data as a stream. Factors such as monitoring financial and banking performance, growth control, and boosting sales and customer happiness all play a role in shaping these services.

The banking and financial industries face a number of significant challenges related to big data. The protection of individual privacy is a major concern when using big data for any purpose. Data quality and compliance with regulations are also taken into account.

Research into big data and finance and banking has not yet achieved its height, despite the fact that every financial and banking product and service is entirely data-based and produces data every second. Therefore, it's easy to say that social media platforms like Facebook and Twitter play an important role in the banking and finance industries.

REFERENCES

1 A. Boumlik and M. Bahaj, "Big data and IoT: A prime opportunity for banking industry," in *Advanced Information Technology, Services and Systems: Proceedings of the International Conference on Advanced Information Technology, Services and Systems (AIT2S-17)*, Held on April 14/15, 2017, Tangier, Springer International Publishing, 2018, pp. 396–407.

2 Mittal, Aditi, and Sumit Gupta. "Emerging role of information technology in banking sector's development of India," *ACADEMICIA: An International Multidisciplinary Research Journal*, vol. 3, pp. 11–17, 2013.

3 R. El-Aziz, S. El-Gamal and M. Ismail, "Mediating and moderating factors affecting readiness to IoT applications: The banking sector context," *International Journal of Managing Information Technology (IJMIT)*, vol. 12, pp. 1–26, 2020.

4 P. Mishra and T. G. Sant, "Role of artificial intelligence and internet of things in promoting banking and financial services during COVID-19: Pre and post effect," in *2021 5th International Conference on Information Systems and Computer Networks (ISCON)*, IEEE, 2021, pp. 1–7.

5 N. Shah, Z. Jhanjhi, F. Amsaad and A. Razaque, "The role of cutting-edge technologies in industry 4.0," in *Cyber Security Applications for Industry 4.0*, edited by R Sujatha, G Prakash, Noor Zaman Jhanjhi, Chapman and Hall/CRC, 2022, pp. 97–109.

6 V. Chang, L. Xiao, Q. Xu and M. Arami, "A review paper on the application of big data by banking institutions and related ethical issues and responses," in *2nd International Conference on Finance, Economics, Management and IT Business*, SciTePress, May 2020, pp. 115–121.

7 Aripin, Zaenal, and Vip Paramarta. "Utilizing Internet of Things (IOT)-based design for consumer loyalty: A digital system integration," *Jurnal Penelitian Pendidikan IPA*, vol. 9, no. 10, pp. 8650–8655.

8   N. Kshetri, "Big data's role in expanding access to financial services in China," *International Journal of Information Management*, vol. 36, no. 3, pp. 297–308, 2016.

9   R. Bhat, S. A. AlQahtani and M. Nekovee, "FinTech enablers, use cases, and role of future internet of things," *Journal of King Saud University-Computer and Information Sciences*, vol. 35, pp. 87–101, 2022.

10 A. Mohaghar, M. R. Sadeghi Moghadam, R. Ghourchi Beigi and R. Ghasemi, "IoT-based services in banking industry using a business continuity management approach," *Journal of Information Technology Management*, vol. 13, no. 4, pp. 16–38, 2021.

11 J. Kumar, "Role of the Internet of Things (IoT) in digital financial inclusion," in *IoT Based Smart Applications*, edited by Nidhi Sindhwani, Rohit Anand, M Niranjanamurthy, Dinesh Chander Verma, Emilia Balas Valentina, Springer International Publishing, 2022, pp. 363–373.

12 H. Alzoubi, M. Alshurideh, B. Kurdi, K. Alhyasat and T. Ghazal, "The effect of e-payment and online shopping on sales growth: Evidence from banking industry," *International Journal of Data and Network Science*, vol. 6, no. 4, pp. 1369–1380, 2022.

13 S. Haripriya, "The role of culture code and IoT technology in successful implementation of marketing intelligence system," *International Journal of Current Engineering and Scientific Research (IJCESR)*, vol. 7, pp. 68–81, 2020.

14 A. Belhadi, K. Zkik, A. Cherrafi, and M. Y. Sha'ri, "Understanding big data analytics for manufacturing processes: insights from literature review and multiple case studies," *Computers & Industrial Engineering*, vol. 137, p. 106099, 2019.

15 R. Dubey, A. Gunasekaran, S. J. Childe, D. J. Bryde, M. Giannakis, C. Foropon and B. T. Hazen, "Big data analytics and artificial intelligence pathway to operational performance under the effects of entrepreneurial orientation and environmental dynamism: A study of manufacturing organisations," *International Journal of Production Economics*, vol. 226, p. 107599, 2020.

16 F. Khanboubi, A. Boulmakoul, and M. Tabaa, "Impact of digital trends using IoT on banking processes," *Procedia Computer Science*, vol. 151, pp. 77–84, 2019.

17 O. N. Bansal and M. Sameer, "IoT in online banking," *Journal of Ubiquitous Computing and Communication Technologies (UCCT)*, vol. 2, no. 04, pp. 219–222, 2020.

18 A. Mohaghar, M. R. Sadeghi Moghadam, R. Ghourchi Beigi and R. Ghasemi, "IoT-based services in banking industry using a business continuity management approach," *Journal of Information Technology Management*, vol. 13, no. 4, pp. 16–38, 2021.

19 A. Boumlik and M. Bahaj, "Big data and IoT: A prime opportunity for banking industry," in *Advanced Information Technology, Services and Systems: Proceedings of the International Conference on Advanced Information Technology, Services and Systems (AIT2S-17)*, Held on April 14/15, 2017 in Tangier. Springer International Publishing, 2018, pp. 396–407.

20 G. Suseendran, E. Chandrasekaran, D. Akila and A. Sasi Kumar, "Banking and FinTech (financial technology) embraced with IoT device," in *Data Management, Analytics and Innovation: Proceedings of ICDMAI 2019*, edited by Neha Sharma, Amlan Chakrabarti, Valentina Emilia Balas, Volume 1. Springer Singapore, 2020, pp. 197–211.

21 F. Almugari, P. Bajaj, M. I. Tabash, A. Khan, and M. A. Ali, "An examination of consumers' adoption of IoT (IoT) in Indian banks," *Cogent Business & Management*, vol. 7, no. 1, pp. 1809071, 2020.

22 H. Ramalingam and V. P. Venkatesan, "Conceptual analysis of IoT use cases in Banking domain," in *2019 IEEE Region 10 Conference (TENCON)*, pp. 2034–2039, October 2019.

23 R. S. Lande, S. A. Meshram, and P. P. Deshmukh, "Smart banking using IoT," in *2018 International Conference on Research in Intelligent and Computing in Engineering (RICE)*, pp. 1–4, August 2018.

24 R. El-Aziz, S. El-Gamal, and M. Ismail, "Mediating and moderating factors affecting readiness to IoT applications: the banking sector context," *International Journal of Managing Information Technology (IJMIT)*, vol. 12, pp. 1–26, 2020.

25 P. H. Patel, C. K. Rathod, and K. Zaveri, "Green IoT (IoT) and machine learning (ML): The combinatory approach and synthesis in the banking industry," *Green IoT and Machine Learning: Towards a Smart Sustainable World*, pp. 297–316, 2021.

26 F. Khanboubi and A. Boulmakoul, "Risk-driven analytics for banking IoT strategy," *IoT, Smart Computing and Technology: A Roadmap Ahead*, vol. 266, pp. 189–215, 2020.

27 R. Li, S. Chen and H. C. Wang, "Using intelligent prediction machine and dynamic workflow for banking customer satisfaction in IoT environment," *Journal of Ambient Intelligence and Humanized Computing*, vol. 14, pp. 1–10, 2021.

13 Investigation of SDN Attacks and Solutions in 5G Mobile Network

*V. Aanandaram, P. Deepalakshmi,
and Sathiyandra Kumar Srinivasan*

13.1 INTRODUCTION

A network architecture model known as software-defined networking (SDN) aims to make networks more resilient, scalable, and programmable. In the context of 5G networks, SDN can play an important role in enabling new capabilities and services needed for 5G use cases such as ultra-low latency, large machine-like communication, and sharing networks. SDN enables 5G networks to have a centralized control plane, where network management and decision-making is centralized, and a distributed data plane, where data transmission is managed by transmission elements such as switches and routers. This separation of the control plane from the data plane allows network operators to have a more flexible and programmatic way of network management and enables them to react quickly to changing network requirements. In addition, SDN enables network sharing, which is a key feature of 5G networks allow carriers to create multiple virtual networks on top of a shared physical infrastructure. Network slicing allows operators to create tailored networks optimized for specific use cases, such as advanced mobile broadband, large-scale machine-type communications, and ultra-low-latency communications. Overall, the combination of SDN and 5G technologies can provide a more flexible and efficient network architecture that can support many new and evolving use cases. 5G network technology (fifth generation), along with SDNs, promises to revolutionize the way communication networks work, making them flexible, efficient, and effective. However, this integration also poses new security challenges, as 5G and SDN technologies have their own set of vulnerabilities and attack vectors.

13.2 TYPES OF SDN ATTACKS IN 5G

The 5G network, being the latest technology in cellular communication, offers numerous benefits such as higher data rates, lower latency, and improved network capacity. However, with the advent of new technologies, security becomes a major concern. The increased complexity and interconnectivity of 5G networks make them vulnerable to various security threats, including SDN attacks. SDN attacks can cause significant harm to 5G networks by compromising network resources, altering

DOI: 10.1201/9781003432869-13

network configurations, and disrupting network traffic. Some of the common SDN attacks in 5G networks include:

Controller Hijacking: In this attack, an attacker compromises the SDN controller that manages the flow of data in the network.
Flow Table Manipulation: Attackers can manipulate the flow table to redirect network traffic or to cause congestion.
Network Resource Exhaustion: Attackers can launch a Denial-of-Service (DoS) attack on network resources, such as switches, to cause network disruption.
Data Tampering: Attackers can alter data as it traverses the network, compromising the confidentiality and integrity of the data.

13.2.1 MAJOR ATTACKS AND VULNERABILITIES IN SDN

13.2.1.1 Insider Threats

With a centralized control plane in SDN, a malicious insider gaining access to the controller has the potential to cause significant damage to the network (Figure 13.1). Network slicing attacks are examples of insider threat attacks against 5G SDN networks [1]. A simple diagrammatic representation for insider threat is shown in Figure 13.2. In 5G networks, network slicing allows the network operators to create more than one (i.e.) multiple virtual networks that share the same physical

FIGURE 13.1   Shows the major 5G SDN vulnerabilities. The same are explained in detail in the subsequent sections.

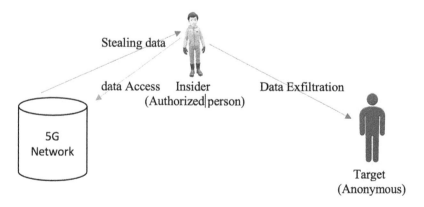

FIGURE 13.2   Insider attack.

infrastructure. Each virtual network or "slice" can be configured with its own policies and quality of service requirements.

Attackers with access to the 5G network can use network slicing to create their own virtual network slice and use it to launch attacks against other slices or the entire network. For example, an attacker can create a slice with high-priority access to the network and use that slice to launch denial-of-service attacks against other slices.

13.2.1.2 Controller Hijacking

The SDN network has an important component named as controller, and an attacker who takes control of the controller can manipulate the behavior of the network, cause a denial of service (DoS), or even redirect traffic to a malicious destination. Figure 13.3 shows the simple view of controller hijacking. In real-time, an attacker hijacks an SDN controller by sending a spoofed "packet-in" message to it. This can cause the controller to misjudge network traffic. An attacker could use this vulnerability to launch a Distributed Denial of Service (DDoS) attack on 5G networks. [2]. By manipulating the traffic flow of a network, an attacker may cause: congestion, overload certain network elements, and disrupt service for legitimate users.

13.2.1.3 Network Function Virtualization (NFV) Security

NFV is a critical component of 5G networks, but virtualizing network functionality also introduces new security risks, such as vulnerabilities or misconfigurations. Figure 13.4 represents an NFV security attack. In real-time, attackers manipulate the VNF (Virtual Network Function) chain mechanism to compromise the integrity and confidentiality of network traffic. An attacker could exploit this vulnerability by manipulating the VNF chaining mechanism to bypass security controls and access sensitive information [3].

In particular, an attacker can manipulate the chain mechanism to force network traffic through malicious VNFs capable of performing various attacks namely eavesdropping, data theft, and data manipulation.

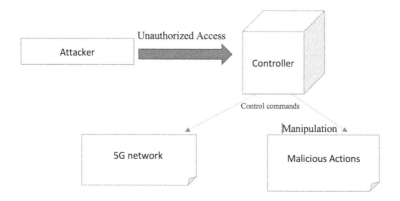

FIGURE 13.3 Controller hijacking.

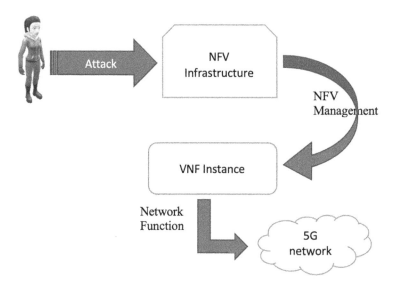

FIGURE 13.4 5G NFV attack.

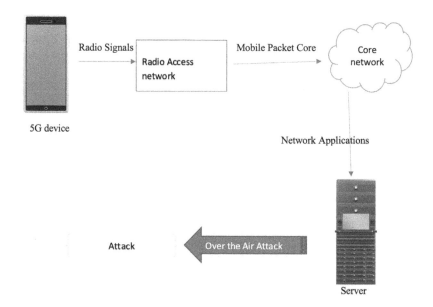

FIGURE 13.5 OTA attack.

13.2.1.4 Over-The-Air (OTA) Attacks

In 5G networks, OTA attacks on the air interface can be used to intercept or modify traffic or interfere with network operations. Figure 13.5 shows the OTA in a simple view.
In real-time, attackers manipulate 5G networks to force users to downgrade to older,
less secure LTE networks. An attacker can exploit this vulnerability by performing an
"LTE to 5G handover request" to force the device to connect to an untrusted network

instead of a trusted 5G network [4]. Attackers can then launch a variety of attacks against your network traffic. Examples: eavesdropping, data theft, data manipulation.

13.2.1.5   Routing Attacks

With SDN, an attacker can manipulate routing information to redirect traffic or disrupt network communication. A real-time example of a 5G routing attack is the "Routing Table Poisoning Attack" reported by Wu et al. [5]. In this attack, an attacker manipulates the routing table of the 5G network to redirect traffic on their network to a malicious target of their choosing as shown in Figure 13.6. This can lead to various attacks like DDoS attacks, data exfiltration, or malware distribution.

13.2.1.6   Rogue Base Stations

In 5G networks, as shown in Figure 13.7, malicious base stations can be used to intercept and monitor user traffic or disrupt network operations. A real-time example of a 5G rogue base station attack is the "stingray attack" used by law enforcement to

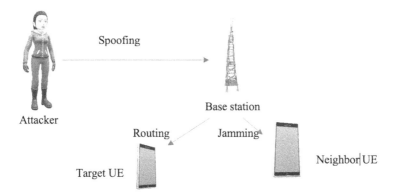

FIGURE 13.6   Routing attack.

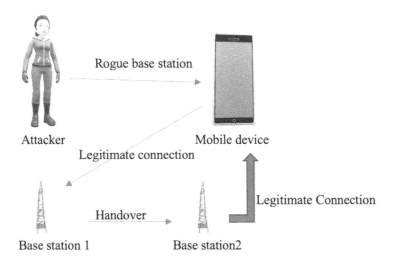

FIGURE 13.7   Rouge base station attack.

intercept cellular communications [6]. Stingray is a type of rogue base station that impersonates a legitimate base station and forces nearby devices to connect.

In a stingray attack, an attacker sets up a rogue base station and uses it to intercept and collect data sent between a user's device and a legitimate network. This may include sensitive information such as phone calls, text messages, and internet traffic. Attackers can also use rogue base stations to inject malware into users' devices or launch other types of attacks. Stingray attacks have been used primarily by law enforcement for surveillance purposes, but they also pose significant security threats to 5G networks. As the use of 5G networks continues to increase, these types of attacks will become more common. It may become a target.

13.2.1.7 API Security

The API used to communicate between a controller and a network device could be a potential entry point for attackers, who could exploit the vulnerability to gain access to sensitive information or damage the network. A real-time example of a 5G API security attack is the "eavesdropping attack" described in the research paper by Li et al. [7]. As illustrated in Figure 13.8, an attacker intercepts and reads sensitive

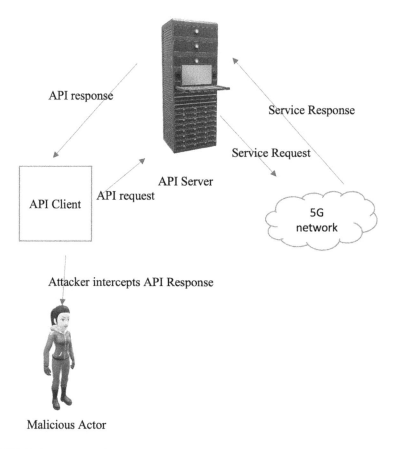

FIGURE 13.8 API security.

information sent between a user's device and the 5G network over an insecure API. They demonstrated how an attacker could exploit this vulnerability by intercepting and decrypting API requests and responses to obtain sensitive information such as user credentials, location data, and payment information. This can be achieved in various ways similar to MITM attacks, network sniffing, and protocol layer attacks.

13.2.1.8 Cryptographic Attacks

5G networks rely on strong cryptography to protect user data and network operations. As shown in Figure 13.9, an attacker could potentially exploit a weakness in an algorithm or cryptographic key to gain access to sensitive information. A real-time example of a 5G cryptographic attack is the "5G AKA key compromise attack" described in a research paper by Yoon et al. [8]. In this attack, an attacker could compromise the integrity of cryptographic keys used in their 5G Authentication and Key Agreement (AKA) protocol to impersonate legitimate users or intercept

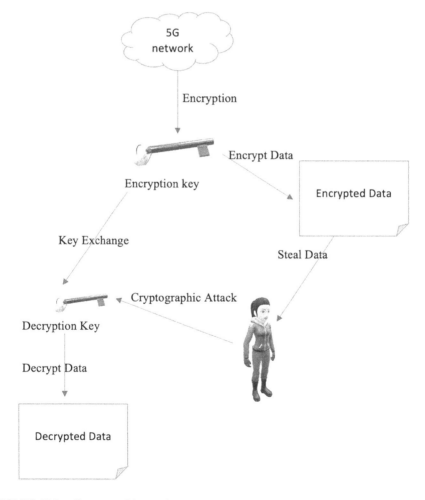

FIGURE 13.9 Cryptographic attack.

communications. In their study, Yoon et al. demonstrated how an attacker could exploit this vulnerability by compromising the long-term secret used by the AKA protocol, either through brute-force, side-channel, or other cryptographic attacks. This allows an attacker to obtain a temporary session key used for secure communication between user devices and the 5G network.

The integration of 5G and SDN technologies presents new security challenges and opportunities. Table 13.1 provides some of the proposed mitigation but it is also essential that network operators and security professionals are aware of these attack vectors and vulnerabilities and deploy strong security measures to protect against them.

TABLE 13.1
Vulnerabilities and Proposed Mitigation in SDN

Attacks and Vulnerabilities	Description	Existing Mitigations
Insider threats	A malicious insider with access to the controller can cause significant damage to the network.	• Network operators can employ a variety of security measures including Access control, network segmentation, and monitoring [9]. • Access control mechanisms can be used to restrict access to networks and specific network resources. • Network segmentation can be used to isolate sensitive parts of the network and limit the impact of a compromised slice. • One can use monitoring to detect and respond to suspicious activity in the network.
Controller hijacking	An attacker who gains control of the controller can manipulate network behavior, causing denial of service or redirecting traffic to malicious destinations.	• Using the "Controller-SDN-Flow-Verifier (C-SFV)" module to detect and filter out all spoofed packet-in messages [10].
Network Function Virtualization (NFV) security	Virtualization of network functions introduces new security risks such as vulnerability to hacking or misconfiguration.	• Using the VNF Chain Integrity Verification (VCI) module to verify the integrity and authenticity of your VNF chain [11]. • The VCI module checks his VNF chain at various points in the network to make sure it hasn't been tampered with by an attacker.
Over-the-air (OTA) attacks	OTA attacks on the air interface can be used to intercept or modify traffic, or to interfere with network operation.	• Using the User-Configured Access Control (UCAC) module to prevent devices from connecting to untrusted networks [12]. • The UCAC module validates network configurations and credentials to ensure devices connect only to trusted networks.

(Continued)

TABLE 13.1
(Continued)

Attacks and Vulnerabilities	Description	Existing Mitigations
Routing attacks	Attackers can manipulate routing information to divert traffic or disrupt network communication.	• Using the Routing Table Verification (RTV) module to verify the integrity and reliability of routing tables in 5G networks [13]. • The RTV engine periodically checks the routing table to ensure that it has not been tampered with by an attacker.
Rogue base stations	Rogue base stations can be used to intercept and eavesdrop on user traffic or disrupt network operations.	• Implementing network authentication protocols: Implementing network authentication protocols like AKA (Authentication and Key Agreement) can help to prevent rogue base stations from accessing the network and intercepting user traffic [14]. • Deploying anti-IMSI catcher technology: There are several anti-IMSI catcher technologies available that can detect and prevent rogue base stations from intercepting user traffic. These technologies can detect and locate rogue base stations and alert network operators to their presence [15].
API security	APIs used to communicate between the controller and network devices could be a potential entry point for hackers or attackers who can exploit vulnerabilities to gain access to sensitive information or cause damage.	• Securing API traffic with Transport Layer Security (TLS) encryption [16], • TLS is a widely used cryptographic protocol that enables secure communication between devices over networks.
Cryptographic attacks	Attackers can exploit weaknesses in cryptographic algorithms or keys to gain access to sensitive information.	• Protecting cryptographic keys using the Post-Quantum Cryptography [17] (PQC) algorithm. • PQC is a type of cryptography designed to resist attacks from quantum computers that can break traditional cryptographic algorithms.

13.3 MITIGATIONS PROPOSED IN LITERATURE

13.3.1 INSIDER THREATS MITIGATION

To reduce the risk of insider threats, network operators should implement robust access control mechanisms such as multi-factor authentication, role-based access control, etc.… to restrict access to sensitive components of the network. Regular security checks and monitoring can also help detect and prevent insider attacks. Role-based access control (RBAC) [18] is a security measure that restricts access to network resources based on user roles or functions. This helps prevent unauthorized access and reduces the risk of insider threats. The researchers suggest using RBAC in 5G SDN networks to limit access to critical network resources and reduce the risk of insider attacks.

Anomaly detection: Anomaly detection is the technique of monitoring network traffic and behavior for unusual patterns or behavior that could indicate an attack. Researchers propose using anomaly detection techniques in 5G SDN networks to detect and prevent insider threats [19].

Multi-factor authentication (MFA): It is a security measure that requires users to provide various forms of authentication before accessing network resources. The researchers propose using MFA in 5G SDN networks to prevent unauthorized access and reduce the risk of insider threats [20].

13.3.2 Controller Hijacking Mitigation

To prevent hijacking, network operators must implement strong and secure communication protocols, namely SSL/TLS, between the controller and the network device. In addition, firewalls, intrusion detection and other security measures should be used to protect the data controllers from external attacks.

Secure Communication Channels: Researchers suggest using secure communication channels such as SSL/TLS to protect communication between controllers and switches in 5G SDN networks [21]. This helps prevent man-in-the-middle attacks and other forms of kidnapping.

Authentication and Access Control: Researchers suggest using authentication and access control measures such as RBAC to restrict access to controllers and other critical network resources [22]. This helps prevent unauthorized access and reduces the risk of hijacking attacks.

Intrusion detection and response: Researchers propose using intrusion detection and response systems in 5G SDN networks to detect and respond to hijacking attacks in real-time [23]. These systems can detect anomalous behavior within the network and initiate automatic or manual responses to mitigate the attack.

13.3.3 Network Function Virtualization (NFV) Security

To secure NFV, network operators must implement security measures such as network segmentation, firewalls, and virtual network functions (VNFs) that are secured by design. They should also perform regular security assessments and vulnerability scans to identify and remediate any security weaknesses.

Identity and access management: The researchers propose using an Identity and Access Management (IAM) system in the 5G SDN NFV environment to make sure that only authorized users and processes can access the network and increase resources. IAM can also enforce security policies at the user or process level [45].

Threat Intelligence Sharing: Researchers propose sharing threat intelligence among various entities within the 5G SDN NFV ecosystem, such as network operators, service providers, and vendors. This improves detection and response to security threats [45].

Software-defined security: Researchers are proposing the use of software-defined security (SDS) in the 5G SDN NFV environment [45]. This includes using software to define and enforce security policies. SDS can provide more flexible and adaptable security than traditional hardware-based security mechanisms. For example, security policies can be updated in real-time based on changing network conditions.

13.3.4 OVER-THE-AIR (OTA) ATTACKS MITIGATION

To prevent OTA attacks, network operators must implement strong encryption algorithms, such as AES and RSA, to protect user data and network activity. They must also use authentication mechanisms, such as digital signatures and certificates, to authenticate the identities of network elements.

Encrypted Communication: A proposed mitigation technique is to use encrypted communication channels between network components and in between the base station and the core network [46]. This prevents attackers from wirelessly intercepting and tampering with data. Additionally, encrypted communication helps protect against other types of attacks namely eavesdropping and man-in-the-middle attacks.

Multi-factor authentication: Another recommended mitigation technique is to use multi-factor authentication (MFA) to access network components. MFA requires some form of identification before granting access such as Password and Fingerprint Scan. This prevents unauthorized access to network components, even if an attacker physically has access to the device [47].

Spectrum Surveillance: Researchers suggest using spectrum surveillance to detect wireless attacks [48]. Spectrum monitoring involves monitoring the radio spectrum for unusual activity, such as unexpected signals or interference. This can help detect attacks that cannot be detected by other means, such as attacks that do not involve network components.

13.3.5 ROUTING ATTACKS MITIGATION

To prevent routing attacks, network operators must implement secure routing protocols, such as BGP and OSPF secure authentication, and use firewalls and detection/prevention systems. Intrusion blocking to protect the network. They should also regularly monitor network traffic and events to detect and respond to suspicious activity.

Network segmentation: A recommended mitigation technique is to use network segmentation to isolate critical network components. This can help prevent an attacker accessing one part of the network from accessing other parts of the network [49]. Additionally, network segmentation can limit the potential impact of a routing attack by limiting the attack to a smaller portion of the network.

Access Control: Another recommended mitigation technique is to use access control mechanisms to limit who can make changes to the network topology [50]. This can help prevent attackers from taking control of the network and making unauthorized changes. Access control can be accomplished through role-based access control, restricting access to certain functions based on a user's role in the organization.

Intrusion detection and prevention: Researchers have proposed the use of this system to detect and prevent routing attacks. These systems monitor network traffic for signs of an attack, such as unusual routing behavior or traffic patterns [51]. If an attack is detected, the system can take action to prevent the attack, such as blocking traffic from a specific source.

13.3.6 ROGUE BASE STATIONS SECURITY

To prevent unauthorized base stations, network operators must implement secure authentication mechanisms, such as digital signatures and certificates, to authenticate the identities of base stations. They should also use firewalls and intrusion detection/prevention systems to protect the network and should regularly monitor network activity to detect and respond to suspicious behavior.

Authentication and Encryption: A recommended mitigation technique is to use encryption and authentication mechanisms to secure communications in-between the core network and the base station. This can help prevent attackers from impersonating a legitimate base station and gaining network access [52]. Authentication can be done through certificates or other authentication mechanisms, while encryption can be used to secure the communication channel.

Signal Strength Monitoring: Another recommended mitigation technique is to monitor the signal strength of base stations in the area [53]. This can help detect rogue base stations that transmit higher-than-normal signals, which could indicate they are trying to interfere with legitimate communications. Signal strength monitoring can be performed using specialized hardware or software tools.

Network segmentation: Similar to the proposed mitigation technique for SDN routing attacks, network segmentation can also be used to isolate critical network components and limit the potential impact of a network attack (i.e.) malicious base station attack [54].

13.3.7 API SECURITY

To secure APIs, network operators must implement strong authentication and authorization mechanisms such as OAuth or JWT, and should use secure communication protocols such as SSL/TLS that help to protect data in transit. They should also perform regular security assessments and vulnerability scans to identify and remediate any security weaknesses.

Access Control: A recommended mitigation technique [55] is to implement access control mechanisms to limit the privileges and actions that API users can perform. This includes role-based access control (RBAC) or attribute-based access control (ABAC) to enforce permissions based on user identity or other attributes.

Safe coding practices: Another recommended mitigation technique is to use safe coding practices when developing APIs to reduce the risk of vulnerabilities such as injection attacks or buffer overflows [56]. This may include input validation, data cleaning, and error handling. API Monitoring and Logging: Similar to the recommended mitigation technique for wireless SDN attacks, monitoring and logging can also be used to detect suspicious or malicious API activity. This may include monitoring API traffic, examining API access logs, and by using an intrusion detection system (IDS) or security information and event management system (SIEM) to analyze data [56].

13.3.8   CRYPTOGRAPHIC ATTACKS MITIGATION

To prevent cryptographic attacks, network operators must use strong encryption algorithms and regularly update encryption keys. They should also implement key management procedures to ensure that encryption keys are securely stored and managed. Cybersecurity is an important aspect of 5G SDN and requires a proactive, layered approach to mitigate the risks associated with these attacks and vulnerabilities. Network operators must continuously assess their security situation and implement security measures to protect against evolving threats.

Strong Key Management: A recommended mitigation technique is the use of strong key management measures to protect cryptographic keys used in the network [57]. This may include periodic key rotation, secure storage of keys and the use of Hardware Security Modules (HSMs).

Authentication and Authorization: Another recommended mitigation technique is to use strong authentication and authorization mechanisms which ensures that only authorized users and devices can access the sensitive data or perform important activities [58]. This may include the use of multi-factor authentication, certificate-based authentication, and access control policies.

Secure communication protocols: The use of secure communication protocols named as Transport Layer Security (TLS) and Datagram Transport Layer Security (DTLS) can help to protect against eavesdropping and other cryptographic attacks [59]. It is important to ensure that the protocols were configured correctly and that all parties involved in the communication are using the same protocol version.

A summary of pros, cons & limitation of these solutions were discussed in Table 13.2 and Table 13.3 provides the techniques to mitigate the attacks in short.

13.4   ARTIFICIAL INTELLIGENCE AND MACHINE LEARNING BASED SOLUTIONS

13.4.1   AIML BASED SOLUTIONS FOR INSIDER THREATS

User Behavior Analytics: AI-powered user behavior analysis can be used to identify and predict unusual behaviors of network users, including insiders, by analyzing the amount of large user activity data. This can help detect potential insider threats in real time and alert network administrators for further investigation. S. Srinivasan, S. Sengupta, and S. K. Ghosh proposed an ensemble machine learning approach for insider threat detection which combines the outputs of multiple models to improve accuracy. The algorithm used is an ensemble machine learning approach, which combines multiple machine learning models to improve accuracy of the insider threat detection. Specifically, the authors used five different machine learning models namely logistic regression, decision tree, random forest, AdaBoost, and Support Vector Machine (SVM). The approach was evaluated on a real-world dataset and

TABLE 13.2
Summary of the Attacks Discussed

Attack Type	Mitigation	Pros	Cons	Limitations
Insider threat	Anomaly detection [24]	• Early detection • Low false positive rate • Flexibility • Real time detection	• High false negative rate • Training required • Limited scalability	• Lack of context • Dependence on data quality • Limited detection capability
	Multi - factor authentication (MFA) [25]	• Increased security • User accountability • Compliance • Customizability	• User resistance • Complexity • Cost	• Vulnerabilities • Compatibility • Dependence on human factors
Controller hijacking	Secure communication channels [26]	• Confidentiality • Integrity • Authentication • Widely adopted	• Resource Intensive • Complexity • Compatibility	• Potential overhead • Limited Scope
	Authentication and access control [27]	• Increased security • User accountability • Customizability • Compliance	• Complexity • User resistance • Cost	• Limited Scope • Dependance on human factors
	Intrusion detection and response [28]	• Early detection • Automated response • customizability • User accountability	• Complexity • False positives • Cost	• Dependence on human factors • Limited Scope

NFV	Identity and access management [29]	• Improved security • Scalability • Simplified management • Auditability	• Complexity • Cost • User resistance	• Limited scope • Dependence on human factors
	Threat intelligence sharing [30]	• Increased awareness • Improved detection • Faster response	• Privacy concerns • Trust issues • Legal and regulatory issues	• Limited scope • Varying quality • Resource constraints
	Software-defined security [31]	• Increased flexibility • Scalability • Reduced cost	• Complexity • Security risks • Standards and interoperability	• Immaturity • Performance • Integration
Over-the-air attack	Encrypted communication [32]	• Increased security • Confidentiality • Authenticity	• Performance • Key management • Compatibility	• Backdoor vulnerability • Limited protection • Encryption strength
	Multi-factor authentication [32]	• Increased security • Stronger authentication • User accountability	• Complexity • User experience • Cost	• False sense of security • Limited protection • Compatibility
	Spectrum surveillance [33]	• Early detection • Comprehensive coverage • Non-invasive	• False positives • Technical complexity	• Limited protection • Real - time detection • Privacy concerns
Routing attack	Network segmentation [34]	• Security • Control • Segmentation • Isolation	• Complexity • Management overhead	• Potential for misconfiguration or mismanagement

(Continued)

**TABLE 13.2
(Continued)**

Attack Type	Mitigation	Pros	Cons	Limitations
	Access control [35]	• Restrictive • Secure	• Inconvenient	• Implementation • Scalability
	Intrusion detection and prevention [36]	• Detection • Prevention	• False negatives	• Scalability • Performance Impact
Rogue base station	Authentication and encryption [37]	• Secure • Prevents impersonation	• Overhead • Complexity	• Dependent on proper implementation and key management
	Signal strength monitoring [38]	• Helps detect rogue base stations • Low cost • Can be performed remotely	• Limited range of detection • May produce false positives • Limited to detecting • Attacks that involve high signal strength	• Limited to detecting attacks that involve changes in signal strength • May not detect more sophisticated attacks
	Network segmentation [39]	• Increased security • Limit potential damage • Easier to manage and monitor	• Increased complexity • Can be costly to implement • Requires proper planning and configuration	• Limited effectiveness against advanced attacks • Still vulnerable to attacks within the same segment
API attack	Access control [40]	• Security • Compliance • Authorization • Accountability	• Complexity • Maintenance • Overhead • Cost	• False positives • Insider threats • Human error • Lack of granularity

Attack	Solution			
	Safe coding practices [41]	• Security • Reliability • Maintainability • Scalability	• Time-consuming • Costly • May impact performance • May require specialized knowledge	• Cannot guarantee complete security • May not be effective against zero-day attacks • May not address vulnerabilities in third-party libraries • May not address security risks in the underlying infrastructure
Cryptographic attack	Strong key management [42]	• Security • Confidentiality • Integrity • Compliance	• Complexity • Cost • Reliance on third-party vendors • May impact performance	• Cannot prevent all attacks • May not address vulnerabilities in other areas of the network • May require specialized knowledge and expertise • May not be feasible in all environments
	Authentication and authorization[43]	• Security • Compliance • Access control • Accountability	• User inconvenience • Cost • Complexity • False positives/negatives	• Cannot prevent all attacks • May be vulnerable to phishing or social engineering • May require additional infrastructure or hardware • May not be feasible in all environments
	Secure communication protocols [44]	• Security • Confidentiality • Integrity • Compliance	• Overhead • Complexity • Compatibility issues • May impact performance	• Cannot prevent all attacks • May be vulnerable to implementation flaws • May require additional infrastructure or hardware • May not be feasible in all environments

TABLE 13.3

Mitigations for the Vulnerabilities of SDN in 5G

Attacks and Vulnerabilities	Mitigation Techniques
Insider threats	• Implement strong access control mechanisms such as multi-factor authentication and role-based access control. • Regular security audits & monitoring.
Controller hijacking	• To implement secure communication protocols such as SSL/TLS. • The use of firewalls, intrusion detection/prevention systems and other security measures.
Network function virtualization (NFV) security	• Implement security measures such as network segmentation and secure VNFs. Regular security assessments and vulnerability scans.
Over-the-air (OTA) attacks	• Implement strong encryption algorithms. Use authentication mechanisms such as digital signatures and certificates.
Routing attacks	• Implement secure routing protocols such as BGP secure and OSPF authentication. • Use firewalls and intrusion detection/prevention systems. • Regularly monitor network traffic and events.
Rogue base stations	• Implement secure authentication mechanisms such as digital signatures and certificates. • Use firewalls and intrusion detection/prevention systems. • Regularly monitor network activity.
API security	• Implement strong authentication and authorization mechanisms. • The use of secure communication protocols such as SSL/TLS. • Regular security assessments and vulnerability scans.
Cryptographic attacks	• Use strong encryption algorithms. • Regularly update encryption keys. Implement key management processes,

achieved a high accuracy rate [60]. They also provided a comprehensive review of various machine learning approaches that have been proposed for insider threat detection. The authors discuss the strengths and weaknesses of different techniques and provide insights into the challenges that should be addressed in future [61].

Behavior-based anomaly detection: This solution involves using ML and AI algorithms to analyze user behavior patterns and detect deviations from normal behavior. By detecting unusual behavior patterns, such as excessive data downloads, unusual connection times, or changes in access patterns, potential insider threats can be identified before significant damage occurs. Zhou et al. (2019) proposed an approach for detecting insider threats in cloud computing environments using machine learning algorithms. The proposed system uses unsupervised learning techniques to detect unusual patterns in user behavior and classify users as normal or abnormal. The system had achieved high accuracy in detecting insider threats along with low false-positive rates. The used algorithm is based on Long Short-Term Memory (LSTM) neural networks for anomaly detection in cloud computing systems. The algorithm involves training the LSTM network on normal system behavior to learn the patterns and correlations between system metrics. The trained network is then used to detect anomalies in real-time by comparing the current system behavior with the learned patterns [62].

Li et al. (2019) proposed an approach for detecting insider threats in enterprise networks using a deep learning-based model. The proposed system analyzes user behavior logs to identify unusual behavior patterns and uses a convolutional neural network (CNN) to classify users as normal or abnormal. The system achieved high accuracy in detecting insider threats with low false-positive rates. The authors proposed an insider threat detection approach based on deep learning, which utilizes a Convolutional Neural Network (CNN) model to detect anomalies in user behavior. Specifically, the authors trained the CNN model using network traffic data, and then used the trained model to classify user behavior as either normal or anomalous. The CNN model operated by performing convolution operations on input traffic data followed by pooling and fully connected layers to extract high-level features and classify the behavior as normal or anomalous [63].

Roychoudhury et al. (2017) proposed an approach for detecting insider threats in mobile devices using machine learning algorithms. The proposed system analyzes user behavior patterns and usage data to detect unusual behaviors and classify users as normal or abnormal. The system achieved high accuracy in detecting insider threats in mobile devices. They used a Random Forest algorithm for behavior-based anomaly detection in mobile devices. The algorithm was trained on a set of features related to user behavior on mobile devices such as app usage and system call records, to classify behavior as either normal or anomalous. The Random Forest algorithm works by creating multiple decision trees, where each and every tree is built using a random subset of the training data and a random subset of the features. The classification decision is then made by aggregating the outputs of all the decision trees in the forest. The authors found that the Random Forest algorithm performed well in detecting insider threats in mobile devices. [64].

Network flow analysis: By analyzing network traffic patterns using ML and AI, it is possible to identify anomalous patterns that may indicate the presence of an insider threat. For example, if someone tries to access a large amount of data outside of their usual scope of work, this could indicate a potential insider threat. Zhang et al. (2018) used a deep autoencoder network to learn normal traffic patterns and detect deviations from those patterns that could indicate the presence of an insider threat. The proposed approach had achieved high accuracy in detecting insider threats in a dynamic network environment. A method based on a deep learning algorithm called Long Short-Term Memory (LSTM) in dynamic environments. LSTM is a type of recurrent neural network (RNN) that can learn long-term dependencies and has been widely used in various sequence learning tasks. The proposed method takes user behavior logs and system logs as input and uses an LSTM model to capture the temporal dynamics of user behavior patterns. The model is trained to differentiate normal behavior from anomalous behavior, and the detection results are further analyzed using a threshold-based method to identify insider threats. The authors demonstrated the effectiveness of the proposed method through experiments on a real-world dataset [65].

Ye et al. (2019) used unsupervised learning algorithms such as k-means clustering and Principal Component Analysis (PCA), to identify anomalous network flow patterns that could indicate the presence of an insider threat. The approach proposed has been evaluated on a real-world dataset and achieved high accuracy in detecting insider threats. The algorithm used in this chapter for insider threat detection is unsupervised learning, specifically clustering-based anomaly detection. The authors used k-means clustering and DBSCAN clustering to group network flows into different clusters, and then identified anomalies based on the characteristics of these clusters [66].

User profiling: By developing detailed user profiles using ML and AI algorithms, it is possible to identify and track user behavior patterns over time. By analyzing these patterns, potential insider threats can be identified based on deviations from normal behavior.

Data-centric security: By using ML and AI algorithms to analyze data access patterns, sensitive data can be identified and protected against potential insider threats. This approach involves classifying data according to its sensitivity and applying access controls based on these classifications.

Synchronous Learning: Synchronous learning involves the use of multiple machine learning and artificial intelligence algorithms to analyze data and detect potential insider threats. By combining the outputs of multiple algorithms, the accuracy of the detection system could be improved and errors can be reduced.

Anomaly Detection: AI-powered anomaly detection algorithms could be used to identify network activity which was anomalous and could indicate an insider attack. Algorithms can analyze network logs and traffic patterns to detect deviations from normal behavior and trigger alerts if needed.

Risk management: AI-based risk management systems can be used to identify and assess risk posed by insiders based on their access level, permissions, and behavior. These systems can use machine learning algorithms to continuously update each user's risk profile and identify those that pose the biggest threat to the network.

Natural Language Processing (NLP): AI-powered NLP algorithms can be used to analyze large amounts of text data, including emails and instant messages, to identify threats latent internals. Algorithms can identify suspicious language patterns, such as those related to insider trading or the sharing of confidential information.

Predictive maintenance: AI-based predictive maintenance algorithms can be used to predict and prevent equipment and system failures, which can be caused by insiders, intentionally or unintentionally. Algorithms can analyze system logs and performance data to detect anomalies and alert network administrators in real time.

While these solutions are not new, they all represent areas where machine learning and artificial intelligence can be applied to improve the accuracy and effectiveness of existing threat detection systems. However, further research and development is needed to create effective machine learning and artificial intelligence solutions that can address the unique challenges posed by 5G insider threats.

13.4.2   AIML BASED SOLUTIONS FOR CONTROLLER HIJACKING

Deep Learning-based Intrusion Detection System: A Deep Learning-based Intrusion Detection System (DIDS) is proposed to detect and prevent hijacking attacks in SDN. The system uses deep neural networks to analyze network traffic and detect anomalous behavior in real time. The algorithm used in this chapter for Deep Learning-based Intrusion Detection System for Controller Hijacking Attacks In SDN is a Convolutional Neural Network (CNN). The proposed system was evaluated on a test basis and showed promising results in detecting and mitigating hijacking attacks [67].

Controller security based on reinforcement learning: K. Alzahrani et al. [68] proposed a reinforcement learning-based approach to improve the security of SDN controllers against hacker attacks. This approach trains the controller to detect and respond to hacking attacks using reinforcement learning algorithms. Specifically, the authors used the Q-learning algorithm to develop an agent that learns to make decisions on how to defend against controller hijacking attacks. The proposed method is evaluated on a test platform and shows improved performance in detecting and mitigating hijacking attacks.

Artificial Neural Network-Based Detection: An artificial neural network (ANN) algorithm is proposed in [69] to detect hijacking attacks in SDN. The algorithm used in this paper for detecting controller hijacking attacks in Software-Defined Networks is a decision tree-based approach. The proposed method uses network stream data and packet headers to train the ANN, which can then detect and mitigate hijacking attacks in real time. The proposed method is evaluated on a test platform and shows improved performance in detecting and mitigating hijacking attacks [69].

Automated encoder-based intrusion detection system: An automatic encoder-based intrusion detection system (IDS) is proposed in [70] to detect and mitigate hijacking attacks in SDN. The proposed system uses an autoencoder to learn the normal behavior of the SDN network and detect anomalies that indicate a hijacking attack. The algorithm used in this paper for the Autoencoder-Based Intrusion Detection System for Controller Hijacking Attacks in SDN is the autoencoder algorithm. The autoencoder is a type of neural network that can be trained to learn a compressed representation of the input data by encoding the data into a lower dimensional space and then decoding it back into its original form. In this paper, the authors used an autoencoder to learn the normal behavior of the SDN controller, and then used it to detect any anomalous behavior that could indicate a controller hijacking attack. The proposed system was evaluated on a test platform and showed improved performance in detecting and mitigating hijacking attacks.

13.4.3   AIML-BASED SOLUTIONS FOR OVER-THE-AIR ATTACKS

Smart Spectrum Monitoring: This solution proposed in [71] uses AI/ML algorithms to monitor the radio frequency spectrum in real-time, identify any unusual or suspicious activity, and generate alerts for potential threats. The article does not mention a specific algorithm used for smart spectrum monitoring in over-the-air attacks. However, the authors discuss the use of machine learning techniques for intelligent spectrum monitoring, such as clustering, classification, and anomaly detection. They also mention the use of deep learning algorithms, such as convolutional neural networks (CNNs) and recurrent neural networks (RNNs), for signal processing and feature extraction from radio frequency (RF) data. The solution can also use machine learning algorithms to predict the likelihood of an attack and take proactive measures to prevent it.

Behavior Analysis: This approach [72] involves using machine learning algorithms to monitor the behavior of devices and users on the network and detect any deviations from normal behavior. This can help identify potential attackers trying to gain access to the network through direct attacks. The author does not specify a particular algorithm. Instead, the authors used a combination of clustering and decision tree analysis to identify anomalous behavior in network traffic and identify rogue devices. The paper also mentions the use of unsupervised learning techniques such as k-means clustering, Principal Component Analysis (PCA), and Density-Based Spatial Clustering of Applications with Noise (DBSCAN) to identify patterns in network traffic.

AI-assisted intelligent deterrence: Machine learning models can be trained to recognize signals from malicious devices attempting to disrupt the network and then actively block those signals to prevent attacks. The paper [73] does not specify a particular algorithm but rather presents a framework that integrates multiple AI techniques, including deep learning, reinforcement learning, and game theory, to design an intelligent jamming system. The system uses a combination of supervised learning and unsupervised learning to identify malicious attacks and select the most effective jamming strategy to prevent the attack.

Reinforcement learning: This can be used to train network security systems to take proactive steps to prevent OTA attacks, such as adjusting network configuration or blocking certain traffic. The author of [74] proposes a novel RL-based security framework that employs the RL algorithm to build a defense mechanism against over-the-air attacks in 5G networks. Specifically, the authors use the Q-learning algorithm to train an agent that can make decisions to mitigate the effects of over-the-air attacks by dynamically adjusting the network configuration.

AI-driven Dynamic Spectrum Allocation: Using AI, spectrum resources can be dynamically allocated in real time, ensuring that the network is not congested and has sufficient bandwidth to support legitimate traffic, preventing OTA attacks. The algorithm used in the paper [75] for dynamic spectrum allocation in 5G networks is a reinforcement learning approach. Specifically, the authors employed a deep Q-network (DQN) algorithm to learn the optimal dynamic spectrum allocation policy.

13.4.4 AIML-BASED SOLUTIONS FOR ROUTING ATTACKS IN 5G SDN

Smart Routing Verification: A study in [76] has proposed an intelligent routing verification system that uses machine learning algorithms to identify abnormal traffic patterns in real time and alert administrators network. The authors use a Random Forest (RF) algorithm as the machine learning model for the proposed system. The system can detect routing attacks with high accuracy and few false positives.

Routing control based on reinforcement learning: Another study [77] has proposed a reinforcement learning-based approach to control routing in the 5G SDN network. The approach used a neural network-based Q learning algorithm to learn the optimal routing policy and mitigate routing attacks. The results show that the proposed method has improved network performance and reduced the impact of routing attacks.

Adversarial machine learning: Adversarial machine learning is another potential solution proposed to detect and mitigate routing attacks in 5G SDN networks. The algorithm used in [78] is a combination of deep neural networks and adversarial training. Specifically, a multi-layer perceptron (MLP) is used as the classifier, and an adversarial example generator is used to generate adversarial examples to train the classifier robustly against attacks. The authors also propose a novel algorithm called adversarial detection and mitigation (ADAM) to detect and mitigate routing attacks using adversarial machine learning. This approach involves training a machine learning model to detect routing attacks by generating hostile traffic that mimics the attacker's behavior. The model is then tested on real traffic to detect and prevent routing attacks.

Deep learning-based network anomaly detection: Deep learning-based network anomaly detection is a promising approach to mitigate path attacks in 5G SDN networks. The algorithm used in this paper [79] for deep learning-based network anomaly detection in software-defined networks is a convolutional neural network (CNN). This approach involves training a deep neural network to detect unusual network traffic patterns that indicate routing attacks. The system can detect and prevent attacks in real-time to ensure the integrity of the network.

Graph-based network analysis: Graph-based network analysis is another potential solution to detect and mitigate routing attacks using machine learning algorithms. The proposed algorithm in this paper is based on the Max-Flow Min-Cut algorithm, which is used to calculate the maximum flow from each controller to the switches it manages to identify potential routing attacks in 5G SDN. This approach involves building a 5G SDN network graph and analyzing it to identify unusual traffic patterns. It then uses the graph to predict future attack patterns and proactively mitigate them [80].

13.4.5 AIML-BASED SOLUTIONS FOR ROGUE BASE STATION ATTACKS

Deep learning-based signal classification: An approach proposed in a recent research paper by Liu et al. [81] uses deep learning techniques such as Convolutional Neural Networks (CNNs) to classify wireless signals and differentiate between legitimate and rogue base stations. The CNN algorithm used in this paper is a type of deep learning algorithm that is commonly used for image classification. However, in this paper, the authors applied the CNN algorithm to the problem of signal classification in mobile networks.

Machine learning anomaly detection: The approach involves training a machine learning algorithm to identify patterns in network traffic and detect anomalies in real time [82]. By continuously monitoring the network, the system can detect the presence of unauthorized base stations and alert network operators. The isolation forest algorithm is a type of machine learning algorithm that is used for anomaly detection in high-dimensional datasets. The algorithm works by randomly partitioning the dataset into subsets and then creating a tree structure to isolate the anomalous observations.

Generative Adversarial Network (GAN) detection: The GAN algorithm used [83] is a type of deep learning algorithm that involves two neural networks: a generator network and a discriminator network. The generator network learns to generate samples that resemble the real data, while the discriminator network learns to distinguish between the real data and the generated samples. This approach involves training a GAN to generate realistic radio signals and then using it to detect rogue base stations. By comparing the generated signal to the actual signal, the system can determine the presence of an unauthorized base station.

Reinforcement learning network security: The reinforcement learning algorithm used in [84] is a type of machine learning algorithm that involves an agent interacting with an environment and receiving feedback in the form of rewards or penalties. The agent learns to take actions that maximize the expected cumulative reward over time. This approach involves training agents using reinforcement learning to detect and mitigate malicious attacks on base stations. Agents can learn optimal security policies by examining the environment and taking actions to maximize reward signals.

13.4.6 AIML-BASED SOLUTIONS FOR API SECURITY

Intelligent API Anomaly Detection: The machine learning algorithms used in [85] include Principal Component Analysis (PCA), Gaussian Mixture Model (GMM), and Support Vector Machine (SVM). PCA is used for dimensionality reduction of the input data, GMM is used for modeling the distribution of the data, and SVM is used for classification of the data into normal and anomalous instances. Use AI/ML-based systems to continuously monitor API traffic, learn what normal traffic patterns look like, and identify anomalies that could indicate an attack. This approach has been used in other security contexts, such as detecting unusual behavior in network traffic.

Behavior-based authentication: The machine learning algorithm used in [86] is a combination of decision tree and k-nearest neighbors (KNN). The approach involves the use of a dataset of user behavior features, such as the number of API calls, the time between API calls, and the types of API calls made. Instead of relying solely on static credentials (e.g., username and password), AI/ML can be used to develop behavioral profiles of API users. The system learns what typical user behavior looks like and can detect deviations in that behavior that could indicate that an attacker is using stolen credentials.

Dynamic API security policies: Security systems can use machine learning to analyze API traffic patterns to dynamically create security policies that adapt to the changing threat landscape. The machine learning algorithm used in [87] is a decision tree-based algorithm. The approach involves the use of a dataset of API usage features, such as the number of requests, the types of requests, and the response times. This approach can be particularly useful for detecting and blocking new, previously unknown attacks.

Adversarial Machine Learning: The approach proposed in [88] involves the use of deep learning algorithms, specifically Convolutional Neural Networks (CNNs), for feature extraction and classification. The proposed approach also involves the use of adversarial training to improve the robustness of the CNNs against adversarial attacks. Adversarial training is a technique where the CNNs are trained on both normal and adversarial examples generated by adding small perturbations to the input data to create misclassifications. The authors used two different adversarial attack methods, Fast Gradient Sign Method (FGSM) and Carlini and Wagner's (CW) attack, to evaluate the performance of their approach. The experimental results showed that the proposed approach achieved high accuracy in detecting both known and unknown adversarial attacks on API calls. Attackers can try to avoid detection by intentionally altering their API traffic to look like benign traffic. An AI/ML-based security system can use adversarial machine learning to detect and block these attempts.

Security-centric API design: The approach involves using machine learning algorithms to analyze the security-centric design of APIs based on their specifications [89]. The authors used a decision tree-based machine learning algorithm to classify the API security design based on a set of predefined security rules. The algorithm takes as input the API specification and a set of security rules and outputs the security-centric design classification. The security rules used in this paper were based on the Open Web Application Security Project (OWASP) API security recommendations, which include authentication, authorization, data validation, and communication security. The proposed approach also involves the use of a feedback mechanism to improve the accuracy of the machine learning algorithm over time. The feedback mechanism involves using the results of the API security testing to update the security rules and improve the accuracy of the algorithm. Finally, a proactive approach to API security might involve integrating machine learning and other AI techniques into the API design process. By integrating security into the API itself, developers have the ability to reduce the attack surface and prevent attackers from exploiting the vulnerability.

13.4.7 AIML BASED SOLUTIONS FOR CRYPTOGRAPHIC ATTACKS

Quantum Key Distribution (QKD): QKD is a cryptographic technique that uses quantum mechanics to establish a shared secret key between two parties. The security of QKD is based on the laws of quantum mechanics and the difficulty of measuring quantum states without disturbing them. The paper discusses various QKD protocols, such as BB84, and the potential attacks that may be launched against these protocols, including intercept-resend attacks, photon-number-splitting attacks, and side-channel attacks. The paper also discusses the limitations of practical QKD implementations and the challenges of scaling these systems to larger networks. Overall, the paper provides a valuable resource for understanding the security of QKD and the potential vulnerabilities that may exist in practical implementations. By leveraging QKD, it is possible to create secure communication channels that are resistant to attacks from quantum computers [90].

Post-quantum encryption using AI/ML: Researchers [91] are also exploring the use of AI/ML techniques to develop and evaluate new post-quantum encryption algorithms. By analyzing the security of different cryptosystems using machine

TABLE 13.4
Impact Level of AIML Solutions

Technique	Security Solution	Technological Impact	Security Level
Insider threats	Machine learning to detect anomalies in network traffic [93–95].	Requires collection and analysis of large amounts of network data, potentially increasing processing power requirements and data storage needs	High
SDN controller hijacking	AI algorithms to monitor network traffic and detect anomalies [96–98].	Causes a slight increase in network latency and processing time, depending on the level of data analysis and network complexity	High
Over-the-air attacks	Machine learning to detect rogue access points [99,100].	Requires additional network sensors /access points to be installed to monitor wireless network traffic, which could increase costs	Medium
Routing attacks	AI algorithms to monitor network traffic and detect anomalies [101,102].	Causes a slight increase in network latency and processing time, depending on the level of data analysis and network complexity	High
Rogue base station attacks	Machine learning to detect rogue base stations [103–105].	Requires additional network sensors to be installed to monitor wireless network traffic, which could increase costs	Medium
API security attacks	AI algorithms to detect unusual API requests and behavior [106–108].	Requires additional API security measures, which can increase the complexity and management of the network	Medium
Cryptographic attacks	Use of blockchain and homomorphic encryption for secure key management [109–111].	Increases the complexity and processing power requirements for the network, as well as the need for specialized hardware and software	High
Cryptographic attacks (key management)	Use of quantum computing to develop more secure encryption keys [112–114].	Requires the development of specialized hardware and software, as well as significant investment in quantum computing technology	High

learning, researchers can identify new cryptographic algorithms that are resistant to attacks from quantum computers.

Quantum blockchain: Quantum blockchain is a new concept that combines the security of blockchain technology with the power of quantum computing. By using quantum computing for encryption and authentication, quantum blockchains can improve protection against attacks on existing cryptographic systems [92]. The level of impact of these is discussed in Table 13.4. Table 13.4 Impact level of AIML solutions

13.4.8 BLOCKCHAIN METHODS FOR CRYPTOGRAPHIC ATTACKS

Blockchain and homomorphic encryption have their own advantages in dealing with cryptographic attacks in 5G SDN. The choice between the two will depend on the specific requirements and security needs of the network. Both solutions can improve network security and increase system accuracy, but it is important to carefully evaluate their pros and cons to determine which solution is best for a particular network. Both old and new methods can play a role in enhancing the security and accuracy of 5G SDN.

Increased security:

- Blockchain: Decentralized and secure ledger system for storing and managing encryption keys and digital signatures.
- Homomorphic Encryption: Enables computations to be performed on encrypted data without decrypting it first.

Improved accuracy:

- Blockchain: Reduces the risk of unauthorized access, tampering, and network disruption
- Homomorphic Encryption: Increases the accuracy of the system by reducing the risk of unauthorized access and tampering

Disadvantages of traditional methods:

- Limited security: Symmetric and asymmetric encryption are vulnerable to brute-force attacks and other types of cyber attacks
- Decreased accuracy: Old methods may result in decreased accuracy due to the risk of unauthorized access and tampering.

13.5   TRADITIONAL VS MACHINE LEARNING (ML) BASED METHODS

In comparison to the traditional security methods, such as firewalls and intrusion detection systems, machine learning (ML) based methods have several advantages in detecting and mitigating SDN attacks in 5G networks.

Improved accuracy: ML algorithms can analyze vast amounts of data in real-time and identify patterns that are indicative of an attack, leading to improved accuracy in detecting SDN attacks. S. S. Ahmed and S. H. Mir. proposed an improved machine learning-based approach for detecting security threats in SDN, which can improve accuracy by analyzing vast amounts of network data and identifying patterns indicative of an attack. The parameters used in this approach to improve accuracy include feature selection, data normalization, and hyperparameter tuning [115]. S. Jafarzadeh, et al. also proposed a deep learning-based approach for detecting network anomalies in SDN, which can improve accuracy by learning from the behavior of the network and identifying patterns indicative of an attack. The parameters used in this approach to improve accuracy include feature selection, model selection, and data augmentation [116].

Adaptability: ML algorithms can learn from the behavior of the network and adapt to new attack patterns, making them more effective in detecting evolving threats. A. Mehdipour et al. proposed [117] an SDN attack detection and response system that uses machine learning techniques to learn and adapt to new attack patterns. The authors use a combination of support vector machines (SVMs) and decision trees to analyze network flow data and detect attacks. T. Wang et al. [118] also proposed an adaptive learning algorithm for SDN security that can dynamically adjust the weights of different features in the ML model based on the importance of each feature in detecting attacks. The proposed algorithm can learn and adapt to new attack patterns over time, leading to improved detection accuracy.

Automation: ML algorithms can automate the detection and mitigation of SDN attacks, reducing the need for manual intervention. Al-Faori et al. [119] used a dataset of simulated SDN attacks to train their machine learning model, which achieved high accuracy in detecting various types of attacks. The system also automatically generated and applied mitigation strategies to contain and prevent the spread of attacks. Bhardwaj et al. [120] proposes a machine learning-based system for automating the mitigation of SDN attacks. The system uses a combination of machine learning algorithms and network flow analysis techniques to detect and classify attacks, and then applies appropriate mitigation strategies to contain and prevent the spread of the attack.

However, ML-based methods also have some limitations, such as the requirement for large amounts of labeled data for training and the potential for false positive or false negative results. Additionally, ML algorithms can be vulnerable to adversarial attacks, where attackers can manipulate the data used for training to evade detection. ML-based methods offer significant advantages in detecting and mitigating SDN attacks in 5G networks compared to traditional security methods. However, it is important to implement a comprehensive security strategy that incorporates both traditional and ML-based methods to ensure the security of 5G networks.

13.6   CONCLUSION AND FUTURE WORKS

5G networks offer significant benefits over previous generations of cellular networks, but they also present new security challenges. SDN attacks pose a major threat to the security of 5G networks and can cause significant harm by compromising network resources, altering network configurations, and disrupting network traffic. While traditional security methods such as firewalls and intrusion detection systems have proven effective in the past, they may not be adequate in detecting and mitigating the latest SDN attacks in 5G networks. Machine learning (ML) based methods offer several advantages over traditional methods, such as improved accuracy, adaptability, and automation. However, it is important to implement a comprehensive security strategy that incorporates both traditional and ML-based methods to ensure the security of 5G networks and to mitigate the risks posed by SDN attacks.

Future research in the security of SDN in 5G networks is the development of self-defending networks. A self-defending network would have the ability to detect, prevent, and recover from security threats in real-time without requiring human intervention. This could be achieved through the integration of artificial intelligence (AI) and machine learning (ML) techniques to enhance the security of the network.

One approach for creating a self-defending network is to use AI and ML algorithms to continuously monitor network behavior and detect anomalies that may indicate an attack. The network could then automatically respond to threats by rerouting traffic, isolating compromised components, or triggering other mitigation actions. Another area of research is the development of secure, decentralized control structures for SDN. Centralized SDN controllers can be a single point of failure, making them vulnerable to attacks. Decentralizing the control structure could increase the resilience of the network and reduce the risk of a successful attack. This could be achieved through the use of blockchain technology to ensure the integrity and security of network configuration data. In addition, there is a need for further research on the development of secure communication protocols for SDN. Communication between SDN components is vulnerable to eavesdropping and tampering, which can compromise the security of the network. The development of secure communication protocols that use encryption and authentication could increase the security of the network. Finally, as new threats emerge, continued research into 5G network security is required. 5G networks are expected to have a longer lifespan than previous generation cellular networks, so it is important to continuously monitor and respond to new security threats as they emerge. This will require close collaboration between research, industry and government to ensure the security and resilience of 5G networks for years to come.

The concept of self-defense networks is a relatively new area of research, and there has been limited work focused specifically on applying this approach to SDN in 5G networks. However, several studies have explored the concept of network self-protection in a broader sense by combining AI and machine learning techniques to improve network security. Authors discussed the challenges and limitations of traditional security mechanisms and propose a new approach to creating self-defense networks by combining artificial intelligence and machine learning techniques [121]. Future work in this area should focus on specific challenges and requirements for SDN security in 5G networks. This may include developing new algorithms and methods for detecting and mitigating SDN attacks in real time, and exploring the possibility of using decentralized governance structures and secure communication protocol. In addition, as 5G networks continue to evolve and become more complex, further research is needed to address new threats. Finally, self-protection networks need to be practically deployed and tested to validate their effectiveness in real-world scenarios. Significant research has been conducted on using machine learning (ML) techniques to improve SDN security in a variety of contexts, including wired and wireless networks. The authors provided a comprehensive overview of the current state of machine learning-based security for SDN [122]. Further work in this area should focus on improving the accuracy and efficiency of ML-based security methods in SDN, especially in the context of 5G networks. This could include developing new algorithms that are tailored to the idiosyncrasies of 5G networks, such as high throughput, low latency, and massive connectivity. In addition, research is needed on the security of emerging 5G network architectures, such as network layering and multiple access edge computing (MEC). Finally, it is necessary to implement and field test ML-based security methods in real 5G networks, to validate their effectiveness and scalability.

REFERENCES

1. A. Giaretta, M. Giordano, A. Capone, and G. Pau. (1 March 2021). "Network slicing in 5G: An insider threat," *IEEE Transactions on Mobile Computing*, vol. 20, no. 3, pp. 1714–1729. https://doi.org/10.1109/TMC.2020.3022152.
2. L. Wu, Y. Zhang, J. Liu, G. Gu, and X. Yang. (2018). "Exploring controller hijacking in software-defined networking-based 5G mobile networks," in *Proceedings of the 2018 ACM SIGSAC Conference on Computer and Communications Security* (pp. 276–291).
3. B. Gökhan, S. Khatun, K. H. Khan, S. Kiyomoto, and K. Sakurai. (2020). "NFVChains: Verifying the integrity of virtual network function chains'" *IEEE Transactions on Network and Service Management*, vol. 17, no. 2, pp. 791–804.
4. R. Borgaonkar, M. Strobel, D. Rupprecht, M. Kohlweiss, and C. Pöpper. (2017). "Breaking LTE on Layer Two," in *Proceedings of the 10th ACM Conference on Security and Privacy in Wireless and Mobile Networks (WiSec)*.
5. L. Wu, Y. Zhang, J. Liu, G. Gu, and X. Yang. (2019). "Enabling dynamic and secure routing in 5G mobile networks," in *Proceedings of the 2019 ACM SIGSAC Conference on Computer and Communications Security* (pp. 1749–1766).
6. A. J. Goldsmith, and W. Wu. (2016). "5G and the future of mobile networks," *IEEE Communications Magazine*, vol. 54, no. 11, pp. 11–17.
7. J. Li, T. Huang, and Q. Z. Sheng. (2020). "5G security and privacy: A survey," *IEEE Communications Surveys & Tutorials*, vol. 22, no. 4, pp. 2695–2730.
8. H. Yoon, K. Lee, J. Lee, S. Lee, and Y. Park. (2020). "Practical attack and improvement of 5G AKA key hierarchy'" *Journal of Communications and Networks*, vol. 22, no. 4, pp. 342–350. https://doi.org/10.1109/JCN.2020.000078.
9. Y. Li, Y. Lu, and K. Huang. (2020). "A survey of 5G security: From access network to core network," *IEEE Communications Surveys & Tutorials*, vol. 22, no. 4, pp. 2104–2144, doi: 10.1109/COMST.2020.2994258.
10. M. S. Alam, M. S. Hossain, M. R. Hasan, A. Alelaiwi, and A. E. Saddik. (2018). "SDN security: A survey," *IEEE Communications Surveys & Tutorials*, vol. 20, no. 4, pp. 3332–3365. https://doi.org/10.1109/COMST.2018.2840680.
11. Y. Jarraya, M. Ben Alaya, and M. R. Senouci. (2018). "A survey on security challenges in network function virtualization," *Journal of Network and Computer Applications*, vol. 115, pp. 1–14. https://doi.org/10.1016/j.jnca.2018.04.008.
12. C. Wang, Q. Zhang, S. Wang, and X. Sun. (2019). "5G security: Untrusted network detection based on UCAC mechanism," in *2019 IEEE International Conference on Computational Science and Engineering (CSE) and IEEE International Conference on Embedded and Ubiquitous Computing (EUC)* (pp. 475–480). IEEE. https://doi.org/10.1109/CSE/EUC.2019.00089.
13. T. Zhang, X. Yang, T. Huang, H. Chen, and X. Li. (2020). "Routing security in 5G networks: Challenges and solutions," *IEEE Communications Magazine*, vol. 58, no. 2, pp. 80–86. https://doi.org/10.1109/MCOM.001.1900367.
14. M. A. Ali, A. Iqbal, and S. Yoo. (2020) "Analysis of authentication and key agreement (AKA) protocol in long-term evolution (LTE) network," *IEEE Access*, vol. 8, pp. 40877–40891. https://doi.org/10.1109/ACCESS.2020.2978952.
15. M. Naveed, M. L. Das, E. C. Ngai, and X. Wang. (2014). "Stingray in action: A comprehensive study of IMSI catcher activities," in *Proceedings of the 2014 ACM SIGSAC Conference on Computer and Communications Security*, pp. 654–665. https://doi.org/10.1145/2660267.2660330.
16. D. Thangavel, K. P. Soman, and P. Poornachandran. (2019). "Enhancing security in software-defined networks through API authentication and authorization," in *2019 IEEE*

International Conference on Distributed Computing, VLSI, Electrical Circuits and Robotics (DISCOVER) (pp. 98–103). IEEE. https://doi.org/10.1109/DISCOVER47537.2019.00024.

17. J. López, and L. Quezada. (2020). "A post-quantum cryptography proposal for 5G networks," in *2020 International Conference on Artificial Intelligence in Information and Communication (ICAIIC)* (pp. 364–368). IEEE. https://doi.org/10.1109/ICAIIC49474.2020.9064753.

18. P. Biswas, A. Mandal, A. Das, and N. Chaki. (2018). "Role-based access control in SDN for 5G networks," in *2018 International Conference on Communication and Signal Processing (ICCSP)*, pp. 154–158. https://doi.org/10.1109/ICCSP.2018.8524429.

19. X. Wang, Y. Li, F. Wu, and D. Wu, (2018). "A SDN-based framework for anomaly detection in 5G network," in *2018 IEEE 14th International Conference on Wireless and Mobile Computing, Networking and Communications (WiMob)*, pp. 1–8. https://doi.org/10.1109/WiMOB.2018.8589123.

20. A. Al-Fuqaha, A. Khreishah, M. Guizani and M. Aledhari (April 2019). "Security in 5G wireless networks: A review," *IEEE Wireless Communications*, vol. 26, no. 2, pp. 120–127. https://doi.org/10.1109/MWC.2019.1800065.

21. Z. Li, Y. Li, F. Wu and D. Wu. (2019). "SDN-based mitigation for controller Hijacking attacks in 5G networks," *IEEE Access*, vol. 7, pp. 168207–168219. https://doi.org/10.1109/ACCESS.2019.2953458.

22. A. Al-Fuqaha, A. Khreishah, M. Guizani and M. Aledhari. (April 2019). "Security in 5G wireless networks: A review," *IEEE Wireless Communications*, vol. 26, no. 2, pp. 120–127. https://doi.org/ 10.1109/MWC.2019.1800065.

23. S. I. Hwang, S. S. Kim, and J. W. Hong. (2019). "A secure SDN architecture to prevent control-plane attacks in 5G networks," *Computer Networks*, vol. 160, pp. 179–191. https://doi.org/10.1016/j.comnet.2019.06.016.

24. M. Shafiq, M. H. U. Rehman, and A. Batool. (2020). "Anomaly detection techniques in 5G SDN networks for insider threat detection and prevention," in *2020 5th International Conference on Computing, Mathematics and Engineering Technologies (iCoMET)* (pp. 1–7). IEEE.

25. S. Raza, T. R. Soomro, J. Arshad, and S. Majeed. (2020). "Multi-factor authentication based access control in 5G SDN networks," in *2020 International Conference on Smart Grid and Smart Cities (ICSGSC)* (pp. 99–103). IEEE. https://doi.org/10.1109/ICSGSC50474.2020.00029.

26. M. H. U. Rehman, A. Batool, and N. Javaid. (2019). "An enhanced security architecture for 5G software-defined networks," *IEEE Access*, vol. 7, pp. 174104–174113. https://doi.org/10.1109/ACCESS.2019.2950504.

27. M. Shafiq, M. H. U. Rehman, and A. Batool. (2020). "Anomaly detection techniques in 5G SDN networks for insider threat detection and prevention," in *2020 5th International Conference on Computing, Mathematics and Engineering Technologies (iCoMET)* (pp. 1–7). IEEE. https://doi.org/10.1109/ICOMET49228.2020.9190883.

28. K. Kaur, and P. Singh. (2020). "An intelligent intrusion detection and prevention system for 5G software-defined networks," in *2020 International Conference on Inventive Research in Computing Applications* (pp. 936–942). IEEE. https://doi.org/10.1109/ICIRCA48275.2020.9199002.

29. X. Chen, X. Lai, B. Fang, and Y. Zhu. (2018). "Identity and access management for cloud-based 5G networks," *IEEE Network*, vol. 32, no. 1, pp. 104–110. https://doi.org/10.1109/MNET.2018.1700259.

30. S. Zeadally, M. F. Siddiqui, and Z. Baig. (2019). "Threat intelligence sharing in 5G networks: Opportunities and challenges," *IEEE Communications Magazine*, vol. 57, no. 4, pp. 50–55. https://doi.org/10.1109/MCOM.2019.1800633.

31. W. Xie, C. Liang, Z. Li, and Y. Chen. (2019). "Software-defined security for 5G networks: A survey," *IEEE Communications Surveys & Tutorials*, vol. 21 no. 4, pp. 3596–3622. https://doi.org/10.1109/COMST.2019.2923177.

32. X. Liu, S. Liu, and F. Hu. (2020). "Security and privacy protection in 5G wireless networks: A survey," *IEEE Access*, vol. 8, pp. 133088–133103. https://doi.org/10.1109/ACCESS.2020.3019584.

33. Y. Wang, H. Zhou, H. Liu, and L. Li. (2020). "A survey on 5G security: Emerging threats and countermeasures," *IEEE Network*, vol. 34, no. 4, pp. 14–20. https://doi.org/10.1109/MNET.011.2000209.

34. S. Zeadally, R. Hunt, and Y.-S. Jeng (2017). "Security issues in software-defined networking and network function virtualization," *IEEE Cloud Computing*, vol. 4, no. 4, pp. 46–52.

35. X. Wang, H. Zhang, Y. Li, W. Xu, and X. Hu. (2020). "Security issues and solutions in 5G networks," *IEEE Network*, vol. 34, no. 4, pp. 176–183.

36. K. Kumar, A. Gurtov, and R. Brännström, (2018). "SDN Security: A Survey," *IEEE Communications Surveys & Tutorials*, vol. 20, no. 4, pp. 3330–3360.

37. J. L. García-Dorado, and M. C. García-Gutiérrez. (November 2018). "Security mechanisms for 5G mobile networks: Challenges and opportunities," *IEEE Communications Magazine*, vol. 56, no. 11, pp. 98–104.

38. F. Liu, L. Wang, X. Lu, and W. Meng. (2014). "Rogue base station detection using signal strength-based techniques," in *Proceedings of the 11th International Conference on Mobile and Ubiquitous Systems: Computing, Networking and Services.*

39. N. Singh, S. Kumar, and S. Tyagi (1 July–August 2020). "Secure wireless communication in 5G networks: Opportunities and challenges," *IEEE Transactions on Services Computing*, vol. 13, no. 4, pp. 744–758.

40. A. Joshi, and S. Shetty. (2016). "Mitigating security risks in RESTful web APIs using access control techniques," *Procedia Computer Science*, vol. 78, pp. 535–542. https://doi.org/10.1016/j.procs.2016.02.089.

41. Y. J. Kim, and Y. S. Park. (2019). "A survey of API security," *Journal of Information Processing Systems*, vol. 15, no. 3, pp. 663–678. https://doi.org/10.3745/JIPS.03.0118.

42. Y. Liang, and H. Huang. (2019). "A survey of key management in blockchain systems," *IEEE Access*, vol. 7, pp. 68870–68889. https://doi.org/10.1109/ACCESS.2019.2912538.

43. S. K. Sood, and R. J. Enbody. (2013). "Cybersecurity threats to mobile devices—Review," *Journal of Cybersecurity*, vol. 2, no. 1, pp. 37–50. https://doi.org/10.1093/cybsec/tyt001.

44. S. Raza, and A. Tauqir. (2019). "Transport layer security (TLS) vulnerabilities and their mitigation," *Journal of Cybersecurity*, vol. 5, no. 1, p. tyz003. https://doi.org/10.1093/cybsec/tyz003.

45. M. S. Ali, S. Li, S. S. Kanhere, and R. Buyya. (2019). "Security and privacy in cloud-assisted wireless networks: Challenges and opportunities," *Journal of Network and Computer Applications*, vol. 136, pp. 52–70. https://doi.org/10.1016/j.jnca.2019.02.021.

46. K. Yang, H. Li, and X. Wu. (April 2019). "Security challenges and solutions in 5G mobile networks," *IEEE Wireless Communications*, vol. 26, no. 2, pp. 120–127. https://doi.org/10.1109/MWC.2019.1800073.

47. K. Yang, H. Li, and X. Wu. (April 2019). "Security challenges and solutions in 5G mobile networks," *IEEE Wireless Communications*, vol. 26, no. 2, pp. 120–127, doi: 10.1109/MWC.2019.1800073.

48. L. Yan, J. Zhang, S. Wang, J. Zhou, and Y. Yang. (2019). "Security and privacy protection in 5G networks: Current status and future directions," *IEEE Access*, vol. 7, pp. 10842–10864. https://doi.org/10.1109/ACCESS.2019.2893036.

49. J. B. Chen, S. Y. Wei, J. L. Wu, and C. C. Chang. (2018). "Securing software-defined networks against advanced persistent threats: A survey," *IEEE Communications Surveys & Tutorials*, vol. 20, no. 1, pp. 650–667. https://doi.org/10.1109/COMST.2017.2762723.

50. J. B. Chen, S. Y. Wei, J. L. Wu, and C. C. Chang (2018). "Securing software-defined networks against advanced persistent threats: A survey," *IEEE Communications Surveys & Tutorials*, vol. 20, no. 1, pp. 650–667. https://doi.org/10.1109/COMST.2017.2762723.

51. F. Lanze, T. Engel, and M. Menth. (Fourthquarter 2018). "Securing software-defined networks: A survey," *IEEE Communications Surveys & Tutorials,* vol. 20, no. 4, pp. 3453–3473. https://doi.org/10.1109/COMST.2018.2862103.

52. S. A. Khan, A. Gani, R. A. Khan, A. Y. Zomaya, and S. Qaisar. (2017). "SDN security: A survey," *IEEE Communications Surveys & Tutorials*, vol. 19, no. 1, pp. 427–455. https://doi.org/10.1109/COMST.2016.2617382.

53. J. R. Kumar, and J. Y. Tham. (February 2019). "Secure SDN controller for preventing rogue base stations in 5G networks," *IEEE Communications Letters*, vol. 23, no. 2, pp. 274–277. https://doi.org/10.1109/LCOMM.2018.2884540.

54. S. A. Khan, A. Gani, R. A. Khan, A. Y. Zomaya, and S. Qaisar. (2017). "SDN security: A survey," *IEEE Communications Surveys & Tutorials*, vol. 19, no. 1, pp. 427–455. https://doi.org/10.1109/COMST.2016.2617382.

55. A. Khan, A. Gani, R. A. Khan, A. Y. Zomaya, and S. Qaisar. (2017). "SDN security: A survey," *IEEE Communications Surveys & Tutorials*, vol. 19, no. 1, pp. 427–455. https://doi.org/10.1109/COMST.2016.2617382.

56. N. Venkatesan, and M. Srivatsa. (2021). "Security and privacy issues in SDN/NFV-based 5G networks: A comprehensive review," *IEEE Access*, vol. 9, pp. 32750–32777. https://doi.org/10.1109/ACCESS.2021.3062339.

57. R. Guo, G. Xu, and L. Huang. (2020). "A survey on security challenges of 5G networks: New cyber-physical domain and Its implications," *IEEE Communications Surveys & Tutorials*, vol. 22, no. 4, pp. 2622–2651. https://doi.org/10.1109/COMST.2020.3025463.

58. M. A. Abdelgadir, M. F. Ahmed, A. S. Alzahrani, A. A. Alsaiari, and A. Al-Rodhaan. (2020). "A comprehensive study of security challenges in 5G networks," *IEEE Access*, vol. 8, pp. 147347–147367. https://doi.org/10.1109/ACCESS.2020.3019016.

59. R. Guo, G. Xu, and L. Huang. (2020). "A survey on security challenges of 5G networks: New cyber-physical domain and Its implications," *IEEE Communications Surveys & Tutorials*, vol. 22, no. 4, pp. 2622–2651. https://doi.org/10.1109/COMST.2020.3025463.

60. S. Srinivasan, S. Sengupta, and S. K. Ghosh. (October 2018). "Insider threat detection using ensemble machine learning approach," *IEEE Transactions on Information Forensics and Security*, vol. 13, no. 10, pp. 2462–2476. https://doi.org/10.1109/TIFS.2018.2837862

61. S. Sengupta, S. Srinivasan, and S. K. Ghosh. (October 2019). "Insider threat detection using machine learning: A review," *ACM Computing Surveys*, vol. 52, no. 5, pp. 1–35. https://doi.org/10.1145/3341640.

62. Y. Zhou, F. Yu, Y. Zhang, J. Liu, and X. Liu. (2019). "Anomaly detection for insider threats in cloud computing systems," *Journal of Cloud Computing*, vol. 8, no.1, pp. 1–16. https://doi.org/10.1186/s13677-019-0127-4.

63. T. Hu, et al. (2019). "An insider threat detection approach based on mouse dynamics and deep learning." *Security and communication networks*, vol. 2019, Article ID 3898951, pp. 12, https://doi.org/10.1155/2019/3898951.

64. P. Roychoudhury, C. H. Tsou, Y. H. Liao, and C. J. Huang. (2017). "A machine learning approach for insider threat detection in mobile devices," *Wireless Personal Communications*, vol. 97, no. 1, pp. 971–987. https://doi.org/10.1007/s11277-017-4211-9.

65. X. Zhang, X. Luo, and J. Zhu. (2018). "Insider threat detection based on deep learning in dynamic environments," *IEEE Transactions on Information Forensics and Security*, vol. 13, no. 11, pp. 2762–2774. https://doi.org/10.1109/TIFS.2018.2835662.

66. L. Ye, R. Zhang, and X. Guan. (2019). "A network flow-based approach to insider threat detection using unsupervised learning," *IEEE Access*, vol. 7, pp. 130926–130938. https://doi.org/10.1109/ACCESS.2019.2931889

67. Abdallah, Mahmoud Said ElSayed (2022). "Effective Deep Learning Based Methods for the Anomaly Detection in Software-Defined Networks." *University College Dublin. School of Computer Science*, http://hdl.handle.net/10197/13338.
68. K. Alzahrani et al. (2021). "Reinforcement learning-based controller security for software-defined networks," *IEEE Access*, vol. 9, pp. 52896–52910.
69. H. Yao et al. (2019). "An artificial neural network-based approach for detecting controller Hijacking attacks in software-defined networks," *IEEE Access*, vol. 7, pp. 166964–166975.
70. L. Liu et al. (2020). "Autoencoder-based intrusion detection system for controller Hijacking attacks in SDN," *IEEE Access*, vol. 8, pp. 110977–110986.
71. M. Chen et al. (June 2020). "Intelligent spectrum monitoring for 5G wireless networks," *IEEE Communications Magazine*, vol. 58, no. 6, pp. 118–124.
72. M. A. Malik et al. (June 2021). "A behavioral analysis approach to detect rogue devices in 5G networks," *IEEE Transactions on Network and Service Management*, vol. 18, no. 2, pp. 355–367.
73. S. Gao et al. (March 2020). "AI-Driven intelligent jamming against Malicious attacks in wireless communication networks," *IEEE Transactions on Communications*, vol. 68, no. 3, pp. 1486–1498.
74. L. Li et al. (July 2020). "A reinforcement learning-based security scheme against over-the-air attacks in 5G networks," *IEEE Transactions on Mobile Computing*, vol. 19, no. 7, pp. 1711–1724.
75. C. Zhao et al. (February 2020). "A reinforcement learning approach to dynamic spectrum allocation in 5G networks," *IEEE Transactions on Vehicular Technology*, vol. 69, no. 2, pp. 2269–2281.
76. K. Chen, et al. (2019). "An intelligent routing verification system based on machine learning in software-defined networking," *2019 IEEE International Conference on Intelligence and Security Informatics (ISI)*.
77. H. T. Le, et al. (2019). "Reinforcement learning for routing control in 5G software-defined networks," *2019 IEEE 31st International Conference on Tools with Artificial Intelligence (ICTAI)*.
78. Qiu, Jing, et al. "Artificial intelligence security in 5g networks: Adversarial examples for estimating a travel time task." *IEEE Vehicular Technology Magazine* 15.3 (2020): 95–100.
79. M. Mirjalili, et al. (2018). "A deep learning-based network anomaly detection system for software-defined networks," *2018 IEEE Symposium on Computers and Communications (ISCC)*.
80. H. Li, et al. (2020). "A graph-based approach for routing security in 5G software-defined networks," in *2020 IEEE/CIC International Conference on Communications in China (ICCC)*.
81. C. Liu, X. Zhang, and X. Wu. (2020). "A rogue base station detection method based on deep learning," in *2020 IEEE 17th International Conference on Mobile Ad Hoc and Sensor Systems (MASS)* (pp. 101–105). IEEE.
82. J. Chen, Y. Yan, Z. Hu, and L. Wu. (2019). "Anomaly detection of rogue base station in 5G network based on machine learning," in *2019 IEEE 5th Intl Conference on Big Data Security on Cloud (BigDataSecurity), IEEE Intl Conference on High Performance and Smart Computing, (HPSC) and IEEE Intl Conference on Intelligent Data and Security (IDS)* (pp. 123–128). IEEE.
83. L. Xu, Y. Zou, L. Wu, and T. Zhang. (2020). "Rogue base station detection using generative adversarial networks," in *2020 IEEE Wireless Communications and Networking Conference (WCNC)* (pp. 1–6). IEEE.
84. H. Saleem, A. Razaque, and A. Malik. (2020). "A survey of machine learning techniques for API security," *International Journal of Advanced Computer Science and Applications*, vol. 11, no. 5, pp. 272–279. https://doi.org/10.14569/IJACSA.2020.0110534.

85. S. S. Khadka et al. (2020). "API anomaly detection: A machine learning approach," in *2020 IEEE 44th Annual Computers, Software, and Applications Conference (COMPSAC)*, pp. 1–6.

86. B. Chen et al. (2018). "Behavioral-based authentication in API access control," in *2018 IEEE 21st International Conference on Computational Science and Engineering (CSE)*, pp. 135–142.

87. A. Afzali-Kusha et al. (1 March–April 2019). "Dynamic security policies in RESTful APIs using machine learning," *IEEE Transactions on Services Computing*, vol. 12, no. 2, pp. 192–205.

88. Z. Wu et al. (July–August 2020). "Adversarial attacks on API calls detection via Robust deep learning," *IEEE Transactions on Dependable and Secure Computing*, vol. 17, no. 4, pp. 882–895.

89. Y. Zhao et al. (2020). "An automated method for API security testing based on API specification and machine learning," *IEEE Access*, vol. 8, pp. 131351–131359.

90. V. Scarani, H. Bechmann-Pasquinucci, N. J. Cerf, M. Dušek, N. Lütkenhaus, and M. Peev. (2009). "The security of practical quantum key distribution," *Reviews of Modern Physics*, vol. 81, no. 3, p. 1301.

91. X. Wang, Z. Chen, and S. Sun. (2019). "A survey of machine learning techniques applied to cryptography," *Journal of Network and Computer Applications*, vol. 127, pp. 95–110.

92. F. Ding, X. Yuan, Y.Guo, Y. Yang, and C. Z. Xu. (2018). "Quantum blockchain using entanglement in time," *Quantum Information Processing*, vol. 17, no. 4, p. 105.

93. L. Janczewski, P. Swierkowski, and J. Wytrebowicz. (2016). "Anomaly detection in the computer network traffic using machine learning methods," *Security and Communication Networks*, vol. 9, no. 17, pp. 4057–4071. https://doi.org/10.1002/sec.1645.

94. A. R. Soltani, A. F. A. Rahman, A. M. A. Latif, and N. A. Latiff. (2017). "Anomaly-based insider threat detection: A survey," *Journal of Network and Computer Applications*, vol. 79, pp. 78–105. https://doi.org/10.1016/j.jnca.2017.01.007.

95. M. Ahmad, A. Mahmood, M. A. Ahmad, and S. S. Hussain (2017). "Anomaly-based intrusion detection in network using machine learning techniques," *International Journal of Advanced Computer Science and Applications*, vol. 8, no. 6, pp. 171–177. https://doi.org/10.14569/IJACSA.2017.080623.

96. Y. Wang et al. (2018). "SDN controller Hijack detection with machine learning," in *2018 IEEE International Conference on Smart Internet of Things (SmartIoT), Xi'an, China*, pp. 221–226. https://doi.org/10.1109/SmartIoT.2018.00044.

97. Y. Kim, S. Lee, S. Kim, and J. Kim (2019). "A study on a method of detecting SDN controller Hijacking attack using machine learning," in *2019 International Conference on Information and Communication Technology Convergence (ICTC), Jeju, Korea (South)*, 2019, pp. 227–232. https://doi.org/10.1109/ICTC46691.2019.8939934.

98. H. M. N. Shah et al. (2021). "Artificial intelligence-based detection and mitigation techniques for SDN controller Hijacking attacks: A survey," *IEEE Communications Surveys & Tutorials*, vol. 23, no. 4, pp. 2406–2439. https://doi.org/10.1109/COMST.2021.3084413.

99. M. A. Baser, and A. S. Uluagac (1 July 2020). "Rogue access point detection using deep learning techniques," *IEEE Transactions on Mobile Computing*, vol. 19, no. 7, pp. 1675–1690. https://doi.org/10.1109/TMC.2019.2912039.

100. E. G. Pascual, and P. R. M. Jr. (2019). "Detection of rogue access points in WLANs using machine learning," in *2019 IEEE 10th Annual Information Technology, Electronics and Mobile Communication Conference (IEMCON), Vancouver, BC, Canada*, pp. 186–190. https://doi.org/10.1109/IEMCON.2019.8936166.

101. F. Lv, J. Wang, and Z. Wang. (2018). "A deep learning based routing security approach for software-defined network," *Journal of Network and Computer Applications*, vol. 102, pp. 64–71. https://doi.org/10.1016/j.jnca.2017.12.002.

102. T. Li, Y. Zhang, K. Li, and W. Li. (2018). "Anomaly detection for software-defined networks: a survey," *IEEE Access*, vol. 6, pp. 29010–29027. https://doi.org/10.1109/ACCESS.2018.2831059.
103. Nakarmi, Prajwol Kumar, Jakob Sternby, and Ikram Ullah. "Applying Machine Learning on RSRP-based Features for False Base Station Detection." *Proceedings of the 17th International Conference on Availability, Reliability and Security*, 2022.
104. H. Yang, H. Huang, X. Liao, and C. Li. (2020). "A deep learning approach for rogue base station detection in mobile communication networks," *IEEE Access*, vol. 8, pp. 52740–52750. https://doi.org/10.1109/ACCESS.2020.2983207.
105. B. Han, J. Zhang, H. Wang, Y. Huang, and Y. Tang. (2021). "Detecting rogue base stations in 5G networks using machine learning," *IEEE Wireless Communications Letters*, vol. 10, no. 1, pp. 168–171. https://doi.org/10.1109/LWC.2020.3035366.
106. H. Thakur, and M. Saini. (2020). "Machine learning based API security testing: A review and a new framework," *International Journal of Advanced Research in Computer Science*, vol. 11, no. 1, pp. 105–109. https://doi.org/10.26483/ijarcs.v11i1.6765.
107. M. H. Almishari, A. T. Alharthi, R. A. Aljehani, H. Y. Alnajjar, and T. Alsboui. (2021). "Anomaly detection in RESTful APIs using machine learning techniques," *IEEE Access*, vol. 9, pp. 74852–74862. https://doi.org/10.1109/ACCESS.2021.3082239.
108. H. Saleem, A. Razaque, and A. Malik. (2020). "A survey of machine learning techniques for API security," *International Journal of Advanced Computer Science and Applications*, vol. 11, no. 5, pp. 272–279. https://doi.org/10.14569/IJACSA.2020.0110534.
109. G. Tack, and R. Jäntti. (2019). "Blockchain-based secure key management for the Internet of Things," *IEEE Internet of Things Journal*, vol. 6, no. 4, 6094–6104. https://doi.org/10.1109/JIOT.2019.2912967.
110. J. López, J. Herranz, F. Almenárez, and R. Romero-Gómez. (2020). "Homomorphic encryption and its applications in industry 4.0," *Sensors*, vol. 20, no. 12, p. 3389. https://doi.org/10.3390/s20123389.
111. T. H. Noor, T. Ramayah, S. A. Rahman, and N. K. Noordin. (2020). "Securing IoT communications using homomorphic encryption," *IEEE Access*, vol. 8, pp. 116704–116717. https://doi.org/10.1109/ACCESS.2020.3003030.
112. A. JavadiAbhari, and A. Karimipour. (October 2021). "A survey on post-quantum cryptography and quantum key distribution," arXiv:2110.02375 [cs.CR]. https://doi.org/10.1145/3465481.3465719.
113. Aithal, P. S. "Advances and new research opportunities in quantum computing technology by integrating it with other ICCT underlying technologies." *International Journal of Case Studies in Business, IT and Education (IJCSBE)* 7.3 (2023): 314–358.
114. C. C. Díaz-Caro, C. Iliopoulos, and P. Wallden. (November 2021). "Efficient post-quantum cryptography with fault-tolerant quantum key distribution," in *Proceedings of the 2021 ACM SIGSAC Conference on Computer and Communications Security*, pp. 1879–1896. https://doi.org/10.1145/3465481.3465544.
115. S. Jafarzadeh, H. Khosravi, A. Al-Fuqaha, and M. Guizani. (September–October 2018). "Deep learning-based anomaly detection for software-defined networks," *IEEE Network*, vol. 32, no. 5, pp. 80–87. https://doi.org/10.1109/MNET.2018.1700182.
116. S. Jafarzadeh, H. Khosravi, A. Al-Fuqaha, and M. Guizani. (September–October 2018). "Deep learning-based anomaly detection for software-defined networks," *IEEE Network*, vol. 32, no. 5, pp. 80–87. https://doi.org/10.1109/MNET.2018.1700182.
117. A. Mehdipour, S. S. Alhadad, and H. T. Chuang. (March 2019). "SDN Attack detection and response system using machine learning techniques," *IEEE Transactions on Network and Service Management*, vol. 16, no. 1, pp. 44–56, https://doi.org/10.1109/TNSM.2019.2893505.
118. T. Wang, J. Z. Zhao, and L. Zhang. (2019). "An adaptive learning algorithm for software-defined network security," *IEEE Access*, vol. 7, pp. 52871–52881. https://doi.org/10.1109/ACCESS.2019.2915952.

119. A. Al-Faori, F. Al-Turjman, S. Al-Emadi, and S. Al-Maadeed. (2018). "A machine learning approach for automated security management of SDN networks," *IEEE Access*, vol. 6, pp. 41898–41910. https://doi.org/10.1109/access.2018.2858627.

120. A.Bhardwaj, A. Verma, and S. Garg. (2018). "Machine learning-based automated mitigation for SDN networks," *IEEE Transactions on Network and Service Management*, vol. 15, no.2, pp. 573–586. https://doi.org/10.1109/tnsm.2018.2834961

121. K. Chen, M. Li, L. Su, and Y. Liu. (2019). "Self-defending networks: A survey," *IEEE Communications Surveys and Tutorials*, vol. 21, no. 2, pp. 1599–1631.

122. M. Hussain, A. Raza, M. Rehan, S. Rho, and S. S. Kim (2019). "Machine learning for security in software-defined networks: A survey," *IEEE Communications Surveys and Tutorials*, vol. 21, no. 4, pp. 3457–3491.

14 Designing Intrusion Detection Systems for Software-Defined Networks Using Deep Learning/Machine Learning Techniques

Vivek Kumar

14.1 INTRODUCTION

The concept of Software-Defined Networking (SDN) is a recent development in the field of computer networking. To improve the existing networking architecture, Nick McKeown came up with the idea of SDNs. SDNs empower network administrators to easily control and manage the network centrally. The objective of SDN is to simplify management and enhance flexibility by centralizing control and reducing maintenance costs. To accomplish this, the layer in the network layer integration is split by programming the network. In traditional networking architecture, the functions of the Application Layer, Data Plane, and Control Plane are combined to perform networking tasks. However, in SDN, these layers are separated, allowing for more centralized and efficient control. However, in SDNs the control plane is separated away and placed centrally. The Control Plane in SDN is designed to provide logical control over the network. It includes a part called Controller, a piece of software that assists the network administrator in centrally organizing network activities. The Control Plane manages the network using programmed instructions, while the Data Plane only forwards information without any programming. The Control Plane uses a central controller to manage the routing rules for forwarding packets from the source host to the destination, ensuring network-wide consistency. This Software-Defined Network technique is used to handle cloud-related services and associated security challenges. The OpenFlow protocol, frequently used in SDN, is utilized for network traffic load balancing, policy direction, and execution.

Security of the network and the data transmitted over it is a critical issue in SDN, requiring the use of appropriate tools and techniques to ensure protection. Malicious actors pose a threat to an organization's confidential data by attempting to access it unauthorized or launch cyber attacks. These actions can compromise the security

DOI: 10.1201/9781003432869-14

of sensitive information. Without a reliable means of data protection, there may be a vulnerability through which an attacker can access the network and steal sensitive information. An intrusion detection system (IDS) is a piece of software/hardware that allows for the monitoring and detection of packets that appear anomalous to determine whether an incursion has taken place. When intrusions happen, related warnings are created and the network administrators are informed. A signature-based IDS has a database of some commonly known attacks, when the IDS encounters any suspicious activity in a network it matches the activity with the attacks in its dataset. If the suspicious activity matches any of the known attacks in the dataset, appropriate action is taken. Anomaly-based IDS works in a different manner; it tries to learn the pattern of the normal traffic in the network and if a monitored suspicious activity varies from the learned pattern by a significant variance, it is labeled as an intrusion. An Intrusion Detection System (IDS) that operates on the basis of anomalies is capable of identifying both familiar and unfamiliar (referred to as zero-day) attacks. In contrast, an IDS based on signatures can only recognize known attacks.

With the advent of high computational power, Machine Learning (ML) and Deep Learning (DL) techniques are now being extensively used for learning unseen patterns in the data. Due to their fast computations and high accuracy, DL/ML techniques are also being used in the area of the development of IDS in SDNs. An SDN is continuously monitored and the traffic flow is regularly recorded, any suspicious activity is manually labeled as malicious or benign. Using advanced feature extraction techniques these collected records are arranged in the form of a dataset containing normal/malicious data samples. A DL/ML-based classifier is then trained on this dataset wherein the classifier learns to distinguish between an intrusion and normal data. Many ML-based techniques like SVM [1], Naïve-Bayes [2], Decision-Tree [3], Random Forest [4], Logistic Regression [5], KNN [6], and DL-based techniques like Neural Networks [7], Recurrent Neural Networks [8], and CNN [9] have been used by the researchers for designing anomaly-based IDS for SDNs. It can be easily observed that most of the research work dedicated to the design/improvement of IDS is directed at ML/DL methods.

In this chapter, we have described the methods and techniques that researchers have proposed for designing efficient IDS using deep learning and machine learning methods. The chapter is structured as follows: the first section, some of the ML-based NIDS are discussed followed by the second section wherein we have described NIDS that are designed using DL techniques, in the third section, we covered the utilization of generative neural networks in the creation of NIDS, finally in Section 14.4 we have concluded the chapter.

14.2 MACHINE LEARNING BASED NETWORK INTRUSION DETECTION SYSTEM FOR SDNS

14.2.1 Network Threat Detection Using SVM

In [10], the authors have proposed a technique for categorizing network threats for NIDS which uses an improved behavior-based support vector machine. The network flow is captured and ID3 decision theory is employed to rule out unusable features and identify the ones which are best for training a support vector classifier.

There are three vital steps that the authors have described for developing the proposed model (1) Reducing the no. of features using ID3 decision tree theory and analyzing the network flow to learn the behavioral features. (2) Using the KDD1999 to evaluate the correctness of the categorization of the SVC and (3) Defending threats by performing signature-based detection for intrusions.

Feature reduction plays an imperative role in improving the training time of machine learning models as well as getting more accurate classification. In the proposed work, the authors have used ID3 decision theory to curtail the no. of features in the feature set. Initially, the algo takes all possible features in set S. Iteratively, the algo. Identifies the feature with maximum information gain and the feature is used to split the set S to produce a reduced set S' on which the procedure is continued. Finally in the order of information gain, a reduced feature set is obtained on which an SVC is trained. For an attribute X in set S, the information gain $IG(X)$ is given by

$$IG(X,S) = H(S) - \sum_{t \in T} p(t) H(T)$$

$$H(S) = -\sum_{t \in T} p(t) \log_2 p(t)$$

$H(S)$ represents the degree of entropy within the dataset S, and T is the subset created after dividing the set S based on attribute X.

For data collection from an SDN environment, the authors have proposed the use of sFlow-RT and Open vSwitch toolset which captures the data from suspicious nodes in a network, the data is preprocessed and is then fed to SVM classifier which is trained to distinguish malignant traffic from the benign traffic. Multiple defense mechanisms have been proposed to prevent malicious traffic and allow legitimate traffic by using a merger of threat detection, traffic categorization, and remediation tools. Figure 14.1 depicts how the sFlow analyzer captures the network information from the SDN controller and using the behavioral feature extraction the raw features are converted to trainable features; the dataset thus created is used to train the SVM.

The authors evaluated the method they proposed using the KDDCUP1999 dataset. They have used k-fold cross-validation to mitigate the risk of over-ambitious learning of the SVM.

14.2.2 INTRUSION DETECTION USING SUPERVISED LEARNING APPROACH

The authors in [11] evaluated various performance measures of different kinds of IDS which were constructed on the principle of anomaly detection for SDNs. Specifically, the authors have compared the performance of some well-known classifiers as a choice for designing IDS, these include ML algorithms like SVM, RF, decision trees, neural network, knn, linear discriminant analysis, neural networks, naive Bayes, extreme machine learning, bagging tree, ADAboost, RUSBoost, and LogitBoost. The authors have used NSL-KDD benchmark for training and testing

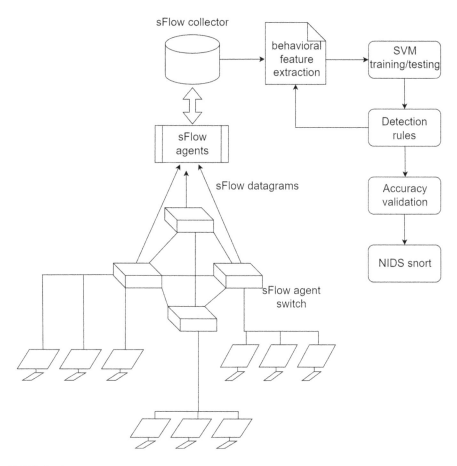

FIGURE 14.1   Data capturing and SVM training for intrusion detection.

of the proposed ML techniques and to compare their performance on the above-mentioned performance metrics.

For feature reduction, the authors have used the PCA [12] technique. PCA is used on the training dataset to reduce its size by turning the data into a fresh set of uncorrelated features, allowing for efficient analysis and improved performance. The authors have experimented with a range of feature values and have analyzed the classifier's performance in terms of the nos. of features they are trained on. The performance metric used by the authors are:-1) Accuracy – It is measure of total nos. of correct classification to the total no. of samples that were fed to the model. In simpler terms, the performance of a classifier is determined by the number of malignant samples correctly identified as malignant (True Positives-TP) and the number of benign samples correctly identified as benign (True Negatives-TN) out of all the tested data samples, we get the following formula for accuracy

$$Accuracy = \frac{TP + TN}{TP + TN + FP + FN}$$

where FN is the total nos. of false negatives which are the nos. of malignant data samples identified as benign and FP is the total nos. of benign data samples that are classified as malignant. The authors also use the False Alarm Rate (FAR), which is calculated as the ratio of false positives upon nos. of benign samples, given by:-

$$\text{Flase Alarm Rate} = \frac{FP}{FP + TN}$$

A good model should give a low FAR. Also, the authors have used F1-score, precision, and recall which are defined as follows:–

$$\text{Precision} = \frac{TP}{TP + FP}$$

$$\text{Recall} = \frac{TP}{TP + FN}$$

$$\text{F1 - Score} = 2 \times \frac{(\text{Precision} \times \text{Recall})}{(\text{Precision} + \text{Recall})}$$

As reported through experiments, the authors have got best results for nine nos. of features in terms of accuracy as shown in Figure 14.2.

The experiments were performed by the authors on an i-5 intel machine running on 12GB

RAM. Figures 14.3 and 14.4 depicts the accuracy and FAR reported for all the classifiers.

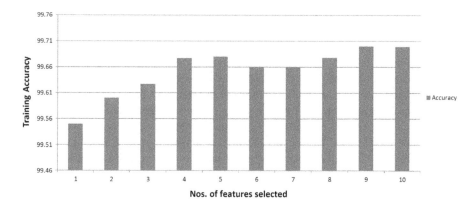

FIGURE 14.2   Training accuracy achieved by the classifiers against the nos. of features they were trained on.

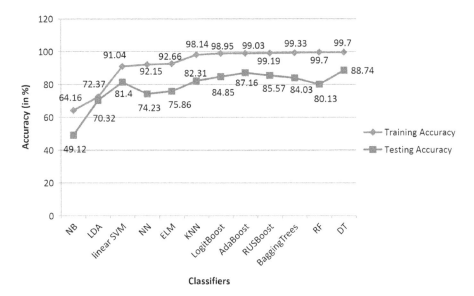

FIGURE 14.3   Accuracy of the classifiers on training and test data set. DT and RF reported the highest training accuracy of 99.70% each while DT achieved the best testing accuracy of 88.74%.

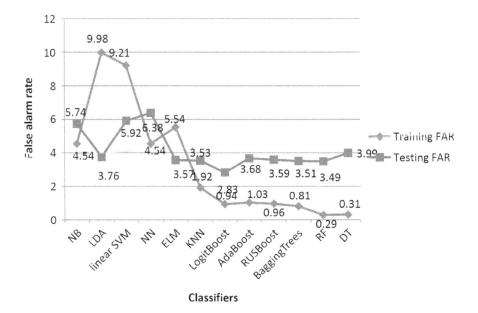

FIGURE 14.4   False alarm rate reported for all the classifiers. RF and DT classifiers showed the least FAR.

14.2.3 INTRUSION DETECTION USING TRAFFIC FLOW FINGERPRINT

In [13] authors have devised a method for detecting intrusion which uses the data captured from the traffic flow through the SDN controller. They have trained a support vector machine for identifying malware in a network. The proposed system (Figure 14.5) comprises an SDN switch that takes control of the network traffic that is coming into a network through external sources and routes it to local area network and vice-versa. The controller act as the central data collection system which regularly monitors the network traffic performs some computations and generates a dataset that comprises the 07 features namely: packet count, byte count, flow time, byte transfer rate, packet transfer rate, packet size, and average packet size. The controller then trains an SVM classifier which classifies the traffic stream as malignant or benign.

The system works as follows: The SDN switch collects the data packets in the network flow and, if there is no specific rule for routing the packet, it forwards it to the controller. The control is then taken by the controller of the incoming packet, decoding it to determine the packet's routing information. The controller acknowledges the switch with the decoded rule and the switch is then able to route the packet it was not able to route earlier. The switch then recurrently uses the decoded rule to route packets it receives in the future. The controller requests information from the switch

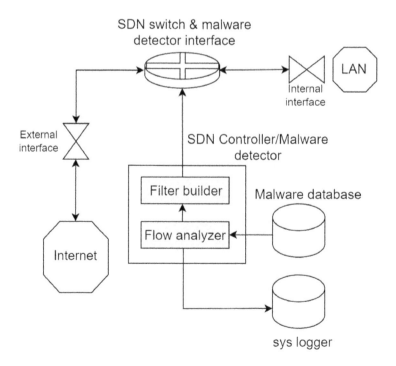

FIGURE 14.5 Architecture of the proposed method.

about the features of the network flow that have been processed through the switch so as to extract the features. When controller gets hold of some of the features like byte nos., packet nos., and flow duration, it can automatically calculate the values of other features like packet rate, byte rate, and packet length.

The authors have used a pre-trained SVM to predict the classification of the collected traffic flow by the controller. If a traffic flow is found to be malignant, necessary actions can be taken by the network administrator ranging from dropping the packet to suspending the network flow altogether.

For experimentation, the authors have mixed the normal data flow with known malicious data flow to create a dataset that is used to train an SVM model. The malware traffic used in the paper contains 11 malware belonging to the categories of Trojan, botnet, and DDoS. For synthesizing the normal data traffic, the authors have configured their laboratory switch which routes the traffic flow to a PC wherein it is ensured that only normal (unaffected) data is being collected.

The information gain method is used to rank the features and authors have chosen only those features which are collectible in the SDN network and which have a high rank. ASVM with a RBF as a kernel function is trained on the training dataset for identification in two classes i.e into benign or malignant categories. During training, the value of hyperparameters like the complexity parameter is fixed to 20 and the kernel parameter is fixed at 2. During testing, the classifier is evaluated for its performance in classifying the test data samples using the performance metrics of true positive (TP) and false positive rate (FP). The test was conducted in four settings: (1) using 33% of the training data and a full set of features, (2) using 50% of the training data and a full set of features, (3) using 33% of the training data and SDN features, (4) using 50% of the training data and sdn features. The result is described in the graph of Figure 14.6.

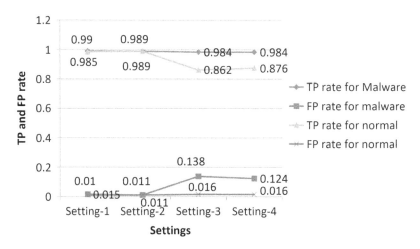

FIGURE 14.6 Experimental results for true positive and false positive rate in different settings.

14.2.4 Decision Tree-Based Intrusion Detection

Authors in [14] have proposed a technique, which detects DDoS attacks of several types in an SDN environment. First, they train an ML classification algorithm on the CIC-DdoS2017 data set and then capture and detect malicious DdoS samples from an SDN. The dataset of SDN dataset is synthesized by the RYU-Controller and Mininet Emulator.

The authors have emulated an SDN environment using Mininet, RYU controller, and have used Wireshark for data capturing. Also, for feature extraction, the authors have used CIC-flow Meter. The Hping3 tool is utilized to create TCP-SYN and UDP flood data traffic, and the incursion data packets are transmitted to the target host in the network with a falsified source id. Similarly, normal data traffic is also generated and is later on mixed with DdoS traffic to make a hybrid data set containing both malicious and normal data samples. For DDoS attacks detection, the authors have employed OpenFlow switches which have flow tables containing the information on network flow in the SDN environment.

As the ML classifier is initially trained using the CIC-DDoS2017 dataset, extraction of similar features is required from the SDN traffic in order to make sure that the trained classifier is deployable in the SDN environment. The 84 features of CIC-DDoS2017 are extracted from the SDN environment using the CICFlowmeter tool. To reduce the nos. of features, the authors have used the mathematical correlation coefficient method which computes how much a particular feature is correlated with the output label of a data sample; the features having high correlation coefficients are extracted for further use. For training and testing purposes, 18 features out of the 84 were used. Figure 14.7 displays the architecture of the proposed model.

For performance evaluation of the ML model, the authors have used metrics including F1-score, precision, and recall. They have employed a total of 03 ML models that are: NB, DT and SVM. The performance of the ML models is compared

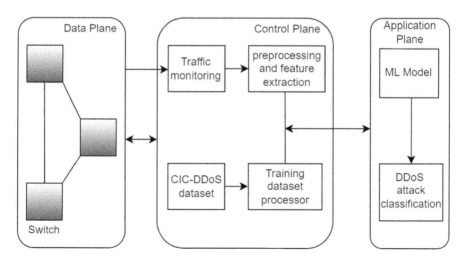

FIGURE 14.7   System model.

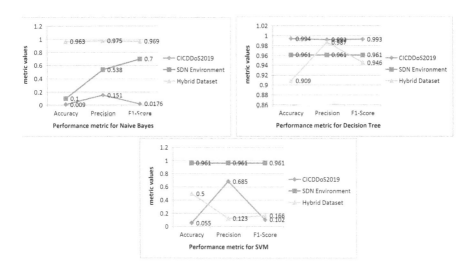

FIGURE 14.8   Performance of ML Classifiers for CICDDoS2019, SDN and Hybrid dataset.

between 03 data sets namely CICDDoS2019, SDN, and hybrid dataset. The results are shown in Figure 14.8.

14.3   NETWORK INTRUSION DETECTION SYSTEM FOR SDNS BASED ON DEEP LEARNING

In this section, we will detail the research on designing Network Intrusion Detection Systems (NIDS) using deep learning. Deep learning techniques, including neural networks, recurrent neural networks, and convolutional neural networks, are widely employed to uncover hidden patterns in data. Universal approximation theorem [15] proves that the multilayer neural networks are universal approximators which means that no matter how complex an unknown relation between data features and output labels is, the neural network has the ability to tune its parameters to learn those relations. This makes a neural network a very powerful learning technique and therefore over the years, thankfully due to the high computational power, neural networks are being extensively used to learn patterns and relations in several fields like optical character recognition, molecule design, healthcare, military, education, etc.

14.3.1   DNN AND GRU-RNN BASED INTRUSION DETECTION SYSTEM

In the design of NIDS, often we see that the features that are to be dealt with are quite large in nos. and the pattern that is shared between the features and their class (anomaly or benign) is unknown. Even though machine learning algorithms have performed fairly well in learning those patterns, researchers have shown that DL methods on the other hand have performed comparatively well. In reference [16], the authors have introduced a DL-based method for intrusion detection in SDN environments, named DeepIDS. Specifically, the authors have used a DNN and a

GRU-RNNto achieve an identification accuracy of 80.7% and 90% respectively. The authors have reported that their IDS doesn't affect the performance of OpenFlow controllers in an SDN.

The proposed architecture (Figure 14.9) consists of 03 modules namely: the consolidator, an anomaly identifier, and a countermeasure deployment. The *collector module* is responsible for data collection from the traffic flow which is then used for classification tasks. For a fixed time interval *T*, the data from the traffic flow is captured recurrently, however, the choice for *T* is tricky as choosing small values of *T* may not allow for sufficient data collection for classification and large values may increase the response time and decrease the throughput. Therefore, *T* is experimentally selected for optimum performance. The *anomaly detector module* employs a DNN which is fed with the data received from the collector module. The authors have claimed that to minimize the overhead of the controller they have limited the neurons present in the hidden layer of the DNN. Both DNN and GRU-RNN [17] have been implemented for designing the IDS. The *Countermeasure deployment module* is responsible for taking further course of action once a dataflow has been identified as malicious flow. The suspicious data sample is parsed for collecting information regarding its source ip, destination ip, etc. and then, the module creates a new entry in the table of openflow switch in order to terminate/suspend any data transfer from the suspicious node. Also, a warning regarding the security breach is given to the network administrators as well.

For performing experiments, the authors have created 03 distinct sub data-set from NSL-KDD each containing 06 features namely vanila set of feature, feature set of traffic, and a hybrid feature set. The performance metrics used for evaluation are:

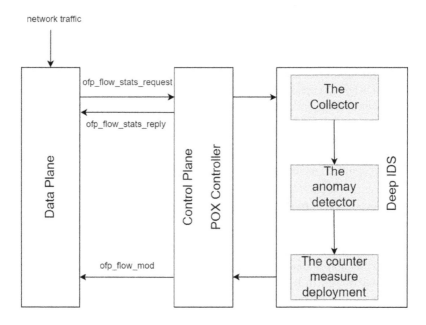

FIGURE 14.9　DeepIDS architecture.

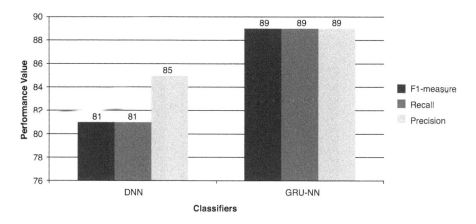

FIGURE 14.10   Comparative performance of DNN and GRU-RNN.

Accuracy, Precision, Recall, and F1-measure. The DNN model was designed for the task of binary classification and a highest accuracy of 80.7% was reported for mixed feature set (Figure 14.10). Therefore, mixed feature set was selected for evaluation and in subsequent experiment, the authors reported the comparative performance of GRU-RNN and DNN, the output in term of accuracy, precision and F1-score are shown in the figure below.

Given the complex learning procedure of the GRU-RNN, there is improvement in precision, recall, and F1-measure.

14.3.2   CNN-LSTM BASED INTRUSION DETECTION SYSTEM

Combining convolutional neural networks (CNN) [18] and long-short term memory (LSTM [19]), authors in [20] have proposed a new hybrid IDS. The authors have claimed that they were able to capture space-time-based features which enhances the model's capability for even 0-day attacks [21]. The model was checked using InSDN[22] dataset, with an accuracy of 96.32% reported.

In the initial stage of the architecture proposed, two convolution layers are utilized to take the spatial features, with output dimensions of 32 and 64. Dimensionality reduction is followed by this layer by employing a max-pooling layer of dimension 2*2. Once the spatial features have been obtained in stage-1, the temporal features are extracted using an LSTM layer. After this, there is a fully connected layer and an output layer. A softmax layer is employed for the purpose of classification in the output layer.

For overcoming the issue of overfitting L2 regularization is used however, the choice for the regularization parameter λ is heuristically searched by conducting several experiments. The final value of λ is chosen to be 0.1 based on experimental results.

The model's delivery is evaluated using all the basic metric used for the purpose in research. For binary classification, the values obtained for these metrics are displayed using bar graphs in Figure 14.11.

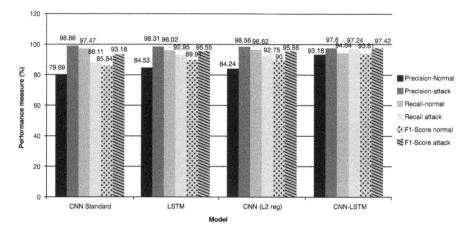

FIGURE 14.11 Comparative performance of the implemented models under normal and attack scenarios.

14.3.3 LSTM-OC-SVM Based Intrusion Detection System

In [23] the authors have proposed an anomaly detection technique for an unbalanced data set using one-class SVM (OC-SVM) and LSTM autoencoder. The model is trained on only data samples of benign class. The use of an LSTM autoencoder mitigates the inability of OC-SVM to work on high-dimensional data. The authors have used InSDN intrusion dataset to perform their experiments and have claimed to achieve high accuracy and low latency.

The authors have used an LSTM autoencoder to memorize the way data is spread and further employed an OC-SVM to train on the compressed representation of the normal data (Figure 14.12). Anomaly detection is ensured by evaluating the reconstruction error of an input data sample, the high value of error indicates that the autoencoder is facing trouble in reconstructing the data as it might be malignant on which it was not trained earlier. In other words, a high reconstruction error signifies intrusion. The authors have justified the choice of LSTM over RNN stating that unlike RNN, LSTM doesn't suffer from vanishing gradient.

The authors have used the InSDN[22] dataset for performing experiments. The choice of InSDN dataset stems from the fact that the it was created as a measure to overcome certain disadvantages of the currently used intrusion data sets like CICIDS2017, NSL-KDD, UNSW-NB15, etc. InSDN dataset has been generated in the context of SDN which makes it a more suitable candidate for designing IDS for SDNs. The dataset contains several attack classes such as Web attacks, DDoS, DoS, Bot-net, Password guessing, FTP, email, etc. It contains a total of 80 statistical features with 275,515 data samples in which 343,939 data samples are of normal category and 68,424 data samples are of attack category. In data preprocessing step, the authors have removed all the socket features from the dataset which reduces the total features to 77. Also, only limited nos. of data samples are used for both training and testing which reduces the running time of the model. Only binary classification has been addressed by the authors.

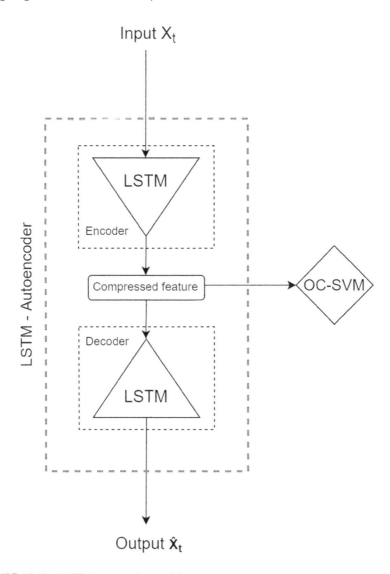

FIGURE 14.12   LIST-Autoencoder model.

The authors have used precision, accuracy and other related parameters for evaluating the performance of their model. The model is trained using data samples of normal category. L2 norm is computed between original datasample X_t and its reconstruction $\widehat{X_t}$. As the model trains on benign data samples, the L2 norm error $e = \| X_t - \widehat{X_t} \|^2$ is quite less for data samples of normal class and is high for malignant data samples. A threshold value for the error is decided above which a test data sample is classified as malignant and below which the model labels it as benign. The authors have tested the model for several values of threshold and the model behaves best for the threshold value of 0.07 as shown in Figure 14.13.

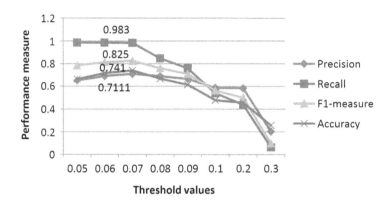

FIGURE 14.13   The performance metrics for difference thresholds.

The authors have claimed that the direct approach for using reconstruction errors for anomaly detection doesn't pay off well given the complexity and heterogeneity of attacks in the dataset, therefore they have used an OC-SVM classifier which is skilled on the probability data distribution space of the normal data samples as shown in Figure 14.13. The performance of OC-SVM model with LSTM-autoencoder-OC-SVM is compared wherein the latter model has performed fairly well. For LSTM-autoencoder-OC-SVM the value of precision, recall, f1-measure and accuracy is 0.93, 0.93, 0.93, and 90.5% respectively, while for OC-SVM the values for these metrics are 0.89, 0.93, 0.91 and 87.5% which shows the superiority of LSTM-autoencoder-OC-SVM over OC-SVM.

14.3.4   RNN-CNN BASED INTRUSION DETECTION SYSTEM

Authors in [24] have proposed an RNN and CNN based IDS for SDNs which automatically extracts features from a traffic flow without human intervention and then learns to classify malicious data within it. The authors have implemented their proposed model using 03 datasets and have reported to achieve reasonable detection accuracy compared some of the previously proposed deep learning based IDS.

For capturing traffic flow, authors have used pcap network data capturing tool. If the captured packet is of type TCP, it is processed according to TCP format. A vectorization layer is utilized to transform the captured packets into a 2-D matrix representation, which improves the efficiency of CNN training when compared to the approach of using the descriptor vector directly for training. The convolutional layer extracts features using convolution operations.

Both CNN and RNN are used for feature extraction. The RNN network is composed of 300 neurons and employs a gated recurrent unit (GRU) architecture, which includes two portals – the portal of updates and the portals of resets – as described in the paper by the authors. The input data is coalesced with data in network by the reset gate while the update gate controls the amount of previously dispensed network flow to be retained. Once the features have been extracted, a linear classifier is trained on the processed dataset.

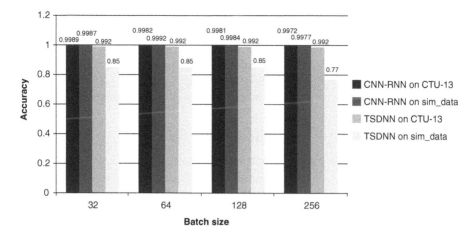

FIGURE 14.14 Comparative performance of CNN-RNN and TSDNN on CTU-13 and sim_data dataset.

For the dataset, some of the network traffic has been generated using mininet and pox simulators of SDNs. The described architecture comprises of 01 switch and 2 hosts, where one host is malicious and another host is the victim. The attack packets are generated at the attacker host and are transmitted to the victim over the network and the flow is captured simultaneously between them. The self-generated data set is called sim_data and beside sim_data, authors have also experimented on CTU-13[25] data set. Comparison has been drawn by the authors on the ability of the classifier for both the dataset. The accuracy achieved by the proposed classifier is compared with an earlier proposed model TSDNN[26] for CTU-13 and sim_data, the results are displayed in the figure below (Figure 14.14).

14.4 GENERATIVE NEURAL NETWORK-BASED NETWORK INTRUSION DETECTION SYSTEM FOR SDNS

Since the introduction of Generative Adversarial Networks (GANs) [27] in 2014, the field of artificial intelligence has witnessed an unprecedented surge in the application of deep learning in almost all the areas imaginable. From MRI image generation to molecule design generation, the generative ability of GANs is being put to use by researchers for getting improved results and novel solution to the real-life problems which were unthinkable a few decades back. The design of IDS in SDNs is also not untouched by generative networks like GANs and Variational autoencoders (VAEs [28]). Most of the research work explores the generative ability of GANs/VAEs to address data imbalance in intrusion datasets. Most of the available intrusion dataset like CICIDS2017, UNSW-NB15, NSL-KDD, etc. suffer from data imbalance where data samples of one type (usually benign) exceeds the data samples of another type (usually malignant) by a large margin. This imbalance makes it challenging to train the machine learning models as they are more prone to bias in favor of benign data samples leading to poor classification results. One way of mitigating the disadvantage of data imbalance is by producing data samples of the undernumbered class to a reasonable no. This can be achieved by training a GAN model on the data of the class which are comparatively few in numbers using the trained generator network of GAN to generate the required numbers of data samples. Another area where GANs are being utilized in securing the computer networks is in the creation of IDS.

14.4.1 GAN BASED ANOMALY DETECTION TECHNIQUE

In [29], the authors have proposed a defense and detection strategy against DDoS attacks using GANs and have also used adversarial training to thwart the threat of adversarial attacks on the proposed NIDS. An adversarial attack on machine learning models aims to exploit certain blindspots in these models which hampers their classification accuracy. The proposed technique offers real-time data traffic monitoring and threat detection using IP flow analysis. They have performed experiments in two scenarios: one with the use of emulated data and another with CICDDoS 2019 public dataset.

The proposed system works in four phases: (1) Data collection phase, wherein the controller of SDN collects the traffic flow from the tables maintained by switches, (2) Data preprocessing phase, wherein the collected data is preprocessed to make it fit for machine learning task, (3) Anomaly detection phase, in which the model analyze real-time data traffic and tries to detects the occurrence of any DDoS attack, (4) Mitigation phase, wherein necessary actions are taken to mitigate the damage incurred by the attack.

In the anomaly detection phase, the model uses a GAN model (Figure 14.15) which is trained on both the normal and DDoS data samples. The generator model of the GAN is a DNN with multiple layers: the 1st layer is a dense layer which is completely connected with 06 neurons followed by 03 more fully connected dense layers with 10, 8 and 6 neurons respectively. The discriminator is also a DNN with multiple

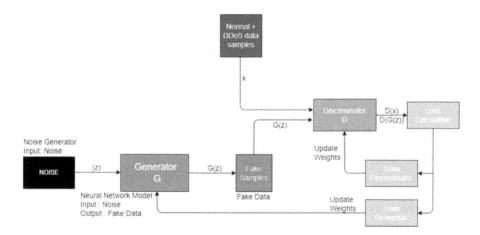

FIGURE 14.15 GAN training.

layers: the first layer is a dense layer which is completely connected with 12 units followed by 03 more fully connected with 10, 6, 1 neurons respectively. The discriminator and generator models are trained adversarially wherein the generator randomly samples data from a noise vector and feeds it to the discriminator. Discriminator's role is to differentiate a synthesized data sample from an actual data sample (from the dataset), the design of the loss functions is structured in a manner that the discriminator virtually feedbacks the generator on the "quality" of the data generated by it and hints at improving the generated data to look more "like" real data samples. Over time, the generator improves its parameters and begins generating data samples that are quite hard to distinguish from the real ones. The trained discriminator acts as a classifier for anomaly detection.

The experiments were performed in Python using Tensorflow [30] and Keras [31] libraries using a machine clocked at 2.21 GHz, primary memory of 8GB, and Microsoft's OS win 10. For evaluation metric, F1-score, accuracy, precision, and recall were used. The experiments were conducted for two scenarios: In the first scenario the dataset used was prepared by emulating an SDN environment using mininet [32] which allows emulating switches, hosts, links, controllers in a single virtual machine. Scapy [33] tool was used to generate network traffic. For inducing DDoS traffic, two DDoS attack types were flooded and the dataset was prepared by tabulating the network features between a host and victim virtual nodes. The evaluation of the IDS on the emulated dataset is shown in Figure 14.16 (second set of bars – GAN) which is compared with previous DL-based IDS which includes: CNN based IDS [34], LSTM-IDS [35], and MLP [36]. In the second case, the performance was assessed using CICDDoS2019. It contains training and test dataset, wherein the dataset used for training contains 12 different types of DDoS attacks. The results obtained on CICIDDoS2019 is shown in Figure 14.17 which also compared with previous works [34][35][36].

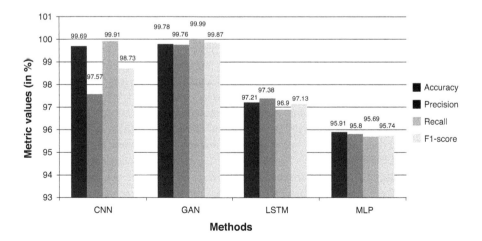

FIGURE 14.16 Discriminatory performance of the model against previously performed similar works (scenario-1).

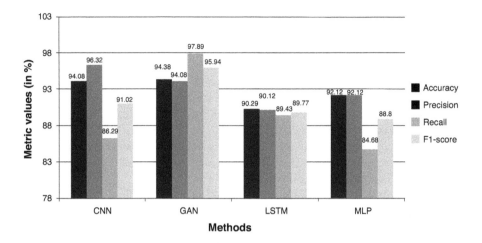

FIGURE 14.17 Evaluation of the proposed model's performance in comparison to previous similar studies (case scenario-2).

14.4.2 ADVERSARIAL AUTO-ENCODER BASED INTRUSION DETECTION

An adversarial auto-encoder (AAE) [37] combines a GAN and an autoencoder which learns the latent space representation of input data by leveraging the adversarial loss of a GAN. It is almost similar in working as a VAE but with a varying loss function in comparison, VAE uses KL-divergence while AAE uses the adversarial loss of the GAN for regularizing the latent space. AAEs are being extensively used for the task of DL-based anomaly detection.

In [38], the researchers have proposed a semi-supervised intrusion detection system that uses minimal data samples for training and deployment. The method uses an adversarial autoencoder and have examined the technique using NSL-KDD dataset, the authors claim that they were able to achieve comparable results by using only 0.1% of the data samples.

An autoencoder is used to compress the features of the input data by using neural networks, it tries to recreate the input data sample and in the process of doing so produces a latent space that preserves the identity of the original data in a few possible dimensions. The basic auto-encoder lacks generative capabilities as we can reduce the dimensions of the input data but cannot generate new data samples; in an adversarial auto-encoder, a GAN is used to overcome this limitation. In the AAE, an encoder module learns the latent space probability distribution $q(z)$ from x and decoder learns to remake x as x' with minimum possible reconstruction error. The GAN model uses the encoder module of the autoencoder as the generator and tries to regularize the latent space distribution $q(z)$ by imposing it to mimic a distribution $p(z)$. As the training process continues, the encoder develops the ability to translate the input data into its latent representation that adheres to the prior distribution $p(z)$. Following training, the encoder can be utilized to produce novel data samples.

In this chapter, the authors have used the AAE (Figure 14.18) as a semi-supervised learning tool. The encoder module employs two latent variables, z1 and z2, instead

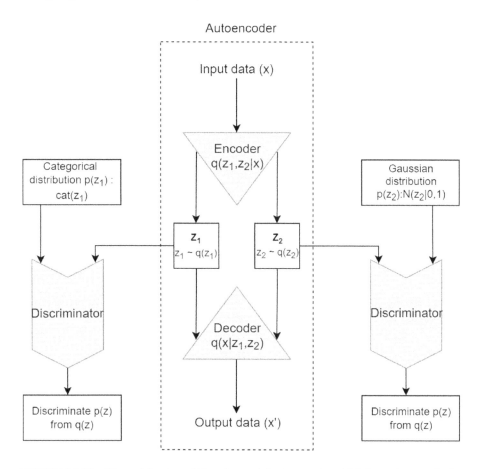

FIGURE 14.18   The architecture of the adversarial autoencoder which is semi-supervised.

of one, to represent the characteristics of the input data. The latent variable $z1$ is used for grasping the features corresponding to the category of the input data ("benign" or "malignant") and latent variable $z2$ is used to grasp the features corresponding to the other features. This differentiation also divides the sampling of the variables. A distribution represented by cat($z1$) is utilized for $z1$, and $N(z2|0, I)$ is used for $z2$. Specifically, two discriminators are used, one for discriminating between categorical distribution cat($z1$) and $z1$ sampled from the encoder module and other discriminator which learns to discriminate between gaussian distribution $N(z2|0, I)$ and $z2$ samples from the encoder module. This arrangement enables a labelled/unlabeled data-specific learning, for an unlabeled data sample both the features and categorical features are learned by using both the discriminators while for labeled data the AAE is trained by using the category of the labeled data. Post training the latent variable $z1$ is able to indicate the inferred category of an input data sample.

The authors have experimented and have claimed that their technique is able to outshine a vanilla DNN in terms of the accuracy in classification in different scenarios

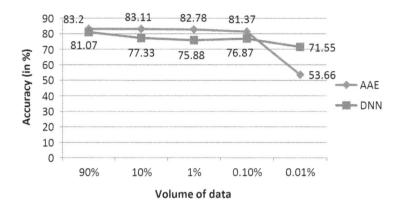

FIGURE 14.19   Comparative performance of DNN and AAE in terms of the volume of data used.

where a fixed percent of data is used for training the models. The Figure 14.19 shows the comparative performance of a DNN and an AAE classifier.

14.4.3   Conditional Variational Auto-Encoder Based Intrusion Detection System

The generative networks have been improved over the years in terms of the quality of the generated data samples as well as they have been tweaked by researchers to generate class-specific data samples too. One such class-specific generative neural network is a conditional variational auto-encoder (CVAE [39]) which can be trained to generate data samples of specific categories. Authors in [40] have proposed an intrusion detection technique which combines an improved CVAE (ICVAE) and a DNN. The CVAE is employed to discover the hidden characteristics of the data samples and subsequently provide a trained decoder which can generate new data samples of attack categories of specific class so as to mitigate the data imbalance problem and to diversify the attack categories which enhances the accuracy of the deep learning model in detecting threats. The ICVAE not only reduces the dimensionality but also sets the initial weight of a DNN which follows ICVAE for further classification tasks. Authors have used NSL-KDD and UNSW-NB15 to examine the proposed ICVAE-DNN model. The authors claim that the proposed detection method outshines other 06 previously proposed technique.

The CVAE is a modified VAE where the encoder and decoder networks are also conditioned on the data label y of an input data samples x. The encoder network is conditioned on x as well as y so the probability distribution that the encoder intends to learn become $Q(z|x,y)$. For the decoder similar changes are performed to condition the decoder to generate data sample x of a given class x, therefore the distribution the decoder intents to learn is $P(x|z,y)$. In an improved CVAE, only the decoder is

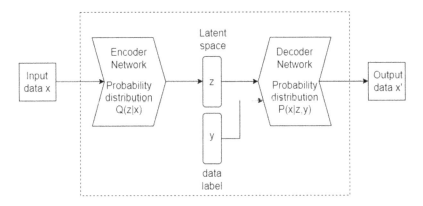

FIGURE 14.20   Architecture of an improved conditional variational autoencoder.

conditioned on the class label, so the distribution for encoder is similar to that of a VAE, $Q(z|x)$. Figure 14.20 shows the architecture of an ICVAE.

For training the ICVAE, the datasets underwent preprocessing wherein numeric features were normalized and the categorical features were encoded to numeric features by using one-hot encoding. Post processing, the number of features in NSL-KDD rose to 122 and for UNSW-NB15 the no. was 196. A multivariate Gaussian distribution was used for the encoder module and a multivariate Bernoulli distribution was used for the decoder module in the ICVAE. Min-max normalization was used to scale the value of all the features between 0 and 1 and the ICVAE was trained using the Adam optimization algorithm. The loss function of the ICVAE consists of two components: KL divergence loss and a reconstruction loss. KL divergence ensures that the encoder-decoder module learns the distribution which follows a standard pre-defined data distribution and the reconstruction loss ensures that the reconstructed data is as closely resembling the input data as possible.

Once the training is complete, the trained decoder is employed to synthesize data points, and are stored in a form of a dataset which is later used to train a DNN. While generating the data samples it is ensured that data of each class is generated proportionally so as to avoid data imbalance. Once the dataset is ready, it is used to train a DNN which learns multiclass classification. The performance of the DNN improves as it trains well on data of each class (normal and attack) and avoids getting biassed toward majority class data samples.

The authors have examined the designed system on datasets: NSL-KDD and UNSW-NB15 and have claimed to achieve better accuracy in comparison to the previous anomaly detection technique which includes, a hybrid spectral DNN based intrusion detection (SCDNN [41]), a self-taught learning based IDS (STL [42]), DNN based IDS [43], Gaussian-bernoulli RBM [44], RNN-IDS [45], ID-CVAE [46], CASCADE-ANN [47], EM clustering [48] and a decision tree based IDS [48]. The comparative performance is shown in the Figure 14.21 below.

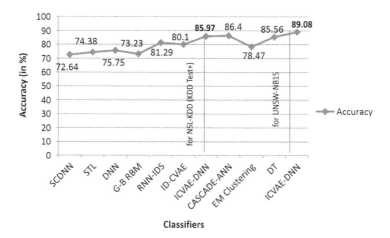

FIGURE 14.21   The comparative performance of the DL-based classifiers on NSL-KDD and UNSW-NB15 in terms of test accuracy. The proposed classifier ICVAE-DNN gives best accuracy for NSL-KDD (85.97%) and UNSW-NB15 (89.08%).

14.5   CONCLUSION

In this chapter, we have discussed how ML and DL approaches are also finding applications in the design of IDS for software-defined networks. Due to the advancement in computational power, ML/DL-based IDS are viable and are offering better performance both in term of latency and correct detection when compared with signature-based intrusion detection techniques.

In the first section, we discussed the published research in ML-based intrusion detection. The ML methods which were discussed in the section included support vector machine, decision tree, NB, LDA, LogitBoost, ADAboost, etc. and we discussed their comparative performance as well. We also discussed that data preprocessing is a crucial step in designing an IDS because an ML algorithm well fed is the machine learning algorithm well trained and even though several researchers use identical ML techniques, the accuracy reported differ due to the preprocessing step. Similarly, we also discussed different techniques that the authors have used for extracting network features from the SDN environment. Unlike other areas where IDS are developed, SDN offers a different challenge for IDS developers because of the underlying complexities of an SDN and we discussed how the researchers have overcome those challenges to extract valuable features from SDN traffic for training their ML models.

In the second section, we shifted our attention to the field of DL-based intrusion detection and discussed various DL techniques that researchers have adopted for designing IDS which included DNN, RNN, CNN, and LSTM. An advantage of the DL methods over ML technique is in terms of automatic feature extraction wherein the DL methods, given their complex structure and impeccable learning capabilities, are able to extract vital features from the dataset without human intervention. This enables the researchers to not worry about feature extraction as the DL model takes care of it while offering application standard detection rates. We also discussed how the researchers have used these techniques in conjunction to produce hybrid models where the individual capabilities of the models empowers the hybrid model to improve its detection rate.

In the last section, we discussed the application of generative neural networks in designing IDS. Generative networks have the capability to generate new data samples by learning the underlying distribution of a given input dataset. The generative models that were discussed in the section included GAN, Adversarial auto-encoder and conditional variational autoencoder. The researchers have commonly used the generative models to mitigate imbalance of data in the existing public datasets wherein, usually the attack data samples are comparatively low in nos. then normal data samples due to which the performance of intrusion detection model is hampered. By generating more number of new data samples of the minority class, the generative models can mitigate the imbalance and provide the ML/DL model with a more diverse data set to train on. Also, a generative model can function as a classifier on its own by using reconstruction errors to detect malignant data samples; however, primarily they are being used for dimensionality reduction and mitigating data imbalance.

REFERENCES

(1) Hadem, P., D. K. Saikia, and S. Moulik. "An SDN-based intrusion detection system using SVM with selective logging for IP traceback."*Computer Networks* 191 (2021): 108015.

(2) Ahmad, A., E. Harjula, M. Ylianttila, and I. Ahmad. "Evaluation of machine learning techniques for security in SDN." *2020 IEEE Globecom Workshops (GC Wkshps.* IEEE, 2020.

(3) Preamthaisong, P., A. Auyporntrakool, P. Aimtongkham, and T. Sriwuttisap. "Enhanced DDoS detection using hybrid genetic algorithm and decision tree for SDN."*2019 16th International Joint Conference on Computer Science and Software Engineering (JCSSE).* IEEE, 2019.

(4) Aliyu, I., M. C. Feliciano, S. Van Engelenburg, D. O. Kim, and C. G. Lim. "A blockchain-based federated forest for SDN-enabled in-vehicle network intrusion detection system." *IEEE Access* 9 (2021): 102593–102608.

(5) Ahmad, A. "Evaluation of machine learning techniques for intrusion detection in software-defined networking."*Faculty of Information Technology and Electrical Engineering,* MS Thesis, 2020.

(6) Ashraf, J., N. Moustafa, A. D. Bukhshi, and A. Javed. "Intrusion detection system for SDN-enabled IoT networks using machine learning techniques."*2021 IEEE 25th International Enterprise Distributed Object Computing Workshop (EDOCW).* IEEE, 2021.

(7) Ujjan, R. M. A., Z. Pervez, and K. Dahal. "Suspicious traffic detection in SDN with collaborative techniques of snort and deep neural networks."*2018 IEEE 20th International Conference on High Performance Computing and Communications; IEEE 16th International Conference on Smart City; IEEE 4th International Conference on Data Science and Systems (HPCC/SmartCity/DSS).* IEEE, 2018.

(8) Tang, T. A., S. A. R. Zaidi, D. McLernon, L. Mhamdi, and M. Ghogho. "Deep recurrent neural network for intrusion detection in sdn-based networks."*2018 4th IEEE Conference on Network Softwarization and Workshops (NetSoft).* IEEE, 2018.

(9) Abdallah, M., N. A. L. Khac, H. Jahromi, and A. D. Jurcut. "A Hybrid CNN-LSTM based approach for anomaly detection systems in SDNs."*The 16th International Conference on Availability, Reliability and Security.* 2021.

(10) Wang, P., K.-M. Chao, H.-C. Lin, W.-H. Lin, and C.-C. Lo. "An efficient flow control approach for SDN-based network threat detection and migration using support vector machine." *2016 IEEE 13th International Conference on e-Business Engineering (ICEBE),* 2016, pp. 56–63, doi: 10.1109/ICEBE.2016.020.

(11) Latah, M., and L. Toker. "Towards an efficient anomaly-based intrusion detection for software-defined networks." *IET Networks* 7.6 (2018): 453–459.

(12) Jolliffe, I. T. "Principal component analysis: A beginner's guide—I. Introduction and application." *Weather* 45.10 (1990): 375–382.

(13) Boero, L., M. Marchese, and S. Zappatore. "Support vector machine meets software-defined networking in ids domain." *2017 29th International Teletraffic Congress (ITC 29).* Vol. 3. IEEE, 2017.

(14) Kousar, H., M. M. Mulla, P. Shettar and D. G. Narayan. "Detection of DDoS attacks in software-defined network using decision tree." *2021 10th IEEE International Conference on Communication Systems and Network Technologies (CSNT).* IEEE, 2021.

(15) Hornik, K., M. Stinchcombe, and H. White. "Multilayer feedforward networks are universal approximators." *Neural Networks* 2.5 (1989): 359–366.

(16) Tang, T. A., L. Mhamdi, D. McLernon, S. A. R. Zaidi, M. Ghogho, and F. El Moussal. "DeepIDS: Deep learning approach for intrusion detection in software-defined networking." *Electronics* 9.9 (2020): 1533.

(17) Rumelhart, D. E., G. E. Hinton, and R. J. Williams. "Learning internal representations by error propagation." *California Univ San Diego La Jolla Inst for Cognitive Science,* 1 (1985): 318–362.

(18) O'Shea, K., and R. Nash. "An introduction to convolutional neural networks." *arXiv preprint arXiv* :1511.08458 (2015).

(19) Hochreiter, S., and J. Schmidhuber. "Long short-term memory." *Neural Computation* 9.8 (1997): 1735–1780.

(20) Abdallah, M., N. A. L. Khac, H. Jahromi and A. D. Jurcut. "A hybrid CNN-LSTM based approach for anomaly detection systems in SDNs." *The 16th International Conference on Availability, Reliability, and Security.* 2021.

(21) Bilge, L., and T. Dumitraş. "Before we knew it: An empirical study of zero-day attacks in the real world." *Proceedings of the 2012 ACM Conference on Computer and Communications Security.* 2012.

(22) Elsayed, M. S., N.-A. Le-Khac, and A. D. Jurcut. "InSDN: A novel SDN intrusion dataset." *IEEE Access* 8 (2020): 165263–165284.

(23) Said Elsayed, M., N.-A. Le-Khac, S. Dev, and A. D. Jurcut. "Network anomaly detection using LSTM based autoencoder." *Proceedings of the 16th ACM Symposium on QoS and Security for Wireless and Mobile Networks.* 2020.

(24) Qin, Y., J. Wei, and W. Yang. "Deep learning based anomaly detection scheme in software-defined networking." *2019 20th Asia-Pacific Network Operations and Management Symposium (APNOMS).* IEEE, 2019.

(25) Garcia, S., S. García, M. Grill, J. Stiborek, and A. Zunino. "An empirical comparison of botnet detection methods." *Computers & Security* 45 (2014): 100–123.

(26) Chen, Y.-C., Y.-J. Li, A. Tseng, and T. Lin. "Deep learning for malicious flow detection." *2017 IEEE 28th Annual International Symposium on Personal, Indoor, and Mobile Radio Communications (PIMRC).* IEEE, 2017.

(27) Goodfellow, I., J. Pouget-Abadie, M. Mirza, B. Xu, D. Warde-Farley, S. Ozair, A. Courville, and Y. Bengio. "Generative adversarial networks." *Communications of the ACM* 63.11 (2020): 139–144.

(28) Kingma, D. P., and M. Welling. "Auto-encoding variational bayes." *arXiv preprint arXiv:1312.6114* (2013).

(29) Novaes, M. P., L. F. Carvalho, J. Lloret, and M. L. Proença Jr. "Adversarial deep learning approach detection and defense against DDoS attacks in SDN environments." *Future Generation Computer Systems* 125 (2021): 156–167.

(30) Abadi, M., Agarwal, A., Barham, P., Brevdo, E., Chen, Z., Citro, C., Corrado, G.S., Davis, A., Dean, J., Devin, M. and Ghemawat, S. "Large-scale machine learning on heterogeneous systems. 2015." Software available from tensorflow. org (2015).

(31) Ketkar, N. "Introduction to keras." In *Deep learning with Python*, Springer Link, ed. Apress, Berkeley, CA, 2017, 97–111.

(32) Lantz, B., and B. O'Connor. "A mininet-based virtual testbed for distributed SDN development." *ACM SIGCOMM Computer Communication Review* 45.4 (2015): 365–366.

(33) Bansal, S., and N. Bansal. "Scapy-a python tool for security testing." *Journal of Computer Science & Systems Biology* 8.3 (2015): 140.

(34) de Assis, M. V. O., L. F. Carvalho, J. Rodrigues and J. Lloret. "Near real-time security system applied to SDN environments in IoT networks using convolutional neural network." *Computers & Electrical Engineering* 86 (2020): 106738.

(35) Priyadarshini, R., and R. K. Barik. "A deep learning based intelligent framework to mitigate DDoS attack in fog environment." *Journal of King Saud University-Computer and Information Sciences* 34.3 (2022): 825–831.

(36) Wang, M., Y. Lu, and J. Qin. "A dynamic MLP-based DDoS attack detection method using feature selection and feedback." *Computers & Security* 88 (2020): 101645.

(37) Makhzani, A., J. Shlens, N. Jaitly, I. Goodfellow, and B. Frey. "Adversarial autoencoders." *arXiv preprint arXiv* 1511.05644 (2015).

(38) Hara, K., and K. Shiomoto. "Intrusion detection system using semi-supervised learning with adversarial auto-encoder." *NOMS 2020-2020 IEEE/IFIP Network Operations and Management Symposium*. IEEE, 2020.

(39) Kingma, D. P., D. J. Rezende, S. Mohamed, and M. Welling. "Semi-supervised learning with deep generative models." *Advances in Neural Information Processing Systems* 27 (2014).

(40) Yang, Y., K. Zheng, C. Wu, and Y. Yang. "Improving the classification effectiveness of intrusion detection by using improved conditional variational autoencoder and deep neural network." *Sensors* 19.11 (2019): 2528.

(41) Ma, T., F. Wang, J. Cheng, Y. Yu, and X. Chen. "A hybrid spectral clustering and deep neural network ensemble algorithm for intrusion detection in sensor networks." *Sensors* 16.10 (2016): 1701.

(42) Javaid, A., Q. Niyaz, W. Sun, and M. Alam. "A deep learning approach for network intrusion detection system." *Proceedings of the 9th EAI International Conference on Bio-inspired Information and Communications Technologies (formerly BIONETICS)*. 2016.

(43) Tang, T. A., L. Mhamdi, D. McLernon, S. A. R. Zaidi, and M. Ghogho. "Deep learning approach for network intrusion detection in software-defined networking." *2016 International Conference on Wireless Networks and Mobile Communications (WINCOM)*. IEEE, 2016.

(44) Imamverdiyev, Y., and F. Abdullayeva. "Deep learning method for denial of service attack detection based on restricted boltzmann machine." *Big Data* 6.2 (2018): 159–169.

(45) Yin, C., Y. Zhu, J. Fei, and X. He. "A deep learning approach for intrusion detection using recurrent neural networks." *Ieee Access* 5 (2017): 21954–21961.

(46) Lopez-Martin, M., B. Carro, A. Sanchez-Esguevillas, and J. Lloret. "Conditional variational autoencoder for prediction and feature recovery applied to intrusion detection in IoT." *Sensors* 17.9 (2017): 1967.

(47) Baig, M. M., M. M. Awais, and E.-S. M. El-Alfy. "A multiclass cascade of artificial neural network for network intrusion detection." *Journal of Intelligent & Fuzzy Systems* 32.4 (2017): 2875–2883.

(48) Moustafa, N., and J. Slay. "The evaluation of network anomaly detection systems: Statistical analysis of the UNSW-NB15 data set and the comparison with the KDD99 data set." *Information Security Journal: A Global Perspective* 25.1–3 (2016): 18–31.

15 The Essence of Software-Defined Network in Big Data Analytics

Saba Farheen N S, Swathi C, Shreya R J,
Sindhu Rajendran, and Gamze Ozel

15.1 INTRODUCTION

The issue of big data is quite current. When personal to geopolitical dimensions are connected to it in an age of information warfare, it becomes a subject of uttermost importance.

Handling this information effectively becomes essential since many firms have a lot of data about their staff, goods, and services. Big data, as defined, is a term used to describe data sets that are too massive or complicated to be handled by conventional data-processing application software. Two effective fields, notably the Hadoop software and MapReduce, are employed to manage these data collections.

The main idea behind the MapReduce technique is to divide a large issue into smaller ones. To put it another way, it takes a collection of data and transforms it into another set of data where each element is broken down into tuples (key/value pairs). The reduction task condenses the input map data tuples into a smaller group of data tuples. Hence by "MapReduce," the reduction task is always carried out after the map job. The ease with which data processing may be spread over several computing nodes is a significant benefit of this approach. The terms "mappers and reducers" refer to the data processing primitives in a MapReduce paradigm. The data processing primitives of a MapReduce paradigm are referred to as mappers and reducers. To separate a data processing program into mappers and reducers is not always simple. The scalability of an application to work on hundreds of servers in a cluster, thousands of them, or even tens of thousands of them just requires a configuration update after it has been created in the MapReduce way. The convenience of scalability makes the MapReduce technique popular among programmers.

Sometimes it is difficult to divide a software application into reducers and mappers. However, as an application is designed according to MapReduce style, scaling to operate on hundreds, thousands, or even tens of thousands of servers in a cluster just takes a configuration update. Many programmers now employ the MapReduce paradigm because of its simplicity in scaling.

DOI: 10.1201/9781003432869-15

271

The open-source framework known as Apache Hadoop can efficiently store and handle gigabytes to petabytes of data. Hadoop allows the clustering of several computers to more effectively analyze massive datasets in parallel than using a single, powerful machine. The scalable large data management system is called Hadoop. Depending on the need, it may operate on a single computer or thousands of computers. Additionally, Hadoop makes it possible to distribute the computing component by allowing data computation to take place on the host or server where the data is located rather than centrally. Hadoop virtually leads the industry in massive data storage because of its versatility.

Hadoop is a management software framework that supports big data analytics. Hadoop can classify, manage, query, and distribute huge unstructured data sets over several nodes in a distributed network environment. The Hadoop distributed file storage system breaks data into small segments and distributes them across many servers (HDFS). By breaking the data down into manageable segments that the nodes can analyze and sort concurrently, Hadoop employs MapReduce to handle the data. The map technique handles the filtering and sorting chores, while the reduction method handles the summary tasks.

Running distributed operations on massive volumes of data is made simple by Hadoop by enabling the use of all the storage and processing capabilities of clustered machines. On top of Hadoop's Building blocks, different services, and applications may be developed. A common option for developing big data infrastructure nowadays is to combine Hadoop with MapReduce. The three main components of a Hadoop network topology are clients, slaves, and masters.

A controller is a group of different service components that are supported by the SDN architecture. Data routing in SDN is more precise and fast since it is based on traffic flow. Performance may be increased by dynamic resource allocation to big data applications by implementing SDN choices in the controller at runtime.

Big data technologies are gaining popularity as a result of the novel methods used to store and retrieve information. Because big data applications are designed for huge datasets, dealing with smaller files presents difficulties. The underlying networks are used by applications like Hadoop to provide seamless consumer services. The main purpose of underlying networks is to manage unpredictable internet traffic. However, the traffic footprint of big data applications differs. In order to provide a better and more reliable infrastructure for big data applications, conventional networks can benefit from SDN.

SDNs and big data are gaining popularity in both educational institutes and industry. The majority of earlier works have typically dealt with these significant areas one at a time. Large data collection, transmission, storage, and processing are all made much simpler by SDN, but the massive amount of data may have a big influence on how SDN is designed and put into practice [1]. Big data computations in cloud statistics facilities, information distribution, collaborative optimization, scientific enormous records architectures, and scheduling issues are just a few of the issues that SDN resolves when it comes to big data programs large data packet performance can be enhanced by proper SDN's neighborhood management. Extensive and challenging to operate are legacy data and communications networks. Different pieces of equipment are involved, all of which are controlled by complicated, closed-source, and proprietary distributed control software. Because the control and data planes are packaged together in traditional IP networks, they are vertically integrated.

Networks are to be made more programmable through SDNs. Software programmers running on top of the network operating system (NOS) allow for the programmability of the network. SDN separates the control and data planes, encourages logical network control centralization, and adds network programming capabilities. Additionally, SDN streamlines network administration and promotes network growth by making it simpler to develop and implement new networking abstractions [2].

Because the data and the control plane in conventional networks are converged and proprietary, they are exceedingly complex and difficult to administer. Another reason is that the device is associated with a different version than the product. It takes a long time to update or generate firmware for each group of goods (i.e. each group of devices has its own configuration and administration interface) [3].These are the reasons that cause network infrastructure problems and greatly limit network creativity, as well as data and control plane separation and network centralization. While the control plane is viewed as a single entity serving as the network's controller or operating system, the data plane is dedicated to effective packet forwarding and programmable packet forwarding devices. Applications and software that control or drive controllers are simpler to create and maintain than conventional networks. Policy implementation can be easily done using SDN and data sets, and represents a model of network evolution and change that creates a new network infrastructure [4].

The tremendous amount of data produced by the global data explosion is frequently referred to as "big data." Big data often comprises a greater volume of unstructured data than standard datasets, demanding more immediate analytics. Moreover, big data opens up fresh possibilities for value discovery, aids in the understanding of hidden value, and poses new organizational and management issues [5].

15.2   UTILITY OF SDN FOR BIG DATA

Traditional network architectures do not support or are incompatible with changing business needs, such as the proliferation of devices, laptops, and mobile phones, and virtualization of machines reducing the need to purchase additional hardware. Consequently, there is a growing demand for more cost-effective high-quality automation and advanced security and management solutions to effectively handle the increasing complexity of IoT device data and big data applications. It also helps in the efficient management of specific newly introduced devices as well as traditional devices such as optical and wireless networks. Network management and control are made simpler with centralized network management. With SDN, it's easy to create automated programs that give organizations the freedom to configure, protect, and optimize their resources [6].

1. By giving the controller access to network intelligence, the forwarding device is made simpler (switch). Since they simply need to respond to commands from the controller and are not required to comprehend and process many algorithms and protocols, these devices are left with relatively minimal capability.

2. Forwarding devices assist controllers in other tasks such as route calculation, link/node monitoring, and network management and diagnostics.
3. The network control plane is separate from management and data planes
   and can be directly programmed.
4. Innovation can be done faster without having to configure every device and
   wait for new versions from vendors.
5. It provides an adaptable network design that safeguards current investments
   while securing the network's future.
6. Since it can swiftly adjust to changing user requests, it improves the experience for users by centralizing network control and providing information to
   more advanced applications.

SDN uses central management to identify faults and does reconfiguration of the identified faults. Proactively handle outages based on expected service unavailability.
SDN will modernize the telecommunications industry. Provider carriers can increase
flexibility and offer on-demand bandwidth and variable bandwidth usage to customers in need of additional flexibility [7].

15.3   SIGNIFICANCE OF SDN FOR BIG DATA

SDN is used for applications with large datasets and makes sense primarily because
of the way applications with large datasets handle facts. Many analyzes of large
datasets involve unstructured data (video, audio, text, email, and other content that
traditional database systems cannot cluster). Big data intelligence is derived from
three basic steps:

1. Splitting data across multiple servers
2. Analyzing all blocks of a dataset, and
3. Merging sequences.

These characteristics have been of immense importance to big data analytics and its
application in the real domain. For example, SDN has facilitated the automation of
community responses and conserves bandwidth when real-time analysis or a higher
reliability is required. Using SDN is a great way to ensure the overall performance
of analyzing large data sets.

Big data may be labeled as unstructured or established. Unstructured data is
poorly organized information that fails to fit into a predefined version. It contains
information gathered from social networking resources that assist organizations in
accumulating statistics on consumer preferences. Salient features of big data are
as shown in (Figure 15.1 Alt text: A circular diagram with interconnected boxes,
each representing salient features of big data such as Velocity, Value, Visualization,
Variety, and Veracity forming a continuous loop.) [8].

- Visualization – Given its enormity, it has been given the term "big data."
  Volume is an enormous amount of data. The volume of data is rather signifi-
  cant. Big data is characterized as having a very huge amount of information.
  As a result, while working with large data, volume is a crucial consideration.

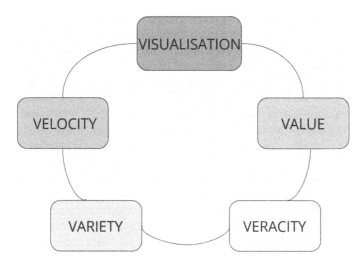

FIGURE 15.1   Five Vs of big data.

- Value – Until it can be turned profitable, the majority of the organization's data is useless. Information must be retrieved from data by changing it into something valuable because data alone is meaningless and irrelevant.
- Veracity: It can be difficult to control the quality and accuracy of the data that is provided, and it can occasionally become chaotic. Big data is unexpected due to the many different data dimensions that it contains, which reduces data ambiguity and inconsistencies from multiple different data types and sources.
- Variety – The term "variety" points to the structured, semi-structured, and unstructured data. It also relates to a variety of sources. There is an influx of data from new sources both inside and outside of an organization.
- Velocity – Velocity is the term used to describe the quick acquisition of data. The rate at which data is produced by sources like social media, machines, mobile phones, networks, etc. is known as big data velocity. A considerable and consistent flow of data is present.

Data transmission is a very difficult task since big data applications need a large amount of data. Because of its effective network management, SDN is regarded as one of the most viable alternatives for reforming the cyber world. Standards for SDN protocols are being developed in practical applications. Today, SDN isn't restricted to implementations, it's a collective term for platforms.

SDN has four characteristics:

- Control plane and data plane are separate.
- Routing decisions are flow-based rather than goal-based.
- Control plane centralization and transfer to the SDN controller or Network Operating System (NOS).
- Software programs that interact with the fundamental data plane components and run on the NOS can program the network.

The collection, data transfer, storage, and computation of big data are made significantly easier by the aforementioned exceptional qualities [9].

The architecture, as well as the operation of SDN, will be greatly affected by big data, a commonly used network application. In particular, the SDN centralized controller can acquire a large volume of data across all multiple levels (that is, from physical to application level) using the perspective of the whole network. Certainly, SDN's architecture and operation can benefit from big data analysis, which uses analytical techniques to extract data-driven information to make appropriate conclusions. For example, the controller may more easily implement traffic engineering to enhance SDN efficiency through big data analysis. These advantageous characteristics can substantially simplify massive data gathering, transmission, storage, and processing. SDN can increase application performance by dynamically allocating resources based on traffic statistics. Additionally, a recent development in network topologies and applications for data centers is to use SDN's capabilities for application-aware networks. Big data applications can leverage SDN-based data centers because a large amount of data is typically handled in them by constantly assigning resources in accordance with the service level agreement of various applications of big data [10].

15.4 CHALLENGES OF SDN

SDN faces several challenges that hinder its overall performance and implementation. The SDN controller must be properly configured to validate the SDN's community topology to avoid manual errors and increase community accessibility. SDN controllers should have the ability to support some path resolution or to quickly redirect website visitors to active hyperlinks when direction/hyperlink failures occur [11]. If the principal controller fails, the new architecture runs a trade controller that can handle the traffic float. Another key issue concerns the fundamental trade-off between the state distribution consistency model, control application consistency requirements, and performance in distributed SDN controllers [12].

- **The additional control plane traffic:** Because of the increased network strain and potential bottleneck, the management of data becomes difficult.
- **Scalability:** One of the main issues with SDNs has been scalability from the start. The primary reason for scalability problems in SDNs is the separation of the data and control planes. Particularly relevant are reactive network architectures, in which the initial forwarding element delivers the first packet of a new flow toward the controller [13].
- **Data distribution among controllers:** In distributed systems, scalability is critically dependent on how data is distributed across controller copies.
- **Availability of Internet routers:** The availability of Internet routers is presently a major problem due to the ubiquity of clouds and their high demands on the network. Therefore, it is essential that increased level of accessibility be arranged on such systems if SDN control frameworks are to act as the foundation of networked applications [14].

15.5   CHALLENGES OF BIG DATA

The actual difficulties with big data are the implementation obstacles. These ought to be managed immediately since if they aren't, the technology might malfunction, which might have a way since if they aren't, the technology might malfunction, which might have some unfavorable consequences. The storing and analysis of extraordinarily massive data and quickly expanding data are among the big data difficulties. Below mentioned are a few challenges pertinent to big data [15].

1. Since data is typically represented inadequately, the purpose of data representation is to make it more comprehensible for computational analysis and user evaluation. However, the original data's value will be reduced, and it can even prevent effective data analysis.
2. Datasets frequently include a great deal of redundant information. Redundancy reduction and data compression are efficient ways to lower the indirect costs of the entire system, provided that the experimental values of the data are unaffected.
3. Vast data would not be supported by the current storage technology. Values hidden in big data typically depend on the recentness of the data. To determine which data should be preserved and which data should be destroyed, a data importance principle based on analytical value should be devised.
4. The big data analytical system must quickly analyze vast amounts of diverse data. Further research is needed on the in-memory database and experimental data based on approximate analysis [16].
5. Most stockholders or suppliers of big data services are now unable to maintain and analyze such massive datasets effectively due to capacity limitations. They must rely on professionals or tools to evaluate such data, which increases the risk of security problems. In order to protect such sensitive data and maintain its security, big data analysis may only be forwarded to a third party for processing when necessary measures are implemented.
6. Big data processing, storage, and transmission will undoubtedly use more and more electricity as data volume and analytical requirements grow. Therefore, while ensuring expandability and accessibility, system-level power consumption control and management methods must be put in place for big data.
7. The big data analysis system must be able to support both recent and upcoming datasets. The computational algorithm should be able to handle increasing and complicated datasets.
8. To fully utilize the possibilities of big data, analysis of big data is interdisciplinary research that calls for collaboration amongst specialists in various domains. To enable scientists and engineers from diverse professions to access various types of data and fully capitalize on their knowledge in order to collaborate to achieve the analytical goals, a thorough big data network architecture must be built [17].

15.6   THE ADVANTAGES OF BIG DATA IN SDN

The SDN approach also creates a foundation to enable data-based applications like virtualization and big data. Traffic engineering and thwarting security intrusions are some of the ways that big data may benefit SDN. The major benefits of software-defined networking for businesses are listed below.

- **Big Data can help SDN prevent security attacks:**
  SDN security is a significant problem. SDN's design is vertically segmented into three primary functional levels, making these three levels vulnerable to malicious assaults. Based on their possible targets, threats posed by SDN can be categorized into three groups: attacks on the infrastructure, at the control level, and at the application level. Big data analysis enables us to thoroughly examine enormous volumes of complex and varied data from several sources in a variety of formats. These data sets enable real-time data comparison, anomaly detection, and cyber-attack defense. It is possible to build multi-dimensional to ultra-high-dimensional datasets online, enabling the real-time detection and prediction of security assaults [18].
- **Big Data Can Help SDN Traffic Engineering:**
  Traffic engineering is a means of improving network performance, by instantly evaluating, estimating, and controlling the behavior patterns of transmitted data through a network. Optimizing network performance and balancing network load are common traffic engineering objectives. It is simple to execute large-scale traffic engineering and network performance enhancement with SDN and big data analysis. A typical SDN-based network consists of several hosts with significant bandwidth requirements. It is quite challenging to implement traffic engineering in these kinds of networks, because information about large data failures and traffic is often easier to obtain via a centralized SDN controller, the combination of big data with SDN for traffic engineering may be a suitable option [19].

15.7   THE ADVANTAGES OF SDN IN BIG DATA

In order to collect massive processing power and extract data that has never been accessible by conventional methods, big-data analytics have been introduced to cloud data centers (CDCs). Big data and SDNs investigate how the two technologies may operate in harmony to deliver services more successfully. SDN may be used to address the primary issue with big-data applications, which is message forwarding across collaborating nodes. Here are a few benefits of SDN for big data. This can be analyzed in (Figure 15.2 Alt text: A diagram with rectangular boxes, each labeled with an advantage of SDN in the context of big data, showcasing the benefits of combining these technologies).

- **Scientific Big Data Architectures Can Benefit From SDN:**
  Scientific research is heavily reliant on data. Some scientific research instruments generate massive amounts of data. Furthermore, some scientific large

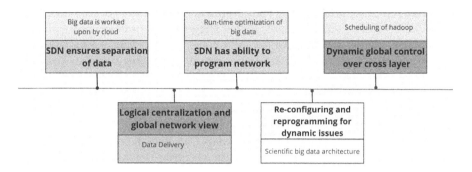

FIGURE 15.2 Advantages of SDN in big data.

data cannot be handled and studied in the same place that it is created for political and technical reasons. The massive volumes of data need to be transferred to various research organizations and university data centers for analysis. However, the current university networks are unable to process such massive amounts of data. As data quantities increase, there is an increasing need for end-to-end network designs and frameworks that are straightforward, efficient, and enable applications to utilize the network most effectively [20].

- **Runtime Programming for Big Data Application Optimization:**
  Due to constantly changing contexts, many big data applications need to be extensively rearranged. Big data applications that demand frequent reconfigurations greatly benefit from SDN's ability to program at runtime. The investigation of SDN programming spans all network levels, including physical architecture, routing, and flow-level traffic. To accomplish precise network control and massive data cooperation, they integrate the SDN controller with optical switching. With a relatively minimal configuration overhead, this integrated network control architecture may enhance outcomes for big data applications by programming the network at runtime using an SDN controller [21].

- **Big Data Processing in Cloud Data Centers Can Benefit from SDN:**
  Big data processing often takes place in cloud data centers. It is critical to efficiently assign and manage cloud data center resources in order to satisfy the Service Level Agreement (SLAs) of different big data applications. The contract that a big data service provider and its client's sign is known as the SLA. Some typical SLAs for big data application performance include latency, process time, rate of failure, reliability, privacy, the amount of data processed, data volume received, data volume emitted, the accuracy of input and output, and data leakage Networking and storage infrastructure are offered as a service and managed by SDN in data centers with SDN [22].

- **Hadoop Scheduling for Big Data Applications Can Benefit from SDN:**
  Hadoop is a powerful technology that integrates data storage, processing, system administration, and a few more components to build a solution that is swiftly taking over as the industry standard for handling large data issues. The goal of this problem is to find solutions for reducing job completion time in Hadoop systems. Because of the absence of a global view for allocating tasks, most existing solutions for this issue are unsatisfactory. SDN is employed to address this issue in Hadoop [23].
- **Data Delivery for Big Data Applications Can Benefit from SDN:**
  Because of the vast amount of data, data transfer is a major difficulty in big data applications. Traffic delivery for big data applications may be accelerated and promoted by an optical network built on SDN. Utilizing physical layer optics, a combined (electrical and optical) method quickens the delivery of traffic for each pattern. Due to the software control plane's SDN compatibility, photonic devices may handle incredibly complex traffic patterns by being dynamically and adaptively configured [24].

15.8   METHODS OF BIG DATA AND SDN

The range of methods used to handle big data grows along with the amount of data generated. The speed, breadth, and depth of meaningful data inspire innovation. The world is run by data, which is examined every second by apps. Different methods are employed to implement big data in various domains and efforts are made to make this more efficient, as seen in (Figure 15.3 Alt text: A visual representation featuring rectangular boxes running from top to bottom, each labeled with different methods of big data analytics such as A/B testing, Data fusion and data integration, Data mining, Machine learning, Natural Language Processing (NLP), and Statistics, providing an overview of approaches available for analyzing big Data.)

The following are the methods of big data analytics:

- **A/B testing:** This approach to data analysis compares several test groups with a control group to see which interventions or other changes improve a particular objective variable.
- **Data fusion and data integration:** Insights can be more effective and accurate than those gained from a single data source by combining several strategies for analyzing and integrating solutions and data from a variety of sources.
- **Data mining:** In order to identify patterns from enormous data sets, data mining, in big data, does data research and combines statistical and machine learning techniques.

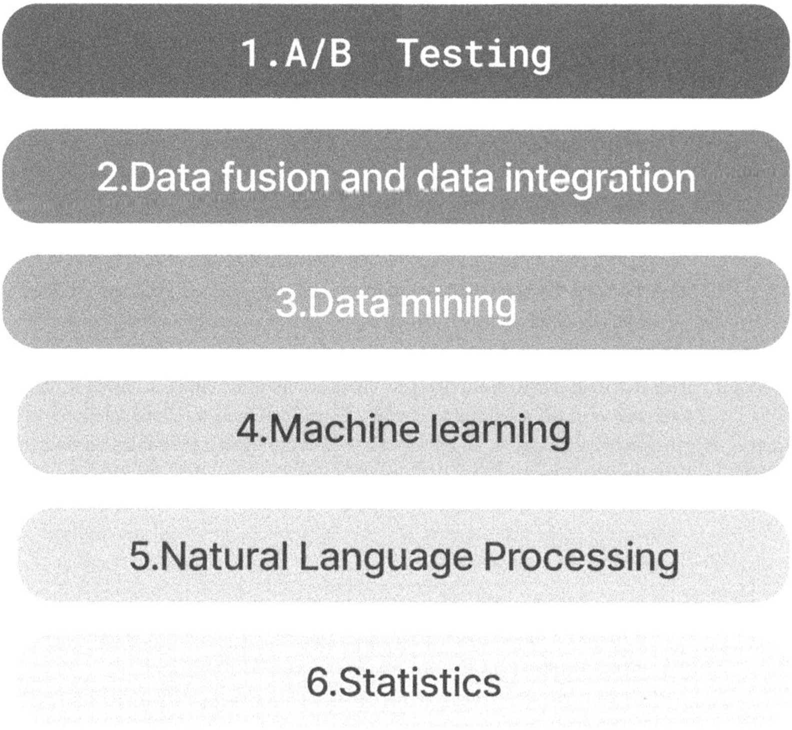

1.A/B Testing

2.Data fusion and data integration

3.Data mining

4.Machine learning

5.Natural Language Processing

6.Statistics

FIGURE 15.3   Types of big data analytics methods.

- **Machine learning:** Machine learning, commonly referred to as artificial intelligence, is used for data analysis. It is a branch of computer science that employs algorithms to make inferences about data. It provides predictions that are difficult for analysts to make manually.
- **Natural Language Processing (NLP):** It is a data analysis tool that uses algorithms to analyze human (natural) language and is a subfield of linguistics known as computer science, and artificial intelligence.
- **Statistics:** In study and experimentation, data are gathered, arranged, and interpreted using this method. Predictive modeling, network analysis, association rule learning, and spatial analysis are further methods for analyzing data.

SDN has been adapted to the necessary work with the help of various methods. The methods are generally associated with a conventional protocol or aided by alternative methods to avoid various blockages like trafficking. The various methods of SDN implementation have been mentioned categorically in Table 15.1.

TABLE 15.1
Different Types of SDN Methods [29]

1. SDN-Based data access network	There are various conventional network methodologies. These are categorized as wired and wireless. The Software-defined networking gets heterogeneous network access with the help of virtual functions of the network. These implement functions such as collaborative services and adaptive reconstruction. Adaptive Reconstruction: The controller redefines the forwarding of the device w.r.t. to GSN's, PSN's control signaling, and approved user installation information. Collaborative Service: Applications of Big data based on requirements In order to coordinate and integrate resources, the controller oversees a number of access networks [25].
2. Network for content delivery based on SDN	Network congestion and application delay occurs when data is received or shared directly over the data center network. Because of this, the content delivery network reacts to user requests for data access in order to lighten the burden on the data center network. The controller conducts appropriate content delivery network operations, such as load balancing, cache management, and priority services, in accordance with the aforementioned applications. • Load Balancing: The controller updates switch forwarding rules to route service requests or data to other agent servers depending on the status information gathered when the CDA or CSA Workload hits a threshold. • Cache-Control: Taking into account the CDA's application needs and cache state, the controller chooses the best policy to deploy to the CDA. • Service with a Priority: The Controller sends the CSA priority control signals pertaining to Application requests. Data clustering and re encapsulation are carried out by CSA, which also sets the transmission order after parsing data Packets using various protocols [26].
3. SDN-Based data center network	The infrastructure of a data center includes computers, heat dissipation systems, network devices (cables, switches, and routers), storage devices, and power distribution systems. A data center contains a data center network (DCN). It has routing/switching devices, related network protocols (such as Ethernet and IP protocols), and network topology. • Bandwidth Control: The controller obtains business operations data from administrators, such as bandwidth statistics, traffic priority information, packet information, etc. A bandwidth allocation scheme is computed by the controller's bandwidth allocation function. With switches, the controller puts the plan into action. • Anomaly Detection: Based on features gleaned from the gathered traffic condition, the controller recognizes traffic. The controller separates anomaly source nodes. Unusual traffic is eliminated. • Communication Control: The communication control function basically gives communication tunnels for different large-scale data centers [27].

(Continued)

TABLE 15.1
(Continued)

4. Big data backbone network using SDN	SDN-supported architecture for Big data is a pillar that puts a network to distribute and layer approach for seeking reliable communication. The prime controller is in the cloud and it periodically gets information from the network. The computational path and QoS are applied by the upper interface of the prime controller. • Path Computation: The backbone controller computes the most effective forwarding path by compiling network routing data from subnet controllers, providing a global view. • QoS Service: The prime controller's network status calculator forecasts future subnet wants of backbone resources. The backbone prime controller notifies the subnet controllers about the forecasted results and tunes the data transfer rate [28].
5. SDN by APIs	SDN makes use of APIs to monitor the state of the network and to modify the network's nature. The SDN controllers and software analytics of the engine of the network assign the APIs to forward and control each constituent of the networking system.
6. SDN overlay model	This model of SDN creates a dynamic tunnel by placing a virtual layer over the existing hardware to various remote data centers. The virtual layer provides bandwidth on numerous channels and distributes to each device, without disturbing the physical network.
7. Hybrid SDN	In this model, the conventional networking methods are combined with SDN in a single environment for the efficient performance of various functions. Some traffic is taken care of by the traditional protocol while others are handled by Software-defined networking.

15.9   APPLICATIONS OF SDN AND BIG DATA

SDN is a promising technology that, when fully integrated with the resource management capabilities provided by the server hypervisors used in data centers, BDMSs (such as Apache YARN and Apache MESOS), may significantly enhance network implementation and QoS. Big data and SDN applications are numerous. These are going to expand and reach every domain due to their extensive linkage to current times. Listed below are a few places that are used in day-to-day life shown in (Figure 15.4 Alt text: A visual representation of rectangular boxes containing text labels that outline the applications of big data running from top to bottom in the order of government and military, Travel and Tourism, Finance and Banking, Health Care, Telecommunication, Social Media, and E-commerce.)

A few more applications of big data are listed below:

1. **Identifying fraud**: In particular, in organizations that include any claims or transaction processing, fraud detection is one of the most striking instances of how big data is used. Real-time analysis of requests and transactions,

the detection of aberrant behavior, and the discovery of significant trends across transactions using big data applications may all revolutionize fraud detection.

2. **Healthcare**: Health businesses are now relying on big data apps to evaluate the data, get insights, and derive more actionable outcomes. They have been able to work with such data more effectively because of recent technological advancements.

3. **Agriculture**: A biotech company uses sensor data to enhance agricultural productivity. Its data environment continuously gathers and records changes

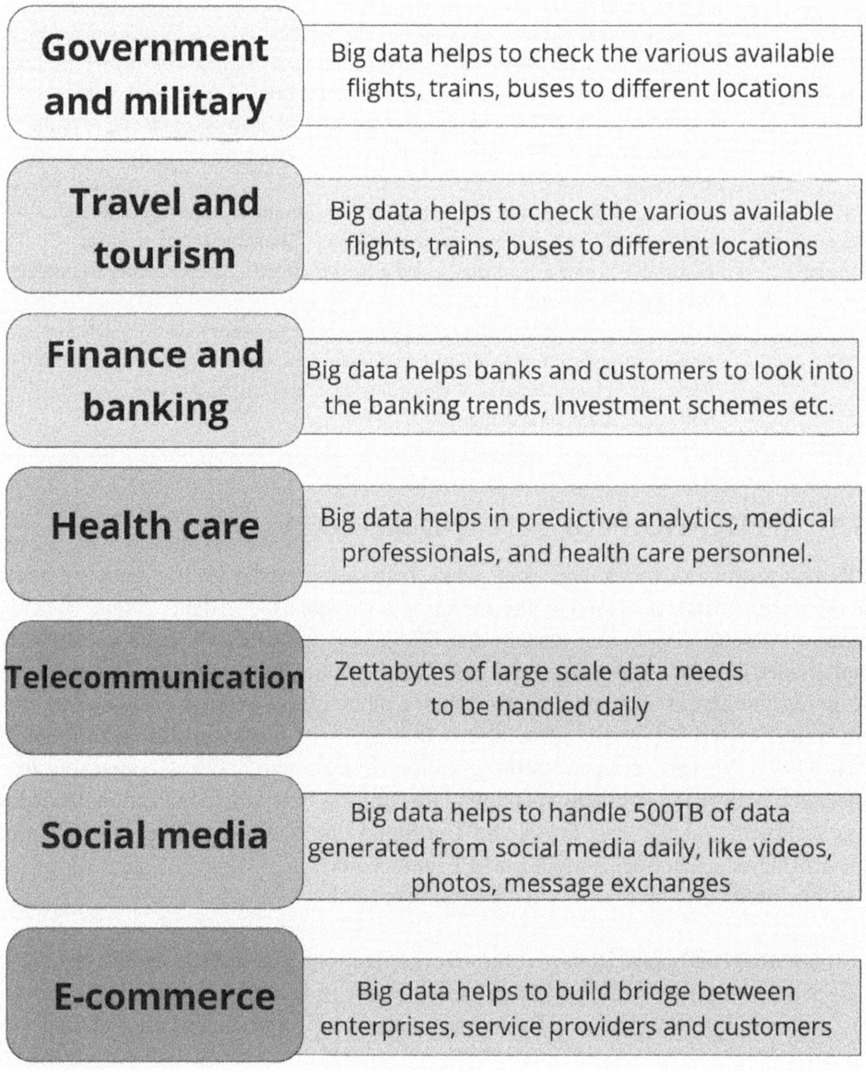

Government and military	Big data helps to check the various available flights, trains, buses to different locations
Travel and tourism	Big data helps to check the various available flights, trains, buses to different locations
Finance and banking	Big data helps banks and customers to look into the banking trends, Investment schemes etc.
Health care	Big data helps in predictive analytics, medical professionals, and health care personnel.
Telecommunication	Zettabytes of large scale data needs to be handled daily
Social media	Big data helps to handle 500TB of data generated from social media daily, like videos, photos, message exchanges
E-commerce	Big data helps to build bridge between enterprises, service providers and customers

FIGURE 15.4 Applications of big data.

in each plant's growth, gene sequencing, and production, as well as the temperature, soil composition, water level, and other variables. Finding the ideal habitat for particular gene types is much easier with the use of such data.

Large volumes of data arrive quickly from many sources. And the outcomes are enormous regardless of the industry. Big data formerly produced more quantifiable, all-encompassing ideas according to the needs of customers. It promotes inductive thinking and is a contentious inversion of the scientific process that puts facts first. Even non-technical staff members may enter data and get data-driven insights in many firms. An elite "analytic culture" emerged. In conclusion, big data is a potent instrument that simplifies tasks in a variety of disciplines if used properly and optimized. In addition to the industries already listed, big data applications are also having a favorable impact on fields including chemistry, data mining, cloud computing, finance, and many more [30].

15.10   APPLICATIONS OF SDN

Numerous business applications exist for SDN. SDN is anticipated to experience increased popularity because of its versatility, simplicity of deployment, and automation-friendly design as shown in Figure 15.5 (Figure 15.5 Alt text: A Hexagonal grid depicting a pictorial representation of SDN applications such as cooperative security, IBN, network setup, Agile operations, RGDD, and SDMN in a clockwise direction.).

Additionally, as more businesses use cloud platforms, SDN is anticipated to aid in the virtualization of networking infrastructure for cloud-based services. In the near future, it is anticipated that this developing technology's responsiveness, automation potential, and cyber security applications will further grow. Listed below are a few applications of SDN:

Security services: Specific virtual services running at the network layer are supported by contemporary virtualization eco-systems. To do this, the SDN platform must be given NFV-like features. This kind of network security lowers risk and fosters an atmosphere that is genuinely proactive, allowing for speedy incident response.

Network Intelligence and Monitoring: One of the key levels in the data center is abstracted by modern SDN technologies. Network designs must process more data than ever before, and they are incredibly complicated. [31].

Applications that must comply with laws and regulations: Major cloud providers now give the option to store and run workloads that must comply with laws and regulations. Organizations may now use dispersed environments and the cloud to expand designs that were previously severely constrained by restrictions.

High-Reliability Applications: The number of new applications and technology is growing rapidly. Due to virtualization, sophisticated technologies like CAD, GIS, and technical, and graphic tools are now used. In the past,

APPLICATIONS OF SDN

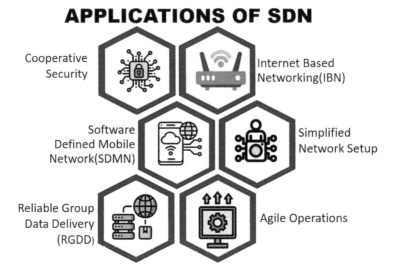

Cooperative Security

Internet Based Networking(IBN)

Software Defined Mobile Network(SDMN)

Simplified Network Setup

Reliable Group Data Delivery (RGDD)

Agile Operations

FIGURE 15.5   Applications of SDN.

these workloads called for bare metal systems with independent connections. However, VDI makes it possible to develop strong desktop experiences as apps are streamed with virtualization. SDN and application control are, however, converging at the network level as well.

Control of distributed systems and cloud assimilation: One of SDN's biggest benefits is that it operates throughout the whole data center. Of this kind connects with scattered locations, clouds, and businesses [32].

15.11   FUTURE PROSPECT

The future of cutting-edge networking and computing technologies is complicated by SDN. Security should not be compromised even if more responsive technologies need to be dealt with. SDN can be employed in provider networks in the long run, but it may be too much for some businesses to handle.SDN needs to be further developed and proven to be a secure and deployable technology [33].

With challenges to overcome, SDN faces a difficult future. The first problem is console/remote functionality with security issues today. Many companies don't want to expose their networks to potential hacker takeovers. The existing state of network management policies and practices, which concentrate on single devices or single pathways, is another problem. Unlike SDN, which is much bigger and more likely to make SDN and related technologies feasible, a network manager can only view how it benefits or destroys the network. Technology today is device-centric, whereas SDN is human-centric. This is a challenging situation for an administrator, especially when one alone can completely change the network, storage, WAN, etc. SDN's potential to benefit the "cloud" has received a lot of attention, however before SDN can be implemented, the "cloud" must be under control. There are also serious problems in the areas of finance, training, and key engagement. In addition to creating a cutting-edge environment for advancement and research and facilitating improvements across multiple fields including design and scalability of switches and controls, as well as network architecture development, performance, and promotion, software-defined networks have paved the way for networking of security. It's clear that Software-Defined Networks continue to excel and a lot of activities are to be witnessed in the years to come. The realization of networks as a service in the cloud computing paradigm, software-defined environments, the application of SDN to carrier transport networks, and other specific domains all demand more research. Experts are studying its programming capabilities to find ways to make network management easier and more efficient, and much work is being done to develop protocols that make programming easier. The academic community has been looking for methods to use SDN to increase the efficiency of big data applications ever since the phrase "big data" gained popularity. In most cases, the bandwidth available as well as the protocols in use create bottlenecks. Thus, optimization is achieved by enhancing current procedures and/or approaches. TCP windows are maintained at lower multiple numbers and subsequently enlarged based on the link situation. The transfer window is again reduced if a problem arises. It is therefore an adaptable process, but bigger file transfers may cause more congestion. The processing times of apps show interesting improvements when request profiles are used.

Future SDN Developments will also be witnessing the use of 5G as SDN helps in creating the framework for 5G. The telecom sector has been evolving quickly for many years. The foundation of 5G technology is the requirement for a more flexible, quick, and agile network, which persisted even as 4G technology advanced. The future will be greatly impacted by 5G technology, which has not yet been completely utilized. SDN will undoubtedly be used in 5G in the future. By doing this, the global telecom sector will embrace open-source networks and 5G as a pairing. Wi-Fi is becoming the most popular method for connecting with one another, whether it be for personal or professional reasons. Businesses may use 5G to aid with connection problems.

In summary, big data connectivity may be addressed by jointly creating big data and SDN. There are immediate issues that need to be solved about how to ideally use SDN to enhance the performance of big data applications and how to ideally use big data to enhance and improve SDN. The technologies used to co-design big data and SDN are briefly reviewed in this article as potential future studies on these subjects [34].

15.12 CONCLUSION

A unique era in the history of data analytics has been created by the availability of big data, inexpensive off-the-shelf gear, and cutting-edge information administration and analysis tools. Because of the convergence of such advancements, we today have the knowledge and resources necessary to examine massive datasets quickly and inexpensively for the first time ever. These characteristics are not hypothetical nor unimportant. They offer unmistakable chances to achieve large improvements in terms of effectiveness, productivity, attrition, and income. Big data causes perspectives to change. Several organizations are using more analytics to drive decisive goals and provide better consumer experiences. Because even small improvements in efficiency and cost savings could have a significant impact, most businesses are converting to big data.

Big data technology is still in its early stages. Advanced analytical approaches are used to handle a number of significant technical issues, including those related to software systems, big data models, and big data architecture that enable big data, as well as grid computing, cloud computing, parallel computing, stream computing. In reality, data-driven apps have existed for many years.

Big data technologies are gaining popularity as a result of the novel methods used to store and retrieve information. Because big data applications are designed for huge datasets, dealing with smaller files presents difficulties. The underlying networks are used by applications like Hadoop to provide seamless consumer services. The main purpose of underlying networks is to manage sporadic internet traffic. But the traffic footprint of big data applications differs. In order to provide a stronger and more reliable infrastructure for big data applications, conventional networks can benefit from SDNs. In this chapter, we provide a number of recommendations that have been made in the literature and examine their benefits and drawbacks. This discovery will serve as the foundation for more study in the area.

REFERENCES

[1] Ranjan, P., P. Pande, R. Oswal, Z. Qurani, and R. Bedi. "A survey of past present and future of software-defined networking." *International Journal* 2.4 (2014): 238–248.

[2] Cui, L., F. Richard Yu, and Q.Yan. "When big data meets software-defined networking: SDN for big data and big data for SDN." *IEEE Network* 30.1 (2016): 58–65.

[3] Alqarni, M. A. "Benefits of SDN for big data applications." *2017 14th International Conference on Smart Cities: Improving Quality of Life Using ICT & IoT (HONET-ICT).* IEEE, 2017.

[4] Hussain, M., N. Shah, R. Amin, S. S. S. Alshamrani, A. Alotaibi and S. M. Raza. "Software-defined networking: Categories, analysis, and future directions." *Sensors* 22.15 (2022): 5551.

[5] Chen, M., and Y. Liu. "Big data: A survey, mobile networks and application." *Mobile Networks and Application* 19.2 (2014): 171. doi: 10.1007/s11036-013-0489-0

[6] Mahmood, W., S. D. Nasir, and I. Waqas. "A research survey on software-defined networking (SDN)." *Proc. of the Ninth Intl. Conf. on Advances in Computing, Control and Networking-ACCN.* 2019.

[7] Drutskoy, D., E. Keller, and J. Rexford. "Scalable network virtualization in software-defined networks." *IEEE Internet Computing* 17.2 (2012): 20–27.

[8] Gudivada, V. N., R. Baeza-Yates, and V. V. Raghavan. "Big data: Promises and problems." *Computer* 48.03 (2015): 20–23.

[9] Ominike, A., E. Seun, A. O. Adebayo and F. Y. Osisanwo. "Introduction to software-defined networks (SDN)." *International Journal of Applied Information Systems* 11 (2016): 10–14.

[10] Kreutz, D., F. M. V. Ramos, P. E. Veríssimo and C. E. Rothenbe. "Software-defined networking: A comprehensive survey." *Proceedings of the IEEE* 103.1 (2014): 14–76.

[11] Sezer, S., S. Scott-Hayward, P. K. Chouhan, B. Fraser, D. Lake, J. Finnegan, N. Vilijoen, M. Miller, and N. Rao. "Are we ready for SDN? Implementation challenges for software-defined networks." *IEEE Communications Magazine* 51.7 (2013): 36–43.

[12] Hakiri, A., A. Gokhale, P. Berthou, and D. Schmidt. "Software-defined networking: Challenges and research opportunities for future internet." *Computer Networks* 75 (2014): 453–471.

[13] Kim, H., and N. Feamster. "Improving network management with software-defined networking." *IEEE Communications Magazine* 51.2 (2013): 114–119.

[14] Goud, K. S., and S. R. Gidituri. "Security challenges and related solutions in software-defined networks: A survey."*International Journal of Computer Networks and Applications (IJCNA)* 9(1) (2022): 22–37. doi: 10.22247/ijcna/2022/211595

[15] Labrinidis, A., and H.V. Jagadish, "Challenges and opportunities with big data." *Proceedings of the VLDB Endowment* 5 (2012): 2032–2033. doi:10.14778/2367502.2367572.

[16] Shah, S. A. R., W. Wu, Q. Lu, L. Zhang, S. Sasidharan, P. DeMar, C. Guok, J. Macauley, E. Pouyoul, J. Kim, S.-Y. Noh. "AmoebaNet: An SDN-enabled network service for big data science." *Journal of Network and Computer Applications* 119 (2018): 70–82.

[17] Peng, S., G. Wang, and D. Xie. "Social influence analysis in social networking big data: Opportunities and challenges." *IEEE Network* 31.1 (2016): 11–17.

[18] Yan, Q., F. R. Yu, Q. Gong and J. Li. "Software-defined networking (SDN) and distributed denial of service (DDoS) attacks in cloud computing environments: A survey, some research issues, and challenges." *IEEE Communications Surveys & Tutorials* 18.1 (2015): 602–622.

[19] Queiroz, W., M. A. M. Capretz, and M. Dantas. "An approach for SDN traffic monitoring based on big data techniques." *Journal of Network and Computer Applications* 131 (2019): 28–39.

[20] Monga, I., E. Pouyoul, and C. Guok. "Software-defined networking for big-data science-architectural models from campus to the WAN." *2012 SC Companion: High Performance Computing, Networking Storage and Analysis*. IEEE, 2012.

[21] Wang, G., T. S. Eugene Ng, and A. Shaikh. "Programming your network at run-time for big data applications." *Proceedings of the First Workshop on Hot Topics in Software-Defined Networks (HotSDN '12)*. Association for Computing Machinery, New York, NY, USA, (2012): 103–108. doi: 10.1145/2342441.2342462.

[22] Han, Y., S.-S. Seo, J. Li, and J. Hyun. "Software-defined networking-based traffic engineering for data center networks." *The 16th Asia-Pacific Network Operations and Management Symposium*. IEEE, 2014.

[23] Qin, P., B. Dai, B. Huang, and G. Xu. "Bandwidth-aware scheduling with sdn in hadoop: A new trend for big data." *IEEE Systems Journal* 11.4 (2015): 2337–2344.

[24] Samadi, P., D. Calhoun, H. Wang, and K. Bergman. "Accelerating cast traffic delivery in data centers leveraging physical layer optics and SDN." *2014 International Conference on Optical Network Design and Modeling*. IEEE, 2014.

[25] Renjie, P., T. Junjie, and X. Ke. "SDN: A service delivery network over end-to-end DHT." *2010 IEEE 2nd Symposium on Web Society*. IEEE, 2010.

[26] Wang, Y., H. Wang, B. Yu, Y. Ma. "A strategy of CDN Traffic optimization based on the technology of SDN." *DEStech Transactions on Computer Science and Engineering* (2017). doi:10.12783/dtcse/iceiti2016/6137.

[27] Aziz, M., M. Aziz, A. F. Hamedani, G. Landi, D. Gallico, K. Christodoulopoulos, and P. Wieder. "SDN-enabled application-aware networking for data center networks." *2016 IEEE International Conference on Electronics, Circuits and Systems (ICECS)*. IEEE, 2016.

[28] Xu, Y., Z. Sun, and Z. Sun. "SDN-based architecture for big data network." *2017 International Conference on Cyber-Enabled Distributed Computing and Knowledge Discovery (CyberC)*. IEEE, 2017.

[29] Yu, S., M. Liu, W. Dou, Xi. Liu, and S. Zhou. "Networking for big data: A survey." *IEEE Communications Surveys & Tutorials* 19.1 (2017): 531–549.

[30] Elshawi, R., O. Batarfi, A. Fayoumi and A. Barnawi. "Big graph processing systems: State-of-the-art and open challenges." *2015 IEEE First International Conference on Big Data Computing Service and Applications.* IEEE, 2015.

[31] Lin, T., J.-M. Kang, H.Bannazadeh, and A. Leon-Garcia. "Enabling SDN applications on software-defined infrastructure." *2014 IEEE Network Operations and Management Symposium (NOMS).* IEEE, 2014.

[32] Li, T., J. Chen, and H. Fu. "Application scenarios based on SDN: an overview." *Journal of Physics: Conference Series.* Vol. 1187. No. 5. IOP Publishing, 2019.

[33] Kim, H., and N. Feamster. "Improving network management with software-defined networking." *IEEE Communications Magazine* 51.2 (2013): 114–119.

[34] Nunes, B. A. A., M. Mendonça, X. Nam Nguyen, K. Obraczka, and T. Turletti. "A survey of software-defined networking: Past, present, and future of programmable networks." *IEEE Communications Surveys & Tutorials* 16.3 (2014): 1617–1634.

16 TCPFlood Defender
TCP SYN Flood Attacks Detection in SDN Environment Using Statistical and Ensemble Machine Learning Methods

K. Muthamil Sudar and P. Nagaraj

16.1 INTRODUCTION

SDN is a novel method for planning and running computer networks that separates the management and forwarding planes of the network. Network components like switches and routers perform both control and data forwarding tasks in a conventional network design. SDN, on the other hand, divides these tasks, enabling more adaptability, scaling, and programmability. In SDN, the network is controlled by a centralized controller, which sets network rules and controls traffic flows. Through a standardized interface called OpenFlow, the controller can interact with the network devices and tell them to forward traffic as needed. One of SDN's main benefits is that it gives network managers more flexibility and dynamic network management. Administrators are better able to modify network rules and configurations because the control plane and data plane are separated, and they can do so without being reliant on the underlying hardware. Data center networking, wide area networks, and even residential networks are just a few of the many uses for SDN. For many new trends, such as cloud computing, network function virtualization, and the internet of things, it is regarded as a crucial enabling technology.

A cyberattack known as a distributed denial of service (DDoS) tries to render a website or online service unavailable by flooding it with traffic from numerous sources. This is accomplished by simultaneously sending a large number of requests to the targeted website or service, which may overload the server and prevent it from responding to valid requests. Amplification attacks, in which the attacker employs a small number of compromised computers to send a large number of requests, botnets (networks of compromised computers), and application-layer attacks are some of the methods used to conduct DDoS attacks. (which target specific parts of a website or service). A DDoS attack can have a significant negative effect by causing

DOI: 10.1201/9781003432869-16

downtime, lost income, and reputational harm to an organization. DDoS attacks are occasionally used as a diversionary strategy to draw attention away from on-going cyberattacks.

TCP (Transmission Control Protocol) flooding is a form of denial-of-service (DoS) attack in which an attacker bombards a target server with numerous TCP connection requests in an effort to overtax its resources and prevent it from responding to legitimate requests. Attacks involving TCP flooding can be reduced by putting in place a number of safeguards, such as traffic filtering, rate limiting, the use of firewalls, and intrusion protection systems. By creating a cookie that the server can use to validate connection requests without having to keep track of every connection attempt, SYN cookies can be used, in particular, to protect against SYN flooding attacks. Traditional TCP flooding attacks can frequently be prevented by implementing a number of security controls, such as traffic filtering, rate limiting, firewalls, and intrusion prevention systems. The increasingly complicated and dynamic SDN TCP flooding attacks, however, may make these defences less effective.

For identifying TCP flooding attacks in Software-Defined Networking (SDN) setups, machine learning can be a useful technique. TCP flooding is a sort of Denial-of-Service (DoS) attack in which an attacker floods a target system with TCP SYN packets, taxing its resources and obstructing the processing of genuine data. In an SDN context, the controller can gather network traffic information from the switches, analyze the information, and spot TCP flooding attack patterns using machine learning methods. Large datasets of network traffic can be used to train machine learning algorithms to find trends and anomalies that can point to an impending assault. Machine learning models can detect both known and undiscovered attacks by analyzing network traffic data in real-time, offering a more proactive and adaptable approach to network security. By examining network traffic data and recognizing patterns that are suggestive of an attack, machine learning algorithms can be trained to recognize these attacks. These patterns may include suspicious IP addresses, strange traffic patterns, and unexpected traffic volumes.

In this chapter, we propose defending mechanism against TCP flooding attacks using ensemble machine learning classifier. Classifiers like Decision tree, Support vector machine, Adaboost and XGBoost are used to construct the ensemble-based machine learning model.

16.2 BACKGROUND AND RELATED WORK

16.2.1 TCP CONNECTION

In applications like browsers, SSH, and mail services, Transmission Control Protocol (TCP), which is connection-oriented and provides a stable communication channel, is essential. Prior to beginning client-server communication, TCP uses a three-way handshake process to guarantee a reliable connection. Figure 16.1 shows the three-way handshake mechanism's sequential operation, which is described later. The client and server devices engage in a three-way handshake process to establish a TCP connection. The following actions are part of the three-way handshake process:

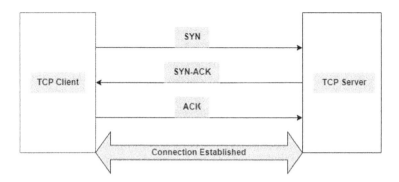

FIGURE 16.1 TCP Three-way handshake mechanism.

- SYN: To make a connection request, the client sends a SYN (synchronize) packet to the server.
- SYN-ACK: The server acknowledges the client's request and establishes a connection by returning a SYN-ACK (synchronize-acknowledge) message.
- ACK: To confirm that the connection has been made, the client sends an ACK (acknowledge) message.

The procedure makes sure that client and server communication is consistent and dependable. The TCP data structure depends on the transmission control block (TCB). Each active TCP connection's transmission activity, including source and destination port numbers, IP addresses, sequence numbers, and an estimate of round-trip timings, is recorded by the TCB. The TCB begins gathering data on the specific connection as soon as the server gets a SYN packet. A SYN-ACK packet is then sent by the server in response to the client. Because the connection hasn't been entirely formed, it is known as a half-open connection. The half-open connection's TCB guarantees a spot in the server queue. The server removes the matching TCB from the queue and initiates communication as soon as it receives the last ACK from the client. The server transmits the SYN and ACK packets to the client computer again if the final ACK signal is not received. Following the three-way handshake, the implementation of a timeout mechanism, and receipt of the RST packet from the client side, the server deletes requests from its queue [1].

16.2.2 RELATED WORK

One of the first and most well-known DDoS attacks in all kinds of networking contexts is TCP flooding. This attack's primary goal is to flood the targeted servers with a large number of half-open connections. This results in network saturation and unresponsiveness of the target server, which prevents authorized users from finishing the TCP connection process [2]. Below, we examined a few related studies to counteract TCP flood assaults.

An SDN-based SYN proxy method (SSP) was suggested by Dang et al. [3] to identify TCP SYN assaults. In SDN contexts, Mohammadi et al. [4] suggested a simple defence against TCP SYN flooding assaults. A thorough strategy to ward off TCP flood attacks in the SDN context was established by Chen et al. [5]. The detection module was added to the SDN OpenDayLight controller. They found the malicious hosts by continuously monitoring the TCP continuing connections. They asserted that the suggested work improves accuracy and reduces overhead by up to 50. Due to constant monitoring and the high number of false alarms caused by the fixed threshold mechanism, the suggested method takes more time to detect an attack in a high volume of data.

In the context of SDN, Tuan et al. [6] looked at how to protect against TCP flood using machine learning technologies like KNN and XGBoost. Swami et al. [7] evaluated TCP SYN flooding attacks in the SDN setting. They calculated the entropy value for the amount of packets per IP and the entropy value of the port for each IP in order to detect assaults and design a flow rule to remove packets in the case of an attack. Their experimental results show that the suggested effort typically reduces the attack by 98% with a low false alert rate. However, when machine learning techniques are used, various network processing times and resource utilization are not assessed. In the IoT setting, Hamza et al's investigation of several volumetric DDoS attacks using SDN monitoring operations [8]. To identify and counteract TCP SYN flood attacks on SDN controllers, Ravi et al. [9] suggested the AEGIS architecture. They activate the detecting module by continuously observing the controller's operation. They asserted that by carefully analyzing the packets, the detecting module in the controller aids in lowering the false alarm rate. High-level traffic scenarios do not analyze resource usage or detection precision. When there is a high degree of packet processing, deep inspection will take more time.

Batool et al.[10] gives a general overview of the many SDN TCP flooding attack types, their traits, and the tools and methods employed to carry out and stop these assaults. Based on their attack vectors, the authors divide SDN TCP flooding assaults into five groups and offer suggestions for how to stop them. A machine learning-based detection strategy for SDN TCP flooding attacks is suggested by Chen et al. [11]. They develop and evaluate multiple machine learning models for spotting such attacks using a dataset of network traffic properties. The outcomes demonstrate that their method is highly accurate in identifying SDN TCP flooding attacks. Sumantra et al. [12] suggests a hybrid method that combines machine learning and deep learning to identify SDN TCP flooding attacks. To categorize network traffic as benign or hostile, the authors combine decision trees and convolutional neural networks. The outcomes show that their method is successful in identifying SDN TCP flooding assaults with high specificity and low false positive rates. In order to counteract SDN TCP flooding attacks, a dynamic traffic engineering approach is suggested by Sun et al. [13]. The authors reduce the impact of the attack by dynamically rerouting traffic away from the target server and toward other network devices using a controller-based technique. The outcomes demonstrate that their strategy is successful in preventing SDN TCP flooding assaults, decreasing packet loss, and enhancing network performance. In order to counteract SDN TCP flooding attacks, Awan et al. [14] suggest a dynamic traffic engineering approach. To lessen the impact of the attack, the authors employ a controller-based strategy to dynamically reroute traffic away from the target server and toward other network devices. The findings demonstrate the effectiveness of their strategy in preventing SDN TCP flooding attacks, lowering packet loss, and enhancing network performance.

The research on SDN TCP flooding attack detection, in conclusion, emphasizes the growing relevance of protecting Software-Defined Networking (SDN) settings. The experiments examined in this review of the literature have shown that machine learning and deep learning algorithms can accurately and efficiently identify SDN TCP flooding attacks. Despite the suggested detection and mitigation methods, additional study in this area is still required. Current detection methods may become ineffective when more complex SDN TCP flooding attacks and evasion tactics emerge. As a result, it is crucial to keep investigating and creating new methods to protect SDN environments from TCP flooding attacks. The literature review emphasizes how crucial it is to keep informed of the most recent security precautions and recommended techniques for SDN TCP flooding attack detection and mitigation.

16.3   PROPOSED WORK

In proposed work, we imposed detection module in the SDN controller to monitor every incoming TCP request from the newly connected OpenFLow switches. Detection module is implemented using two methods such as statistical-based and machine learning-based techniques. The main objective is to identify the half-open connections in the server queue and remove it as quick as possible which helps to process the legitimate requests.

16.3.1   STATISTICAL-BASED TECHNIQUES

Statistical methods are frequently employed to identify flooding attacks in their early phases. Network traffic analysis is one of the most used statistical-based techniques for looking for anomalies that point to a DDoS attack. By looking at the amount, regularity, and patterns of network traffic, this can be accomplished. For instance, abrupt spikes in traffic coming from a particular region or IP address may be a sign of a DDoS attack. Entropy, probability distribution, and t-statistic measures are examples of statistical-based procedures that can achieve good accuracy [15]. A dataset's entropy is a gauge of its randomness or unpredictability. Entropy analysis in the context of network traffic is figuring out the entropy of the packet payload or other network variables like source, destination, and port numbers. Because DDoS attackers frequently employ randomized or faked IP addresses to generate high volumes of traffic, a spike in entropy can be a sign of an assault. The fundamental tenet of entropy-based DDoS detection is that, whereas regular network traffic frequently results from random generation, resulting in a greater entropy value, DDoS activity frequently has a predictable distribution of values. Therefore, depending on the amount of unpredictability in the network traffic, it is possible to identify DDoS attacks by analyzing the entropy of the traffic Figure 16.2 shows the working function of proposed methodology.

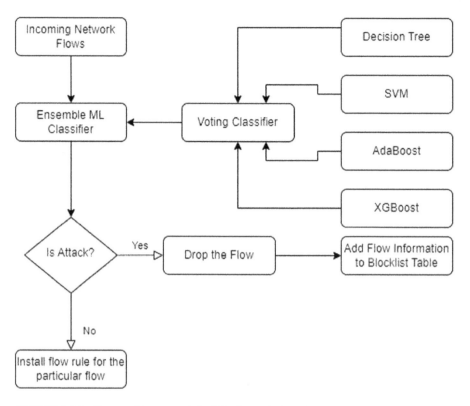

FIGURE 16.2   Proposed framework for DDoS attack detection.

16.3.2   MACHINE LEARNING-BASED TECHNIQUES

Building models that can identify patterns and relationships in data and use that knowledge to make predictions or choices about new data is the aim of machine learning (ML). This is accomplished by training the model to recognize patterns and correlations in a sizable dataset of labelled data. Once trained, the model can be used to forecast or select on previously unobserved data.

In the creation of traditional IDS, machine learning-based techniques are frequently employed and have seen significant success in both wired and wireless networks [16]. In a similar vein, numerous researchers have also applied machine learning strategies in SDN-focused settings. These methods are used to look for malicious activity by analyzing different aspects of network flows. We found that ensemble machine learning classifiers outperform single classifiers in terms of accuracy and processing power after analyzing noteworthy machine learning-based IDS.

In proposed work, we used four classifiers such as Decision tree, SVM, AdaBoost and XGBoost to construct ensemble classifier module. In most cases, ensemble learning's predictive power exceeds that of its component techniques. To combine the classification output, we use soft voting technique.

16.3.4   C4.5 Decision Tree

The C4.5 technique is frequently used in applications for data mining and machine learning, and it is efficient when handling datasets with continuous and discrete attributes [17]. Recursively dividing the training set into subsets based on the values of the input attributes, the C4.5 algorithm then chooses the attribute with the best information gain ratio to make the next split. This statistical technique results in the construction of a decision tree.The predominant properties to check for sensing the DDoS attacks are,

- Is the network experiencing abnormally high traffic or requests?
- Is the traffic or requests coming from a single IP address or a small group of IP addresses?
- Is the traffic or requests coming from known malicious IP addresses or a suspicious geographic location?
- Is the traffic or requests legitimate traffic from a user or a group of users?
- Is the traffic or requests coming from a botnet or a large number of different IP addresses?

Algorithm for Decision Tree
  Input: Dataset D, Set of features F
  Output: Decision Tree

1. *If all data points in D have the same class label, return a leaf node with that label.*
2. *If the set of features F is empty, return a leaf node with the majority class label of the data points in D.*
3. *Select the best feature f from F to split D. The best feature is the one that results in the highest information gain or lowest impurity.*
4. *Create a new internal node with f as its decision attribute.*
5. *Split the data points in D into subsets based on the possible values of f.*
6. *For each subset, repeat the above steps recursively with the remaining features and data points.*
7. *Return the root node of the decision tree*

16.3.5   Support Vector Machine

SVM tries to find a hyperplane that separates the input data into two classes while maximizing the margin between the classes [18]. Compared to other machine learning methods like decision trees and neural networks, SVMs are less prone to overfitting. By examining network traffic and spotting patterns that point to an attack, SVMs can be used to discover DDoS attacks. To learn how to distinguish between the two, SVMs can be trained on a sizable dataset of network traffic that includes instances of both normal and attack traffic. The SVM can be used to categorize new incoming traffic as legitimate or possibly malicious after being trained. The methods for using SVM to detect DDoS attacks are as follows:

- Gather information about network activity, such as packet size, rate, and direction.
- From the network traffic statistics, extract features. A few characteristics that can be employed for SVM are the mean packet size, standard deviation of packet size, and the number of packets per second.
- Indicate whether the network activity is legitimate or malicious. To achieve this, train the SVM using a dataset of known threats along with regular traffic.
- Utilize the labelled network traffic sample to train the SVM.
- Test the SVM's efficacy in identifying DDoS attacks using a different dataset of network traffic data.
- To increase the DDoS detection's precision, tweak the SVM's settings and feature selection.
- Utilize the SVM to watch traffic in real-time and identify DDoS attacks on the network infrastructure.

Algorithm for Support Vector Machine:

Input:

A training dataset D containing labelled network traffic samples.

A kernel function K, which defines the similarity between two data points.

C, a parameter that controls the trade-off between maximizing the margin and minimizing the classification error.

γ, a parameter that controls the shape of the decision boundary.

Output: SVM Classifier

1. *Preprocess the dataset D to extract relevant features, such as packet size, packet rate, or packet entropy.*
2. *Split the dataset into two parts: a training set and a validation set.*
3. *Train an SVM model on the training set using the kernel function K, the parameter C, and the parameter γ. The SVM model learns to separate normal traffic from DDoS traffic by finding a hyper plane that maximizes the margin between the two classes.*
4. *Adjust the C and γ or using a different kernel function till getting the best hyper plane.*

16.3.6 AdaBoost

AdaBoost (Adaptive Boosting) combines several weak classifiers to produce a strong classifier with the goal of increasing the accuracy of a machine learning model. A strong classifier is a model that can confidently and reliably categorize the data, as opposed to a poor classifier that only slightly outperforms random guessing. [19]. AdaBoost is advantageous for IDS use because it can handle imbalanced datasets, where the proportion of malicious occurrences is substantially smaller than that of benign examples. AdaBoost can effectively raise the detection rate while lowering the false alarm rate by concentrating on the hard-to-classify instances, which frequently represent malicious instances.

16.3.7 XGBoost

Extreme Gradient Boosting (XGBoost) is a distributed, scalable gradient-boosted decision tree (GBDT) machine learning framework [20]. The top machine learning library for regression, classification, and ranking issues, it offers parallel tree boosting. Comprehending the machine learning ideas and techniques that supervised machine learning, decision trees, ensemble learning, and gradient boosting are built upon is essential to understanding XGBoost. In supervised machine learning, a model is trained using algorithms to discover patterns in a dataset of features and labels, and the model is then used to predict the labels on the features of a new dataset.

1) AdaBoost and XGBoost with Decision Trees:
  • Collect and preprocess data: Collect data from your dataset and preprocess it to extract relevant features.
  • Split the data into training and testing sets: Divide the dataset into a training set and a testing set. The training set is used to train the AdaBoost algorithm, and the testing set is used to evaluate its performance.
  • Train a Decision Tree: Train a decision tree on the training set.
  • Use AdaBoost to create a strong classifier: Use AdaBoost to create a strong classifier by combining multiple decision trees. AdaBoost assigns higher weights to the misclassified examples, which leads to the creation of a strong classifier.
  • Evaluate the performance: Evaluate the performance of the AdaBoost algorithm on the testing set. You can use metrics such as accuracy, precision, and recall to evaluate its performance.
  • Deploy the model: Once you are satisfied with the performance of the model, deploy it in your system to detect data anomalies or make predictions.

2) AdaBoost and XGBoost with SVMs:
  • Collect and preprocess data: Collect data from your dataset and preprocess it to extract relevant features.
  • Split the data into training and testing sets: Divide the dataset into a training set and a testing set. The training set is used to train the AdaBoost algorithm, and the testing set is used to evaluate its performance.
  • Train an SVM: Train an SVM on the training set.
  • Use AdaBoost to create a strong classifier: Use AdaBoost to create a strong classifier by combining multiple SVMs. AdaBoost assigns higher weights to the misclassified examples, which leads to the creation of a strong classifier.
  • Evaluate the performance: Evaluate the performance of the AdaBoost algorithm on the testing set. You can use metrics such as accuracy, precision, and recall to evaluate its performance.
  • Deploy the model: Once you are satisfied with the performance of the model, deploy it in your system to detect data anomalies or make predictions.

16.3.8 VOTING CLASSIFIER

A voting classifier is a machine learning model that gains experience by training on a collection of several models and forecasts an output (class) based on the class with the highest likelihood of being the output. To predict the output class based on the highest majority of votes, it merely averages the results of each classifier that was passed into the voting classifier. A voting classifier receives the output from the four classifiers in order to determine whether an attack or regular traffic actually occurred. We use soft voting technique to make the final detection of attack or normal instance. In soft voting, the forecast made for each output class is based on the average probability assigned to that class. A voting classifier is used to increase the forecasts' stability and precision. The voting classifier can capture various aspects of the data and lessen the effect of the weaknesses of individual models by combining multiple models. Furthermore, it may be more resilient to overfitting and anomalies.

16.4 EXPERIMENTAL SETUP

We simulate an SDN environment to assess the effectiveness of our proposed framework by utilizing a Python-based POX and the Mininet simulation tool. Data plane host machines and OpenFlow switches are provided with device functions. In addition to employing the Scapy tool to create TCP flooding attacks with spoof IP numbers. Scapy'sRandShort() function is utilized to develop assaults from BoNeSi [21–24] to produce legitimate traffic, random source port numbers, and using Wireshark to record and examine attack and normal behavior connections.

16.4.1 CAIDA DATASET

DDoS (Distributed Denial of Service) attacks and their effects on network traffic can be researched using the CAIDA (Center for Applied Internet Data Analysis) Dataset. The dataset contains a range of data sources that can be used to recognize and assess DDoS assaults, such as DNS query data, BGP routing data, and passive and active measurement data. Every 20 seconds, the CAIDA dataset's TCP packet information is examined. TCP ports and IP addresses both grow significantly during an attack, meaning that each IP address has a disproportionately large number of ports open at any given time.

16.4.2 FEATURE SELECTION

The CAIDA dataset consists of network traffic data and provides valuable insights into various aspects of the Internet's structure, performance, and behavior. The dataset contains a wide range of features, but the importance of specific features may vary depending on the research or analysis objectives. Here are some important features commonly found in the CAIDA dataset:

  (i) *Source IP Address:* The IP address of the source device or host from which the network traffic originates. It helps in understanding the source of the traffic and identifying potential patterns or anomalies.

(ii) *Destination IP Address:* The IP address of the destination device or host to which the network traffic is directed. It helps in analyzing traffic patterns, identifying communication patterns, and detecting potential security threats.

(iii) *Packet Size:* The size of the packets in the network traffic. It provides information about the volume of data being transmitted and can be useful for capacity planning and performance analysis.

(iv) *Protocol:* The network protocol used for communication, such as TCP (Transmission Control Protocol), UDP (User Datagram Protocol), or ICMP (Internet Control Message Protocol). It helps in understanding the nature of the network traffic and its behavior.

(v) *Port Numbers:* The port numbers associated with the network traffic. Ports are used to identify specific services or applications running on devices. Analyzing port numbers can help in identifying network services, detecting potential vulnerabilities, or understanding traffic patterns.

(vi) *Timestamp:* The timestamp indicating when the network traffic occurred. It enables the analysis of temporal patterns, identifying trends, and understanding the dynamics of network behavior.

(vii) *Autonomous System (AS) Number:* The AS number represents a group of IP addresses under the control of a single administrative entity (Autonomous System). It helps in analyzing the routing infrastructure and understanding the relationships between different entities in the network.

(viii) *Flow Duration:* The duration of a flow, which represents a sequence of packets sharing common characteristics (e.g., source IP, destination IP, protocol). Flow duration can provide insights into the duration of network connections, the persistence of communication, or potential anomalies.

(ix) *Traffic Volume:* The total amount of data transmitted during a network flow. It helps in analyzing the volume of traffic, detecting outliers, and understanding the load on the network.

(x) *Network Latency:* The time delay experienced in the transmission of network traffic. Analyzing latency can help in assessing network performance, identifying bottlenecks, or detecting anomalies.

16.5   PERFORMANCE EVALUATION

True Positive (TP) rate or Detection rate: It measures the percentage of actual DDoS attacks that are correctly identified by the detection system. False Positive (FP) rate or False alarm rate: It measures the percentage of legitimate traffic that is mistakenly identified as a DDoS attack by the detection system. True Negative (TN) rate or Specificity: It measures the percentage of legitimate traffic that is correctly identified as legitimate traffic by the detection system. False Negative (FN) rate or Miss rate: It measures the percentage of actual DDoS attacks that are incorrectly classified as legitimate traffic by the detection system.The accuracy, precision, recall, and F1 measure evaluation metrics were utilized to calculate the performance of the Machine learning module. The ratio of genuine positives and negatives to the total number of evaluations is used to measure accuracy (A).Precision (P) identifies the positive data that was accurately classified out of all the positive classified data. Recall (R) measures the classification accuracy of the model for true positives. The F-score is calculated by averaging recall and accuracy. Performance measures are illustrated in Figures 16.3–16.10. Table 16.1 shows the comparative analysis of performance measures.

16.6   CONCLUSION

Statistical-based and machine learning-based mechanisms are proposed to defend against TCP flooding attacks. Statistically based strategies aid in early attack detection but have a high false alarm rate. Machine-learning based techniques aid in the accurate and low false alarm rate detection of the attack. Decision tree, SVM, adaboost, and XGboost approaches were our go-to base classifiers. For the ensemble

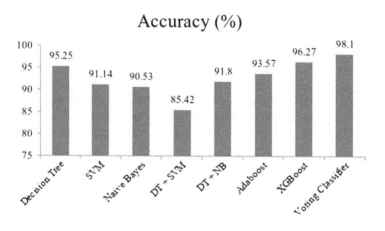

FIGURE 16.3   Performance measure – Accuracy.

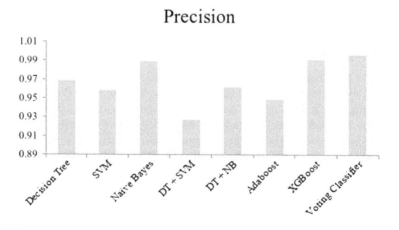

FIGURE 16.4   Performance measure – Precision.

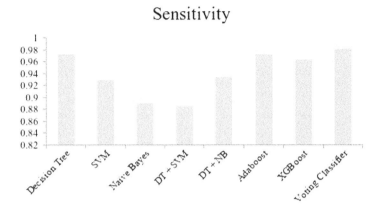

FIGURE 16.5   Performance measure – Sensitivity.

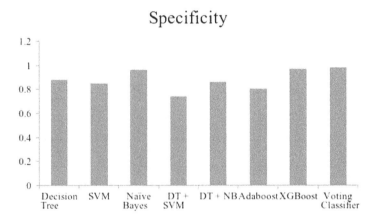

FIGURE 16.6   Performance Measure – Specificity.

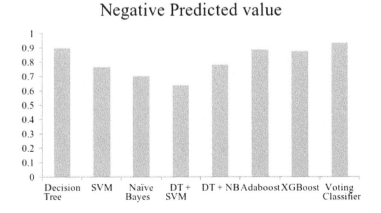

FIGURE 16.7   Performance evaluation – negative predicted value.

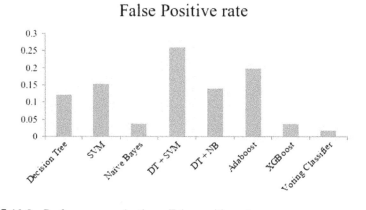

FIGURE 16.8 Performance evaluation – False positive rate.

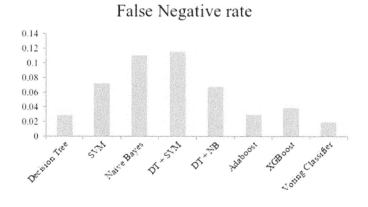

FIGURE 16.9 Performance evaluation – False negative rate.

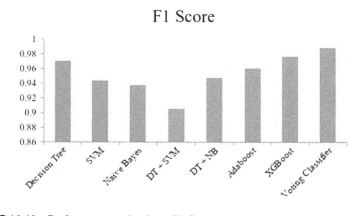

FIGURE 16.10 Performance evaluation – F1 Score.

TABLE 16.1
Performance Evaluation

Models	Sensitivity	Specificity	Precision	Negative Predicted Value	False Positive Rate	False Negative Rate	Accuracy (%)	F1 Score
Decision Tree	0.9719	0.8807	0.9679	0.8945	0.1193	0.0281	95.25	0.9699
SVM	0.9284	0.8484	0.9578	0.762	0.1516	0.0716	91.14	0.9429
Naïve Bayes	0.8898	0.9628	0.9888	0.7023	0.0372	0.1102	90.53	0.9367
DT + SVM	0.8849	0.7405	0.9266	0.6348	0.2595	0.1151	85.42	0.9053
DT + NB	0.9333	0.8613	0.9614	0.7771	0.1387	0.0667	91.8	0.9471
Adaboost	0.9715	0.8032	0.9481	0.8837	0.1968	0.0285	93.57	0.9597
XGBoost	0.9623	0.9642	0.9901	0.8735	0.0358	0.0377	96.27	0.976
Voting Classifier	**0.9807**	**0.982**	**0.9951**	**0.9321**	**0.018**	**0.0193**	**98.1**	**0.9878**

combination estimator, we employed a soft voting classifier. Based on the attacks with the highest probability selected by the basic classifiers, the voting classifier finds the attack. For detecting DDoS attacks, ensemble learning has shown to be a promising method. Ensemble learning has the potential to significantly increase the reliability and accuracy of DDoS detection systems by merging numerous models. The risk of false positives or false negatives can be decreased by using a variety of models to recognize various attack patterns. Ensemble learning can also adjust to the dynamic nature of DDoS attacks by routinely updating and retraining the ensemble's models. With ensemble learning, it is possible to identify even subtle patterns and anomalies in network traffic that may indicate a DDoS attack is underway.

REFERENCES

1. Sudar, K. M., Deepalakshmi, P., Singh, A., & Srinivasu, P. N. (2022). TFAD: TCP flooding attack detection in software-defined networking using proxy-based and machine learning-based mechanisms. *Cluster Computing*, 26(2), 1–17.
2. Muthamil Sudar, K., RubaSoundar, K., Vinoth, P., Nagaraj, P., & Muneeswaran, V. (2023). Detection of DDoS attack using machine learning techniques in software-defined networking. *Handbook of Research on Current Trends in Cybersecurity and Educational Technology*, 19–36.
3. Dang, V. T., Huong, T. T., Thanh, N. H., Nam, P. N., Thanh, N. N., & Marshall, A. (2019). SDN-based SYN Proxy—A solution to enhance performance of attack mitigation under TCP SYN Flood. *The Computer Journal*, 62(4), 518–534.
4. Mohammadi, R., Javidan, R., & Conti, M. (2017). SLICOTS: An SDN-based lightweight countermeasure for TCP SYN flooding attacks. *IEEE Transactions on Network and Service Management*, 14(2), 487–497.
5. Chen, K.Y., Junuthula, A. R., Siddhrau, I. K., Xu, Y., & Chao, H. J. (2016). SDNShield: Towards more comprehensive defense against DDoS attacks on SDN control plane. In IEEE *Conference on Communications and Network Security (CNS)*, 28–36.
6. Tuan, N. N., Hung, P. H., Nghia, N. D., Tho, N. V., Phan, T. V., & Thanh, N. H. (2020). A DDoS attack mitigation scheme in ISP networks using machine learning based on SDN. *Electronics*, 9(3), 1–7.
7. Swami, R., Dave, M., & Ranga, V. (2021). Detection and analysis of TCP-SYN DDoS attack in software-defined networking. *Wireless Personal Communications*, 1, 1–23.
8. Hamza, A., Gharakheili, H. H., Benson, T. A., & Sivaraman, V. (2019). Detecting volumetric attacks on lot devices via sdn-based monitoring of mud activity. In *Proceedings of the ACM Symposium on SDN Research*, 36–48.
9. Ravi, N., Shalinie, S. M., Lal, C., & Conti, M. (2020). AEGIS: Detection and mitigation of TCP SYN flood on SDN controller. *IEEE Transactions on Network and Service Management*, 18(1), 745–759.
10. Batool, S., Zeeshan Khan, F., Qaiser Ali Shah, S., Ahmed, M., Alroobaea, R., Baqasah, A. M., … & AhsanRaza, M. (2022). Lightweight statistical approach towards TCP SYN Flood DDoS attack detection and mitigation in SDN environment. *Security and Communication Networks*, 2022, 1–14.
11. Chen, Y., Hou, J., Li, Q., & Long, H. (2020, December). DDoS attack detection based on random forest. In *2020 IEEE International Conference on Progress in Informatics and Computing (PIC)* (pp. 328–334). IEEE.
12. Sumantra, I., & Gandhi, S. I. (2020, July). DDoS attack detection and mitigation in software-defined networks. In *2020 International Conference on System, Computation, Automation and Networking (ICSCAN)* (pp. 1–5). IEEE.

13. Sun, J. R., Huang, C. T., & Hwang, M. S. (2022). A SYN flooding attack detection approach with hierarchical policies based on self-information. *ETRI Journal*, 44(2), 346–354.
14. Awan, M. J., Farooq, U., Babar, H. M. A., Yasin, A., Nobanee, H., Hussain, M.,… & Zain, A. M. (2021). Real-time DDoS attack detection system using big data approach. *Sustainability*, 13(19), 10743.
15. Sudar, K. M., Beulah, M., Deepalakshmi, P., Nagaraj, P., & Chinnasamy, P. (2021, January). Detection of distributed denial of service attacks in SDN using machine learning techniques. In *2021 International Conference on Computer Communication and Informatics (ICCCI)* (pp. 1–5). IEEE.
16. Muthamil Sudar, K., & Deepalakshmi, P. (2020). A two level security mechanism to detect a DDoS flooding attack in software-defined networks using entropy-based and C4. 5 technique. *Journal of High Speed Networks*, 26(1), 55–76.
17. Awan, M. J., Farooq, U., Babar, H. M. A., Yasin, A., Nobanee, H., Hussain, M.,…& Zain, A. M. (2021). Real-time DDoS attack detection system using big data approach. *Sustainability*, 13(19), 10743.
18. Deepa, V., Sudar, K. M., & Deepalakshmi, P. (2018, December). Detection of DDoS attack on SDN control plane using hybrid machine learning techniques. In *2018 International Conference on Smart Systems and Inventive Technology (ICSSIT)* (pp. 299–303). IEEE.
19. Deepa, V., Sudar, K. M., & Deepalakshmi, P. (2019, March). Design of ensemble learning methods for DDoS detection in SDN environment. In *2019 International Conference on Vision Towards Emerging Trends in Communication and Networking (ViTECoN)* (pp. 1–6). IEEE.
20. Sudar, K. M., Nagaraj, P., Deepalakshmi, P., & Chinnasamy, P. (2021, January). Analysis of intruder detection in big data analytics. In *2021 International Conference on Computer Communication and Informatics (ICCCI)* (pp. 1–5). IEEE.
21. Sudar, K. M., & Deepalakshmi, P. (2020). Comparative study on IDS using machine learning approaches for software-defined networks. *International Journal of Intelligent Enterprise*, 7(1–3), 15–27.
22. MuthamilSudar, K., & Deepalakshmi, P. (2021). An intelligent flow-based and signature-based IDS for SDNs using ensemble feature selection and a multi-layer machine learning-based classifier. *Journal of Intelligent & Fuzzy Systems*, 40(3), 4237–4256.
23. Sudar, K. M., Deepalakshmi, P., Ponmozhi, K., & Nagaraj, P. (2019, December). Analysis of security threats and countermeasures for various biometric techniques. In *2019 IEEE International Conference on Clean Energy and Energy Efficient Electronics Circuit for Sustainable Development (INCCES)* (pp. 1–6). IEEE.
24. Sudar, K. M., Nagaraj, P., Ganesh, M., Yadav, D. A., Kumar, K. M., & Muneeswaran, V. (2022, June). Analysis of seminary learner campus network behaviour using machine learning techniques. In *2022 7th International Conference on Communication and Electronics Systems (ICCES)* (pp. 1117–1122). IEEE.

Index